Language Change

English as a Lingua Franca (ELF) has become ubiquitous in today's globalized, mobile and fast-changing world. It is clear that it will have an unprecedented impact not only on how we communicate but also on our understanding of language use and change. What exactly ELF brings to our life and to language theory is a question which requires an interdisciplinary take. This book gathers together leading scholars from World Englishes, typology, language history, cognitive linguistics, translation studies, multilingualism, sociolinguistics and ELF research itself to seek state-of-the-art answers. Chapters present original insights on language change, based on theoretical approaches and empirical studies, and provide clear examples of social, interactional and cognitive changes that ELF instigates. The picture which unfolds on the pages of this book is complex, dynamic and makes a convincing case for the importance of English as a Lingua Franca on language change at a global scale.

ANNA MAURANEN is Professor and Research Director at the University of Helsinki, and President of the Finnish Academy of Science and Letters. Her research includes ELF, academic discourses, corpus linguistics, translation and modelling speech. She is co-editor of *Applied Linguistics* and *Changing English* (2017), and author of *Exploring ELF* (2012) and *Linear Unit Grammar* (2006).

SVETLANA VETCHINNIKOVA is University Lecturer in the Department of Languages, University of Helsinki. Her current interests include chunking at different levels of language organization, individual variation and modelling language as a complex system. She is author of *Phraseology and the Advanced Language Learner* (2019) and co-editor of *Changing English* (2017).

Language Change
The Impact of English as a Lingua Franca

Edited by

Anna Mauranen
University of Helsinki

Svetlana Vetchinnikova
University of Helsinki

CAMBRIDGE
UNIVERSITY PRESS

University Printing House, Cambridge CB2 8BS, United Kingdom

One Liberty Plaza, 20th Floor, New York, NY 10006, USA

477 Williamstown Road, Port Melbourne, VIC 3207, Australia

314–321, 3rd Floor, Plot 3, Splendor Forum, Jasola District Centre, New Delhi – 110025, India

79 Anson Road, #06–04/06, Singapore 079906

Cambridge University Press is part of the University of Cambridge.

It furthers the University's mission by disseminating knowledge in the pursuit of education, learning, and research at the highest international levels of excellence.

www.cambridge.org
Information on this title: www.cambridge.org/9781108492850
DOI: 10.1017/9781108675000

© Cambridge University Press 2021

This publication is in copyright. Subject to statutory exception and to the provisions of relevant collective licensing agreements, no reproduction of any part may take place without the written permission of Cambridge University Press.

First published 2021

A catalogue record for this publication is available from the British Library.

Library of Congress Cataloging-in-Publication Data
Names: Mauranen, Anna, editor. | Vetchinnikova, Svetlana, editor.
Title: Language change : the impact of English as a lingua franca / edited by Anna Mauranen, Svetlana Vetchinnikova.
Description: Cambridge, UK ; New York : Cambridge University Press, 2021. | Includes bibliographical references and index.
Identifiers: LCCN 2020023263 (print) | LCCN 2020023264 (ebook) | ISBN 9781108492850 (hardback) | ISBN 9781108729819 (paperback) | ISBN 9781108675000 (epub)
Subjects: LCSH: English language–Globalization. | English language–Variation–Foreign countries. | English language–Political aspects–Foreign countries. | English language–Social aspects–Foreign
countries. | Lingua francas.
Classification: LCC PE1073 .L3585 2020 (print) | LCC PE1073 (ebook) | DDC 420.9–dc23
LC record available at https://lccn.loc.gov/2020023263
LC ebook record available at https://lccn.loc.gov/2020023264

ISBN 978-1-108-49285-0 Hardback
ISBN 978-1-108-72981-9 Paperback

Cambridge University Press has no responsibility for the persistence or accuracy of URLs for external or third-party internet websites referred to in this publication and does not guarantee that any content on such websites is, or will remain, accurate or appropriate.

Contents

List of Figures	*page* vii
List of Tables	x
List of Contributors	xii
Acknowledgements	xv
List of Abbreviations	xvii

Introduction: Dynamics of Change from Different Perspectives
and on Different Scales 1
ANNA MAURANEN AND SVETLANA VETCHINNIKOVA

Part I Pooling Perspectives

Introduction 11
ANNA MAURANEN

1 *Calling* Englishes *As* Complex Dynamic Systems: Diffusion and Restructuring 15
EDGAR W. SCHNEIDER

2 English as a Lingua Franca in the Context of a Sociolinguistic Typology of Contact Languages 44
WILLIAM CROFT

3 How Writing Changes Language 75
EWA DĄBROWSKA

4 ELF and Translation As Language Contact 95
ANNA MAURANEN

5 Present-Day Standard English: Whose Language Was It Anyway? 123
TERTTU NEVALAINEN

6 Beyond Language Change: ELF and the Study of Sociolinguistic Change 152
JANUS MORTENSEN

Part II Zooming in on ELF

Introduction — 175
SVETLANA VETCHINNIKOVA

7 ELF, Language Change, and Social Networks: Evidence from Real-Time Social Media Data — 179
MIKKO LAITINEN AND JONAS LUNDBERG

8 ELF and Language Change at the Individual Level — 205
SVETLANA VETCHINNIKOVA AND TURO HILTUNEN

9 Are Multilinguals the Better Academic ELF Users? Evidence from a Questionnaire Study Measuring Self-Assessed Proficiencies — 234
PETER SIEMUND AND JESSICA TERESE MUELLER

10 The Role of Co-Textual and Contextual Cues for Intelligibility in ELF Interactions — 267
VERONIKA THIR

11 Exploring the Pragmatics of Computer-Mediated English as a Lingua Franca Communication: Multimodal and Multilingual Practices — 291
RINO BOSSO

12 Development of Shared Multilingual Resources in ELF Dyadic Interaction: A Longitudinal Case Study — 311
AKI SIEGEL

13 The Role of Translanguaging in ELF Advice Sessions for Asylum Seekers — 336
ALESSIA COGO

Index — 356

Figures

1.1	The S-curve as a diffusion model in population biology (from Mobus & Kalton 2015: 215)	*page* 22
1.2	S-curve shapes in the diffusion of *do*-support in different environments (from Kroch 1989: 223, after Ellegård 1953)	23
1.3	Relationship between *recall* and *recollect* in World Englishes	32
1.4	Relationship between *aid* and *assist* in World Englishes	33
1.5	Relationship between *assume* and *suppose* in World Englishes	33
1.6	Changing frequencies of *assume* and *suppose* in Indian English 1978 vs. 2000	34
1.7	Frequencies of meanings of *learn* in WEs	35
1.8	Diachronic change of proportions of three meanings of *learn* in Indian English	36
2.1	The exoteric language continuum	53
2.2	A scale of social organization	56
2.3	The neogenic language continuum	64
3.1	Results for Dimension 1 ("Involved v. informational"). Reproduced from Biber 1995, p. 289	85
5.1	Frequency of verbal *-s* (vs. *-th*) in the CEEC	131
5.2	Frequency of *-th* (vs. *-s*) between 1460 and 1539	132
5.3	Frequency of *-s* (vs. *-th*) between 1540 and 1619	133
5.4	Thomas Cromwell (painted by Hans Holbein between 1532 and 1533; public domain via Wikimedia Commons)	134
5.5	Frequencies of *has* vs. *hath* and *doth* vs. *does* in print in the seventeenth century (EEBO)	139

5.6	Agreement sensitive to subject type (eWAVE Feature 181; the darkest markers show where the feature is pervasive or obligatory)	143
5.7	Third-person -s generalized to all persons (eWAVE Feature 171; the darkest markers show where the feature is pervasive or obligatory)	143
5.8	Invariant zero marking (eWAVE Feature 170; the darkest markers show where the feature is pervasive or obligatory)	144
7.1	The rate of addition of new user accounts in the NTS	186
7.2	Cumulative frequency diagram of user accounts and tweets	186
7.3	Boxplots of the median values for the four account types for friends (top) and followers (bottom)	191
7.4	Friends and followers per Swedish and English (ELF) accounts (only NTS-Human-Active)	193
7.5	Friends vs. followers for passive, bot, and verified accounts	194
7.6	Share of English distribution per account type	196
7.7	Friend cohorts (top) and follower cohorts (bottom) when using a ten-cohort division	198
7.8	Friend cohorts using ten tweets as their threshold value	199
8.1	Proportions of *it's* and *it is* per PERSON	215
8.2	Proportions of *it's* and *it is* per SYNTACTIC STRUCTURE, PERSON	216
8.3	Proportions of *it's* and *it is* per PRIMING, grouped by PERSON	220
8.4	Proportions of *it is* and *it's* per CHUNKING, grouped by PERSON	222
9.1	Age ranges of the students in the sample	247
9.2	Age ranges of the instructors in the sample	248
9.3	Monolingually raised students' (left) and instructors' (right) L1s by frequency	249
9.4	Multilingually raised students' (left) and instructors' (right) L1s by frequency	250
9.5	Monolingually raised vs. multilingually raised students' average self-assessed proficiency levels	251
9.6	Monolingually raised vs. multilingually raised instructors' average self-assessed proficiency levels	252
9.7	Reading comprehension among multilingually raised vs. monolingually raised students	253
9.8	Spoken production among multilingually raised vs. monolingually raised students	254
9.9	Spoken production among multilingually raised vs. monolingually raised instructors	255

9.10	Written expression in multilingually raised vs. monolingually raised instructors	256
10.1	Types of miscommunication according to their severity in the experimental data	277
11.1	Image of disinfectant	301
11.2	Image of a kettle	303
11.3	Image of a sweeping and mopping tool	304
11.4	Image of a ladle	305
11.5	Image of a juice squeezer	306
11.6	Image of an Allen wrench	307

Tables

1.1	Relationship between *recall* and *recollect* in World Englishes	*page* 31
1.2	Relationship between *aid* and *assist* in World Englishes	32
1.3	Relationship between *assume* and *suppose* in World Englishes	32
1.4	Changing frequencies of *assume* and *suppose* in Indian English 1978 vs. 2000	34
1.5	Frequencies of meanings of *learn* in WEs	35
1.6	Diachronic change of proportions of three meanings of *learn* in Indian English	35
1.7	Diachronic comparison of "intrusive *as*" in Indian English	38
2.1	African lingua francas in large-scale societies that pre-date European expansion	58
2.2	African lingua francas that emerged from long-distance trade with Europeans	59
2.3	North American pidgins and lingua francas that likely emerged with European contact	61
2.4	Linguistic knowledge in Gapun village, Papua New Guinea in 1987	63
2.5	Linguistic knowledge in western and central Kenya in 1968	63
2.6	African lingua francas that emerged in the creation of new states (empires)	66
2.7	African lingua francas that emerged in the creation of European colonies	67
3.1	Vocabulary richness in selected spoken and written genres (adapted from Hayes & Ahrens 1988)	76
5.1	The Corpus of Early English Correspondence: its original version (CEEC), Extension (CEECE) and Supplement (CEECSU)	130
7.1	The count of tweets and accounts in the NTS-Human-Active dataset	189
7.2	The network sizes for four account types	189
8.1	Individual subcorpora and Non24	212

8.2	Most frequent five-grams involving *it is/it's* for each of the individual commenters	223
8.3	Distribution of speaker-specific chunks across syntactic categories	223
8.4	Syntactic categorization used with examples	232
8.5	Pre-nuclear cases and comparative constructions	233
10.1	Speaker information for the two pairs of ELF users	274
10.2	Tasks and conditions per pair	276
10.3	Comprehension difficulties	279
10.4	Non-understandings that occurred in the absence of sufficient co-textual and contextual cues	281
10.5	Non-understandings where listeners did not profit from a co-textual or contextual cue	282
10.6	Non-understandings where a co-textual and/or contextual cue contributed to loss of intelligibility	282
10.7	Misunderstandings	284
12.1	Recording date and length	316
12.2	The number of word search sequences (WS) and the number of WS that include code-switching (CS)	317
13.1	Data collected	341

Contributors

RINO BOSSO is a PhD candidate at the Department of English and American Studies, University of Vienna. His research project "Exploring Computer-Mediated English as a Lingua Franca" investigates the pragmatic strategies adopted by members of a multicultural Hybrid Community to realize pragmatic meaning, and achieve mutual understanding, in online ELF communication.

ALESSIA COGO is Senior Lecturer in Applied Linguistics at Goldsmiths, University of London, where she is also director of the MA in Multilingualism, Linguistics and Education. She is currently involved in research concerning ELF and critical pedagogy, ELF and EMI and ELF in asylum-seeking contexts. She is editor-in-chief of the *ELT Journal*.

WILLIAM CROFT is Professor Emeritus at the University of New Mexico. His books include *Typology and Universals, Explaining Language Change, Radical Construction Grammar, Cognitive Linguistics* (with D. Alan Cruse) and *Verbs: Aspect and Causal Structure*. He is currently working on *Morphosyntax: Constructions of the World's Languages* for Cambridge University Press.

EWA DĄBROWSKA is Humboldt Professor for Language and Cognition at the Friedrich-Alexander-Universität in Erlangen and Professor of Linguistics at the University of Birmingham. She is also the President of the UK Cognitive Linguistics Association and was previously editor-in-chief of *Cognitive Linguistics*.

TURO HILTUNEN is Senior Lecturer in English at the University of Helsinki, Finland. His main scholarly interests include phraseology and grammar, English for academic purposes, the language of science and medicine from the early modern period to the present day, and the language of Wikipedia.

MIKKO LAITINEN is Professor of English at the University of Eastern Finland. He obtained his PhD in the University of Helsinki in 2007. He is one of the two founding members of Data Intensive Sciences and Applications (DISA), a multidisciplinary consortium involving computer scientists, mathematicians and social scientists at Linnaeus University.

JONAS LUNDBERG received a PhD in Theoretical Physics from Umeå University in 1994 and a PhD in Computer Science at Linnaeus University in 2014. He is currently Associate Professor in Computer Science at Linnaeus University. His main research interests are in program analysis, software engineering and applied machine learning.

ANNA MAURANEN is Professor and Research Director at the University of Helsinki, and President of the Finnish Academy of Science and Letters. Her research includes ELF, academic discourses, corpus linguistics, translation and modelling speech. She is co-editor of *Applied Linguistics* and *Changing English* (2017), and author of *Exploring ELF* (2012) and *Linear Unit Grammar* (2006).

JANUS MORTENSEN is Associate Professor of Language Policy at the Centre for Internationalisation and Parallel Language Use (CIP), University of Copenhagen. His research interests include language policy, English as a Lingua Franca, university internationalization, interaction in transient social configurations and sociolinguistic change.

JESSICA TERESE MUELLER is a linguist and clinical psychologist with interests in multilingualism, second and foreign language acquisition and community interpreting within the field of applied linguistics. In the field of psychology, her research and clinical work has been focused on eating disorders, substance abuse disorders, mother–child attachment and psycho-oncology.

TERTTU NEVALAINEN is Professor and Director of the Research Unit for Variation, Contacts and Change in English at the University of Helsinki. Her research interests include corpus linguistics, historical sociolinguistics and language change. She has published, among others, *Historical Sociolinguistics: Language Change in Tudor and Stuart England* (with Helena Raumolin-Brunberg, 2017).

EDGAR W. SCHNEIDER is Chair Professor of English Linguistics at the University of Regensburg, Germany. He is an internationally renowned sociolinguist, known best for his "Dynamic Model" (*Postcolonial English,* CUP

2007). He has published many books and articles and lectured on all continents, including many keynote lectures.

AKI SIEGEL is Senior Lecturer at Linnaeus University, Sweden. She completed her PhD in Applied Linguistics at Newcastle University, UK. She is interested in analysing changes and learning occurring through interactions, and considering the ways in which classroom teaching and learning can be improved based on empirical evidence.

PETER SIEMUND has been Professor of English Linguistics at the University of Hamburg since 2001. He pursues a cross-linguistic typological approach in his work on reflexivity and *self*-intensifiers, pronominal gender, interrogative constructions, speech acts and clause types, argument structure, tense and aspect, varieties of English, language contact and multilingual development.

VERONIKA THIR is a doctoral student at the Department of English at the University of Vienna, where she worked as a university assistant from 2015 to 2019. Her main research interest lies in phonological intelligibility in English as a Lingua Franca communication.

SVETLANA VETCHINNIKOVA is University Lecturer in the Department of Languages, University of Helsinki. Her current interests include chunking at different levels of language organization, individual variation and modelling language as a complex system. She is author of *Phraseology and the Advanced Language Learner* (2019, Cambridge) and co-editor of *Changing English* (2017, De Gruyter).

Acknowledgements

It has been a real pleasure to put this book together. The authors have shown enthusiasm and commitment to this little-researched but exciting interface between several established and new angles on language change on the one hand, and the ongoing changing of English on the other, which is happening fast and on a large scale right under our noses.

Most of the papers in the volume spring from the presentations given at the ELF and Changing English, 10th Anniversary Conference of English as a Lingua Franca, which we hosted at the University of Helsinki on 12–16 June 2017. In this regard, we wish to extend our thanks to all the conference participants, who engaged in lively discussion of the presentations on the spot and made it such an unforgettable event. We would also like to thank the Federation of Finnish Learned Societies for funding the organization of the conference and the University of Helsinki for providing the venue. The conference was a culmination of a four-year consortium project, Changing English (ChangE): Users and Learners Worldwide, made possible by the Academy of Finland, whose funding we gratefully acknowledge.

As editors we have enjoyed working with the excellent authors and with the reviewers of the articles and believe the end product makes a difference in its theoretical depth and empirical breadth. In the spirit of open discussion and with the generous consent of the reviewers, we would like to use this opportunity to thank them and give credit to their important work openly. Our gratitude goes to (in alphabetical order) Michael Barlow, Jean-Marc Dewaele, Maria Grazia Guido, Spencer Hazel, William Kretzschmar, Salla Kurhila, Merja Kytö, Christian Mair, Simo Määttä, Päivi Pahta, Kaisa Pietikäinen and Devyani Sharma. Thank you very much for your insightful and thought-provoking reviews! You made this volume better. We would also like to thank the anonymous reviewers of the entire volume whose helpful comments we tried to take on board.

At the late stages of the book, Nina Mikušová has been a great help in compiling the various files required for production and preparing the index. Her careful and methodical work was, as always, invaluable.

The book would not have been possible without the wonderfully professional editorial and production teams at Cambridge University Press, so thank you Commissioning Editor Rebecca Taylor, Editorial Assistant Isabel Collins, Content Manager Laura Simmons, Copy-Editor Clare Diston and Project Manager Divya Arjunan; your cheerful attitude, clear notions and firm but humane deadlines made the backbone of the process.

Helsinki 31 October 2019
Anna Mauranen
Svetlana Vetchinnikova

Abbreviations

AAVE	African American Vernacular English
ABSL	Al-Sayyid Bedouin Sign Language
ACE	Asian Corpus of English
AGT	automatically generated tweets
AmE	American English
API	application programming interface
ARCHER	A Representative Corpus of Historical English Registers
BELF	Business English as a Lingua Franca
BES	bilingual English speaker
BNC	British National Corpus
BrE	British English
CA	conversation analysis
CALP	cognitive academic language proficiency
CC	control condition
CDS	Complex Dynamic Systems
CEEC	Corpus of Early English Correspondence
CEECE	Corpus of Early English Correspondence Extension
CEECSU	Corpus of Early English Correspondence Supplement
CEFR	Common European Framework of Reference for Languages
CMC	computer-mediated communication
CMELF	Computer-Mediated English as a Lingua Franca
COBUILD	Collins Birmingham University International Language Database
CoRD	Corpus Resource Database
CS	code-switching
CT	Complexity Theory
CTF	Corpus of Translated Finnish
DH	digital humanities
DOI	digital object identifier
EAAVE	Earlier African American Vernacular English
EC	experimental condition
EEBO	Early English Books Online

EEBO-TCP	Early English Books Online Text Creation Partnership
EFL	English as a Foreign Language
ELF	English as a Lingua Franca
ELFA	Corpus of English as a Lingua Franca in Academic Settings
EModE	Early Modern English
ESOL	English for speakers of other languages
ET	English translation
EU	European Union
eWAVE	electronic World Atlas of Varieties of English
FECC	Finnish-English Contrastive Corpus
fMRI	functional magnetic resonance imaging
FO	Finnish original
GB	Great Britain
GeoIP	geographic location of internet protocol
GPS	Global Positioning System
HC	Helsinki Corpus of English Texts
HC	hybrid community
ICE	International Corpus of English
IMR	individual multilingual repertoire
IP	Internet Protocol
IPC	inferior parietal region
KASELL	Korean Association for the Study of English Language and Linguistics
LALME	Linguistic Atlas of Late Mediaeval English
LVC	language variation and change
ME	Middle English
MICASE	Michigan Corpus of Academic Spoken English
MOOC	Massive Open Online Course
MRP	multilingual resource pool
NBES	non-bilingual English speaker
NNS	non-native speaker
NS	native speaker
NSR	Northern Subject Rule
NTS	Nordic Tweet Stream
OE	Old English
p.c.	personal communication
RQ	research question
SAD	single ancestor-dialect
SAVE corpus	South Asian Varieties of English corpus
SLA	second language acquisition
SLU	second language use
STG	superior temporal region

UID	uniform information density
VOICE	Vienna-Oxford International Corpus of English
VWFA	visual word form area
WE	World Englishes
WS	word search sequence

Introduction

Dynamics of Change from Different Perspectives and on Different Scales

Anna Mauranen and Svetlana Vetchinnikova[1]

Languages undergo continual change, but not at constant speed. External and internal dynamics affect the speed as well as the different scales at which change occurs. Among important external factors, societal change, mobility and the ensuing language contact create conditions of stability or instability and upheaval. Language-internal changes may be triggered off by external changes, for instance when these lead to lively contact between languages or varieties, but internal changes may also begin seemingly autonomously, and may affect different subsystems, or one or more subsystems at different stages. In this volume both internal and external processes of language change are addressed, with a focus on contemporary processes and on English, although not exclusively, so that historical lines of development are included, as are other languages. Throughout the volume, the contributions highlight social contexts of various sizes and kinds, and social processes interacting with linguistic ones. A few chapters also delve into cognitive processes and individual users, thus ensuring that a range of scales is covered in addressing the issues of change and the specific phenomenon of English as a global lingua franca.

English is a particularly interesting kind of language use in the contemporary world, because it has ushered in a qualitatively new linguistic development, one that not only commands a wider reach than any other language before, but at the same time is spoken far more by its second-language (L2) users than its first-language (L1) users. Its most common use today is as a lingua franca, which means it is spreading in a qualitatively new fashion, as a global, transregional lingua franca, or, as Croft puts it (this volume, Chapter 2), 'the primary exoteric lingua franca' in many domains of the globalized world. In this role, as a means of communication between people who do not share a mother tongue, it is now used across spaces and domains, transcending traditional community divisions by nationality, culture or geographic location. Such a change in uses and practices calls for rethinking traditional principles of

---

[1] The authors are listed in alphabetical order.

analysis and categorization, along with sources and directions of influence. It also throws the dynamicity and complexity of language in sharp relief: a global-scale lingua franca may be exceptionally sensitive to change and complex influences, but in which ways, if any, does it differ from the ways in which any language use is complex and dynamic?

What we want to achieve in this volume is to bring different research traditions to bear on the issue of how the emergence of English as a Lingua Franca (ELF) as a relatively recent research field touches upon other, more established fields of study that relate to English, and to the study of language more generally. By bringing together very different perspectives, we also want to contribute to a more ambitious goal: new conceptualizations of the dynamics of language change in the context of relationships within language, between languages, and between languages and their environments.

Contact, Change and Mobility

It is relatively well established that language contact is one of the major drivers of language change, and even though change takes place via many different routes and for a plethora of reasons, contact is a fundamental characteristic of ELF, and a common thread in this book. Contact is approached from a variety of perspectives leading to different kinds and levels of contact, each author specifying their own particular take on the concept and its relation to the data with which they are engaging. Several chapters are concerned with multilingual speakers engaging in direct face-to-face contact or digital interaction, translating texts and sometimes falling back on their different languages in otherwise English-based interactions. Speakers of different linguistic backgrounds have presumably always, since prehistoric days, met and communicated over trade, war, hunting or exchanging spouses, and we know hunter-gatherers to have already been mobile. Today mobility takes place on an unprecedented scale, and has gained entirely novel forms in digital discourses which may or may not accompany physical mobility. All these kinds of social and communicative contact involve contact between speakers of different languages and different varieties – 'polylectal' speakers (cf. Ross 2003), in short.

Breadth and Heterogeneity of Social Contacts

The kinds of social contacts that specifically characterize ELF have turned out to be elusive for attempts at defining them. Many scholars have noted the unsuitability of traditional notions of speech community for capturing the nature of the social formations where ELF is used – many contacts are transient encounters, as Jenkins (2015) points out, and along similar lines, Mortensen

(2017 and this volume, Chapter 6) talks about transient communities. On the other hand, many ELF communities can be seen to resemble Wenger's (1998) communities of practice (Seidlhofer 2011). Mauranen (2018) in turn suggests that they are diffuse, network-based multilingual communities where English is a dominant lingua franca.

Early modern London, a city with a fluid social structure, gave rise to verbal -*s* as a result of 'the heterogeneity of contacts between speakers of different regional and social backgrounds' (Nevalainen this volume, Chapter 5). Today's social contacts can be considered even more heterogeneous as individuals engaging in ELF communication are not only of different social backgrounds, but also come from different social structures: for example, the social position of a student can be very different around the world. In this volume we observe the communication of university students in a student dormitory in Vienna (Bosso, Chapter 11) and in Japan (Siegel, Chapter 12), as well as advice sessions for refugees and asylum seekers at a UK charity centre (Cogo, Chapter 13) – the social contexts of which are as far from each other as possible, representing both privileged and necessity-driven mobility.

The heterogeneity of today's social contacts can also be seen in an impressive variety of L1 backgrounds which are attested in different communicative settings and thus are potentially in direct contact. Siemund and Mueller (Chapter 9) count ninety-three different L1 backgrounds in their study of multilingualism among university students and instructors. Cogo lists a dozen languages the staff of the charity speaks and a dozen which refugees/asylum seekers speak, with the overlap between them of about five languages. Mauranen (Chapter 4), drawing on the ELFA corpus, deals with speakers of more than fifty different L1s. In fact, a high degree of complex multilingualism in terms of the number of languages in speakers' backgrounds and those available in the situational contexts is an aspect of most chapters in Part II of this volume.

To further complicate matters, the fluency of speakers engaging in ELF interaction varies just as widely. For example, some of Cogo's informants in Part II are clearly the least fluent, whereas students in Bosso's study seem to be more fluent than students in Siegel's study. Thir (Chapter 10), in her study of the ability of ELF users to benefit from co-textual and contextual cues to aid phonological intelligibility in comprehension, estimates the participants to be at an upper-intermediate or low-advanced level in English. While fluency is rarely taken up by ELF scholars, it clearly has an influence on the strategies different speakers use to manage interaction and negotiate meaning. Importantly, this affects not only those who are less fluent, but also those who perceive their interlocutors to be less fluent. The strategies and communicative practices adopted range from gesturing, mimicking and use of co-textual and contextual clues to code-switching, translanguaging and using digital tools and multimodal resources, and involve both common as well as unconventional means (see Cogo, Bosso, Siegel and Thir this volume). Thus, ELF interaction seems to provide ground not only for the diffusion of innovative forms, but also for novel communicative means and practices, such as glossing standard but low-frequency lexical items with pictures, or searching for a picture of an L1 word instead of an English translation (see Bosso this volume).

The relationship between the breadth of social contacts and ELF is vividly demonstrated in Laitinen and Lundberg's study (Chapter 7), who show that those who tweet in ELF have larger social networks, weaker ties and therefore, as is reasonable to hypothesize, enjoy social conditions favourable for diffusing innovations and acting as agents of change. The reverse relationship is probably also true: in order to reach out to a wider social circle, one needs to adopt ELF as the language of communication. In this sense, the prophecy of the second president of the United States, quoted in Nevalainen, that English will be 'the general medium of Correspondence and Conversation among the Learned of all Nations, and among all Travellers and Strangers' due to the increasing number of speakers of English and their wide contacts with speakers of other languages, is largely fulfilled, as, for example, Franzman et al. (2015) also suggest.

Multilingualism

Breadth and heterogeneity in social contacts make multilingualism a ubiquitous feature of ELF communication, and one of the most prominent themes in this volume; we see a complex interplay between multilingualism in the mind, multilingual features in interaction and a potential impact of both on language change.

Multilingualism impacts individuals cognitively beyond the social level. Mauranen investigates language contact at three levels: cognition, interaction and language as a collective entity. For cognition she argues that, while languages in a multilingual's mind exert an unavoidable influence on each other, as demonstrated in previous research (e.g. Pavlenko 2014), it is nevertheless important to approach the issues from fresh angles, since the mechanisms and the manifestations of such influences have turned out to be hard to pin down. Considering together relatively neglected domains of multilingual activity – either investigated in relative isolation or simply under-researched, like translation and ELF – and bringing them to bear on the study of multilingual cognition shows intriguing commonalities and differences which help track down tricky questions of priming effects, for example. Siemund and Mueller hypothesize that it is cognitively advantageous for subsequent language acquisition to have more than one home language, and thus those who are multilingually raised reach higher proficiency in ELF. At the same time, a social impact is also observable. As already mentioned, Laitinen and Lundberg show that it is individuals who use more than one language in their tweets who have larger social networks, counted in the number of friends and followers, especially if one of these languages is ELF. Thus, from the perspective of social network theory and taking into account Laitinen and Lundberg's findings, it would seem to be above all networked multilingual individuals who have the potential for acting as innovators and agents of change.

We can then take a different perspective and look at how multilingualism manifests itself in interaction. It seems that the extent to which multilingual practices are adopted depends on a variety of social factors. In Bosso's study we can only see a very covert type of multilingualism: international students living in a student dorm in Vienna seem to recognize the potential lack of intelligibility of English low-frequency vocabulary, and therefore the nature of English they are using as a lingua franca, through their reliance on multi-modal practices such as using pictures in their messages. However, they do not resort to any explicitly multilingual practices such as code-switching. In contrast, in the seemingly similar context of a student dorm in Japan, Siegel observes not only explicit code-switching between a Japanese and Thai speaker, but also a change over time in their recognition of shared multilingual resources: such resources gradually become part of their communication. Finally, the amount of code-switching in Cogo's study is such that she argues for a need of a theoretical shift and conceptualization in terms of translanguaging which emphasises the 'permeability of languages and linguistic repertoires' (Cogo this volume, Chapter 13). Still, she points out that there would be even more space for translanguaging practices if not for the ideological pressures which limit them to specific contexts and points in interaction.

With respect to the plethora of multilingual practices ELF speakers engage in in different social contexts, it is instructive to go back to Croft's chapter on sociolinguistic typology of contact languages. He argues that it is social factors or traits, namely community size and degree of stratification, which determine the way languages will be used in a situation of contact. He draws our attention to a surprising fact: the absence of lingua francas and pidgins – languages which arise specifically for the exoteric function or communication between members of different speech communities – in areas of high linguistic diversity, such as Papua New Guinea. The explanation he offers is that an exoteric language emerges only in contact with a large-scale stratified society. Thus, long-distance trade with such a society gives rise to a lingua franca, while in contrast, communication between neighbouring small-scale egalitarian societies can be managed by local (receptive) bi-/multilingualism.

Synchronic Variation and Standardness

ELF is typically regarded as non-standard English, as we see discussed in many of the chapters in this volume, especially in Part II. Nevalainen shows in her chapter how, in the historical perspective, English has had a long history of pre-standard stages, changing standards and more or less pervasive or widely adopted standards. The last is what one might call a 'weak' standard, one that is there but is not too overpowering, so that local and regional usages develop and live on despite the existence of a standard. With ELF we see a pervasive language use that is not regional, not local and not standard – but not always very far from Standard English either, like in the case of written academic texts. What makes global ELF a particularly interesting research domain is that it coexists with a few national standards (UK, US, Australian, Canadian, South African, etc.) based on native-speaker use, while actual ELF develops in interaction, giving rise to spontaneous norms without external norms. Thus, among these islands of somewhat different standards, bottom-up self-regulation emerges without top-down regulation. Tensions between communicative effectiveness or expedience, favouring spontaneous self-regulation, and social prestige, favouring standards, add to the dynamics of variation, regulation and change.

Standardness has a strong ideological underpinning: it is advocated as language at its 'best': the richest in vocabulary, the most sophisticated – and 'correct' – in grammatical structure, the most appropriate in register, the most idiomatic in phraseological expression, the most fluent in speech and elegant in accent. Since English as an L2 is most commonly associated with learning English as a foreign or second language through classroom instruction and often relatively early stages of learning, native speakers not only constitute the target set up for learners, but are always at an advantage in comparison, and ascribed the possession of the 'best' version of the language. However, in her chapter, Dąbrowska (Chapter 3) clearly shows that such key aspects of individual language ability as phonological representation, vocabulary size and grammatical complexity are all determined to a large extent by the amount of print exposure. The amount of print exposure does not equal the categories of native and non-native speakers. Quite the contrary, many speakers of ELF, professionals in academia, diplomacy and international relations, are likely to have experienced vast amounts of print exposure. Thus, the 'best' versions of the language might not necessarily belong to native speakers.

The issue of individual speakers versus language in the community is raised in several chapters. Dąbrowska describes how writing changes language in the individual mind and how cumulatively such changes lead to changes at the level of the community. Mauranen likewise explores language contact at the individual and the communal levels, but also posits a third level of social interaction as the mediating force between the two. She argues that the effects of language contact percolate upwards from the individual to collective usage through social interaction. Conversely, individuals are primed by the usage in interaction but also beyond it, to adopt features from 'above', absorbing them in their personal repertoires. Croft, adopting an evolutionary perspective, defines language as a population of actual utterances produced in a speech community, in turn defined as a population of persons interacting with each other. Schneider (Chapter 1) assumes a complex dynamic systems perspective and points out that constructions diffuse by replication both individually and communally. Vetchinnikova and Hiltunen (Chapter 8) conceptualize language as a complex system of idiolects and examine micro-processes of language change, such as priming and chunking, at both the individual and the communal level of language representation, comparing them to each other. Recognizing individuals under the disguise of the communal has implications for understanding synchronic variation, especially in the current situation of increased mobility and migration.

Vetchinnikova and Hiltunen's study shows that when a communal corpus displays an alternation between, for example, two variant forms, it does not necessarily mean that each individual alternates between these two forms in the same proportion. What this can suggest instead is the split between those individuals who prefer one form and those who prefer the other, both being remarkably consistent in their choices. Thus, variation can be tied to the actual people rather than to nationality, culture, geographic location or any other criterion by which a language community is commonly defined. In diffusion, then, the forms are 'reshuffling', to use Schneider's expression, because people are reshuffling by migrating from one place to another. That is, forms can travel together with the idiolects which bear them.

The process itself is not new, as we see from Nevalainen's close focus on the individual within the wider social environment. In Early Modern English, migrants from the North brought the third-person singular -*s* variant to London, replacing the southern -*(e)th* variant: early modern London was a city of immigrants, as Nevalainen writes. She gives examples of two individual speakers, Thomas Cromwell, who was born south-west of London and was a consistent -*(e)th* user, and Henry Machyn, who apparently arrived in London from the North and continued to use the -*s* variant. The difference of today's Global English from Early Modern English is in the scale of migration and the heterogeneity of social contacts.

Internal Dynamics

Several chapters in this volume directly address the question of internal processes of language variation and change, such as regularization, simplification, generalization and lexical conditioning.

Nevalainen points out that the replacement of the third-person singular -(*e*)*th* by the northern -(*e*)*s* variant is a case of simplification, since the original northern English system of present-tense verbal inflections was more complex. She also predicts that the current system is at an intermediate stage in the regularization process and may continue to regularize. Verbal -*s*, for example, may at some point in the future be replaced by the suffixless or zero variant which can at present be observed in some pidgin and creole varieties, as well as in ELF interaction.

Contact-induced processes in translations and ELF, as discussed by Mauranen, reveal some shared contact-induced developments, which indicate simplification in certain respects, but also complexification, and above all new preferences among existing grammatical patterns. Simplification would seem to be at its clearest in lexis, where the most common words tend to become proportionally even more common. This effect is nevertheless found only among the very highest-frequency lexis, and an overarching simplification is not supported. In syntax, calquing is common in both translation and ELF, resulting in new lexicogrammatical patterns in the affected language, while altered syntactic preferences are also in evidence. At the same time, both show a measure of loosening up of conventional patterns, which would appear to originate in a reinterpretation of patterns as productive instead of conventionalized and lead to increased variability.

Schneider takes up the phenomenon of the spread of *as* in constructions such as *call as/term as* in Asia (cf. *consider as/regard as*). He notes that the process follows the common route observed in the diffusion of innovations, as it is lexically conditioned to be adopted with different verbs to various extents, but the 'lexical anchor' drives the innovation to new contexts. The process is similar to lexicosyntactic calquing (Silva-Corvalan 1998) and appears in translations and cross-linguistic influences discussed in Mauranen's chapter. In this respect it is interesting to recall that the diffusion of verbal -*s* also showed signs of lexical conditioning: high-frequency verbs *have* and *do* resisted the change.

Vetchinnikova and Hiltunen looked at the variation between the contracted and the full form *it's* versus *it is* and show that at the individual level there is an effect of priming and chunking on the tendency to contract. That is, if an individual produced a contracted form, s/he is more likely to contract it again in immediate proximity. Likewise, if *it's/it is* is part of a chunk in one's individual chunk repertoire, it is more likely to occur in a contracted form. Since both factors, cognitive in nature, work at the individual level, this may lead to more divergence in individual preferences and individual language use.

The chapters in this volume have adopted various units of analysis – from individual speakers to social formations such as societies, countries, tribes and groups, and a number of linguistic categories, including grammatical or lexical forms, pragmatic items or 'linguemes'. Besides these, units of analysis involving multimodal elements such as gestures and images are taken up, and newer, typically digital elements also make an appearance: emoji and tweets shape our notions of what counts as a unit of communication. Many of these may very well be closely intertwined with ELF as the language of the globalized world, with the growing needs to communicate across boundaries and borders, even when conventional notions of proficiency, fluency or standardness fail to be relevant. These may indicate the shape of things to come.

REFERENCES

Franzmann, Andreas, Jansen, Axel & Münte, Peter. 2015. Legitimizing science: Introductory essay. In Axel Jansen, Andreas Franzmann & Peter Münte (eds.), *Legitimizing Science: National and Global Publics (1800–2010)*, 11–34. Chicago, IL: University of Chicago Press.

Jenkins, Jennifer. 2015. Repositioning English and multilingualism in English as a Lingua Franca. *Englishes in Practice* 2(3), 49–85.

Mauranen, Anna. 2018. Second language acquisition, World Englishes, and English as a Lingua Franca (ELF). *World Englishes* 37, 106–119.

Mortensen, Janus. 2017. Transient multilingual communities as a field of investigation: Challenges and opportunities. *Journal of Linguistic Anthropology* 27(3), 271–288.

Pavlenko, Aneta. 2014. *The Bilingual Mind*. Cambridge: Cambridge University Press.

Ross, Malcolm. 2003. Diagnosing prehistoric language contact. In Raymond Hickey (ed.), *Motives for Language Change*, 174–198. Cambridge: Cambridge University Press.

Seidlhofer, Barbara. 2011. *Understanding English as a Lingua Franca*. Oxford: Oxford University Press.

Silva-Corvalan, Carmen. 1998. On borrowing as a mechanism of syntactic change. In Armin Schwegler, Bernard Tranel & Myriam Uribe- Etcxebarria (eds.), *Romance Linguistics: Theoretical Perspectives*, 225–246. Amsterdam: John Benjamins.

Wenger, Etienne. 1998. *Communities of Practice. Learning, Meaning, and Identity.* Cambridge: Cambridge University Press.

Part I

Pooling Perspectives

Introduction
Anna Mauranen

Linguistic processes have often been recognized as being inextricably entwined with social processes, sometimes also with cognitive processes. It would be possible to go further and embrace the fact that language is both a social and a cognitive phenomenon, and that, therefore, linguistic processes are social processes and at the same time also cognitive processes. This holistic picture would seem to emerge from much of the discussion in the papers to hand, albeit not made explicit in any of them.

The set of articles in this first part of the current volume paints the big picture and addresses theoretical issues related to language contact and language change. All originate from different theoretical traditions but come together in that they all engage with dynamism in language: we know that language is in a perpetual state of change, but we know far less about the possible causes that bring this change about. Clearly, phenomena and processes that are involved in change can be internal or external to language, and models involving either or both are familiar in linguistic research.

Major threads running through these papers include change and dynamism, contact and different levels of language processes. **Edgar W. Schneider** starts out by outright focusing on change as dynamism. He presents a model that comprises all possible Englishes, core Englishes and World Englishes, as well as English as a Lingua Franca (ELF): Complex Dynamic Systems. This theoretical model, which originates in sciences but has also been adopted in social sciences, including linguistics, offers tools for dealing with change, and a perspective on language that is both holistic and processual. Schneider concentrates on analysing certain lexical and syntactic phenomena to illustrate the strengths of the model. Processes of lexicosemantic diffusion cater both to a measure of stability in language and to providing prerequisites for qualitative changes over time. His other case is syntactic restructuring, which reflects self-organization in language, and moving from chaotic states towards order. Schneider also points out that many open questions still remain quite unexplored and unanswered in the pursuit of manifestations and processes of Complex Dynamic Systems in linguistic phenomena. This field of research is still in its early stages.

William Croft proposes a sociolinguistic typology of contact languages, showing how ELF can be placed in this framework. He looks at different types of contact languages in diverse social settings, thus also present-day ELF in relation to the general processes of language contact and change. Along with Nevalainen's and Mortensen's papers, he also orients to societal changes and circumstances as key components of language contact and change. Croft distinguishes between different kinds of contact languages, albeit on a continuum: esoteric, used within a speech community; exoteric, used between communities; and neogenic, which arise when different speech communities merge into a new societal unit. He stresses the role of social circumstances in giving rise to the different kinds of language contact and contact languages. He shows how English has functioned as a neogenic language a number of times throughout its history in different parts of the world. In today's world, however, one of its principal roles is to function as the primary exoteric lingua franca in the globalized world, notably in domains like science, commerce and popular culture.

Both of the previous papers have been concerned with macro-level phenomena – language as a whole and entire communities or societies. **Ewa Dąbrowska**'s approach brings in the individual's cognitive level along with the communal level. Her take on what changes language takes a step in a new direction, not only with respect to this volume, but in relation to most linguistic research: she is concerned with the effects that writing might have on language. Her main focus is on the individual mind, and how the availability of visual representation helps lift off some of the load on the working memory, which helps in processing more complex sentences. This presumably also provides access to a wider range of contexts of use to an individual in a literate society, including more register variation. Among other things, writing enables communication with relative strangers, with whom shared knowledge cannot be assumed to the extent that it is possible in small communities, and which therefore necessitates greater communicative explicitness – which is a comparable development in ELF, and also in translation, as Mauranen's paper shows. Dąbrowska also makes the important point that the few studies of the effects of literacy have been made on languages with a long tradition of literacy, while non-European, oral languages have remained mainly outside, and even though they are known to be different in many ways, have not been included in relevant theorizing yet.

ELF is compared with translation by **Anna Mauranen**, who takes both as embodiments of language contact. Both change people's linguistic intuitions, including those concerning their L1, through engagement in multilingual activity. Mauranen looks into similar processes and phenomena in ELF and translation, and notes that enhanced explicitness characterizes both – a process Dąbrowska suggests was enabled by literacy. She adds one more level to the cognitive and the macro-social: the interactional or micro-social, which she implicates in a crucial mediating role in the diffusion of influences across individuals towards collective social levels. This is particularly important in analysing ELF, which in contrast to standardized languages lacks top-down regulation. A crucial mechanism in passing on influences between individuals in mainly spoken interaction (as in ELF) and in text-mediated interaction (typically in translation), in her view, is priming, which thus also plays a central role in the diffusion of innovations and changes. She posits that the specific interest value of ELF lies in its character as a second-order contact, which is both complicated and complex in the sense of Complex Dynamic Systems, outlined in Schneider (see also Vetchinnikova and Hiltunen in Part II).

Terttu Nevalainen combines historical and sociolinguistic perspectives in her approach to change in English, which takes up an extended case study of the third-person verbal ending *-s* with its variants. Her analysis draws interesting parallels between ELF today and the longer temporal trajectory of Standard English in England. Contact between languages and dialects plays a major role in both, and very similar variation and structural simplification phenomena are discernible from the diachronic and the synchronic vantage points. Like the previous articles in this section, Nevalainen alternates between the micro and macro levels, showing how different social strata, mobility and developments in the societal structures contributed to adoption or rejection of given forms. At the same time, variability in individuals' usage not only persisted for decades, but was also remarkably widespread, so that around half of the individual writers in the data retained more than one variant form in their usage. To the much-debated issue of whether Standard English is a help or hindrance to effective communication, she usefully remarks that code fixation is in itself a process, never final and complete.

Finally, **Janus Mortensen** suggests that we might not want to limit ourselves to investigating the ways in which ELF changes English, but more ambitiously extend our horizons to include the ways in which it changes social practices. Mortensen draws his illustrative examples from the university domain, where internationalization has brought ELF into the daily lives of students, professors and administrators alike. The development in Denmark that Mortensen describes has run along similar lines in many European countries, and has not been an uncontroversial process, perhaps showing indeed how closely language is intertwined with social processes – or indeed how language is in itself a social phenomenon. By focusing on a specific context where ELF use has been mapped fairly thoroughly over recent years, Mortensen's article also bridges the transition from the general issues discussed in the first part of this volume towards a variety of more specific cases and contexts that are addressed in Part II.

1 *Calling* Englishes *As* Complex Dynamic Systems: Diffusion and Restructuring

Edgar W. Schneider

1 Introduction

Traditionally, descriptive linguistic perspectives on varieties of English, both diachronic, regional, and social ones, as well as World Englishes (WEs; Schneider 2007, 2011a; Mesthrie & Bhatt 2008) or novel English as a Lingua Franca (ELF) uses (Seidlhofer 2011; Pitzl & Osimk-Teasdale 2016; Jenkins et al. 2018) have largely been feature-based – documented and analyzed distinctive and conspicuous properties on the levels of lexis, pronunciation, and grammar. This approach characterizes major reference resources, such as the two-volume *Handbook* by Kortmann et al. (2004) or the eWAVE (Kortmann & Lunkenheimer 2012; http://ewave-atlas.org/). Often these features are compared to some "reference" norm, most commonly standard British English (BrE). Heuristically, this constitutes important groundwork, to understand the character of varieties and the nature of change in them, and also for practical applications – for example, in language policy development and teaching. Theoretically and ideologically, however, the feature-based approach can also be regarded as problematic, especially if it remains focused on a single phenomenon, disregarding contexts and systemic embedding. Most fundamentally, it is in line with a basic "reductionist" tendency of sciences, to be found in linguistics as well, which breaks complex entities down into smallest units, which are then classified and described with respect to their types of mutual relations (constructions in language).

It has been felt and argued that such a categorial approach abstracts too strongly from complex realities, reducing them to relations more readily suitable for the human mind to grasp. This is not to reject feature-based descriptions altogether – they may be heuristically helpful and provide a baseline for more comprehensive perspectives and for understanding interactions between the components of a language. But a call for a more comprehensive, integrative approach is justified. Complicated and multifactorial systems like human language are marked by continuous and multiple interactions, ongoing changes, and other properties. So instead of asking, "Which features (sounds, words, constructions) does variety X have?" and

"Where has this feature come from?" (a legitimate but reductionist and outside-dominated view), it is more appropriate to ask, "How is the (sub)system xy organized in context Y (determined by speakers at place P and time T)?" and "How have these relationships evolved (through time, place, and various input factors)?" This paper presents and reinforces a call for an independent, systemic perspective, the adoption of a novel (suitable) framework from the sciences that promises to be suitable, inspiring, and enlightening for language development as well: the theory of Complex Dynamic Systems (CDS).

It is worth noting that the same applies to ELF usage as well (cf. Mauranen 2017, 2018; Jenkins et al. 2018). There have been studies of "ELF features," but conventionally ELF is not regarded as "a variety" (though there are alternative views as well; cf. Laitinen 2018), lacking stability and depending very much on specific usage contexts. But in principle ELF clearly also constitutes a manifestation of usage, continuously recreated and situationally dependent and constantly reorganized in this process, thus manifesting the core property of auto-organization and emergence. Larsen-Freeman (2018) explores the relationship between ELF and what she calls "Complexity Theory" (CT), and explicitly suggests "design features for an ELF research agenda informed by CT" (51). In ELF communication, speakers enact "a languaging episode" and "soft-assemble" and thereby transform their language resources (53), she suggests. Similarly, Mauranen (2017, 2018: 12–13, 16–20) focuses on interaction as central to ELF and connects this with CT.

2 The Theory of Complex Dynamic Systems and Linguistic Applications

Over the last few decades, CDS theory has been established and growing vigorously in the natural and social sciences and in mathematics, showcasing a wide range of successful applications in biology, medicine, social organization, the description of natural phenomena, technology, businesses, and more. It captures basic properties of many different domains in life, highlighting complex systemic relationships and their interconnected, perpetually developing nature.

The theory is associated with varying labels (e.g. Systems Science, Complexity Science, or theory of Complex Adaptive Systems). It has evolved through and become influential in various subdisciplines of the sciences since roughly the 1960s, after precursor disciplines since the earlier twentieth century (for a historical survey of the discipline see Mobus & Kalton 2015: 32–40), and is well established by now as a novel, all-encompassing explanatory framework. CDS theory argues strongly against reductionism and categorial and deterministic thinking. While there is a wide body of writings and applications, no generally accepted, canonical framework exists as yet; it is a "holistic" and "cross-disciplinary" approach, an emerging "meta-science" (Mobus & Kalton 2015: 3). Properties of CDS will be outlined in Section 3, but for reasons of space I cannot go into the history and other applications of the theory (see Bossomaier & Green 2000; Johnson 2009; Holland 2014; Mobus & Kalton 2015).

CDS theory is closely related to chaos theory, one of its major precursor frameworks, based on non-linear equations in mathematics. The precise relationship between both approaches is unclear, perhaps controversial. While some scholars insist that CDS theory is essentially independent of chaos theory (Kretzschmar, p.c.), most books on CDS theory tend to incorporate concepts from chaos theory, regarding the latter as a branch of the former (see, e.g. Guastello et al. 2009: e.g. p. 3). The core property of non-linearity is usually taken to be shared (Mufwene et al. 2017: 2; Larsen-Freeman 2018: 52) or even central to both disciplines: "Non-linear behaviour is one of the cornerstones of complexity" (Bossomaier & Green 2000: 7; cf. Mobus & Kalton 2015: 202, 251–252, 592). Given that CDS is often explicitly viewed as a "meta-theory" (Guastello et al. 2009: 2; Mobus & Kalton 2015: 3; Larsen-Freeman 2018: 51), this is a reasonable position, which I also adopt. I shall therefore include some components that are typical of chaotic systems (e.g. the interrelationship of order and chaos, or bifurcation) in my discussions below, a view that is shared by Vetchinnikova (p.c.).

Many application domains have been discussed in the CDS literature; the only one I am aware of that lists language as a CDS, in very general terms, is Holland (2014). In linguistics, claims of the applicability of CDS theory to language have increasingly been voiced over the last few years and decades, although this is clearly still a marginal line of thinking. Some early and general suggestions include Lindblom et al. (1984) on self-organization, Hopper (1987) on grammar as emergent, and Schneider (1997a) on chaos theory as a possible model for dialect variability and change. A few references in passing on the possible suitability of chaos theory for explaining patterns of language can be found in writings by Salikoko Mufwene, David Lightfoot, and a few others – in very general terms, though. Early work by Larsen-Freeman (e.g. 1997) employed this theory in applied linguistics, notably to explain aspects of language acquisition; similarly, Nick Ellis has contributed important psycholinguistic studies from this perspective (e.g. 2008, 2011). Some conceptual parallels with usage-based linguistics are evident, a relationship explicitly stated in Bybee (2010), a book that in a chapter of its own posits "Language as a Complex Adaptive System" and mentions some similarities between both approaches. Mauranen (2017, 2018), Larsen-Freeman (2018), and Vetchinnikova (2017) have related complex systems theory to ELF usage.

A few important recent monographs, beginning with Larsen-Freeman and Cameron (2008), explicitly make claims as to the suitability of CDS theory for language, also in their titles. Most importantly, Ellis and Larsen-Freeman's (2009) collection contains a programmatic "position paper" entitled "Language Is A Complex Adaptive System" (Beckner et al. 2009, also known as the "Five Graces Group"). They state that "[t]he study of Complex Adaptive Systems, Emergentism, and Dynamic Systems Theory is a relatively recent phenomenon, yet it is revolutionizing our understanding of the natural, physical, and social worlds" (Ellis & Larsen-Freeman 2009: vi). The contributions in these books survey core properties of complexity and chaos that determine language behavior as well, but they do so in rather general terms (with hardly any structural examples) and from a strongly applied perspective (highlighting the relevance of this approach for language teaching and acquisition). Finally, Kretzschmar (2015), after a thematically related precursor volume (Kretzschmar 2009), presents CDS theory as an alternative view to determinism and reductionism. Strongly fueled by quantitative observations of Linguistic Atlas data distributions, he highlights the ubiquity of "A-curve" distributions (closely related to the "80/20 rule," known also in the business world): the fact that we often find a small number of types with very high token frequencies (the prototypical representatives of a category) and then an increasingly large number of rare types (the "long tail" of a graphic A-curve display, which holds the potential for increase and change when any of the rare forms, for whatever reason, increase in frequency).

While all these authors, and a few more, consider CDS theory to be a suitable approach for languages, it still seems clear that CDS thinking in linguistics largely constitutes a niche today – growing in importance, but clearly not yet mainstream thinking. There have also been initial, tentative applications to language change and ELF, the topic of this volume (Mauranen 2017, 2018; Vetchinnikova 2017; Larsen-Freeman 2018). The applicability of the theory has been intuitively sensed, projected, and suggested, but it still needs to be expanded and filled with life. Consequently, in this paper I focus on processes of variation and change in English, integrating examples from the history of English, from regional and social varieties, and from WEs – recognizing the holistic nature of the CDS approach.

3   Properties of Complex Dynamic Systems in English(es)

In this section I discuss a range of core properties of CDS, briefly characterizing their fundamental nature, their applicability to language in general, and possible applications to aspects of English. The issues to be addressed include systemness, complexity, perpetual dynamics, network relationships, the alternation between order and chaos, the "butterfly effect," bifurcation, emergentism, and a system's self-organizing capacity. Further properties of CDS are disregarded here for the time being and for possible future consideration, including non-linearity, fractals (but see Vetchinnikova 2017 [esp. p. 279], who views similarities in the patterns of chunking between the cognitive and the communal planes as an indication of the fractal structure of language), and attractors (cf. Larsen-Freeman 2018: 52).

3.1 Systemness

In CDS theory, "a system is a whole of some sort made up of interacting or interdependent elements or components integrally related among themselves" (Mobus & Kalton 2015: 73f). It is self-evident and axiomatic in linguistics that this holds for language as well – for example, in Saussure's structuralism that language is a "system of signs" in which units on several levels (phonemes, morphemes, lexemes; phrases, clauses; constructions) enter mutual (syntagmatic and paradigmatic) relations of various kinds. Systemness is thus a prerequisite for but not yet a manifestation of complexity.

This is equally obvious and uncontroversial in varieties of English. Here is a trivial example from WEs, a prototypical structure found in Colloquial Singaporean English:

(1)   *I dunno lah* (from an informal conversation; source: Schneider 2011a: 160)

Even this simple three-word pattern allows us to identify a number of systemic language-internal relations between clause constituents of several kinds. The words represent a basic syntagmatic pattern (S-Aux-Neg-V-A$_{\text{[sentence adverbial/discourse marker]}}$). The "underlying" items *do + not + know* are syntagmatically fused to yield *dunno*. The (typically Singaporean) discourse marker *lah* takes a syntagmatic role as sentence adverbial modifying the matrix clause proposition, with specific semantics ("assertion"); and in itself it represents an element of a subsystem, potentially contrasting with other Singlish discourse markers such as *lor* (which would mean "compromise"), *meh* (indicating "uncertainty"), and others.

3.2 Complexity

This property is even embedded in the name of CDS. It is defined as a large number and different types of objects or agents and by regular interactions between them, operating on several hierarchical organization levels.[1] Its applicability to languages (and to Englishes) is equally uncontroversial

---

[1] It is noteworthy that being complex in the CDS sense is not the same as merely being "complicated." The latter certainly constitutes a condition for the former, but complex systems are characterized by the entire set of properties discussed in this paper, most importantly emergentism and auto-organization.

(cf. a series of recent publications on complexity in languages, e.g. Miestamo et al. 2008; Sampson et al. 2009; Culicover 2013; Newmeyer & Preston 2014).

It operates on two levels: the intralinguistic and extralinguistic. Language-internal relations are conventionally understood as hierarchies of units that build utterances: sounds build morphemes, which are parts of lexemes, which in turn constitute phrases, and these function in clauses; clauses are constituents of utterances and sentences, which build discourse and texts. An additional, recursive level of complexity arises from the fact that some of these units can be mutually hierarchically constitutive: phrases are constituents of clauses, and clauses can be constituents of phrases. Language-externally, speakers can be viewed as agents, of which there are large numbers with varying acquisition backgrounds and idiolects, adopting varying identities and social roles and attributing different prestige assignments to their utterances. For example, in the Dynamic Model of the evolution of Postcolonial Englishes (Schneider 2007), political factors determine identities of and relationships between settlers and indigenous groups, and the sociolinguistic interactions between them are decisive for the process of "structural nativization," the emergence of locally characteristic language patterns, and the evolution of New Englishes – clearly also a process with many agents, hierarchies, and levels of complexity involved. For ELF usage, comparable social complexity levels include "individual human beings, their contact zones, and globalized networks" (Larsen-Freeman 2018: 54).

3.3   Perpetual Dynamics

CDS are always in flux, marked by continuously ongoing changes and modifications of systems over time, a perpetual process that never stops. Obviously, the same applies to language and to English(es): language transmission from one generation to the next, also involving constant processes of change, is equally perpetually continuing. In fact, it is not even or mainly across generations that linguistic forms and habits are being passed on – every single utterance always reiterates, reproduces linguistic usage, is shaped by and at the same time may be taken to have an influence on earlier and later utterances produced by surrounding speakers. We need to recognize that there has been an unbroken chain of transmission from Germanic to Old English (OE) to Middle English (ME) to Early Modern English (EModE) to Modern English – with more or fewer contact effects filtered in at different points of time, but without any interruption. And we have to note that this pattern of continuous transmission comprises not only "Standard English" and regional dialects but all varieties, all elements of the "English Language Complex" (Mesthrie & Bhatt 2008: 1–10). English has equally continuously been passed on (and partly been transformed in this process) to regional and colonial dialects; with this in mind, Singlish, Indian English, Nigerian Pidgin English, and all other "New Englishes" and contact varieties are all equally continuations and dynamic reinstantiations of what once was OE, daughter varieties or complex interacting branches of an overall system of "English(es)!"

This process of transmission comprises both elements of continuity – perpetuation across time without substantial modification (e.g. practically all varieties of English have a sound /p/, a lexeme *hand*, and an NP pattern with a Det-Adj-N constituent sequence) – and discontinuity – that is, change, innovation, and the adoption of elements from contact languages (e.g. Singlish has subject omission in *Can!*, Indian English has the lexeme *dhoti*, and Nigerian Pidgin English has a second-person plural pronoun *una* – all "picked up" at some point along the way through time and space, for some reason, and not shared by the others).

As an illustration of these principles, I want to briefly recapitulate the development of modal verbs in English(es), from the beginnings to some present-day branches (cf. Lightfoot 1979; Denison 1993: 292–339; Fischer & van der Wurff 2006: 146–152). As is well known to language historians, in pre-OE times some Proto-Indo-European perfect verb forms were semantically reinterpreted as (resultative) present forms (the so-called preterite present verbs). In OE these verbs had full verb properties: they were main verbs and some had direct objects, two properties that their German cognates have retained to the present day (e.g. *ich kann das*), but that English lost along the way (*I can that); also, they had non-finite forms, unlike today's English modals. In the transition from ME to EModE these verbs were reanalyzed as auxiliaries (modal auxiliaries, more precisely), increasingly gaining the distinctive so-called NICE properties (being used in special ways for negation, inversion in interrogatives, "code" in elliptical structures, and emphasis). Furthermore, they no longer allow direct objects and cannot be used without full verb predicates (cf. *I can do that*), they come to lack non-finite forms, and their semantics changes in distinctive ways (getting restricted to epistemic or deontic meanings). In present-day English many modals have been shown to be losing ground, to the point of partly disappearing (e.g. in the cases of *may* for permission, *ought to,* or *shall*); conversely, new modals (e.g. *gonna, gotta, wanna*) keep emerging, and the use of semi-modals (e.g. *be going to, have to*) is increasing (Leech et al. 2009: 71–117). In regional dialects, alternative options and properties have been retained or have emerged. For example, in Southern AmE (American English) double modals can be found (e.g. *I might could do that*), in a pattern that violates the Modern English rule of allowing only one modal in a clause, but that may be seen as continuing the OE property of the combinability of preterite presents, with special pragmatic functionality (e.g. implying tentativeness). In WEs, frequency shifts of modal usage are common; for example, *shall* occurs very frequently in Kenya but is very rare in

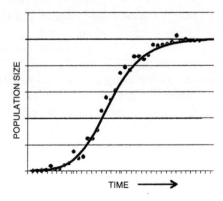

Figure 1.1 The S-curve as a diffusion model in population biology. (from Mobus & Kalton 2015: 215)

Hong Kong (Collins & Yao 2012). So, it's a *perpetuum mobile*, a continuous reshuffling process, with old forms retaining old properties only in some varieties but gaining new functions in others, with the frequency of individual forms waxing and waning from one variety to another, with relations constantly changing in a process that never ends.

Interestingly enough, in both frameworks the notion of the S-curve as a typical instantiation of the diffusion dynamism, a model of the phase and state transitions that an innovation passes through, has been identified. For CDS, Mobus and Kalton state that "[t]he S-shape of the logistic function is generated when processes are characterized first by an exponential rise followed by an exponential deceleration to level off at a maximum" (2015: 215). Figure 1.1 shows how new properties spread in a population over time, following the typical phases of a slow start, a quick rise through the population, and a slow trailing off, observed to be a common process in population biology.

In sociolinguistics, since Bailey (1973) the S-curve has also been the generally accepted model for how linguistic innovations spread in social space (Kroch 1989; Labov 1994: 65–67; Nevalainen 2015), in a characteristic "slow-quick-quick-slow" pattern. Change is thus understood as incremental, not discontinuous – but non-linear!

Figure 1.2 documents a well-known application to the history of English, based on work by Ellegård (1953). The graph shows the spread of *do*-support in different constructions during the EModE period (adapted by Kroch 1989: 223) – in each environment it diffuses in an S-curve form. Nevalainen (2015) puts the model to the test and finds it largely confirmed and basically descriptively adequate for the vast majority of longitudinal changes investigated.

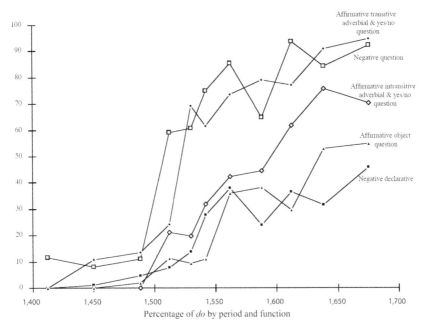

Figure 1.2 S-curve shapes in the diffusion of *do*-support in different environments.
(from Kroch 1989: 223, after Ellegård 1953)

3.4   Network Relationships

In CDS, "systems are ... networks of relations," "the components are connected in various relations" (Mobus & Kalton 2015: 137), often indirectly, in a chainlike fashion. Again, this is evidently relevant to language and Englishes as well, and can be viewed from two perspectives.

The language-external perspective recognizes the fact that the development of linguistic forms depends upon social relationships between speakers; Thomason and Kaufmann (1988), for instance, explicitly stated that "the history of a language is a function of the history of its speakers" (4). Similarly, in the so-called second wave of variationist sociolinguistics, the concept of social networks is crucial to speakers' speech behavior, as shown in work by Jim and Lesley Milroy in Belfast (Milroy & Milroy 1985; L. Milroy 1987; Milroy & Llamas 2013). In Postcolonial Englishes, as based on the Dynamic Model (Schneider 2007), a unilateral implication between various factors is posited: "history and politics" determine speakers' "identity constructions," which in turn determine sociolinguistic conditions of contact and interaction, and these are decisive for linguistic developments and structural effects. Thus, there is a network dependency leading from external conditions to internal structural properties.

In a language-internal perspective, interrelationships between items, constructions, and language levels can be taken to illustrate the network principle. The loss of endings in the history of English, and consequently the change of the character of English from a largely synthetic to a largely analytic language, a most fundamental modification, presents a nice example of this. Indo-European, Germanic, and OE were strongly synthetic languages, rich in inflectional endings. The change started inconspicuously with the "Germanic Main Stress Rule," which fixed stress on the first syllables of words in pre-OE times. Stressed initial syllables cause a weakening of the phonation stream in later, especially final syllables, which in turn produce the weakening of full vowel qualities (to schwa) in final syllables. In OE this reductive tendency was amplified (presumably) by intensive contact with the Scandinavians' Old Norse, supporting the loss of endings. So, gradually, most inflectional endings disappeared. For example, OE *sunu*, with a full final vowel, became weakened ME *sune*, and ultimately uninflected Modern English *son*. The loss of endings, however, needed to be compensated for by new grammatical means of expressing syntactic functions, so English developed a fixed subject-verb-object word order and the strengthening of function words. A former accusative ending became replaced by the direct object position immediately after the verb; the dative ending gave way to the preposition *to* plus the noun; the verbal subjunctive was weakened substantially, its function being taken over by modal verbs and modal adverbs, and so on. So the radical change of the character of English, unique among the Germanic languages, was motivated by a series of reasons and step-by-step influences, leading from stress to phonology to morphology to syntax. Today in some WEs – for example, China English – the trend continues further, since due to substrate effects of analytic Sinitic languages, the *-s* suffix on verbs (for the third-person singular) or nouns (for plural) is often omitted (Schneider 2011b).

3.5 The Interplay of Order and Chaos

The coexistence of order and chaos, in different subsystems and at different times, is a constitutive property of "chaotic systems": they are characterized by "pockets of order" inside "chaos" (Gleick 1987; Johnson 2009: 15–16), "a complicated mix of ordered and disordered behavior" (Johnson 2009: 15). Transition from order and/or simplicity to chaos and/or complexity proceeds via phases of "turbulence."

Obviously this applies to languages and Englishes as well: at any point in time, there are subsystems that are relatively orderly (i.e. consist of a relatively small number of units with clear functional assignments and clear mutual delimitation) and subsystems that are disorderly (marked by a large number of units, fuzziness, and functional overlaps). And this is constantly subject to change: ordered subsystems may be disrupted and break down, but conversely systematicity may emerge in formerly chaotic subsystems.

As a suitable example from the history of English, extending back across millennia, let us look at the dissolution of the English strong verb system and counter-tendencies towards regularization. The starting point in Indo-European shows a perfectly regular and predictable distribution of forms: verbs have four stem forms for different functions, which receive different degrees of stress (full/weak/none/none) and consequently develop different vowel realizations (-e-/-o-/-Ø-/-Ø-). In a second stage, towards Germanic and OE, turbulence comes in via effects of interfering conditioned sound changes, which modify stem vowels in different phonological environments. Simplifying things a bit, the stem vowels are changed variably depending on whether an /i/, an /u/, a nasal or liquid, a consonant cluster beginning with a nasal or liquid, or any other sound follows, impacting the system and illustrating how internal effects may generate disequilibria (Mauranen, p.c.). These changes produce five classes (and more subclasses) of "strong verbs," each of which, combined with the different base vowels of Indo-European, is marked by very many different but still predictable vowels in specific verb forms. Together with a sixth verb class (from a different source), other verbs joining the pattern, and occasional lengthening tendencies in some forms, a highly complex but still largely predictable system emerges. Further turbulence kicks in between OE and ME with the reduction of four stem forms to the three we find in Modern English. Which form survived varied strongly from one word and one dialect to another, so any leftover regularity breaks down by this point. During EModE the process of standardization and authoritative sources like Johnson's *Dictionary* of 1755 established some conventions as to which forms count as accepted in English, but in regional and social dialects we find even more turbulence, irregularity, and chaos. In Earlier African American Vernacular English (EAAVE), for instance, we find forms such as *bring – brung, fight – fit, sit – sot, fetch – fotch, catch – cotch, take – tuck/tooken*, and many more (Schneider 1989: 90–114). Hence, the modern set of irregular English verb forms can be considered as wholly chaotic, but at the same time a product of a gradual breakdown of order towards chaos.

Conversely, however, there have been counter-tendencies towards regaining order in expressing past tense. One is regularization, based on the cognitive principle of regularity and compositionality: a consistent association of a particular form (the dental suffix *-ed*) and a specific meaning ("past"), added to verbs, produces a large number of "weak" verbs in OE (classified as "regular" verbs today), and attracts some strong verbs to join the regular set (e.g. the strong OE verb *helpan-healp-hulpon-holpen* became regular in Modern English: *help-helped-helped*). Again, this tendency is even stronger and more widespread in regional and social dialects without the pressures of standardization and norming – in EAAVE, for example, we find *knowed, growed, gived, runned*, and other similar forms. Some of these are also found in some WEs. A second tendency increasing order in past-tense formation is the growing association of the "ideaphone" /ʌ/ with the notion of "past-ness" identified by Cheshire (1994). Again, this is strongest in dialects, where we find not only the standard forms *run, struck, wrung, done,* and *sunk*, but also *drug, tuck,* or *brung* as past-tense forms. In Canadian English *snuck* is replacing *sneaked*, with this ongoing change forming "a classic S-curve" (Chambers 2006–2007: 27).

3.6 The "Butterfly Effect"

The widely known "butterfly effect" – popularly understood as the flapping of the wings of a butterfly causing a tornado some time later in a totally different place – is technically known as "sensitivity to initial conditions," a characteristic property of chaotic systems, resulting from non-linear equations: very slight differences of initial states lead to unpredictably large divergences down the road; amplification may lead to a qualitative leap in the system. This has important consequences for the time flow of such systems: as a matter of principle, their evolution is explainable from hindsight but unpredictable in advance.

Consequently, the history and development of English (or any language) can be explained but not predicted, because small-scale distinctions (possibly via affecting other levels of organization) may have far-reaching qualitative effects. A very strong example of such a process in the history of English, the loss of endings and its causes and steps, was discussed earlier in Section 3.4: a small-scale phonotactic change (the fixing of stress) about 2,000 years ago has ultimately led to the fundamental transformation of the typological character of English, from synthetic to analytic.

Another example of a possible butterfly effect is the different effects of a sound change known as "replacive lengthening" in English versus German, summarized in example (2), which ultimately led to qualitative lexical effects:

(2) Replacive lengthening
Shared condition (West Germanic):
V N > V: Ø / ___ C$_{\text{[voiceless velar fricative]}}$ (= χ [x])
Widened variant condition (Anglo-Frisian; i.e. in English but not German):
V N > V: Ø / ___ C$_{\text{[voiceless fricative]}}$ (= also f, s, þ)

In this Germanic sound change, nasals (N) were lost between vowels (V) and fricatives but produced a lengthening of the preceding vowel. All across West Germanic this change operated only before voiceless velar fricatives; only in Anglo-Frisian (which later produced English) did it occur before other voiceless fricatives as well. So, in both German and English some base forms of verbs have nasals (*denken, bringen*; *think, bring*, etc.), but the past-tense forms, where the velar stops were assimilated to become velar fricatives and hence the above condition applied, have none (*dachte, brachte*; *thought, brought*). But before other fricatives, due to the slight variation in the conditions of the sound change, the nasal was removed in English but not cognate German words, yielding *five – fünf*; *us – uns*; *other – andere*; and others. Hence a minute constraint difference of a sound change of some 1,600 years ago has yielded noticeable phonotactic differences in lexical shapes today.

3.7   Bifurcation

This term describes the fact that a single category (of a CDS) splits into two. It is also a characteristic pattern in chaotic systems, described in "catastrophe theory," developed by the mathematician René Thom as a branch of chaos theory (cf. Guastello et al. 2009: 12–15). Bifurcations are a simple ("first-order") type of "catastrophe," a functional discontinuity and sudden qualitative change at a specific, mathematically derived point, a transition point into chaos where a system may or may not change direction.

Obviously this principle manifests itself in Englishes and languages as well; for example, in instances of a single unit splitting into two, exemplified in (3).

(3)   Examples of bifurcation in Englishes

(a)   in phonology:

phonemic split: ME /u/ > modE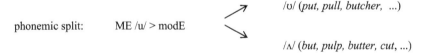

(b)   in lexis:

lexical splits, e.g.:   ME *flure*

similarly: *urban/urbane, metal/mettle, shade/shadow, skirt/shirt; catch/chase*, ...

(c)   in grammar (WEs):

2 passive constructions in Singapore English: ↗ *he kena play out*
                                                    ↘ *he was cheated*

3.8 Emergentism

Emergentism is another core property of CDS: smaller, less complicated entities interact, form new linkages, and jointly build gradually more complex functional units. This can be seen as a manifestation of the importance of a cooperative, complexity-building principle in life (instead of an emphasis on competition and fragmentation).

Again, this principle is evidently applicable to English(es) and languages as well. Larsen-Freeman states that "[a]s new forms emerge through adaptation and co-adaptation, they self-organize into coherent patterns" (2013: 104). Beckner et al. put it pointedly: "[l]inguistic patterns are not preordained by God, genes, school curriculum, or other human policy. Instead, they are emergent" (2009: 18).

A basic manifestation of this property in languages is simply the principle of compositionality: small units jointly build larger constituents with a different function. This is illustrated by any higher-level construction (words built from sounds, phrases from words, clauses from phrases, etc.); for example, in the build-up of complex lexemes and idioms (e.g. *spill the beans, kick the bucket*), complex prepositions (*in spite of*; cf. Bybee 2010), and chunking and phraseologisms (constructions like *to tell you the truth, what is more, after all*). It further expands to more abstract compositional patterns – schematic constructions like the comparative correlative *the Xer, the Xer* (e.g. *the older, the merrier*), or indirect object constructions with the scheme $SVO_{indir}O_{dir}$ (e.g. *he gave me a book*). And of course the principle operates equally in varieties of English, building systematic patterns and formal relationships. In WEs, for example, we find local, partly patterned word-formation products (e.g. Indian English *chai wallah, rikshaw wallah*; Malaysian English *botak head*; Philippine English *to back-carry, to gift-give*; New Zealand English *sharemilker*; etc.), localized phraseologisms (e.g. Kenyan English *look at someone with bad eyes, break a leg* 'make pregnant without being married'), and localized construction types (e.g. Singaporean English *Can or not? – Can, lah!*). Hoffmann (2014) hypothesizes that the emergence of mainly substantive constructions characterizes early phases of a new variety's evolution in the Dynamic Model, as opposed to "meso-constructional" schematic constructions that occur at later stages.

3.9 Auto-Organization

This term denotes another core property of CDS, a "twin process" to emergence and a central component of evolution in general: a system's self-organizing capacity to evolve towards higher-order, more complex subsystems and organization levels. A "spiraling cycle of increasing complexity," forming structures and leading to order (from chaos), has been observed. Mobus & Kalton (2015: 459–461, 476) further state that "systems can self-organize (i.e. become more complex) ... evolution is understood as a systematically produced trajectory of increasing complexity that need not be teleologically headed anywhere."

Obviously this growth of systemic relations to increase complexity constitutes also a core property of languages and English(es). Two related concepts in linguistics are worth mentioning in particular. In a classic book on language, Edward Sapir (1921: ch. 7) introduced the notion of "drift" in languages, an inbuilt trajectory of "unconscious," long-term change towards more consistent typological properties (e.g. the loss of endings in English). Rudi Keller (1994) posited the operation of an "invisible hand" in language change, an unintended directionality of evolutionary processes of linguistic change as the product of collective human agency.

An example from English dialects illustrates the emergence of systematically organized subsystems through time: Anderwald's (2001) work on an emerging polarity-based systemic opposition in past-tense copula forms in dialects of British English (based on the 10 million-word corpus of spoken colloquial English that is part of the British National Corpus [BNC]). Her starting point is the observation that the past-tense forms of the English copula (*was – were*) show an irregular, unusual distribution, with the choice of a verb form based on the grammatical person of the subject, different from the behavior of main verbs (*I was – you(sg.) were – she was – we/you(pl.)/they were*). This is a case of irregularity without a function (a residual trace of an earlier language stage), and as such is prone to be removed.

A simple "solution," found in many dialects, is the choice of a single form throughout all grammatical persons – most likely the majority form *was*, which yields *I/you/she/we/they was*, a pattern that is common in some dialects (e.g. African American Vernacular English or Southern AmE). However, the relationship gets more complex when polarity, commonly expressed by phonologically weak morphological clitics (*-n't*), comes in. Anderwald's (2001) analysis shows that positive *was* and negative *weren't* are spreading in all grammatical persons in BrE dialects. Since this is an unexpected, counter-intuitive result, it is worth asking why this is the case. The new distribution not only marks positive versus negative polarity (the important piece of information "yes or no?") by the (phonetically rather weak) clitic *–n't*, but strengthens it by distinct stem choices added: *was* always signals positive information, *were* marks negative propositions. In other words, this ongoing reorganization of a formal subsystem in BrE dialects marks priority given to the distinct expression of polarity over the traditional, synchronically unmotivated English person-number system. Clearly this can be interpreted as an evident self-organizing tendency in BrE dialects, based on the strength and impact of cognitive factors and principles!

3.10 Englishes as Complex Dynamic Systems: Intermediate Summary

In sum, many properties and characteristics of CDS have been found to operate in the evolutionary trajectories of (W)Es as well, so it seems clear that languages in general and Englishes in particular are CDS indeed.

Still, the principles and properties of CDS are fairly abstract and fundamental; they need to be filled with life by more down-to-earth application and exemplification. Essentially, the mechanisms of implementing these principles in detail are the processes of linguistic change, which are widely familiar from investigations of change, commonly divided into internal (cognitive) and external (social) causes. The next section looks into two exemplary kinds of processes and mechanisms of change and asks how they can be integrated into a CDS perspective, namely diffusion and restructuring. By necessity, these outlines will have to remain exemplary.

4 Select Mechanisms of Change in a CDS Perspective

4.1 Diffusion

Diffusion can roughly be defined as the fact that constructions (i.e. linguistic forms, constituents, or features) are continuously passed on through time and space, both individually (simply via individual usage, by repetition and replication, leading to that construction's entrenchment in speakers' minds) and communally (in speech communities with shared habits of their own, and across generations). All constructions (or units) come up with a certain performance frequency, but this frequency of use of all features may change (rise or fall) in the diffusion process: a quantitative "reshuffling" of options and alternatives, with some waxing and others waning, takes place perpetually. Basically, this is a well-known process, and it explains the phenomenon that the same forms appear in different varieties at varying frequency rates. Many studies of WEs, especially in the corpus-linguistic tradition, pursue such a perspective. Frequency comparisons of select choices, in partial linguistic systems, can be found for BrE versus AmE (e.g. Algeo 2006; Leech et al. 2009; Rohdenburg & Schlüter 2009) and also across several WEs (Hundt & Gut 2012; Collins 2015; Werner et al. 2016; etc.).

The example domain to which this idea will be applied here, hardly ever addressed so far in variationist studies, is lexicosemantic diffusion. My basic hypothesis is that the mutual meaning delimitation within semantic spaces constitutes a particularly volatile domain, since frequencies of word meanings operate below the level of conscious awareness, and hence no impact of prescriptive rules is to be expected. These appear to be conditions likely to generate frequency shifts quite readily. Emerging frequency differences between variant meanings of polysemic words may introduce variety-specific preferences (so that one specific meaning of a polysemic word becomes preferred strongly in a given variety), or also the possible disappearance of low-frequency variants (so that rare meanings of certain words fall into oblivion in some varieties). I choose two domains of exemplification of shifting semantic spaces: first, varying lexical choices within a semantic field, between near-synonyms (I investigate as examples *recall – recollect, aid – assist,* and *assume – suppose*), and second, changing meanings of polysemic verbs (the example being three different meanings of the verb *learn*).

Methodologically, my data source is the widely familiar ICE corpora (cf. http://ice-corpora.net/ice/), which consist of one million words each, contain 60 percent spoken and 40 percent written texts, and are largely identical in design. The corpora were searched with AntConc, and all verb forms were lemmatized. For Indian English only, in addition to ICE-India, whose texts date from the late 1990s to the early 2000s, I investigate a second, older corpus, the Kolhapur Corpus of Indian English, with texts from 1978 (slightly different in composition, since it follows the design of the "Brown Corpus," but I assume that the mutual proportions of meanings investigated here are not affected by this). The availability of both corpora allows a diachronic comparison over an interval of more than twenty years, a period of vibrant change.

Tables 1.1–1.3 and Figures 1.3–1.5 show word frequencies of words in three pairs of synonyms, *recall* and *recollect, aid* and *assist,* and *assume* and *suppose,* respectively. Note that the absolute frequencies and the fact that in some pairs one word is much less common than the other are not what counts here; it is the mutual relationships within the pairs that is of interest for the diffusion issue. We do find substantial differences: lexical choices are passed

Table 1.1 Relationship between *recall* and *recollect* in World Englishes
highly sig. at $p < .001$ ($\chi^2 = 94.2$, 5df) overall, $p < .001$ India vs. others (Fisher's exact).

	recall	*recollect*
Great Britain	52	3
India	41	27
Hong Kong	107	1
Singapore	63	4
East Africa	76	2
Nigeria	54	2

Table 1.2 Relationship between *aid* and *assist* in World Englishes
highly sig. at p < .001 (χ^2 = 49.3, 5df) overall, p < .001 Africa vs. others (Fisher's exact).

	aid	*assist*
Great Britain	16	23
India	21	34
Hong Kong	15	59
Singapore	24	61
East Africa	24	224
Nigeria	12	94

Table 1.3 Relationship between *assume* and *suppose* in World Englishes
highly sig. at p < .001 (χ^2 = 107, 5df) overall, p < .001 Africa vs. others and India vs. others (Fisher's exact).

	assume	*suppose*
Great Britain	129	364
India	59	508
Hong Kong	77	261
Singapore	123	339
East Africa	790	1,809
Nigeria	93	172

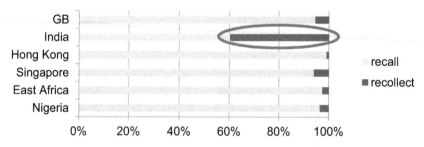

Figure 1.3 Relationship between *recall* and *recollect* in World Englishes
highly sig. at p < .001 (χ^2 = 94.2, 5df) overall, p < .001 India vs. others (Fisher's exact).

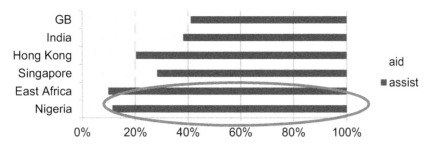

Figure 1.4 Relationship between *aid* and *assist* in World Englishes highly sig. at p < .001 (χ^2 = 49.3, 5df) overall, p < .001 Africa vs. others (Fisher's exact).

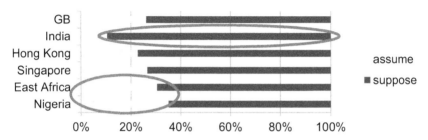

Figure 1.5 Relationship between *assume* and *suppose* in World Englishes highly sig. at p < .001 (χ^2 = 107, 5df) overall, p < .001 Africa vs. others and India vs. others (Fisher's exact).

on at varying and changing (relative) frequencies. The data show that *recollect* in India, as well as *assist* in Nigeria and East Africa, get strongly adopted; *assume* is stronger in Nigeria and East Africa than anywhere else; and *suppose* (as opposed to *assume*) becomes the predominant choice in India.

For the latter pair, Table 1.4 and Figure 1.6 prove the impression of an emerging significant frequency difference gained in Table 1.3 and Figure 1.5, providing evidence that diachronic change is indeed going on in Indian English: a substantial increase of *suppose* in the recent past can be observed, while the use of *assume* has declined somewhat. So it seems we see ultimately varying lexical choices developing, due to different intensities of entrenchment, and possibly increasing effects via feedback loops.

My second sample inquiry into diffusion concerns the transmission of polysemy: are all meanings of a polysemic word passed on equally, at consistent proportions? I look into the three basic meanings of the verb *learn*, illustrated in (4), with definitions, examples from the WE ICE corpora, and typical syntactic complementation patterns:

Table 1.4 Changing frequencies of *assume* and *suppose* in Indian English 1978 vs. 2000;
highly sig. at p < .001 (Fisher's exact).

	assume	suppose
India 1978 Kolhapur	87	124
India 2000 ICE	59	508

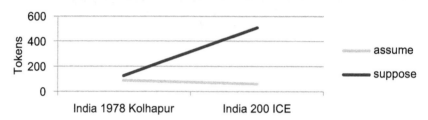

Figure 1.6 Changing frequencies of *assume* and *suppose* in Indian English 1978 vs. 2000;
highly sig. at p < .001 (Fisher's exact).

(4)   Polysemy of *learn*: three main meanings

a)   'receive information,' e.g. *that night I learned that I have a skill* ... (ICE-HK s2a-037.txt) [+ *that/about/wh**]

b)   'store information,' e.g. *he learned a number of Malay words* (ICE-Sing s2a-066.txt) [+ NP]

c)   'acquire ability to do sth.,' e.g. *I learned to cultivate an ego* (ICE-Ind, w2f-012.txt) [+ *to*]

Table 1.5 and Figure 1.7 show the varying frequencies of the different meanings by variety. In all New Englishes the meaning 'receive information' is expressed consistently less frequently than in Great Britain, and the same, except for Singapore, applies to 'acquire ability.' What we are witnessing here appears to be a "focusing" process: in all New Englishes, especially in India, the core meaning "store information" is gaining ground at the expense of the two other, more marginal meanings.

Does the diachronic comparison substantiate this observation? Table 1.6 and Figure 1.8 show the distributions for the two Indian English corpora.

Indeed, the Indian data confirm the evidence for the focusing process: across the interval of slightly more than two decades, the core meaning "store information" is expanding, while the secondary meanings are losing ground. This makes perfect sense in the light of what we know about principles of language

Calling Englishes *As* Complex Dynamic Systems

Table 1.5 Frequencies of meanings of *learn* in WEs
highly sig. at p < .001 (χ^2 = 35.3, 10df).

	learn 'receive info'	*learn* 'store info'	*learn* 'acquire ability'
Great Britain	31	224	34
India	24	324	33
Hong Kong	54	560	55
Singapore	27	376	79
East Africa	61	659	65
Nigeria	46	489	69

Table 1.6 Diachronic change of proportions of three meanings of *learn* in Indian English
n.s. (p < .1, χ^2 = 4.61, 2df) overall; sig. at p < .05 "store" vs. others (Fisher's exact).

	learn 'receive info'	*learn* 'store info'	*learn* 'acquire ability'
India 1978 Kolhapur	28	206	24
India 2000 ICE	24	325	32

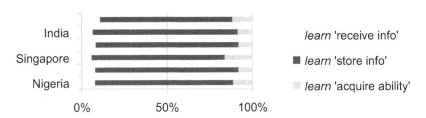

Figure 1.7 Frequencies of meanings of *learn* in WEs
highly sig. at p < .001 (χ^2 = 35.3, 10df).

change: languages display a tendency towards "isomorphism," a clear one-to-one match between form and meaning. It appears that this trend, restoring order and simplicity, is strongly effective in the growth of new varieties of English.

Hence, overall, the above data suggest that lexicosemantic diffusion will change the balance between word-meaning frequencies in the process of these being passed on to new, emerging varieties: some meanings, apparently mainly the central ones, are favored and come to be used more regularly,

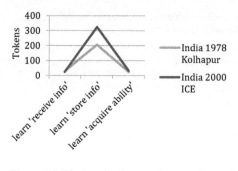

Figure 1.8 Diachronic change of proportions of three meanings of *learn* in Indian English
n.s. (p < .1, χ^2 = 4.61, 2df) overall; sig. at p < .05 'store' vs. others (Fisher's exact).

while others are disfavored, are used less frequently, and ultimately may fall into oblivion. Systemic relations keep being reshuffled, a process that possibly may lead towards qualitative change in the long run.

4.2 Restructuring

This process (understood in a general, not generative sense) also relates to a change in conventionalized form–meaning mappings, in this case in syntactic constructions: viewed from the two sides of a construction, it denotes either different meanings coming to be associated with a given form (e.g. a construction being parsed in a novel fashion), or different forms developing for the same meaning. The process has also been documented and studied in some earlier work on WEs; for example, on ditransitives in Indian English (Mukherjee & Hoffmann 2006). Basically this is a familiar pattern, but it gets used more frequently and with new types of verbs in India (e.g. *she wanted to gift him a dream*; Mukherjee & Hoffmann 2006: 163).

The example investigated here is complex transitive constructions, notably the spread of *as* connecting object and object-complement constituents in New Englishes (which provided the motivation for this paper's title). Structurally, the relevant background observation is that in "complex transitive complementation" patterns (Quirk et al. 1985), also known as "small clauses" (Aarts 1992), a non-finite object clause consisting of object + object complement follows the matrix verb. The copular relationship between these constituents can be realized in formally alternative ways, shown in (5): by *to be*, not at all (i.e. by "zero"), or by *as*.

(5) Alternative structural realizations of complex transitive complementation

S	V	[O	~copula	Ocomp]$_{\text{small clause}}$
I	consider	John		my friend
I	consider	John	to be	my friend
I	consider	John	as	my friend

The word *as* in this pattern is somewhat strange, and clearly difficult to interpret and to classify. Its part of speech assignment is unclear – in this pattern it has been viewed as a preposition, conjunction, or just generically a "particle." Its function is quasi-copular, and it is fully equivalent to *to be* as an alternative pattern – but it is clearly not a verb (cf. Schneider 1997b). The pattern is lexically idiosyncratic, tied to specific verbs: *I consider/regard John as my friend* is grammatical, but **I believe/think John as my friend* is not.

The construction appears to be spreading to new verbs, notably *call*, in Asia. For example, in an abstract of a Korean paper at the KASELL (Korean Association for the Study of English Language and Linguistics) meeting (KASELL 2013: 201) I came across the clause "initial forms such as ... are **called as** 'combining forms'" (my emphasis). The phenomenon, labeled "intrusive *as*," was studied systematically by Lange (2016) and, compared to learner Englishes, by Koch et al. (2016). It is found mainly with *call, name,* and *term,* and also with *declare, deem,* and other verbs. Examples can be seen in (6).

(6) Sample structures with "intrusive *as*" (from Lange 2016)
*The main temple is **called as** Rang-Mahal* (India)
*an examination system that **declares** a majority of its students **as** failures* (Nepal)
*Maldives has been **named as** the Indian Ocean's leading tourism destination* (Maldives)
*He likes to be **called as** Sam* (Sri Lanka)
*Moin Khan should be **named as** next captain* (Pakistan)

Based on data from the SAVE newspaper corpus, Lange (2016) studied the occurrence of the pattern in South Asian Englishes in general. Select quantitative findings are reported in (7). The numbers report the frequencies of the respective forms with *as*, normalized to frequency of occurrence per one million words; percentages document the proportions of uses with *as* out of all uses of the respective verbs.

(7) Absolute and relative frequencies of "intrusive *as*" by lexemes and select varieties (after Lange 2016)
call as: India 2.9 (1.4%), Bangladesh, Pakistan, Sri Lanka 2.3 (1.3–1.8%)
name as: all 8.2–12.8 (19–31%)
term as: India 32 (72%), Sri Lanka (52%), Maldives (56%), all (40%)
declare as: India 16 (25.6%), Bangladesh 13 (16%), Sri Lanka 8.6 (23%)

Clearly, the spread of this pattern with *as* is a pan-South Asian process. It is being established most systematically in India, and also, not quite as strongly, in Sri Lanka. The varying strengths of evolutionary trajectories may be seen as progress along an S-curve.

Table 1.7 Diachronic comparison of "intrusive *as*" in Indian English.

	Kolhapur - 1978			ICE-Ind wr ca2000		
	N	with *as*	% with *as*	N	with *as*	% with *as*
call (as)	623	17	4.6	349.2	36.8	10.5
term (as)	38	16	42.1	16.1	11.5	71.4
declare (as)	24	6	25	32.2	4.6	14.3
name (as)	4	3	75	39.1	4.6	11.8
deem (as)	29	0	0	16.1	0	0

It is also strongly lexically conditioned, having been adopted to varying extents with different verbs. The strongest case of embracing the new pattern is *term as*, a construction on its way to becoming the predominant choice. This is in line with what we know about the spread of linguistic innovations in general (and with Kretzschmar's 2015 observations on A-curves): a new "lexical anchor" drives the progress of a familiar structure into innovative contexts (e.g. with new verbs), at varying strengths. The restructuring of "intrusive *as*" clearly represents a case of grammatical change in progress in South Asian Englishes.

As before, Table 1.7 investigates the diachronic spread of the form in Indian English. It compares data from 1978 (the Kolhapur Corpus, all written texts) to Lange's (2016) data from the written ICE component only, produced around 2000. Again, this is obviously identified as a lexically constrained restructuring process: a clear increase of *term as* and *call as* (unlike the other verbs) can be observed.

4.3 Summary Assessment: Mechanisms of Change in a CDS Perspective

How can these processes be viewed in a CDS perspective?

Diffusion clearly constitutes an essential element in the perpetual dynamism of languages. It guarantees a certain amount of stability; at the same time, it is a prerequisite for a transition towards qualitative change if the frequencies of alternative choices diverge over time – for example, via an S-curve: one form becomes more frequent and wins out, while another decreases and falls into disuse in the long run. These trends may then lead to bifurcation.

Restructuring is a manifestation of qualitative change, a relevant step towards emergentism and auto-organization, and also an intermediate stage in the path from chaos to order. In the above example, for instance, the spread of *call/term as* works towards establishing a more systematic and transparent form–meaning mapping, and thus introduces a pocket of order in a complex (and possibly chaotic) subsystem.

Both diffusion and restructuring show that evolution is incremental: there are no major leaps; development proceeds gradually, in step-by-step processes, even if these may be leading to massive changes in the long run. Hence they are also potentially associated with the "butterfly effect." From a linguistic perspective, the interesting questions are which verbs and which varieties lead the change. Which choices happen to be gaining decisive momentum?

All these processes thus constitute major mechanisms of implementing CDS principles, leading towards self-organization, emergentism, changes from chaos to order or vice versa, increasing complexity, and so on.

5 Conclusion: Englishes as Complex Dynamic Systems

Given the above arguments, examples, and evidence, it seems obvious that all Englishes, including today's WEs, are Complex Dynamic Systems! And, as stated initially, the same applies to ELF usage, which has the same potential for constant dynamism in interaction, the growth of complexity, the emergence of innovative structural relationships in specific contexts, etc.

This paper thus represents another call for a change of framework and perspective towards a holistic and processual perspective, rather than upholding a reductionist and segmenting, categorial view, in line with new tendencies in the sciences. At this stage we need steps towards implementing this new perspective, building bridges between both ways of understanding Englishes.

Clearly, this is just a starting point, and many open questions remain. Possible perspectives include the following: which properties of Englishes (or languages in general) can meaningfully be viewed as "attractors," a core notion in chaos theory ("preferred states," after Larsen-Freeman 2018: 52)? How do mechanisms of linguistic change as manifestations of self-organization relate to comparable processes in other systems? What is the precise relationship between the notion of complexity as widely applied in linguistics, meaning something like "complicated" (implying that a system is rich in choices and distinctions; cf. Miestamo et al. 2008; Culicover 2013), and complexity in the technical sense of CDS theory (cf. Mauranen 2017; Mufwene et al. 2017: 3)? Can a loss of marking and hence (linguistic) complexity (e.g. of endings in the history of English) be meaningfully interpreted as a case of "entropy," the loss of energy in all CDS, based on laws of thermodynamics, indicative of the ageing of systems? How exactly does the notion of scale-free distributions, highlighted in Kretzschmar (2015) and related to Mandelbrot's concept of "fractals", manifest itself in language structures? Much of this has to do with the question of the level of granularity a researcher is aiming at – are we going for the "big picture" (necessarily rather abstract, then), or are we interested in the interpretation of details and minute developments? (On the other hand, complexity is supposed to be independent of scale, as Kretzschmar 2015 strongly argues.)

CDS theory offers a generic and fundamental perspective on language evolution, a "meta-theory," projecting abstract principles and forces. There is a need to "translate" them, to "boil them down" to specific observations and investigations, to individual explanations of language change in (World) Englishes. In other words, the theory needs to be adopted, adapted, developed, specified, and filled with life from the perspectives of language variation and change, as well as language history and evolution. In my view, working this out will be worth the effort.

REFERENCES

Aarts, Bas. 1992. *Small Clauses in English. The Nonverbal Types.* Berlin: Mouton de Gruyter.
Algeo, John. 2006. *British or American English? A Handbook of Word and Grammar Patterns.* Cambridge: Cambridge University Press.
Anderwald, Lieselotte. 2001. Was/were variation in non-standard British English today. *English World-Wide* 22, 1–22.
Bailey, Charles-James 1973. *Variation and Linguistic Theory.* Arlington, VA: Center for Applied Linguistics.
Beckner, Clay, Richard Blythe, Joan Bybee, Morten H. Christiansen, William Croft, Nick C. Ellis, John Holland, Jinyun Ke, Diane Larsen-Freeman & Tom Schoenemann. 2009. Language is a complex adaptive system: Position paper. *Language Learning* 59(s1), 1–26.
Bossomaier, Terry R. J. & David G. Green (eds.). 2000. *Complex Systems.* Cambridge: Cambridge University Press.
Bybee, Joan. 2010. *Language, Usage and Cognition.* Cambridge: Cambridge University Press.
Chambers, J. K. 2006–2007. Geolinguistic patterns in a vast speech community. *Linguistica Atlantica* 27(28), 27–36.
Cheshire, Jenny. 1994. Standardization and the English irregular verbs. In Dieter Stein & Ingrid Tieken-Boon van Ostade (eds.), *Towards a Standard English 1600–1800*, 115–133. Berlin, New York: Mouton de Gruyter.
Collins, Peter (ed.) 2015. *Grammatical Change in English World-Wide.* Amsterdam: Benjamins.
Collins, Peter & Xinyue Yao. 2012. Modals and quasi-modals in New Englishes. *In Hundt & Gut* 2012, 35–53.
Culicover, Peter. 2013. *Grammar and Complexity: Language at the Intersection of Competence and Performance.* Oxford: Oxford University Press.
Denison, David. 1993. *English Historical Syntax.* London, New York: Longman.
Ellegård, Alvar. 1953. *The Auxiliary Do: The Establishment and Regulation of Its Use in English.* Stockholm: Almqvist & Wiksell.
Ellis, Nick C. 2008. The dynamics of second language emergence: Cycles of language use, language change, and language acquisition. *The Modern Language Journal* 92(2), 232–249.

2011. The emergence of language as a complex adaptive system. In James Simpson (ed.), *The Routledge Handbook of Applied Linguistics*, 666–679. London: Routledge.

Ellis, Nick C. & Diane Larsen-Freeman (eds.). 2009. *Language as a Complex Adaptive System*. Malden, MA: Wiley & Sons.

Fischer, Olga & Wim van der Wurff. 2006. Syntax. In Richard Hogg & David Denison (eds.), *A History of the English Language*, 109–198. Cambridge: Cambridge University Press.

Filppula, Markku, Juhani Klemola, Anna Mauranen & Svetlana Vetchinnikova (eds.). 2017. *Changing English. Global and Local Perspectives*. Berlin, Boston: Mouton de Gruyter.

Gleick, James. 1987. *Chaos. Making a New Science*. New York: Viking.

Guastello, Stephen J., Matthijs Koopmans & David Pincus (eds.) 2009. *Chaos and Complexity in Psychology. The Theory of Nonlinear Dynamic Systems*. Cambridge: Cambridge University Press.

Hoffmann, Thomas. 2014. The cognitive evolution of Englishes: The role of constructions in the Dynamic Model. In Sarah Buschfeld, Thomas Hoffmann, Magnus Huber & Alexander Kautzsch (eds.), *The Evolution of Englishes. The Dynamic Model and Beyond*, 160–180. Amsterdam: Benjamins.

Holland, John H. 2014. *Complexity. A Very Short Introduction*. Oxford: Oxford University Press.

Hopper, Paul J. 1987. Emergent grammar. *Berkeley Linguistic Society* 13, 139–157.

Hundt, Marianne & Ulrike Gut (eds.). 2012. *Mapping Unity and Diversity World-Wide*. Amsterdam: Benjamins.

Jenkins, Jennifer, Will Baker & Martin Dewey (eds.). 2018. *The Routledge Handbook of English as a Lingua Franca*. London, New York: Routledge.

Johnson, Neil. 2009. *Simply Complexity. A Clear Guide to Complexity Theory*. Oxford: Oneworld Publications.

KASELL (Korean Association for the Study of English Language and Linguistics). Dec. 2013. *Proceedings*. Seoul: KASELL.

Keller, Rudi. 1994. *On Language Change: The Invisible Hand in Language*. London: Routledge.

Koch, Christopher, Claudia Lange & Sven Leuckert. 2016. "This hair-style called as 'duck tail'": The 'intrusive *as*'-construction in South Asian varieties of English and Learner Englishes. *International Journal of Learner Corpus Research* 2(2), 151–176.

Kortmann, Bernd, Edgar W. Schneider et al. (eds.). 2004. *A Handbook of Varieties of English*. 2 vols. Berlin, New York: Mouton de Gruyter.

Kortmann, Bernd & Kerstin Lunkenheimer (eds.). 2012. *The Mouton World Atlas of Variation in English*. Berlin, Boston: Mouton de Gruyter.

Kretzschmar, William R., Jr. 2009. *The Linguistics of Speech*. Cambridge: Cambridge University Press.

2015. *Language and Complex Systems*. Cambridge: Cambridge University Press.

Kroch, Anthony. 1989. Reflexes of grammar in patterns of language change. *Language Variation and Change* 1, 199–244.

Labov, William. 1994. *Principles of Linguistic Change*. Vol. 1: *Internal Factors*. Cambridge, MA, Oxford: Blackwell.

Laitinen, Mikko. 2018. Placing ELF among the varieties of English. In Sandra C. Deshors (ed.), *Modeling World Englishes: Assessing the Interplay of Emancipation and Globalization of ESL Varieties*, 109–131. Amsterdam: Benjamins.

Lange, Claudia. 2016. The 'intrusive *as*'-construction in South Asian varieties of English. *World Englishes* 35(1), 133–146.

Larsen-Freeman, Diane. 1997. Chaos/complexity science and second language acquisition. *Applied Linguistics* 18(2), 141–165.

2013. Complexity Theory/Dynamic systems theory. In Peter Robinson (ed.), *The Routledge Encyclopedia of Second Language Acquisition*, 103–106. New York: Routledge.

2018. Complexity and ELF. In Jenkins et al. (eds.), 51–60.

Larsen-Freeman, Diane & Lynne Cameron. 2008. *Complex Systems and Applied Linguistics*. Oxford: Oxford University Press.

Leech, Geoffrey, Marianne Hundt, Christian Mair & Nicholas Smith. 2009. *Change in Contemporary English. A Grammatical Study*. Cambridge: Cambridge University Press.

Lightfoot, David. 1979. *Principles of Diachronic Syntax*. Cambridge: Cambridge University Press.

Lindblom, Björn, Peter MacNeilage & Michael Studdert-Kennedy. 1984. Self-organizing processes and the explanation of language universals. In B. Butterworth, Bernard Comrie & Östen Dahl (eds.), *Explanations for Language Universals*, 181–203. Berlin, New York: de Gruyter.

Mauranen, Anna. 2017. A glimpse of ELF. In Filppula et al. (eds.), 223–253.

2018. Conceptualising ELF. In Jenkins et al. (eds.), 7–24.

Mesthrie, Rajend & Rakesh Bhatt. 2008. *World Englishes*. Cambridge: Cambridge University Press.

Miestamo, Matti, Kaius Sinnemäki & Fred Karlsson (eds.). 2008. *Language Complexity: Typology, Contact, Change*. Amsterdam: John Benjamins.

Milroy, Jim & Lesley Milroy. 1985. Linguistic change, social network and speaker innovation. *Journal of Linguistics* 21, 339–384.

Milroy, Lesley. 1987. *Language and Social Networks*. 2nd ed. Oxford: Blackwell.

Milroy, Lesley & Carmen Llamas. 2013. Social networks. In J. K. Chambers & Natalie Schilling (eds.), *The Handbook of Language Variation and Change*, 409–427. Malden, MA, Oxford: Wiley-Blackwell,

Mobus, George E. & Michael C. Kalton. 2015. *Principles of Systems Science*. New York: Springer.

Mufwene, Salikoko S., Christophe Coupé & Francois Pellegrino. 2017. *Complexity in Language. Developmental and Evolutionary Perspectives*. Cambridge: Cambridge University Press.

Mukherjee, Joybrato & Sebastian Hoffmann. 2006. Describing verb-complementational profiles of New Englishes: A pilot study of Indian English. *English World-Wide* 27, 147–173

Newmeyer, Frederic J. & Laurel B. Preston (eds.). 2014. *Measuring Grammatical Complexity*. Oxford: Oxford University Press.

Nevalainen, Terttu. 2015. Descriptive adequacy of the S-curve model in diachronic studies of language change. In Christina Sanchez-Stockhammer (ed.), *Can We*

Pitzl, Marie-Luise & Ruth Osimk-Teasdale (eds.). 2016. *English as a Lingua Franca: Perspectives and Prospects*. Berlin, Boston: de Gruyter Mouton.
Quirk, Randolph, Sidney Greenbaum, Geoffrey Leech & Jan Svartvik. 1985. *A Comprehensive Grammar of the English Language*. London, New York: Longman.
Rohdenburg, Günter & Julia Schlüter. 2009. *One Language, Two Grammars? Differences between British and American English*. Cambridge: Cambridge University Press.
Sampson, Geoffrey, David Gil & Peter Trudgill (eds.). 2009. *Language Complexity as an Evolving Variable*. Oxford: Oxford University Press.
Sapir, Edward. 1921. *Language*. New York: Harcourt, Brace & Co.
Schneider, Edgar W. 1989. *American Earlier Black English. Morphological and Syntactic Variables*. Tuscaloosa: University of Alabama Press.
    1997a. Chaos theory as a model for dialect variability and change? In Alan R. Thomas (ed.), *Issues and Methods in Dialectology*, 22–36. Bangor: Department of Linguistics, University of Wales.
    1997b. *As* as "is". Is *as* "is"? In Udo Fries et al. (eds.), *From Aelfric to the New York Times. Studies in English Corpus Linguistics*, 33–50. Amsterdam: Rodopi.
    2007. *Postcolonial English: Varieties around the World*. Cambridge: Cambridge University Press.
    2011a. *English around the World: An Introduction*. Cambridge: Cambridge University Press.
    2011b. English into Asia: From Singaporean ubiquity to Chinese learners' features. In Anne Curzan & Michael Adams (eds.), *Contours of English and English Language Studies: In Honor of Richard W. Bailey*, 135–156. Ann Arbor: University of Michigan Press.
Seidlhofer, Barbara. 2011. *Understanding English as a Lingua Franca*. Oxford: Oxford University Press.
Thomason, Sarah Grey & Terrence Kaufman. 1988. *Language Contact, Creolization and Genetic Linguistics*. Berkeley, Los Angeles: University of California Press.
Vetchinnikova, Svetlana. 2017. On the relationship between the cognitive and the communal: a complex systems perspective. In Filppula et al. (eds.), 277–310.
Werner, Valentin, Elena Seoane & Cristina Suárez-Gómez (eds.). 2016. *Re-Assessing the Present Perfect*. Berlin: de Gruyter.

2 English as a Lingua Franca in the Context of a Sociolinguistic Typology of Contact Languages

William Croft

1 Introduction

This chapter will situate English as a lingua franca in the context of a sociolinguistic typology of contact languages. A sociolinguistic typology of languages is a typology of languages based not on their structural or semantic traits, but on the traits of the communities that speak the language, and/or how the language is used in social interaction.

Of course, there are many ways in which one could construct a sociolinguistic typology of languages, just as there are many ways in which typologists construct structural or semantic typologies of languages. There are not many sociolinguistic typologies of languages at present. One example is Trudgill's typology that relates structural linguistic "complexity" to different types of societies according to various social traits (Trudgill 2011).

The sociolinguistic typology I am interested in here is rather different from Trudgill's. The primary social trait relevant to lingua francas and other contact languages is how language is used, or in some cases not used, in social interaction with individuals outside one's own speech community, that is, linguistic communication between individuals who speak different languages. English as a lingua franca is one example of this type of linguistic communication. But English as a lingua franca, or even lingua francas in general, represents just one way that a language is (or is not) used in intersocietal communication. We can reach a better understanding of the social circumstances under which a lingua franca such as English is used by constructing a sociolinguistic typology of contact languages.

This chapter proposes such a typology. The typology is then used to propose some universals about sociolinguistic types of contact languages and other social traits of the speech communities using those contact languages, specifically community size and degree of stratification. The hypothesis is tested against a sample of contact languages. It turns out that the critical cases for the hypothesis are non-European contact languages, so much of this chapter will not be devoted to English as a contact language. Nevertheless, I argue that understanding how language is used in intersocietal communication across a

ELF in the Context of Contact Languages 45

wide range of situations that do not involve English or even other European languages will shed light on our understanding of English as a lingua franca.

1.1 An Evolutionary Framework for Integrating Social and Structural Traits of Languages

Contact languages are of interest due to both their structural and their social traits. In order to analyze contact languages and how they arise, we need a framework that integrates both structural and social traits of languages. The framework I use is an evolutionary framework, which I will briefly introduce here; the relevance of this framework to contact languages is described in the following section (see also Mufwene 2001 for a similar framework).

An evolutionary framework is a framework for understanding the dynamics of speech communities and languages that uses concepts from the philosophy of biology (Hull 1988). An evolutionary framework is not the opportunistic use of analogies from the evolution of biological species to languages and language change. It abstracts away to leave only commonalities in processes that take place in biological systems and cultural systems such as language. This abstraction leads to a coherent, highly general theory of evolution.

The evolutionary framework is a theory of change by replication. Replication is a process that creates new entities based on an old entity. The fundamental properties of a *replicator* (the entity that gets replicated) are:

- Replicated units can themselves be replicated, that is, they form *lineages*.
- Replicated units possess much of the structure of the original, that is, there is *inheritance* of much of the structure of the original.
- Replication is mostly faithful, or conversely, replication can introduce *variation*.
- Replication is *cumulative*, that is, replication can produce heritable variation.

In Croft (2000), a monograph presenting this evolutionary framework, I argue that tokens of linguistic structure in utterances are replicators. Each time I produce an utterance – or for that matter, in each sentence I write here – I replicate sounds, words, and constructions from prior utterances that I have heard or produced myself. In Croft (2000), I introduced the term *lingueme* to describe tokens of linguistic structure in utterances. Linguemes form lineages: I, or another speaker, may further replicate one of the linguistic structures in my utterance. A replicated lingueme possesses much of the structure of the original (otherwise communication could fail because the listener cannot recognize the form). Lingueme replication is mostly faithful, but it introduces variation; this is of course demonstrated in instrumental phonetics for sounds (Ohala 1989), and also in the expression of the same meaning by words and constructions (Croft 2010). Finally, lingueme replication is cumulative: this is how language changes can persist.

Language use therefore involves replication of linguemes by speakers in the course of communicative interaction. Evolutionary change – that is, change by replication – is a two-step process: generation of variation, and selection (propagation) of the novel variants. Hull (1988) proposes a Generalized Theory of Selection that abstracts away from the specifics of biological mechanisms of evolution. The process of replication of the replicator generates variation, as noted above. Hull posits another abstract role, the *interactor*, which is an entity that interacts with its environment in such a way that it causes differential replication, that is, some replicators are replicated more than others. That process of environmental interaction is *selection*: it leads to differential replication, which can proceed to the point of the fixation of the replicators selected for, and the extinction of the replicators selected against – that is, an evolutionary change.

This is, of course, a highly abstract analysis of the evolutionary process. In Croft (2000), I described how this abstract theory of selection is instantiated in language change, in a way that unifies several theories of language that are commonly treated as independent, although they are generally grouped together as "functionalist" theories.

The first step in the process is replication. Replication occurs in conversational interaction, that is, when we talk to each other. These processes of formulation and understanding utterances are described by theories of cognitive linguistics that draw on conceptualization and verbalization of experience, and of social cognition to describe social interaction (Croft 2009).

The process of communication – that is, perception and production of language – generates variation in the replication process. As noted above, the generation of variation has long been observed in phonetics, and it also occurs in grammar and lexicon, in terms of the variation in expressing a specific experience on different occasions (Croft 2010). I have described the variation in production of grammar and lexicon as "exemplar semantics."

Once this variation has been produced in replication, speakers may come to associate particular variants with social valuation, which leads to differential replication, or as it is called in linguistics, propagation. This is the domain of sociohistorical linguistics, which analyzes the social aspect of language variation and change.

Finally, the effect of the processes of generating variation, and selection of variants, feeds back into the grammatical knowledge of speakers. The knowledge a speaker has about their language changes over their lifetimes, reflecting the language use that they have been exposed to, as well as the nature of human memory. This aspect of the process is described by the usage-based model.

The context of this evolutionary process of language change is the speech community. From an evolutionary perspective, a speech community is a population. The concept of a population is an equally important element of the evolutionary framework. A population is not an idealization, but an actual historical entity, or as it is said in philosophy, a spatiotemporally bounded entity. The population of speakers is defined not by some essential property, such as, for instance, being a native speaker of the language. Instead, it is defined by some interactional property. For biological species, which are also populations of individuals, the interactional property is interbreeding, and more importantly, its converse, reproductive isolation relative to other populations. For a speech community, the interactional property is communication, and its converse, communicative isolation relative to other speech communities (Croft 2000: 17–19). Of course, speech communities are never completely communicatively isolated – but neither are biological species, especially plant species.

The fact that communicative isolation is never complete is the domain of language contact, which is the topic of this chapter. Before we turn to language contact in the evolutionary framework, we must note two other important populations in the evolutionary approach to language. In the evolutionary approach, a language is not an idealization either, governed by rules that don't exist in any speaker's head. A language is a population of utterances, namely the utterances that are produced in a speech community: actual utterances, no matter what their grammatical form or phonetic realization is. It is actual utterances that speakers replicate, and actual utterances that form the grammatical knowledge of a speaker, as assumed in the usage-based model.

The other population is the population of linguemes, that is, the structural traits of the language that are the units of replication. Again, this is not an idealized set of phonemes, morphemes, words, and constructions, but the actual sounds, word forms, and syntactic patterns in utterances that have been produced in a speech community. The speech community, the language, and the "grammar" are all actual historical entities, not idealizations representing an abstract grammar. The population of linguemes is what Salikoko Mufwene calls the linguistic feature pool (Mufwene 2001: 4) in his closely related evolutionary model, which I will draw on in the remainder of this chapter.

1.2   Language Contact from an Evolutionary Perspective

In the evolutionary framework described in Section 1.1, a language is the population of actual utterances produced in an actual speech community. A grammar is the population of actual linguemes that are replicated in those utterances (compare Langacker's definition of a grammar as "a structured inventory of conventional linguistic units"; Langacker 1987: 56–76). The linguemes form lineages – that is, sequences of replications – as they are replicated by speakers in the speech community. Since utterances are made up of combinations of linguemes, and different utterances are made up of different combinations from the same set of linguemes, the population of utterances is tightly woven together by the lineages of the linguemes that make them up.

A speech community is a population of persons who communicatively interact with each other and are relatively communicatively isolated from other persons. The critical word in these definitions for contact languages is *relative* communicative isolation. There is a popular view of biological evolution and biological species that their reproductive isolation is very high. The popular view is that plants or animals evolve when their population splits up: the populations do not interbreed any more, certain biological traits get selected in one population but not another, and so the species divides into two or more new species, each adapted to its biological environment. The linguistic equivalent is the divergence of languages (that is, their linguistic features or linguemes) when a speech community splits and the two speaker populations no longer communicatively interact – communicative isolation. This is part of what is sometimes called "normal transmission": a speaker learns a first language in childhood through to adulthood, without "interference" from exposure to another language from another speech community during acquisition, or even afterwards.

The popular view of biological evolution is incomplete, to say the least. Many biological populations are not fully reproductively isolated, and many species (especially plant species) have hybrid origins. The same is even more true of languages. No speech community is totally communicatively isolated. The traditional tree model, in which a speech community splits up and each new community's language changes due to communicative isolation from the others, is almost never the reality. Human societies are always in some degree of contact with other societies – indeed many other societies – due to migration, including conquest. In this respect, language evolution and biological evolution are alike. However, a language may also recruit linguemes from any language, not just languages that are genetically closely related to it. There is no barrier to adoption of linguemes based on how different or mutually unintelligible two languages are. (Even in biology, microorganisms can insert genes into a distantly related organism; but I do not think it is as easy or as extensive as contact effects on languages.)

Let us look at the process of language contact from an evolutionary perspective more closely. Consider a simple case such as the English word *faith*, borrowed from French. English and French are both Indo-European languages. That is, they are assumed to have split from a single prehistoric speech community; in fact, English and French also split from fragments of the

Indo-European speech community, that is, the Germanic and Romance speech communities.

Old French *feid/feit* are descendants in a lineage of replications from Latin *fidēs*. Through language contact as a result of the Norman invasion of England, Middle English "borrowed" *feid/feit* as *feith/feth*. What does that mean? It means that some speakers in the English speech community, who also interacted to some degree with the French speech community, replicated the Old French word in utterances in the English speech community, consisting mostly of English linguemes; from there, other English speakers continued to replicate *feith*, later orthographically replicated as *faith*, in utterances produced in the English speech community.

In this case, a lingueme lineage "jumped" from the interwoven tapestry of French linguemes in the French speech community to be woven into the tapestry of English linguemes in the English speech community. This was made possible originally by a member of the English speech community speaking with a member of the French speech community. The process is often called "horizontal" transmission, but this is a misnomer, since all lineages are "vertical"; what is distinctive is that the lineage jumps from one lingueme population to another.

This is the simplest case: a single lingueme lineage jumps from one population to another, and we pretend that it was the result of a single English speaker talking to a single French speaker. The reality, of course, is that most contact situations involve many speakers in many social-communicative interactions. And the nature of the social structures of the respective speech communities, the roles of the individuals in those social structures, and what happens to those social structures when individuals from the two (or more) societies interact, influence how many and which linguemes jump from one lingueme population to the other.

The question of how, when, and why this happens is very difficult to answer because of the complexity of social structures and social interactions. We can only address the question at a coarse level of description of social structure, and also at a very coarse level of types of linguemes. In the last subsection of this section, we will offer a coarse classification of linguemes, and in the following sections of this chapter, a coarse classification of types of social interaction using language. Although it is at a coarse level, it does appear to lead to certain universal patterns of sociolinguistic typology.

1.3   Linguistic Features, or Linguemes

Linguemes can be divided into two broad types: substance linguemes and schematic linguemes (Croft 2000: 203). *Substance linguemes* are linguemes in which a pairing of form and meaning is replicated. Substance linguemes may be grammatical morphemes such as English *-ed* "past" or *will* "future," basic vocabulary items such as *nose* and *sit*, or other, non-basic vocabulary items such as English *opossum* and *jihad*. (I have deliberately chosen examples of non-basic vocabulary with non-Germanic origins, but the point here is that they are now words of English.)

Schematic linguemes, on the other hand, are linguemes in which only form or only meaning is replicated. An example of a form-only schematic lingueme is the phonetic realization of a phoneme – for example, trilled vs. uvular /r/ in various continental Western European languages. An example of a meaning-only schematic lingueme is the recruitment of a predicative possession construction, such as the verb "have," combined with a verb denoting an event to express the meaning of the perfect – neither the phonological form of "have" nor the participial verb form is specified – or patterns of co-expression such as a single verb used for both "know a person" and "know a fact." The form-only schematic linguemes are the primary subject of study for phonological typology, and the meaning-only schematic linguemes are the primary subject of study for morphosyntactic and semantic typology.

The distinction between substance and schematic linguemes does not correspond to the distinction between lexical and grammatical elements of language. Lexical items are mostly substance linguemes, as with English *head* or German *Kopf*: each is a pairing of form and meaning. However, word-formation patterns and patterns of semantic extension from one meaning to another are schematic linguemes. For example, English *headhunter* describes a traditional cultural activity with a compound; German uses the same compound pattern but with different forms (*Kopfjäger*; Görlach 2001: 148). English has extended the term metaphorically to personnel recruitment, and so has German (ibid.). On the other hand, the English grammatical inflection *-ed* is a substance lingueme, contrasting with zero expression of the present: it is a particular form paired with a particular meaning. However, the pattern of contrasting verbal forms for past and non-past tenses is a schematic lingueme: the pattern of the tense contrast, found in many languages (Dahl and Velupillai 2013), does not specify any particular phonological form. Hence lexical "borrowing" may involve substance linguemes (word forms as well as meanings) or schematic linguemes (calques), and grammatical "borrowing" may involve substance linguemes (grammatical forms as well as meanings) or schematic linguemes (typological traits).

We now turn to the classification of types of social interaction, and types of social structure, that we want to relate to these types of linguemes.

2 Towards a Sociolinguistic Typology of Languages with Respect to Intersocietal Contact

My starting point for the proposed sociolinguistic typology is a distinction between the uses of a language proposed by Thurston (1989). Thurston distinguishes between esoteric and exoteric languages. *Esoteric languages* are languages used for communication among members of the same speech community. *Exoteric languages* are languages used for communication between members of different speech communities that remain distinct, that is, the communication is not a result of the fusion of the speech communities.

The distinction between esoteric and exoteric is based on the communicative situation, in particular the speech community membership(s) of the interlocutors. It is not an inherent property, social or otherwise, of the language. From this latter fact follow a number of corollaries. First, a language may be both esoteric and exoteric at the same time, that is, a language may have both esoteric and exoteric functions. Second, a language may change its social type as defined over time. An esoteric language may develop exoteric functions, or an exoteric language may develop esoteric functions. Also, a language that has both esoteric and exoteric functions may come to be restricted to just exoteric function or just esoteric function. Of course, in these processes of social change of language use, language structure may also change, leading to a structural divergence of what was once a single language serving multiple functions or changing functions. This is part of what makes the social processes linguistically interesting (although the social processes are interesting in themselves as well).

To Thurston's (1989) esoteric and exoteric types a third type must be added. I qualified the definition of an exoteric language as one in which the interlocutors come from different speech communities that remain distinct. But there is another possible reason why speakers from two different communities are communicating. It could be because the two communities, or at least the relevant subgroups of the communities, are coming together to create a new unitary speech community, for whatever reason. This is one way in which an exoteric language becomes esoteric, but it is a particularly significant way in which this happens. I will call such languages *neogenic* languages.

One can describe pidgins and creoles, two types of contact languages with similar functions to a lingua franca, in terms of this sketch of a sociolinguistic typology of languages. Pidgins are standardly, if simplistically, described as exoteric languages, at least at first; one of their commonest uses is in trade relations. Structurally, the lexical substance linguemes of a pidgin are drawn from multiple sources, though one source almost always dominates, the so-called lexifier language. The grammatical substance linguemes are generally reduced from those of the lexifier language, and many grammatical schematic linguemes and also some grammatical substance linguemes originate in the other source languages, the so-called substrate languages. Creoles are standardly described as esoteric languages, the languages of a speech community where a pidgin has acquired native speakers, namely the speakers of the speech community. In this theory, similarities in the sources of the creole's linguemes to those of pidgins are due to the descent of creoles from pidgins.

Mufwene's theory of creole formation (Mufwene 2001, 2005, 2008) is a theory in which creole formation is a case of language neogeny: the creation of a new language accompanying the creation of a new society in a colonial context. Mufwene supports his theory in a number of ways. First, pidgins and creoles largely have independent geographical locations and origins (Mufwene 2008: 35, Map 1). Second, creoles emerged largely from plantation colonization in the European expansion post-1500, a social process by which a new speech community was formed from the fusion of several groups: speakers of non-standard varieties of European languages such as English and French; speakers of minor European languages such as Gaelic and Breton; enslaved or indentured speakers of either local languages (e.g. Native American languages) or languages from where the slaves or indentured servants were taken (e.g. Africa). These groups formed a speech community to the extent that there was communicative interaction between them, and the language of the speech community is the result of the linguistic utterances produced in that interaction. Third, the structures of the creole – both schematic and substance linguemes, in our terms – can be traced to the languages of the speech communities from which the speakers came who fused into the plantation community. Finally, the likelihood of the structures of a source language surviving to become part of the creole is partly a function of demography (the proportion of speakers), as well as of socioeconomic power structures in the new society.

Of course, the formation of creoles is only one specific case of a neogenic language, just as the formation of pidgins is only one specific case of an exoteric language. They represent only two types of social contact situations leading to two types of contact languages. In this chapter, I will relate the neogenic process of creole formation, and the exoteric process of pidgin formation, to the function of lingua francas in the larger context of types of exoteric and neogenic languages. The simple definitions of esoteric, exoteric, and neogenic languages hide a continuum of social language types for each of the three broad categories. The continua for exoteric and neogenic languages, both relevant to English as a lingua franca, will be briefly described in the next two sections, along with their apparent structural and social correlates.

3 The Exoteric Language Continuum and Its Relation to Social Organization

3.1 Pidgins and the Exoteric Language Continuum

Pidgins represent only one extreme end of the exoteric language continuum; see Figure 2.1. To get there, I will begin from the other end of the continuum and proceed through the intermediate types.

The first type, receptive multilingualism, represents the minimum exoteric use of the esoteric languages of the speech communities in contact. In receptive multilingualism, each interlocutor uses their own esoteric language. Exoteric communication succeeds because each interlocutor has at least passive knowledge of the other interlocutor's (otherwise esoteric) language. This type of exoteric communication was described as "semi-communication" by Haugen (1966a) in the Scandinavian context, as "dual-lingualism" by Lincoln (1979/1980) in an Austronesian context, and is now referred to as *receptive multilingualism* (see, for example, ten Thije and Zeevaert 2007). Receptive multilingualism appears to preserve the esoteric nature of the languages, in that only the speech community member uses their esoteric language in production.

The more widely reported type of bi-/multilingualism is where both interlocutors both know and produce one or more of the esoteric languages of their respective speech communities. Such bilingualism may be *symmetric*: either (or both) languages may be used exoterically. This is the next step in the continuum. Or bilingualism may be *asymmetric*, in that one of the two (or more) languages spoken by the interlocutors is the preferred or exclusive language for exoteric use. Asymmetric bilingualism suggests that one of the esoteric languages in the contact situation is coming to be construed as a specifically exoteric language, in addition to serving as an esoteric language for one of the interlocutors. The asymmetry of bilingualism is a scale, of course: some languages may be more likely than others to be used exoterically, depending on a variety of social factors.

Bi-/Multilingualism used for exoteric function between communities speaking those languages esoterically may have certain structural effects. Stable multilingualism leads to general maintenance of core substance linguemes – grammatical morphemes and basic vocabulary – in the respective speech communities, although non-basic vocabulary linguemes may be borrowed. (These generalizations are probabilistic, of course.) Although some have

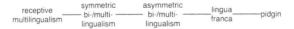

Figure 2.1 The exoteric language continuum.

claimed more extensive borrowing in small-scale (low-population) societies, surveys of borrowing patterns indicate that this is not the case (Alpher and Nash 1999; Bowern et al. 2011), and language phylogenies can be recovered even when there has been up to around 40 percent of borrowed vocabulary (Greenhill et al. 2009; Bowern et al. 2011).

However, there may be exchange of schematic linguemes, possibly extensively where the societies are in close contact. The most extreme reported case is from the village of Kupwar in India (Gumperz and Wilson 1971). The first example shows where the Kupwar varieties of Indo-Aryan languages have adopted the morphosyntactic construction for person inflection (contrast the standard Hindi-Urdu construction) from Kannada, a Dravidian language spoken in the village. The second example shows where the Kupwar varieties of Kannada and Marathi have adopted the Indo-Aryan construction for predicate nominal constructions (Gumperz and Wilson 1971: 157, 158):

(1)	Kupwar Kannada	yəlli	hog	idi	ni
		where	gone	were(2sg)	you
	Kupwar Marathi	kəttə	gel	hotas	twa
	Kupwar Urdu	khã	gəe	te	tu
	Hindi-Urdu	kəhã	gə-ii	th-ii	tu
		where	gone	were-F	you
	"Where did you go?"				

(2)	Kupwar Urdu	ye	tumhar-ə	ghər	həy
		this	your-suff.	house	is
	Kupwar Marathi	he	tumc-ə	ghər	hay
	Kupwar Kannada	id	nim-d	məni	eti
	Kannada	i-du	nim	mənə	
		this	your	house	
	"This house is yours."				

The sociolinguistic situation in Kupwar is likely to be an extreme case, in that the caste divisions in Indian society lead to a high degree of social separation combined with cohabitation in the same village. There is thus a high degree of exoteric communication combined with a high degree of social segregation. Nevertheless, it is found elsewhere – for example, in Oceania (e.g. Thurston 1987), where it has been called "metatypy" (Ross 1996).

The next step is for a language to be more fully separated from its esoteric function, and to come to be used as an exoteric language even in a contact situation where none of interlocutors uses the language esoterically (that is, none are native speakers of that language). A language that has reached this independent degree of exoteric use is generally called a *lingua franca*. A simple example of a lingua franca is the use of English in scientific conferences, say, in Europe, where English may be used by European scientists, none of whom are native English speakers.

At this point, exoteric language use has passed beyond the control, so to speak, of the native speakers. This divergence in communicative context may lead to divergence in language structure. For example, there are many lexical items in English as a lingua franca in Europe that are not part of English as an esoteric language in Britain or the United States, as evidenced in Manfred Görlach's *A Dictionary of European Anglicisms* (Görlach 2001).

The last step of separation from any esoteric function is represented by *pidgins*. Pidgins are exclusively used for exoteric function, possibly a highly restricted function related to certain types of trade or other exchange between distinct societies. Although pidgins may primarily draw their lexicon from a single source, the restricted exoteric function means that both the lexicon and the range of syntactic constructions employed may be limited in comparison to the esoteric language that provides most of the lexicon of the pidgin.

3.2 Exoteric Languages and Social Organization

A number of researchers have observed what they considered a puzzle: the absence of lingua francas or pidgins in areas of high linguistic diversity:

the number of reported pidgins is surprisingly small given the linguistic diversity of Papua New Guinea and the number of trading networks in which there was contact between [Austronesian] and other languages. (Mühlhäusler et al. 1996: 417)

basically in the whole interior of Canada, despite the diversity of languages and despite the multiple interethnic contacts ... no pidgins are recorded. (Bakker and Grant 1996: 1152)

The headwaters of the Xingu river in the Brazilian state of Mato Grosso constitute an area of extraordinary ethnic and linguistic diversity .... The tribes of the Upper Xingu entertain close economic and cultural relations ..... Yet, no lingua franca seems to have developed. (Adelaar 1996a: 1345)

Currently, there exists no obvious sociolinguistic or historical explanation for the apparent scarcity of indigenous contact languages in the Southwest; for this area showed as much linguistic diversity, and experienced as extensive intertribal and interethnic contacts, as other regions in North America. (Drechsel 1996: 1216; California is also cited in this regard; ibid.: 1215)

I suggest that the explanation for this apparent anomaly has to do with social organization. Although the analysis of social structure is a complex and controversial area, there are two parameters of variation on which there appears to be some consensus: scale (population size) and stratification.

Societies vary considerably in scale. The smallest-scale societies appear to number in the hundreds or low thousands; such societies were found in many parts of the globe before European expansion, and many such societies have survived into the beginning of the twenty-first century.

Societies may also be broadly divided into egalitarian and stratified. Egalitarian societies are those in which "there are few differences between members in wealth, status, and power" (McDowell 2017: 4). Although egalitarian societies do have leaders, they are not hereditary. Stratified societies do have major differences in wealth, status, and power (some anthropologists also distinguish an intermediate category of ranked societies, but we will ignore that distinction here).

Egalitarian societies are small-scale, and large-scale societies are stratified, presumably since it would be difficult to manage a large-scale society without some degree of stratification. However, societies up to some intermediate scale (numbering in the thousands) may also be egalitarian. Thus, we can posit roughly a single scale, with some overlap at intermediate population size, from small-scale egalitarian societies to large-scale stratified societies; see Figure 2.2.

All of the areas described in the quotations above are occupied by small-scale, egalitarian societies. This is, of course, why there is also great linguistic diversity in these areas: each small-scale society has its own language; without higher-level social integration, the languages will diverge over time; and these areas have been occupied by such communities for a long period of time.

My hypothesis is that *it is only when there is contact with larger-scale, stratified societies that lingua francas and pidgins – that is, exclusively exoteric languages – emerge*. In other words, the scale of degrees of exotericity in Figure 2.1 correlates with the scale of social organization in Figure 2.2: if at least one of the languages in contact is farther to the right on the scale in Figure 2.2, then the exoteric language used in contact may be farther to the right on the scale in Figure 2.1. We will explore this hypothesis in the remainder of Section 3, but I first want to suggest a reason for this correlation between social organization and type of exoteric language use.

The question is: why do small-scale egalitarian societies make do with multilingualism in areas of great linguistic diversity (by definition), but

Figure 2.2 A scale of social organization.

larger-scale, stratified societies use more exclusively exoteric languages? My suggestion is that the difference may be due to the engagement (or not) in direct, long-distance trade. Small-scale, egalitarian societies do not carry on direct, long-distance trade, that is, individuals do not regularly travel long distances to trade items. Instead, they trade with neighboring communities. For this reason, multilingualism with the local languages will mostly suffice for exoteric function. This is not to deny that trade items may travel long distances through chains of local trade, or that a few individuals may travel long distances beyond neighboring communities. But the trade is not frequent enough or broad enough to motivate the emergence of a lingua franca.

In contrast, large-scale societies have the reach and the resources to engage in long-distance trade with sufficient frequency and breadth to give rise to exclusively exoteric languages. This trade may, of course, involve small-scale egalitarian societies as counterparties, so the latter may also use the exoteric language for trade. The exoteric language is usually, though not always (see Sections 3.4–3.5), a descendant of the esoteric language of the large-scale society. In the extreme case of social asymmetry between the trading societies and minimal interaction in trade contact, a pidgin will arise as the exoteric language.

Pidgins based on European languages – the best-described pidgins – are of this type: they originate with large-scale, stratified European societies, and they are used with long-distance, colonial trade. The more interesting cases that will test the hypothesis are well-documented, non-European lingua francas and pidgins. The question is: are the non-European languages that give rise to lingua francas and pidgins also farther to the right in the scale of social organization in Figure 2.2? If so, then the hypothesis is supported.

The examples of non-European lingua francas and pidgins discussed in the following sections are based primarily on the surveys in *Status and Use of African Lingua Francas* (Heine 1970) and *Atlas of Languages of Intercultural Communication in the Pacific, Asia, and the Americas* (Wurm et al. 1996). These two sources cover most of the world outside the Eurasian continental region where most of the large-scale, stratified, colonizing societies originated.

3.3 African Lingua Francas before, or in Apparent Absence of, European Contact

A number of lingua francas in Africa arose before European contact with sub-Saharan Africa. These lingua francas fall into two categories. The first is the languages of states of ultimately Near Eastern origin. Arabic, including a pidginized form, functioned as a major lingua franca for trade between the Arab Empire and sub-Saharan societies (Heine 1970: 115–118). The second is the languages of sub-Saharan states (called "empires" in the African historical

Table 2.1 *African lingua francas in large-scale societies that pre-date European expansion.*

Arabic pidgins	Arab caliphates, states
Swahili	Zenj Empire
Kanuri	Kanem-Bornu Empire
Hausa	Hausa states
Songhai	Songhai Empire (15c.–16c.)
Mandingo > Malinke, Dyula, Bambara; pidginized Kambe	Mali Empire (11c.)
Maba	Wadai Empire (17c.)

tradition) that arose as a result of contact with Near Eastern origin states, as a result of long-distance trade with Arab states across the Sahara Desert or the Indian Ocean. Their language was used for political integration but also for trade, and often remained in the latter function after the political collapse of the empire.

The Zenj Empire arose as a result of trade along the Indian coast, and Swahili spread with it (ibid.: 83). Kanuri developed into a lingua franca along with the Kanem-Bornu Empire (ibid.: 112). The Hausa "states" developed as a result of trade between the Arab states and the rainforest peoples, leading to Hausa's use as a lingua franca (ibid.: 151–153). It appears that Songhai became a lingua franca with the advent of the Songhai Empire, and was clearly a lingua franca by the empire's height in the fifteenth to sixteenth centuries (ibid.: 159–160). The vicissitudes of the Mali Empire, starting in the eleventh century, led to a series of lingua francas: Mandingo (ibid.: 164), which split into Malinke (ibid.: 165), Dyula (ibid.: 166), and Bambara (ibid.: 164), and also apparently gave rise to the pidginized Kangbe (ibid.: 170–171). Much later, the Wadai Empire was founded in the seventeenth century in what is now eastern Chad by an Arab leader, but Maba as the language of the capital and surrounding area became the lingua franca of the empire (ibid.: 115).

These lingua francas are summarized in Table 2.1.

3.4 African Lingua Francas in the Context of European Contact

Some societies that controlled trade between Africans and Europeans gave rise to lingua francas. The Duala managed trade between the British and the Cameroon interior from the eighteenth century (Heine 1970: 125). The Wolof benefited from early contact with the Europeans and managed trade on the Senegalese coast (ibid.: 147–148). The Ovimbundu managed trade between Europeans and Bantus in southwest Africa from the nineteenth century (ibid.: 54–55). Other lingua francas are associated with regional trade networks that

ELF in the Context of Contact Languages 59

Table 2.2 *African lingua francas that emerged from long-distance trade with Europeans.*

Duala	*British and the Cameroon interior*
Wolof	*Europeans on the Senegalese coast*
Ovimbundu	*European and Bantus in SW Africa*
Mbum	*Adamawa Plateau*
Gbaya	*western Central African Republic*
Lwena	*Angola-Congo-Zambia border area*
Jukun	*Benue River*
Kituba, Lingala	*Congo River*
Sango	*Ubangi River*
Tshiluba	*Lualaba River*

arose well after European contact, presumably as a consequence of that contact and the increased trade it stimulated. This appears to be true of Mbum (Adamawa Plateau; ibid.: 130), Gbaya (western Central African Republic; ibid.: 130), Lwena (the Angola-Congo-Zambia border area; ibid.: 56), and Jukun (Benue River; ibid.: 129).

There is one category of lingua francas that might have arisen before the emergence of states as a result of Near Eastern or European state contact. These lingua francas are found on the Congo River and its tributaries. On the Congo River itself, the early phases of Kituba (Heine 1970: 68) and Lingala (ibid.: 73) may antedate European contact, and there may have been a lingua franca preceding Lingala (ibid.: 72) there as well. However, Samarin argues against this view (Samarin 1990/1991). Early Sango may have been a trade language on the Ubangi River before European contact (Heine 1970: 131), but Samarin argues persuasively against this view also (Samarin 1982). On the Lualaba River, Tshiluba may have been a pre-European lingua franca (Heine 1970: 65).

The African lingua francas that emerged (certainly or presumably) from long-distance trade with Europeans are summarized in Table 2.2.

3.5 North American Lingua Francas and Trade Pidgins

There are a number of trade pidgins and lingua francas reported in North America (Silverstein 1996). Initial European contact was by signs and interpreters. In some cases, interpreters knew only local languages (Silverstein 1996: 118); in other cases, it appears that some languages were more widely known, at least among certain individuals, but early European reports were unsophisticated and may describe dialect continua or a bilateral pidgin devised for use with Europeans (ibid.: 119). However, soon after European contact, extended trade networks and political integration led to some languages becoming lingua francas in the narrow sense, including pidginized forms. Of the latter, the ones that were based largely on indigenous languages and achieved some degree of stability were Montagnais Jargon (early seventeenth century, French-Montagnais contact), Pidgin Delaware (seventeenth century, Delaware-Dutch/Swedish/English; see also Goddard 1997), Apalachee-Spanish jargon (early eighteenth century, Apalachee-Spanish), Mobilian Jargon (eighteenth to nineteenth centuries, lower Mississippi societies-French/English), Chinook Jargon (Pacific Northwest Coast societies-English), and Pidgin Eskimo, an Inuit-European variety and an Eskimo-Athapaskan variety (Silverstein 1996: 121–131).[1]

Of the post-contact varieties discussed by Silverstein, two have been argued to be pre-contact in origin: Chinook Jargon and Mobilian Jargon. Hymes (1980) offers some early reports that might be evidence of a pre-contact pidgin antedating Chinook Jargon, but Samarin (1986: 25–26) questions their reliability and the inferences that can be drawn from them. Hymes proposes that Chinook Jargon arose as a result of pre-contact slave trading in the Columbia River area, but a detailed study of slavery on the Pacific Northwest Coast concludes that extensive slave trading did not occur in the area before contact (Donald 1984: esp. 152–153; see also Samarin 1986: 29). Also, large-scale migrant labor, not small-scale, localized slavery, can give rise to a contact language, but that language is a creole, not a pidgin (Samarin 1986: 29, 30; see Section 4).

These considerations do not rule out the possibility that Chinook Jargon arose as a trade pidgin in pre-contact times. However, linguistic diversity does not require a lingua franca or pidgin for trade, as noted above, and it is likely that trade was restricted to particular members of the society (Samarin 1986: 28–29; see above). Also, the evidence offered by Donald (1984) suggests that long-distance, intensive trading networks appear to have arisen as a result of European contact (ibid.; compare Silverstein 1996: 127). Moreover, the European vessels were manned by a large number of indigenous Alaskan and Siberian people, further stimulating the rise of a pidgin (Samarin 1988).

The case for Mobilian Jargon existing before European contact is weaker. The earliest explorers do not mention a lingua franca or a pidgin, and they used interpreters, as did the Indians among themselves (Crawford 1978: 21–29); there is no positive evidence for a pre-contact origin (Silverstein 1996: 124; Drechsel 1997: 294). After the Europeans established settlements in the Gulf

---

[1] Silverstein suggests the Eskimo-Athapaskan pidgin arose before direct European contact (Silverstein 1996: 120), but Samarin notes that the earliest statement about a pre-contact Eskimo-Athapaskan pidgin (by Stefánsson) was made 200 years after the first European contact in the Arctic (Samarin 1986: 23).

Table 2.3 *North American pidgins and lingua francas that likely emerged with European contact.*

Montagnais Jargon	early 17c., French-Montagnais
Pidgin Delaware	17c., Dutch/Swedish/English-Delaware
Apalachee-Spanish Jargon	early 18c., Spanish-Apalachee
Mobilian Jargon	18c.–19c., French/English-lower Mississippi
Chinook Jargon	English-Northwest Coast
Pidgin Eskimo	European-Inuit/Athapaskan
Plains Sign Language	18c.–20c., European-Gulf Coast, Great Plains

area at the end of the seventeenth century, a lingua franca was reported, and the first examples of the pidgin were recorded (Drechsel 1997: 215–244). Mobilian Jargon was used among Native Americans, and between them and Europeans and Africans, peaking in the eighteenth century (ibid.: 254). Drechsel speculates that a pidgin must have been used among the pre-contact chiefdoms (ibid.: 285–286), but as we have seen, this is by no means a necessary conclusion. Silverstein argues that Mobilian arose as a pidginized western Muskogean language spoken with the French, with possible contributions from Apalachee-Spanish and from Algonquian languages used in the Mississippi tributaries (Silverstein 1996: 120, 124, 125).

Finally, it has been suggested that Plains Sign Language was a pre-European lingua franca (Taylor 1975, 1981). A Native sign language is reported in the Gulf Coast area by early-sixteenth-century European explorers. Plains Sign Language spread north and west from the Gulf Coast after European contact (eighteenth to twentieth centuries). Plains Sign Language may have originated among stratified societies in the Gulf Coast area – Native North America included stratified societies in that area – but it spread as a lingua franca only after European contact and the social changes brought about thereby (Samarin 1987).

Table 2.3 summarizes the North American pidgins or lingua francas that appear to have emerged in long-distance trade with Europeans.

3.6   Pidgins in Papua New Guinea before European Contact

A few pre-contact pidgins have been reported from Papua New Guinea. Although these were used by societies that were at a stage of incipient stratification, they arose in circumstances that favored their rise even at this stage.

There were a number of bilateral pidgins involving Yimas, a language spoken on the Sepik River. Pidgin Yimas is in fact several bilateral pidgins, each used with a particular linguistic community (Mühlhäusler et al. 1996:

419, based on unpublished work by Jeff Williams; Foley 1988 describes the Yimas-Arafundi pidgin). The Yimas pidgins are used by individual clans, reflecting a common pattern where trade is exclusive to particular families or elites (e.g. Johnson and Earle 2000: 156, 214, 238, 252, 267). Mühlhäusler et al. also cite reports of other bilateral pidgins in the Middle Sepik River area (1996: 420–421). All of these Papuan societies are small scale and egalitarian, but they are found on a major river and have specialized economic niches. In particular, the Yimas are fisherfolk, and incipient stratification has been reported for the Sepik fisherfolk societies (Harrison 1987: 492).

Two bilateral pidgins were used by the Austronesian Motu people for their *hiri* or long-distance trading voyages from the Port Moresby area to the Gulf of Papua (Dutton 1983, 1996). The long-distance trade was required because of the poor agricultural environment of the Motu (Oram 1982: 5) and were undertaken only when necessary (ibid.: 26). The Motu traded with the Eleman and Koriki; they stayed for at least one or two months (Oram 1982: 15) and were largely segregated from the local people (Dutton 1983: 87). The trading languages were predominantly based on Toaripi (an Eleman language) and Koriki respectively; they were the Motu's trading partners. The pidgins were used only in this trade. The Motu were organized as tribes without an overarching political structure (Oram 1982: 3). However, in some villages, headmen were hereditary (ibid.), and more significantly, the Motu villages did not make war on one another (ibid.: 9), which suggests an emerging regional political identity, a first step towards a larger-scale, stratified society. It appears that the long-distance trade necessitated by food shortages, combined with the long-term absence and the segregation from the local people during the stay of the traders, were the motivating factors for the emergence of the bilateral pidgin in this small society.

It is very difficult to try to infer social organization, trade, and exoteric language use in areas prior to European contact without written records. The changes wrought by European contact were dramatic, and often obscured or erased previous social organization and trading patterns. For example, in Africa, "[s]ince the arrival of the European the contacts between the various ethnic groups had considerably enlarged on account of the stamping out of tribal warfare and the improved means of communication" (Heine 1970: 74). Trade with Europeans along the West African and Congolese coasts led to intensification of long-distance trade with inland tropical forest societies that did not have direct contact with Europeans (ibid.: 68, 72). While it is clear that European contact led to social changes that favored the emergence of exclusively exoteric languages, it is not clear that those social structures existed prior to European contact.

3.7 Social Changes and Changes in the Type of Exoteric Language

The survey of non-European lingua francas and pidgins in Sections 3.3–3.6 support the hypothesis that exoteric languages farther to the right of the exoteric language continuum in Figure 2.1 are used when at least one of the societies in contact is larger scale and more stratified, that is, it falls towards the right of the scale of social organization in Figure 2.2.

The survey of synchronic contact situations in those sections can be further supported by historical changes in the type of exoteric language used in some cases. That is, we can observe the shift from multilingualism for exoteric communication to lingua francas. There is some evidence that lingua francas tend to replace symmetrical multilingualism as societies become larger and more stratified. Tables 2.4 and 2.5 present data from Gapun village, Papua New Guinea in 1987 (Kulick, 1993: 118, fn. 2), and western and central Kenya in 1968 (Heine 1970: 102).

The data from Gapun village documents the loss of multilingualism in a small-scale, egalitarian society that is now part of Papua New Guinea. Taiap is the esoteric language, spoken only in the village (Kulick 1993: 94). Tok Pisin is the lingua franca and also the state language of Papua New Guinea; it was

Table 2.4 *Linguistic knowledge in Gapun village, Papua New Guinea in 1987.*

	languages spoken (passive knowledge)		
Sex and age of speakers	esoteric language	lingua franca	neighboring esoteric languages
Male, > 50yr	Taiap	Tok Pisin	Kopar, Adjora, one or two others
Male, > 40yr; Female, > 35yr	Taiap	Tok Pisin	Kopar *or* Adjora
> 14yr	Taiap	Tok Pisin	(Kopar *or* Adjora)
< 14yr	(Taiap)	Tok Pisin	

Table 2.5 *Linguistic knowledge in western and central Kenya in 1968.*

Mother tongue only	13.3%
Mother tongue + vernacular(s)	0.6%
Mother tongue + vernacular(s) + lingua franca(s)	17.6%
Mother tongue + lingua franca(s) only	68.5%
Lingua francas: Swahili 85.5%, English 27.8%	

introduced into Gapun after World War I (ibid.: 95; see Section 4.1 for further discussion of the evolution of Tok Pisin). The oldest male speakers in 1987 were multilingual in several of the local esoteric languages, as well as Tok Pisin, which was at first just another language for intercultural communication. Younger villagers gradually abandoned the use of the local languages in favor of Tok Pisin. The youngest speakers have even abandoned the village language (see Section 4.1).

By 1968 Kenya had been under state control for two centuries and contact with Arab and European states had altered trading patterns in the interior for many more centuries. By that time, virtually none of the multilingual speakers had knowledge of only local vernaculars (esoteric languages), and the vast majority had knowledge of the lingua franca(s) only. Almost all of the multilingual speakers knew Swahili, and about one-third knew English, a more recent lingua franca, as well.

Both the Gapun and Kenya situations involve not just larger-scale societies but also the creation of new societies: the countries of Papua New Guinea and Kenya respectively. I turn to these processes in the next section.

4   The Neogenic Language Continuum

In Section 2, I presented Mufwene's arguments for creoles as neogenic languages, and not as the descendants of pidgins, which are exoteric languages (Mufwene 2001, 2005, 2008). Creoles, like pidgins, also represent one extreme of a continuum of neogenic languages; see Figure 2.3. Again, I describe the continuum starting from the opposite end.

The opposite extreme from a creole, in which there are significant contributions of linguemes from multiple sources, is a neogenic language that arises almost exclusively from a single source. This is *language shift*: the language of the new society eventually shifts to that of the dominant community in the new society. The neogenic language continuum in Figure 2.3 appears to be associated with relatively large-scale societies, although the degree of social asymmetry or stratification (that is, the degree of dominance of one group) appears to play a role, as well as the size of the dominant group relative to that of the other groups brought together in neogeny. Again, the crucial test cases for this hypothesis are non-European contact languages in neogeny, since the European languages are spoken by already large-scale, stratified societies.

Figure 2.3 The neogenic language continuum.

4.1 Language Shift and Lingua Francas

Language shift is commonly associated with the creation of a large-scale, or at least larger-scale, society by conquest or by other means of socioeconomic incorporation. This is most often observed in the creation of modern nation-states, but it also took place in the creation of empires in the past, such as the Roman Empire.

Of course, the initial effect of incorporation is the creation of a multilingual society. Language shift does not happen overnight; it frequently takes several generations for a complete shift to take place. But the incorporation of societies speaking different languages into a new state also leads to larger-scale interactions between the component societies that require an exoteric language. The dominant group's language usually serves as the lingua franca for the longer-distance intersocietal communication that develops within the newly established state. This sort of lingua franca is therefore the result of incomplete, or not yet complete, language shift. As time goes on, increased economic and political integration of the state leads eventually to complete language shift, unless of course the state or empire breaks up, as happened with the Roman Empire. In the case of the Roman Empire, Latin persisted as a lingua franca among the ecclesiastical and secular elite for many centuries.

Where lingua francas of this type are attested outside the Eurasian area occupied by states since ancient times, they are associated with states, either before or after European contact. Many African lingua francas are primarily languages used for political integration of states, although they may also be used in trade (see Section 3). The Abyssinian Empire emerged long before European contact, leading to the use of Amharic as the language among the incorporated societies (Heine 1970: 107). The Mosi "states" evolved into "empires," presumably in response to increased trade across the Sahara and with societies in contact with Europeans, and Mosi concomitantly became a lingua franca (ibid.: 161–162).

After European contact in Africa, lingua francas arose in newly formed African states. Some African societies responding to European state contact created states as a political defense, incorporating local societies. The Bambara Empire arose first after the destruction of the Songhai Empire by the Moroccans in the sixteenth century, and survived until the nineteenth century, benefiting from its central location between Arab and European trade routes. Bambara became a lingua franca as a result (Heine 1970: 168). The Ful formed an empire in the nineteenth century at the expense of the Hausa and Bambara states, and the Ful dominated the political administration under French colonialization; as a result, Adamawa Ful has become a lingua franca (ibid.: 128–129). The rise of the Ashanti Empire in the eighteenth century led to Twi being used as a lingua franca (ibid.: 141–142).

Table 2.6 *African lingua francas that emerged in the creation of new states (empires).*

Amharic	*Abyssinia*
Mosi	*Mosi Empire*
Bambara	*Bambara Empire (16c.–19c.)*
Adamawa Ful	*Ful Empire (19c.)*
Twi	*Ashanti Empire (18c.)*

Table 2.6 summarizes the lingua francas of African states (empires) created before European contact or in response to European contact.

Other African languages became lingua francas in Africa when European states established state colonies and used the local society, or rather one of the local speech communities, as its administration. Susu had brief prominence around 1790 but is now a contemporary lingua franca in the Sierra Leone estuary (Heine 1970: 146). Ewe became a lingua franca after the Germans took control of the Slave Coast (ibid.: 140). Ga became a lingua franca in the nineteenth century after German missionaries chose it for missionary work (ibid.: 144). Bulu may have been a lingua franca before its choice by American missionaries in the late nineteenth century, but its clear expansion occurred around that time (ibid.: 119–121). After the British took control of Sierra Leone in the nineteenth century, Mende and Temne came to be used as lingua francas as the peoples moved from the interior towards the coast (ibid.: 145). Yoruba had been a lingua franca in Dahomey and Togoland in the late nineteenth century under German administration (ibid.: 139). Tswana became a lingua franca after the establishment of the Bechuanaland Protectorate (now Botswana; ibid.: 52). The Nyanja and their language spread as a lingua franca as the people expanded after the creation of the Nyasaland Protectorate (now Malawi; ibid.: 60–61). Ganda became a lingua franca as the British extended their administration through the Kingdom of Buganda (now Uganda; ibid.: 105–106). Ewondo (Yaoundé) became a lingua franca as a result of the German colonization of Cameroon (ibid.: 122–124), as did Bali to a lesser extent (ibid.: 126–127).

Table 2.7 summarizes the African (non-European) lingua francas of newly created European colonies.

In Central and South America, Nahuatl and Quechua functioned as lingua francas for the Aztec and Inca states respectively, while the Linguas Gerais of Brazil originated in the Portuguese colonial era (Holm 1989: 605–606; Adelaar 1996b).

In Oceania, Tok Pisin began as an exoteric trade language, that is, a pidgin. It is a seeming counterexample to Mufwene's theory (Mufwene 2001, 2005,

Table 2.7 *African lingua francas that emerged in the creation of European colonies.*

Susu	*Sierra Leone estuary, ca. 1790*
Ewe	*German Gold Coast*
Ga	*German missionary work*
Bulu	*American missionary work*
Mende, Temne	*British Sierra Leone*
Yoruba	*German Dahomey, Togoland*
Tswana	*Bechuanaland Protectorate*
Nyanja	*Nyasaland Protectorate*
Ganda	*British Uganda*
Ewondo, Bali	*German Cameroon*

2008) because it "creolized" in Papua New Guinea. However, Tok Pisin "creolized" because it became a neogenic language, that is, the language of a colony and later a nation-state, namely Papua New Guinea. In other words, Tok Pisin began as an exoteric pidgin, then expanded to become a lingua franca in the exoteric sense, and then came to be a lingua franca in the neogenic sense. It expanded in function, and as the lingua franca of a newly created state that incorporated a large number of small-scale societies, those latter societies shifted to the lingua franca. In this sense, a pidgin became a "creole," but via processes that are quite general to language neogeny.

It is interesting to compare the development of Tok Pisin in this framework to the development of Latin after the Roman Empire. Latin served as a lingua franca for the Roman Empire, leading to shift of many languages under its jurisdiction. After the Roman Empire collapsed, Latin persisted as a lingua franca among the ecclesiastical and secular elite for many centuries. By this point, the Romance languages had diverged, and due to its elite prestige, Latin was also used as an elite lingua franca in states with Germanic and Slavic languages. In other words, Latin moved from being a lingua franca in the neogenic sense during the Roman Empire to being a lingua franca in the exoteric sense in Europe, extending long after the fall of the Roman Empire. In other words, Latin and Tok Pisin as lingua francas changed sociolinguistic functions in opposite directions over their respective histories.

4.2 Neogeny from Closely Related Varieties: Koiné and Standard

The next step on the neogenic language continuum is the creation of a *koiné* or a *standard* language out of a set of closely related varieties that have been joined in a newly created state society. A koiné is an exoteric variety used for interdialect communication, in trade or in an incipient state. It differs from complete language shift in that there are multiple sources; however, the sources are closely related varieties. Likewise, a standard language for a state also has multiple sources. Following the classic model of standardization of Haugen (1966b/1972), adapted to the current framework, the steps in the process are: (i) selection of a set of linguemes from different varieties; (ii) codification (in evolutionary biological terms, fixation) of the linguemes for the standard; (iii) elaboration of linguemes for the many functions of the state; and (iv) acceptance by the speech communities in the state, that is, complete language shift to the standard. The standardization process is well documented since it is a concomitant of writing, and there are a number of case studies – for example, French (Lodge 1993), Latin (Clackson and Horrocks 2007), and Greek (Horrocks 2010).

4.3 Neogeny Involving Speakers of Sharply Distinct Varieties: Restructured Varieties and Creoles

The next step in the neogenic language continuum is a *restructured variety*. Restructured varieties are language varieties that have undergone some degree of simplification in comparison with the original language. Restructured varieties stand between simple language shift and creolization in structure and also in demography. Holm (2004) examines five partly restructured varieties, each descended from a different European language (African-American Vernacular English, Afrikaans, Brazilian Vernacular Portuguese, Non-Standard Caribbean Spanish, and vernacular lects of Réunionnais French). Holm concludes that the most significant factor leading to restructuring is the ratio of non-native to native speakers of the European language in the newly created colonial society: the ratio is larger than in simple language shift, but smaller than in creolization.

Restructuring differs from creolization only in degree, not kind. The results of language neogeny are a complex function of the proportion of speakers of the different source languages, the number of different source languages, the social relations between the different linguistic groups of speakers, and so on. In all cases, a new society is created, and a new language with it. The makeup of the new language is the result of a complex but at least partly predictable process, in part due to the major role of demography (see also Tria et al. 2015).

Restructuring differs from language shift only in degree, not kind. For example, Southern Irish English has a few schematic linguemes from Irish Gaelic, including: wider use of the progressive than in British English (3a–b); use of *after* combined with the progressive to express perfect meaning (3d); wider use of the cleft construction (3d–e); and use of elliptical verb phrases instead of *yes/no* in answers to polarity questions (3f–h) (Trudgill and Hannah 1994: 106–107):

(3) a. I'm seeing it very well.
b. This is belonging to me.
c. I'm after seeing him. (= "I have seen him")
d. It was very ill that he looked.
e. Is it stupid you are?
f. Are you going?   – I am.
g. Is it time?   – It is.
h. Did he come?   – He did not.

And phonetic schematic linguemes are frequently drawn from the original language of the shifting speakers; this is, of course, what is known as an accent.

Mufwene also argues that restructuring differs from language shift, and in fact from so-called normal language transmission, only in degree, not in kind (Mufwene 2008). Mufwene points out that the history of Indo-European and its descendants is one of migration into South Asia and into Europe in multiple waves, conquest, the breakup of empires and states, bilingualism of conquered speech communities for generations until those communities eventually shift, and so on. The amalgamation of speech communities into the societies that spoke the Celtic, Germanic, Romance, and Slavic protolanguages and then the splitting and amalgamation into the societies speaking the modern Indo-European languages is no less complex or "abnormal" than the amalgamation that led to the creoles in the plantation colonies of the New World. As a consequence, Mufwene argues that creole languages, as well as restructured varieties, are descendants of the European languages that provide the bulk of the core substance linguemes of these languages (Mufwene 2005, 2008).

5   Conclusions

Incomplete communicative isolation is the norm in virtually all speech communities. There is almost always some degree of exoteric language function between distinct speech communities in socioeconomic interaction. And in addition to fission of societies – the classic family tree and normal transmission model of language change – there is constant fusion of societies as well.

This chapter proposes a sociolinguistic typology of languages into esoteric, exoteric, and neogenic languages. Each of these three types (esoteric languages are not discussed here) are actually continua of language types that arise under different social circumstances, and evolve with different types of linguistic structures and different combinations of linguemes from different speech communities that have been or continue to be in contact. Although I hope that the sociolinguistic typology presented here sheds some light on the relationship between social contact, social organization, and the evolution of languages, it is only a beginning. At best it suggests necessary conditions, not sufficient conditions, for the types of contact languages that emerge.

I conclude with a few remarks on where English as a lingua franca fits into this sociolinguistic typology. English was spoken by a large-scale, stratified society by the time it emerged into the historical record as the language of the English kingdoms. For this reason, it is not surprising that it functioned and now functions as a lingua franca, typical of language contact in asymmetric social contexts. In fact, English functions as a lingua franca in both ways described in this chapter.

English has functioned as a lingua franca in the context of language neogeny multiple times over. As the British Isles were united under the British kingdom, English functioned as a lingua franca for the state in interaction with the Celtic speech communities that were conquered in the process; language shift has been completed by Manx and Cornish (although there is a Cornish language revival movement), and English is the dominant language in Scotland (by far) and in Wales.

As the Europeans colonized the rest of the world, the English language served as a neogenic lingua franca in the United States and Canada, Australia and New Zealand, and South Africa, as well as a number of smaller colonies where the English population came to vastly dominate the speech community (through violence as well as immigration). English has become a lingua franca also in countries such as India and Nigeria, where there was not significant migration from the British Isles.

The dominance of Britain and then the United States led to the adoption of English as a lingua franca not just between different speech communities in a new society (nation-state) in the process of linguistic integration and ultimately language shift, but also between different speech communities that are not so united. As science, commerce, and popular culture have become globalized, English has become the primary exoteric lingua franca in all of these domains (for example, this is why this chapter is written in English). Of course, English is not always the lingua franca in these various social contexts, but it would require going well beyond this chapter to explore the social circumstances that lead to the use of English or another language as the lingua franca for the exoteric social interaction.

REFERENCES

Adelaar, Willem F. H. 1996a. Areas of multilingualism in northern South America. In Stephen A. Wurm, Peter Mühlhäusler & Darrell T. Tryon (eds.), *Atlas of Languages of Intercultural Communication in the Pacific, Asia and the Americas* 1345. Berlin: Mouton de Gruyter.

1996b. The Tupí-Guaraní languages of Atlantic South America, and Línguas Gerais. In Stephen A. Wurm, Peter Mühlhäusler & Darrell T. Tryon (eds.), *Atlas of Languages of Intercultural Communication in the Pacific, Asia and the Americas*, 1333–1334. Berlin: Mouton de Gruyter.

Alpher, Barry & David Nash. 1999. Lexical replacement and cognate equilibrium in Australia. *Australian Journal of Linguistics* 19, 5–56.

Andersen, Henning. 1988. Center and periphery: adoption, diffusion, and spread. In Jacek Fisiak (ed.), *Historical Dialectology: Regional and Social*, 39–83. Berlin: Mouton de Gruyter.

Bakker, Peter & Anthony P. Grant. 1996. Interethnic communication in Canada, Alaska and adjacent areas. In Wurm et al. (eds.), 1107–1169.

Blythe, Richard A. & William Croft. 2012. S-curves and the mechanisms of propagation in language change. *Language* 88, 269–304.

Bowern, Claire, Patience Epps, Russell Gray, Jane Hill, Keith Hunley, Patrick McConvell & Jason Zentz. 2011. Does lateral transmission obscure inheritance in hunter-gatherer languages? *PLoS ONE* 6, e25195.

Clackson, James & Geoffrey Horrocks. 2007. *The Blackwell History of the Latin Language*. Chichester: Wiley-Blackwell.

Clark, Herbert H. 1996. *Using Language*. Cambridge: Cambridge University Press.

Crawford, James M. 1978. *The Mobilian Trade Language*. Knoxville: University of Tennessee Press.

Croft, William. 2000. *Explaining Language Change: An Evolutionary Approach*. Harlow, Essex: Longman.

  2009. Toward a social cognitive linguistics. In Vyvyan Evans & Stéphanie Pourcel (eds.), *New Directions in Cognitive Linguistics*, 395–420. Amsterdam: John Benjamins.

  2010. The origins of grammaticalization in the verbalization of experience. *Linguistics* 48, 1–48.

Dahl, Östen. 2004. *The Growth and Maintenance of Linguistic Complexity* (Studies in Language Companion Series, 71). Amsterdam: John Benjamins.

Östen Dahl, Viveka Velupillai. 2013. The past tense. In Matthew S. Dryer & Martin Haspelmath (eds.), *The World Atlas of Language Structures Online*. Leipzig: Max Planck Institute for Evolutionary Anthropology. Available at http://wals.info/chapter/66, accessed on January 28, 2019.)

Donald, Leland. 1984. The slave trade on the Northwest Coast of North America. *Research in Economic Anthropology* 6, 121–158.

Drechsel, Emanuel J. 1996. Native American contact languages of the contiguous United States. In Wurm et al. (eds.), 1213–1239.

  1997. *Mobilian Jargon: Linguistic and Sociohistorical Aspects of a Native American Pidgin*. Oxford: Oxford University Press.

Dutton, Tom. 1983. Birds of a feather: a pair of rare pidgins from the Gulf of Papua. In Ellen Woolford & William Washabaugh (eds.), *The Social Context of Creolization*, 77–105. Ann Arbor: Karoma Publishers.

  1996. Hiri trading languages. In Wurm et al. (eds.), 233–236.

Foley, William. 1988. Language birth: the processes of pidginization and creolization. In Frederick J. Newmeyer (ed.), *Linguistics: The Cambridge Survey, vol. IV*, 162–183. Cambridge: Cambridge University Press.

Goddard, Ives. 1997. Pidgin Delaware. In Sarah G. Thomason (ed.), *Contact Languages: A Wider Perspective*, 43–99. Amsterdam: John Benjamins.

Görlach, Manfred (ed.). 2001. *A Dictionary of European Anglicisms*. Oxford: Oxford University Press.

Greenhill, Simon J., Thomas E. Currie & Russell D. Gray. 2009. Does horizontal transmission invalidate cultural phylogenies? *Proceedings of the Royal Society B* 276, 2299–2307.

Gumperz, John J. & Robert Wilson. 1971. Convergence and creolization: a case from the Indo-Aryan/Dravidian border. In Dell Hymes (ed.), *Pidginization and Creolization of Languages*, 151–167. Cambridge: Cambridge University Press.

Harrison, Simon. 1987. Cultural efflorescence and political evolution on the Sepik River. *American Ethnologist* 14, 491–507.

Haugen, Einar. 1966a/1972. Semicommunication: the language gap in Scandinavia. *Sociological Inquiry* 36, 280–297. Reprinted in Anwar S. Dil, *The Ecology of Language: Essays by Einar Haugen*, 215–236. Stanford: Stanford University Press.

1966b/1972. Dialect, language, nation. *American Anthropologist* 68, 922–935. Reprinted in Anwar S. Dil, *The Ecology of Language: Essays by Einar Haugen*, 237–254. Stanford: Stanford University Press.

Heine, Bernd. 1970. *Status and Use of African Lingua Francas*. München/New York: Weltforum Verlag/Humanities Press.

Holm, John. 1989. *Pidgins and Creoles, Vol. II: Reference Survey*. Cambridge: Cambridge University Press.

2004. *Languages in Contact: The Partial Restructuring of Vernaculars*. Cambridge: Cambridge University Press.

Horrocks, Geoffrey. 2010. *Greek: A History of the Language and Its Speakers*. Chichester: Wiley-Blackwell.

Hull, David L. 1988. *Science as a Process: An Evolutionary Account of the Social and Conceptual Development of Science*. Chicago: University of Chicago Press.

Hymes, Dell. 1980. Commentary. In A. Valdman & A. Highfield (eds.), *Theoretical Orientations in Creole Studies*, 389–423. New York: Academic Press.

Johnson, Allen W. & Timothy Earle. 2000. *The Evolution of Human Societies: From Foraging Group to Agrarian State*, 2nd ed. Stanford: Stanford University Press.

Kulick, Don. 1993. Growing up monolingual in a multilingual community: how language socialization patterns are leading to language shift in Gapun (Papua New Guinea). In Kenneth Hyltenstam & Åke Viberg (ed.), *Progression and Regression in Language*, 94–121. Cambridge: Cambridge University Press.

Langacker, Ronald W. 1987. *Foundations of Cognitive Grammar, Vol. I: Theoretical Prerequisites*. Stanford: Stanford University Press.

Lincoln, Peter C. 1979/1980. Dual lingualism: passive bilingualism in action. *Te Reo* 22/23, 65–72.

Lodge, R. Anthony. 1993. *French: From Dialect to Standard*. London: Routledge.

Lupyan, Gary & Rick Dale. 2010. Language structure is partly determined by social structure. *PLoS ONE* 5(1), e8559.

McDowell, Paul. 2017. Political anthropology: a cross-cultural comparison. In Nina Brown, Luara Tubelle de González & Thomas McIlwraith (eds.), *Perspectives: An Open Invitation to Cultural Anthropology*. Portland, OR: Lumen Learning.

Available at www.perspectives.americananthro.org/Chapters/Political_Anthropology.pdf, accessed August 22, 2018.

Mufwene, Salikoko. 2001. *The Ecology of Language Evolution*. Cambridge: Cambridge University Press.

2005. *Créole, écologie sociale, évolution linguistique*. Paris: L'Harmattan.

2008. *Language Evolution: Contact, Competition and Change*. London: Continuum.

Mühlhäusler, Peter, Tom Dutton, Even Hovdhaugen, Jerry Williams & Stephen A. Wurm. 1996. Precolonial patterns of intercultural communication in the Pacific Islands. In Wurm et al. (eds.), 401–437.

Ohala, John. 1989. Sound change is drawn from a pool of synchronic variation. In Leiv Egil Breivik & Ernst Håkon Jahr (eds.), *Language Change: Contributions to the Study of Its Causes*, 173–198. Berlin: Mouton de Gruyter.

Oram, Nigel. 1982. Pots for sago: the *hiri* trading network. In Tom Dutton (ed.), The *Hiri* in History: Further Aspects of Long Distance Motu Trade in Central Papua, 3–33. Canberra: The Australian National University.

Ross, Malcolm D. 1996. Contact-induced change and the comparative method: cases from Papua New Guinea. In Mark Durie & Malcolm D. Ross (ed.), *The Comparative Method Reviewed: Irregularity and Regularity in Language Change*, 180–217. Oxford: Oxford University Press.

Samarin, William J. 1982. Colonization and pidginization on the Ubangi River. *Journal of African Languages and Linguistics* 4, 1–42.

1986. Chinook Jargon and pidgin historiography. *Canadian Journal of Anthropology/Revue canadienne d'anthropologie* 5, 23–34.

1987. Demythologizing Plains Sign Language history. *International Journal of American Linguistics* 53, 65–73.

1988. Jargonization before Chinook Jargon. *Northwest Anthropological Research Notes* 22, 219–238.

1990/1991. The origins of Kituba and Lingala. *Journal of African Languages and Linguistics* 12, 47–77.

Silverstein, Michael. 1996. Dynamics of linguistic contact. In Ives Goddard (ed.), *Handbook of North American Indians, Vol. XVII: Language*, 117–136. Washington, DC: Smithsonian Institution.

Taylor, Allan R. 1975. Nonverbal communications systems in native North America. *Semiotica* 4, 329–374.

1981. Indian lingua francas. In Charles A. Ferguson & Shirley Brice Heath (eds.), *Language in the USA,* 175–195. Cambridge: Cambridge University Press.

ten Thije, Jan D. & Ludger Zeevaert (eds.). 2007. *Receptive Multilingualism: Linguistic Analyses, Language Policies and Didactic Concepts*. Amsterdam: John Benjamins.

Thomason, Sarah G. & Terrence Kaufman. 1988. *Language Contact, Creolization and Genetic Linguistics*. Berkeley and Los Angeles: University of California Press.

Thurston, William R. 1987. *Processes of Change in the Languages of North-Eestern New Britain* (Pacific Linguistics, Series B, No. 99). Canberra: Department of Linguistics, Research School of Pacific Studies, The Australian National University.

1989. How exoteric languages build a lexicon: esoterogeny in West New Britain. In R. Harlow & R. Hooper (ed.), *VICAL 1, Oceania Languages: Papers from the*

Fifth International Conference on Austronesian Linguistics, 555–579. Auckland: Linguistic Society of New Zealand.

Tria, Francesca, Vito D. P. Sevedio, Salikoko S. Mufwene & Vittorio Loreto. 2015. Modeling the emergence of contact languages. *PLoS ONE.* doi:10.1371/journal.pone.0120771.

Trudgill, Peter. 2011. *Sociolinguistic Typology: Social Determinants of Linguistic Complexity.* Oxford: Oxford University Press.

Trudgill, Peter & Jean Hannah. 1994. *International English*, 3rd ed. London: Edward Arnold.

Wurm, Stephen, Peter Mühlhäusler & Darrell T. Tryon (eds.). 1996. *Atlas of Languages of Intercultural Communication in the Pacific, Asia, and the Americas.* Berlin: Mouton de Gruyter.

3 How Writing Changes Language

Ewa Dąbrowska[1]

1 Introduction

As any introductory linguistics text will tell you, spoken language is the basic mode, or language in its "natural" state, in the sense that both historically and developmentally, the spoken form precedes the written form. Written language is a relatively recent innovation and is not universal: that is to say, many languages do not have a written form, and it is thus regarded as a somewhat artificial add-on – artificial because it has to be explicitly taught and it is strongly influenced by prescriptivist notions. What most textbooks don't tell you is that the availability of the written form has a profound influence on language structure and representation at both the individual level (mental grammar) and the social level (language as a conventional system shared by a community of speakers). In this paper, I discuss some of these effects and their implications for how we think about language.

2 Individual Level

2.1 Vocabulary

The effect of writing at the individual level is perhaps most obvious when we consider vocabulary: experience with written language results in a massive growth of vocabulary. Although we acquire basic vocabulary early in development through face-to-face interaction with our caretakers, most of the words we know have been learned through incidental exposure in written texts (Dąbrowska 2009) – "we" being speakers living in modern industrialized societies. This is because, past the early stages of acquisition, we already know nearly all the words we encounter in speech. Consider the figures in Table 3.1, which provides information about the lexical richness of selected

---

[1] This research was funded by the Alexander von Humboldt Foundation (grant number ID-1195918).

Table 3.1 *Vocabulary richness in selected spoken and written genres (adapted from Hayes & Ahrens 1988).*

	Proportion of text from 5,000 basic lexicon	Rank of median word	Number of rare words per 1,000 tokens
College graduates in conversation with friends and spouses	.94	496	17.3
Popular prime-time TV	.94	490	22.7
Children's books	.92	627	30.9
Adult books	.88	1,058	52.7
Newspapers	.84	1,690	68.3
Scientific articles	.70	4,389	128.0

spoken and written genres, based on corpus data analyzed by Hayes and Ahrens (1988). As we can see, even children's books are lexically richer than adult conversation or prime-time television, and newspapers contain almost four times as many rare words (defined as words with a rank higher than 10,000 in the reference frequency list) as casual conversation among educated adults. Not surprisingly, numerous studies have shown that vocabulary size correlates strongly with measures of print exposure, with correlation coefficients varying from .56 to .80 (Stanovich & Cunningham 1992; Cunningham & Stanovich 1997; Dąbrowska 2018). Crucially, the correlations remain significant even after controlling for general ability and reading comprehension, showing that the relationship is not due simply to the fact that people with higher abilities also have larger vocabularies (for discussion, see Stanovich & Cunningham 1992).

Cunningham and Stanovich (1998) conclude that, compared to writing, speech is lexically impoverished; but perhaps a better way of putting it would be that, compared to speech, writing is lexically enriched. As a result, the later stages of literacy acquisition involve, to a large extent, the acquisition of new vocabulary (cf. Biemiller 2003).

2.2   *Phonology*

Learning to read and write also has profound effects on speaker's phonological knowledge and processing. In particular, there is considerable evidence that phoneme awareness – that is to say, the ability to segment words into phonemes – is a consequence of acquiring an alphabetic writing system. Research with illiterates and pre-literates has shown that they do very poorly on phoneme segmentation tasks (such as adding or deleting a single consonant at the beginning of a word, or naming words beginning with a particular consonant), but have no problems with phonological tasks involving larger units such as syllables or rhymes (Morais et al. 1979, 1986; Adrián et al. 1995; Kurvers et al. 2006). A clever study by Read et al. (1986) has shown that this is also true of people literate in a non-alphabetic writing system. Read et al. exploited the fact that (at the time their research was conducted) some Chinese speakers learned only the traditional logographic system, while others also learned to write in pinyin (a system for transliterating Chinese using the Roman alphabet). They found that speakers who only knew the traditional system were 21 percent correct on phoneme segmentation tasks, whereas speakers who learned both the traditional system and pinyin were 83 percent correct.

It may seem that phoneme awareness is an aspect of metalinguistic knowledge that has little to do with ordinary language processing. However, there is substantial evidence that learning to read has a major effect on how we process speech. Illiterates have difficulty repeating pseudowords, and often substitute real words (Reis & Castro-Caldas 1997; Castro-Caldas et al. 1998). What is more, Castro-Caldas et al. (1998) found different patterns of brain activation in literates and illiterates while repeating pseudowords; interestingly, there were no differences for real words.

Further research revealed that illiterates process speech more slowly than literate speakers. Huettig et al. (2011) investigated visual orienting behaviour in high- and low-literate Hindi speakers. Participants listened to spoken sentences containing a target word (e.g. *magar* "crocodile") while looking at a visual display with four objects: a phonological competitor (*matar* "peas"), a semantic competitor (*kachuwa* "turtle"), and two unrelated distractors. The authors found that the high literates shifted their gaze to the phonological competitor as soon as phonological information became available, and shifted their gaze away from the phonological competitor as soon as the acoustic information mismatched. Low literates, in contrast, moved their gaze to the phonological competitor only when there was no semantic competitor, and only after a considerable delay compared to the high-literate speakers. The reason for this, the authors argue, is that their phonological representations are under-specified, or less finely grained. Mishra et al. (2012) conducted a similar experiment, but using stimuli in which the target noun was preceded by an adjective that strongly collocates with it. Such stimuli encourage anticipatory eye movements, and indeed, the authors found that the high-literacy group started to shift gaze to the target object well before the onset of the target noun. Low literates, in contrast, looked at the target more than a second later, and well after the onset of the target. This suggests that literacy enhances the ability to predict upcoming spoken language input. Studies of children learning to read and adults with dyslexia provide corroborating evidence for this conclusion (see Huettig 2015).

Further evidence comes from research on inexperienced writers. Ehri (1985) found that children's spelling errors frequently reflect their mispronunciations:

in other words, children who wrote *bisaco* for *bicycle, crans* for *crayons,* and *chrak* for *truck* pronounced these words as /baɪsəko/, /krænz/, and /tʃrʌk/, respectively. A more systematic spelling error that Ehri observed were {e}–{i} substitutions, such as *gist* for *guessed, ind* for *end, git* for *get, melk* for *milk, nicks* for *necks,* and *levd* for *lived.* Interestingly, when the children pronounced these words, they produced a vowel that was intermediate between /e/ and /ɪ/. This suggests that learning the spelling of a word may help to entrench its conventional pronunciation, particularly when vowel segments are involved.

A number of other studies have found widespread effects of orthography on the online processing of speech. In a classic study conducted by Seidenberg and Tanenhaus (1979), participants listened to pairs of words and had to decide if they rhymed. The authors found that reaction times were shorter for orthographically similar rhymes (*tie – pie*) than for orthographically dissimilar ones (*tie – rye*). Similarly, Jakimik et al. (1985), using an aural lexical decision task, found priming effects for orthographically similar words, but not for words which were similar in pronunciation only: for example, *barber* primed *bar* and *napkin* primed *nap,* but *laundry* did not prime *lawn* and *record* did not prime *wreck.* A number of more recent studies (e.g. Pattamadilok et al. 2007; Perre et al. 2009; Ziegler et al. 2008) report orthographic consistency effects in speech perception: that is to say, lexical decision times for auditorily presented words are shorter, and error rates lower, in words from orthographically consistent neighbourhoods, that is, words with rhymes that can be spelled in only one way (e.g. the ending /ʌk/, as in *duck, luck, suck, tuck,* etc., is always spelled "uck"), compared to words from orthographically inconsistent neighbourhoods (such as words ending in /-ip/, which can be spelled either "-eep," as in *deep*, or "eap," as in *heap*). Perre et al. (2009) showed that the consistency effect peaks at around 350 ms after word onset (i.e. before lexical access), showing that it is a fast, automatic process, and it is observable in the left temporoparietal area – an area known to play a role in phonological processing – but not in visual areas of the brain.

Perhaps the most dramatic demonstration of how written presentation can affect the mental representations of words comes from a study by Bürki et al. (2012). The authors exploited the fact that, in French, a schwa in the initial syllable is frequently reduced: for example, the word *seringue* "syringe" can be pronounced either [sərẽg] or [srẽg]. Unlike in English, the difference is categorical (i.e. the schwa is either fully present or entirely absent), and while the schwa variant reflects the spelling, the reduced variant is much more frequent. In the experiment, French speakers had to learn novel words containing initial consonant clusters, such as [plur]. The words were presented auditorily while participants saw pictures of the referent. The training was spread over four days, and participants heard each word about twenty-six times. On the last day of training, the participants were given a single exposure to the written form of the words. Half of the words were spelled with an [e] in the initial syllable (e.g. *pelour*) and the other half contained a consonant cluster (*plour*). During post-tests conducted on the following day, participants were asked to name the pictures and to categorize phonological forms as either "old" (i.e. presented during the training phase) or "new." Bürki et al. found that participants were much more likely to use the schwa variant in the production task, and to falsely recognize the schwa variant on the categorization task, if the written version of the word contained an {e}. In other words, a single exposure to the written form was enough to restructure representations acquired on the basis of multiple auditory presentations in the earlier part of the experiment. Thus, "orthography 'contaminates' phonology during the process of learning to read and write, thus altering the very nature of the phonological representations themselves" (Perre et al. 2009).

Further evidence demonstrating the effects of literacy on phonological processing comes from brain imaging studies. Petersson et al. (2007) investigated activation in the STG (superior temporal region; that is, Brodmann areas 22, 41, and 42) and the IPC (inferior parietal region; that is, Brodmann areas 39 and 40). The STG is involved in the processing of speech, and earlier research (e.g. Dehaene-Lambertz et al. 2002) has shown that even infants are left-lateralized in the STG when processing speech or speechlike stimuli. The IPC is known to be involved in phonological processing, reading, and working memory. Petersson et al. tested two groups: literate and illiterate women from a fishing village in southern Portugal who had very similar social backgrounds; most of the literates had about four years of schooling. The authors conducted two experiments. In Experiment 1, participants were asked to repeat real words and nonce words; in Experiment 2, the participants listened to, and tried to memorize, word pairs. In both experiments, literates showed more activation in the left IPC than the right, while illiterates showed the opposite pattern. In contrast, both groups showed a similar level of left-hemisphere dominance in the STG.

Another study by Dehaene et al. (2010) also revealed interesting differences between literates and illiterates. The authors used fMRI to study brain activation during the processing of linguistic and visual stimuli in illiterates and in early and late literates. They found considerable differences between groups during speech perception, with some regions being activated less and some more. In particular, the VWFA (visual word form area) – an area of the brain that is hypothesized to be involved in letter and word recognition – was highly activated during an *auditory* lexical decision task in literates, but showed no activation in illiterates. Furthermore, activation in the left of the planum temporale (a region involved in phonological processing) in response to spoken language in literate participants was double that in illiterates. For auditory decision tasks, the differences between groups were even larger.

To summarize: learning to read and write in an alphabetic writing system results in enhanced phoneme awareness and more finely grained phonological representations, which in turn leads to more efficient speech processing, particularly for non-words. Furthermore, the brains of literate individuals show a different pattern of connectivity, and language processing is more strongly left-lateralized in literate than in illiterate speakers. This is interesting, since left-hemisphere specialization is frequently cited as evidence for an innate adaptation for language. Yet research with illiterate speakers shows that the asymmetry is partly a consequence of learning to read and write.

2.3 Grammar

> By age 5, children essentially master the sound system and grammar of their language and acquire a vocabulary of thousands of words .... The development of complex (i.e., multi-clause) sentences usually begins some time before the child's second birthday and is largely complete by age 4.
> Hoff 2009

> It is safe to say that except for constructions that are rare, predominantly used in written language, or mentally taxing even to an adult (like *The horse that the elephant tickled kissed the pig*), all parts of all languages are acquired before the child turns four.
> Pinker 1995

> It is well known, however, that children acquire most of their grammar by the time they are three years old.
> Hirsh-Pasek & Golinkoff 1999

As the above quotations illustrate, it is often asserted that grammatical development is largely complete by age five, four, or even three. However, there is growing evidence that complex syntax and some aspects of morphology – including full passives, the past perfect, some derivational affixes, relative clauses and subordinate clauses generally, and nominalizations – continue to develop well into adolescence (Hunt 1977; Nippold 1998; Berman 2007; Nippold et al. 2007; Kaplan & Berman 2015) or even later (Hartshorne et al. 2018).

These "late-blooming" structures are likely to be acquired through exposure to written language. This is because they are characteristic of writing (e.g. complex sentences are three times more common in picture books for preschoolers than in child-directed speech; see Cameron-Faulkner & Noble 2013), and tend not to be fully acquired by speakers who are not regularly exposed to written language. For example, they do not appear in heritage speakers who are not literate in the heritage language (Montrul 2008). Moreover, there are correlations between print exposure and both comprehension (Street & Dąbrowska 2010; Dąbrowska 2018) and production (Montag & MacDonald 2015) of constructions such as passives and relative clauses, which are considerably more frequent in written language. Finally, Pakulak and Neville (2010) report significant correlations between linguistic proficiency and education ($r = .37$) and how much participants were read to as children ($r = .23$), though – interestingly – not between linguistic skills and adult reading behaviour.

Admittedly, the evidence for a relationship between morphosyntactic knowledge and reading is, at present, suggestive rather than conclusive. Clearly more research is needed in this area – ideally studies that, like the speech-perception studies discussed in the preceding section, compare cognitively normal adult illiterates with low and high literates.

3 Reasons for Literacy Effects

The preceding discussion suggests that learning to read and write has profound effects on speakers' mental representations of the phonology, lexicon, and grammar of their language. How do these effects come about? We have already discussed one aspect of this phenomenon. Becoming literate in an alphabetic writing system requires phonological awareness and eventually leads to finer-grained phonological representations. This, in turn, has far-reaching effects on phonological processing, and in particular, better phonological short-term memory, as evidenced, for example, by better memory for pseudowords (Reis & Castro-Caldas 1997). This, in turn, is likely to make it easier to learn new words, resulting in faster vocabulary growth, and could also enhance the processing of complex sentences (Daneman & Merikle 1996).

Learning to read and write also results in improved metalinguistic abilities: that is to say, literates are better than illiterates and pre-literates at attending to the form of an utterance. This kind of advantage is presumably conveyed by any kind of literacy, not just alphabetic literacy, and is perhaps best illustrated by a series of studies conducted by Tarone et al. (2007) that compared the performance of low-literate and moderately literate adult Somali immigrants learning English as a second language on linguistic tasks involving question formation. Crucially, all participants were at the same level of proficiency, yet the low-literate and moderately literate groups differed in a number of interesting ways.

Study 1 used a task developed by Philp (2003) that involves repetition of recasts. Participants performed a question elicitation task; if they produced an ungrammatical question, the researcher corrected them and knocked on the table, at which point the participant was supposed to repeat the correction, as in the following example:

(1)   Participant trigger: *What she doing?*
        Researcher recast: *What is she doing?* [two knocks]
        Participant recall: *What is she doing?*

More literate participants performed better, particularly when two or more changes were required, presumably because of better phonological short-term memory and/or increased ability to attend to form. Study 2 involved elicited imitation; that is to say, participants had to repeat eight-syllable questions – a more difficult task than repeating recasts, and again, more literate participants did better. The final study examined the use of semantically redundant grammatical morphemes in oral narratives. Tarone et al. (2007) found that the low-literacy group produced bare verbs in contexts requiring a tensed form more frequently than the moderate-literacy group (64 percent versus 50 percent of the time). The more literate participants supplied tense marking more frequently (50 percent versus 36 percent) and were more likely to supply plural marking (77 percent versus 48 percent). Perhaps most interestingly, the moderate-literacy group produced almost twice as many dependent clauses, and 3.5 times as many relative clauses as the low-literacy group. Typical examples of utterances produced by moderate and low literates are given in (2) and (3).

(2) Moderate literate: The monkeys took all his hats.
    Low literate: A lot of monkey they take his hat.

(3) Moderate literate: Her mom says, "Come in now, in a car."
    Low literate: Her mother they say, "We going right now."

Admittedly, Tarone et al.'s (2007) study involved adult second language learners. It doesn't follow that the same effects will necessarily be observable in child first language learners (and, of course, children acquiring English as a first language learn to form questions long before they learn to write). However, we know that learning to read and write is associated with the development of metalinguistic abilities, and that metalinguistic abilities, in turn, correlate with first language grammatical comprehension, even in monolingual adults (Dąbrowska 2018).

The third, and probably most important, way in which literacy may affect individual grammatical development is relevant for relatively high-literate participants only. When children first begin to write, their written productions are much simpler and contain more grammatical errors than their spoken productions. Throughout the school years, both spoken and written language continue to improve, which is evident in measures such as length of T-unit (roughly, a main clause plus any dependent clauses attached to it) and the subordination index (average number of clauses per T-unit). However, written language improves more quickly, so that it eventually becomes syntactically more complex than the child's speech. Interestingly, this happens at different times for different measures (for example, at about age nine for length of T-unit and about age fifteen for subordination index, see Scott 1988).

The greater syntactic complexity of written texts produced by skilled writers is doubtless due to the fact that writing is produced under less time pressure than speech and can be edited; moreover, the presence of the written representation eases the load on working memory. Thus, writing provides a processing crutch that enables speakers to produce more complex structures than they would otherwise be able to produce. Furthermore, writing may act as training wheels for language production in the sense that structures that are initially produced with the aid of the written medium may then find their way into the speech of highly literate speakers.

4   Effects on Language at the Community Level

Some of the effects of writing on language are evident relatively quickly – virtually as soon as language users begin to produce extended written texts (Mithun 1984; Biber 1995); others may take considerably longer to develop. One would expect that, in the long run, the cumulative effect of these individual changes would lead to changes at the level of the community language. Unfortunately, there is surprisingly little research on this, largely because the idea that languages develop, and possibly complexify, as a result of the introduction of writing was for a long time a taboo subject in linguistics, since it seemed to hark back to the old idea that traditional societies have "primitive" languages. Today, we know that this is not the case; the languages spoken by traditional societies of intimates are in many ways more complex than "industrial" languages – particularly with regard to morphology, and possibly also phonology (Lupyan & Dale 2010; Trudgill 2011, 2015) – and an increasing number of researchers are beginning to examine the relationship between writing and complexity.

4.1   Standardization

One area where the effects of writing on language are relatively uncontroversial is standardization. While standardization is, to a large extent, a sociopolitical phenomenon, it also has an important linguistic dimension, namely variation reduction (cf. Deumert & Vandenbussche 2003). Milroy and Milroy (2012) point out that standardization nearly always involves suppression of optional variability, as the result of which languages become more regular. (It should be noted, however, that once a written standard is established, it tends to be more conservative than speech, and often preserves irregularities that have been levelled out in speech.) Standardization involves the selection of particular variants, the codification of norms in dictionaries, grammars, style manuals, etc., and subsequently diffusion throughout the community. It may also involve elaboration, when new forms – typically lexical items, but occasionally also grammatical structures – are created to increase the expressive power of the language (see Joseph 1987). Importantly, writing is a prerequisite for standardization, since it makes it possible to establish prescriptive models and to plan and edit texts. Initially, standards are developed for writing; however, spoken standards sometimes develop later on the basis of the written model. (Finnish provides an excellent example of this; see Paunonen 2006.)

Standardization is a gradual process that may take several centuries. For example, for most European languages the process began towards the end of the sixteenth century, when the first reference grammars of the major (and some minor) European languages were published. The process gathered speed with the introduction of compulsory elementary education, which in most European countries happened in the late eighteenth or early nineteenth centuries, and was further supported by nineteenth- and twentieth-century ideas of romantic nationalism (see Deumert & Vandenbussche 2003).

4.2 Register Variation

Another fairly uncontroversial area where writing has a lasting effect on language is register variation. A tradition of literacy results in the development of written registers, which differ in many ways from spoken registers (see, e.g., Biber 1995, 2009), as well as from each other. As Biber (2009: 81) observes:

> Spoken registers are surprisingly similar to one another in their typical linguistic characteristics, regardless of differences in communicative purpose, interactiveness, and preplanning ... in contrast, written registers have a much wider range of linguistic diversity.

For example, classroom discourse is more like conversation than like written academic prose. This is also true of academic discourse (cf. Mauranen 2004, 2012). Interestingly, oral poetry is the only spoken genre that patterns like written texts. Biber speculates that this is most likely to due to the fact that traditional oral poetry is composed by individuals with exceptional memory and undergoes numerous rounds of planning and revision, both of which lead to greater use of more elaborate vocabulary and grammar.

The gradual diversification of written registers is clearly demonstrated by Biber's (1995) multidimensional analysis of registers in the ARCHER corpus, a multigenre historical corpus of English which spans the period from 1600 to 1999. Figure 3.1 shows the development in Dimension 1, which Biber dubs "involved v. informational." Dimension 1 is characterized by features such as frequency of verbs, pronouns, stance devices, and finite dependent clauses (all characteristic of "involved interactive discourse") on the one hand, and frequency of nouns, attributive adjectives, long words, and prepositional phrases

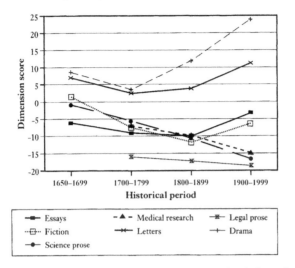

Figure 3.1 Results for Dimension 1 ("Involved v. informational"). Reproduced from Biber 1995, p. 289

(all characteristic of "informational production") on the other. As can be seen from the figure, Dimension 1 scores during the earliest point (1650–1699) ranged from −6 (for essays) to 9 (for drama); by the latest period (1990–1999), scores ranged from −19 (legal prose) to 24 (drama).

One particularly interesting case of the linguistic changes resulting from the introduction of literacy is the recent history of Somali, described by Biber and Hared (1991). Somali underwent a development similar to English, but over a much less protracted period of time. Before 1972, all public written communication in Somalia was conducted in Arabic, English, or Italian. In 1972, President Siyaad Barre declared that Somali should be the only official language of government and education. This led to mass literacy campaigns, the establishment of a standardized orthography, and the publication of a variety of texts, including national newspapers, textbooks, and fiction. In their study, Biber and Hared (1991) conducted a multidimensional analysis of texts published during the seventeen years following the introduction of literacy (1973–1989). The linguistic developments during this period were quite dramatic. Before 1972, the scores on Dimension 1 ("structural elaboration"), ranged from −1 to 10; following the introduction of literacy, the range was from −5 to 10. For Dimension 2 ("lexical elaboration," comprising features such as hapax legomena, type-token ratio, nominalizations, compound verbs, and word length), the range of register variation pre-1972 was 2–8; at the time of research, the range was from −15–8.

Thus, a tradition of literacy contributes to the development of a variety of written registers, thus considerably extending the range of register variation. Although this can occur very quickly, as in the case of Somali, in more typical cases this process takes several centuries.

4.3 Vocabulary

Much more problematic is the idea that the existence of a written tradition has an effect on vocabulary size. To my knowledge, the first modern linguist to suggest in writing that languages with a literate tradition have larger vocabularies than oral languages was Deutscher, who makes the following observations:

> Linguists who have described languages of small illiterate societies estimate that the average size of their lexicons is between three thousand and five thousand words. In contrast, small-size bilingual dictionaries of major European languages typically contain at least fifty thousand entries. Larger ones would contain seventy to eighty thousand. Decent size monolingual dictionaries of English contain about a hundred thousand entries . . . . Some researchers have estimated the passive vocabulary of an average English-speaking university student at about forty thousand words. (Deutscher 2010: 110)

More recently, Dixon (2016: 172) estimated the vocabulary size of the "non-major" languages as between 5,000 and 10,000 words. (It is probably no coincidence that both of these publications are aimed at a popular rather than an academic audience: the statement is so controversial that it is unlikely to get past an academic reviewer.)

It goes without saying that such estimates should be treated with caution. Obviously, languages such as English, Spanish, or German are much better described than languages spoken by small, illiterate societies, and this is likely to be reflected in the size of their dictionaries. Furthermore, publishers may inflate the number of entries in dictionaries for marketing purposes, and this is less likely to be the case with poorly described languages, where there is less competition. However, given the magnitude of the differences (3–10K versus 50–100K), it is likely that Deutscher and Dixon are onto something real.

To a large extent, these differences in vocabulary size are due to societal complexity, and in particular the amount of specialization, rather than directly due to writing: the languages of complex industrial societies contain a large number of words that are used predominantly by particular occupational or social groups (e.g. plumbers, artists, computer programmers, cross-country skiers, people who knit, etc.). However, it is arguably writing that makes complex societies possible in the first place. Moreover, as we saw earlier, people living in large industrial societies typically acquire most of their vocabulary through the written medium, and in this sense, universal literacy contributes to vocabulary growth.

4.4 Complex Hypotactic Syntax

There is also some evidence that a tradition of literacy may have an effect on the development of complex hypotactic syntax, and in particular, clausal subordination. Languages differ considerably both in the frequency of subordination and the number of subordination markers in their grammars. Global languages such as English boast a variety of complementizers and subordinators and allow recursive subordination, as in example (4), taken from Karlsson (2007), which contains a main clause, a finite verb complement clause, a non-finite verb complement clause, an adverbial clause embedded within another adverbial clause, and a non-restrictive relative clause modifying the subject of the finite complement clause.

(4) If, as often happened, she asked him to tell her about it, she thought that he, who had been so kind, would understand.

At the other extreme, it has been claimed that some languages lack subordination altogether. Such claims have been made, most famously, for Pirahã (Everett 2005, 2012), which, according to Everett, lacks any recursive constructions, but also for several other languages, including Inuktitut (Kalmar 1985), Iatmul (Foley 1986), and ABSL[2] (Aronoff et al. 2008; Meir et al. 2010). They are, however, controversial, and have been challenged by other linguists. For example, Nevins et al. (2009) argue that the Pirahã suffix -*sai*, which Everett analyzes as a marker of old information, is actually a complementizer. The controversy is not likely to disappear any time soon, as during the early stages of syntacticization, it is often difficult to determine if a clause is grammatically dependent or independent (cf. Hurford 2012), and the distinction is arguably a matter of degree (Cristofaro 2014).

Somewhat less controversially, it has been argued that some languages – including Mohawk, Gungwinggu, Kathlamet (Mithun 1984), Biblical Hebrew (Givón 1991), Akkadian (Deutscher 2000), Old English (O'Neil 1977), and Old Chinese (Pulleyblank 1995) – make minimal use of subordination. For instance, Mithun (1984) reports that the proportion of subordinate clauses in oral narratives in her data was 2 percent for Kathlamet, 6 percent for Gungwinggu, and 7 percent for Mohawk. Oral narratives in English, in contrast, have on average 34 percent subordinate clauses – in other words, subordinate clauses in English narrative are five times more frequent than in Mohawk, and seventeen times more frequent than in Kathlamet.[3]

---

[2] Al-Sayyid Bedouin Sign Language.
[3] It should be noted that the figures given by Mithun may be an overestimate, since she counted all borderline cases as subordinate. Moreover, her Mohawk informants were literate in English, and the Gungwinggu informants could not write but knew some English. Only the Kathlamet

Crucially, all languages that have been claimed to lack subordination, or make very little use of it, are oral languages spoken by traditional "societies of intimates." Conversely, all languages with an established tradition of literacy have subordination. Furthermore, for languages with long histories of literacy, we see clear historical trends towards more use of subordination, and a greater variety of subordinate constructions (Kortmann 1997; Martowicz 2011). A similar trend can be found in the depth of subordination. Karlsson (2009) argues that there are strict constraints on the depth of clausal embedding actually found in real texts (up to two levels of embedding in clause-initial positions and up to three in clause-central positions), and that it takes about 500 years of written tradition for languages to reach their complexity maxima.

A "health warning" is in order here. I am not suggesting that the use of a written form is *necessary* for the development of subordination. It is clear that the majority of, and perhaps all, oral languages use some subordination devices. However, the availability of the written form facilitates the development of more complex subordinate structures, for reasons described in Section 3: the need to be more explicit on the one hand, and time to reflect when composing the message on the other.

Finally, it is worth noting that a language may be affected by writing indirectly through contact with a written language. For example, a number of native American languages, including Quechua, Guarani, and Otomi, borrowed complementizers and subordinators from Spanish on quite a large scale (see, for example, Bakker 2012; Bakker & Hekking 2012). Although, as far as we can determine, all of these languages already had some subordination prior to the arrival of European colonizers, contact with Spanish resulted in the development of a wider variety of subordinate constructions and a considerable increase in their text frequency.

5 Conclusion

The differences between speech and writing are partly due to the different contexts of use (specifically, the need to be more explicit in writing) and partly to the fact that the availability of a visual representation eases the load on working memory, thus making it possible to produce and understand more complex sentences. The research reviewed here shows that the acquisition of literacy has profound implications for the linguistic system at the individual level, and, more controversially, also at the level of the speech community, in that a tradition of literacy leads to changes in register, vocabulary, and morphosyntax.

informant could not read and did not know a language with a literary tradition, and it is interesting to note that Kathlamet had the lowest proportion of subordinate clauses.

A final qualification is in order. I am not arguing that writing is necessary for the developments described above. Rather, its role is better described as a facilitating or enabling one. Without doubt, other factors also contribute to vocabulary growth and to an increase in embedding complexity and the range of register variation. For example, communicating with people with whom one shares relatively little knowledge (e.g. strangers, or people who occupy a different social "niche") requires the speaker to be more explicit and thus results in the use of more complex syntax (Wray & Grace 2007), as well as creating opportunities for learning new vocabulary. (This is also true in an English as a Lingua Franca context: see Seidlhofer 2011; Mauranen 2012.) Similarly, certain genres such as retold narratives or oral poetry may promote the emergence of features similar to what we find in written language. Repeated retelling allows the storyteller to reuse the same sentence fragments, thus easing working memory load and allowing more focus on form. As a result, in later retellings, the narrative becomes increasingly elaborated but also compact, in the sense that more information is packed into fewer words (see Biber 2009).

It is clear that the research on the effects of writing on language is still in its infancy. While there are a number of excellent studies demonstrating the effects of the acquisition of an alphabetic writing system on phoneme awareness and speech perception, the evidence for effects in vocabulary and morphosyntax is much sparser and mostly correlational. Further research will be necessary to establish precisely which aspects of language are influenced by writing, and the details of how this happens. However, the evidence that is already available makes it clear that familiar European languages with a long tradition of literacy – and in particular, English, with its global language status – differ in substantial ways from oral languages, and therefore linguistic theories developed primarily on the basis of such languages may not be applicable to all languages.[4]

REFERENCES

Adrián, José Antonio, Jesus Alegria & José Morais. 1995. Metaphonological abilities of Spanish illiterate adults. *International Journal of Psychology* 30, 329–353.

Aronoff, Mark, Irit Meir, Carol Padden & Wendy Sandler. 2008. The roots of linguistic organization in a new language. *Interaction Studies* 9, 131–150.

Bakker, Dik. 2012. Three languages from America in contact with Spanish. In Jeanette Sackel & Thomas Stolz (eds.), *Amerindiana: Neue Perspektiven auf die indigenen Sprachen Amerikas*, 171–195. Berlin: Akademie Verlag.

---

[4] For further discussion of the dangers of generalizing from modern languages to languages spoken by "societies of intimates," see Trudgill 2015.

Bakker, Dik & Ewald Hekking. 2012. Clause combining in Otomi before and after contact with Spanish. *Linguistic Discovery* 10(1), 42–61.

Berman, Ruth A. 2007. Developing linguistic knowledge and language use across adolescence. In Erika Hoff & Marilyn Shatz (eds.), *Blackwell Handbook of Language Development*, 347–367. Oxford: Blackwell Publishing.

Biber, Douglas. 1995. *Dimensions of Register Variation: A Cross-Linguistic Comparison.* Cambridge: Cambridge University Press.

2009. Are there linguistic consequences of literacy? Comparing the potentials of language use in speech and writing. In David R. Olson & Nancy Torrance (eds.), *Cambridge Handbook of Literacy*, 75–91. Cambridge: Cambridge University Press.

Biber, Douglas & Mohamed Hared. 1991. Literacy in Somali: Linguistic consequences. *Annual Review of Applied Linguistics* 12, 260–282.

Biemiller, Andrew. 2003. Vocabulary: Needed if more children are to read well. *Reading Psychology* 24, 323–335.

Bürki, Audrey, Elsa Spinelli & Gareth Gaskell. 2012. A written word is worth a thousand spoken words: The influence of spelling on spoken-word production. *Journal of Memory and Language* 67, 449–467.

Cameron-Faulkner, Thea & Claire Noble. 2013. A comparison of book text and Child Directed Speech. *First Language* 33, 268–279.

Castro-Caldas, Alexandre, Karl Magnus Petersson, Alexandra Reis, Sharon Stone-Elander & Martin Ingvar. 1998. The illiterate brain: Learning to read and write during childhood influences the functional organization of the adult brain. *Brain: A Journal of Neurology* 121(6), 1053–1063.

Cristofaro, Sonia. 2014. Is there really a syntactic category of subordination? In Jyrki Kalliokoski, Laura Visapää & Helena Sorva (eds.), *Contexts of Subordination*, 73–91. Amsterdam: John Benjamins.

Cunningham, Anne E. & Keith E. Stanovich. 1997. Early reading acquisition and its relation to reading experience and ability 10 years later. *Developmental Psychology* 33(6), 934.

1998. What reading does for the mind. *American Educator* 22, 1–8.

Dąbrowska, Ewa. 2009. Words as constructions. In Vyvyan Evans & Stéphanie Pourcel (eds.), *New Directions in Cognitive Linguistics*, 201–223. Amsterdam: John Benjamins.

2018. Experience, aptitude and individual differences in native language ultimate attainment. *Cognition* 178, 222–235.

Daneman, Meredyth & Philip M. Merikle. 1996. Working memory and language comprehension: A meta-analysis. *Psychonomic Bulletin & Review* 3, 422–433.

Dehaene, Stanislas, Felipe Pegado, Lucia W. Braga, Paulo Ventura, Gilberto Nunes Filho, Antoinette Jobert, Ghislaine Dehaene-Lambertz, Régine Kolinsky, José Morais & Laurent Cohen. 2010. How learning to read changes the cortical networks for vision and language. *Science* 330(6009), 1359–1364.

Dehaene-Lambertz, Ghislaine, Stanislas Dehaene & Lucie Hertz-Pannier. 2002. Functional neuroimaging of speech perception in infants. *Science* 298(5600), 2013–2015.

Deumert, Ana & Wim Vandenbussche. 2003. Standard languages: Taxonomies and histories. In Ana Deumert & Wim Vandenbussche (eds.), *Germanic Standardizations: Past to Present.* Amsterdam: John Benjamins.

Deutscher, Guy. 2000. *Syntactic Change in Akkadian: The Evolution of Sentential Complementation*. Oxford: Oxford University Press.
   2010. *Through the Language Glass. Why the World Looks Different in Other Languages*. New York: Metropolitan Books.
Dixon, R. M. W. 2016. *Are Some Languages Better than Others?* Oxford: Oxford University Press.
Ehri, Linnea C. 1985. Effects of printed language acquisition on speech. In David R. Olson, Nancy Torrance & Angela Hildyard (eds.), *Literacy, Language and Learning: The Nature and Consequences of Reading and Writing*, 333–367. New York: Cambridge University Press.
   2005. Cultural constraints on grammar and cognition in Pirahã: Another look at the design features of human language. *Current Anthropology* 46, 621–646.
   2012. *Language: The Cultural Tool*. London: Profile Books.
Foley, William A. 1986. *The Papuan Languages of New Guinea*. Cambridge: Cambridge University Press.
Givón, Talmy. 1991. The evolution of dependent clause morpho-syntax in Biblical Hebrew. In Elizabeth Closs Traugott & Bernd Heine (eds.), *Approaches to Grammaticalization*, vol. 2, 257–310. Amsterdam: John Benjamins.
Hartshorne, Joshua K., Joshua B. Tenenbaum & Steven Pinker. 2018. A critical period for second language acquisition: Evidence from 2/3 million English speakers. *Cognition* 177, 263–277.
Hayes, Donald P. & Margaret G. Ahrens. 1988. Vocabulary simplification for children: A special case of "motherese"? *Journal of Child Language* 15, 395–410.
Hirsh-Pasek, Kathy & Roberta Michnick Golinkoff. 1999. *The Origins of Grammar: Evidence from Early Language Comprehension*. Cambridge, MA: MIT Press.
Hoff, Erika. 2009. Language development at an early age: Learning mechanisms and outcomes from birth to five years. *Encyclopedia of Early Childhood Development*. www.child-encyclopedia.com/sites/default/files/textes-experts/en/622/language-development-at-an-early-age-learning-mechanisms-and-outcomes-from-birth-to-five-years.pdf. Accessed March 15, 2013.
Huettig, Falk, Niharika Singh & Ramesh K. Mishra. 2011. Language-mediated visual orienting behavior in low and high literates. *Frontiers in Language Sciences* 2, 285. doi: 10.3389/fpsyg.2011.00285.
Huettig, Falk. 2015. Literacy influences cognitive abilities far beyond the mastery of written language. In Ineke van de Craats, Jeanne Kurvers & Roeland van Hout (eds.), *Adult Literacy, Second Language, and Cognition. LESLLA Proceedings 2014*, 115–128. Nijmegen: Centre for Language Studies.
Hunt, Kellog W. 1977. Early blooming and late blooming syntactic structures. In Charles L. Cooper & Lee Odell (eds.), *Evaluating Writing*, 91–104. Buffalo, NY: State University of Buffalo.
Hurford, James R. 2012. *The Origins of Grammar: Language in the Light of Evolution II*, vol. 2. Oxford: Oxford University Press.
Jakimik, Jola, Roland A. Cole & Alexander I. Rudnicky (1985). Sound and spelling in spoken word recognition. *Journal of Memory and Language* 24, 165–178.
Joseph, John Earl. 1987. *Eloquence and Power: The Rise of Language Standards and Standard Languages*. London: Pinter.

Kalmar, Ivan. 1985. Are there really no primitive languages? In David R. Olson, Nancy Torrance & Angela Hildyard (eds.), *Literacy, Language and Learning*, 148–166. Cambridge: Cambridge University Press.

Kaplan, Dafna & Ruth Berman. 2015. Developing linguistic flexibility across the school years. *First Language* 35, 27–53.

Karlsson, Fred. 2007. Constraints on multiple center-embedding of clauses. *Journal of Linguistics* 43, 365–392.

2009. Origin and maintenance of clausal embedding complexity. In Geoffrey Sampson, David Gil & Peter Trudgill (eds.), *Language Complexity as an Evolving Variable*, 192–202. Oxford: Oxford University Press.

Kortmann, Bernd. 1997. *Adverbial Subordination: A Typology and History of Adverbial Subordinators Based on European Languages*. Berlin: de Gruyter.

Kurvers, Jeanne, Ton Vallen & Roeland van Hout. 2006. Discovering features of language: Metalinguistic awareness of adult illiterates. In Ineke van de Craats, Jeanne Kurvers & Martha Young-Scholten (eds.), *Low-Educated Second Language and Literacy Acquisition: Proceedings of the Inaugural Symposium Tilburg 2005*, 69–68. Utrecht: LOT.

Lupyan, Gary & Rick A. Dale. 2010. Language structure is partly determined by social structure. *PLoS ONE* 5(1), e8559.

Martowicz, Anna. 2011. *Origin and Functioning of Circumstantial Clause Linkers: A Crosslinguistic Study*. PhD thesis, University of Edinburgh.

Mauranen, Anna. 2004. Talking academic: A corpus approach to academic speech. In Karin Aijmer (ed.), *Dialogue Analysis VIII: Understanding and Misunderstanding in Dialogue*, 201–217. Tübingen: Max Niemeyer.

2012. *Exploring ELF: Academic English Shaped by Non-Native Speakers*. Cambridge: Cambridge University Press.

Meir, Irit, Wendy Sandler, Carol Padden & Mark Aronoff. 2010. Emerging sign languages. In Marc Marschark & Patricia Elizabeth Spencer (eds.), *Oxford Handbook of Deaf Studies, Language, and Education*, vol. 2, 267–280. Oxford: Oxford University Press.

Milroy, James & Lesley Milroy. 2012. *Authority in Language: Investigating Standard English*. London: Routledge.

Mishra, Ramesh K., Niharika Singh, Aparna Pandey & Falk Huettig. 2012. Spoken language-mediated anticipatory eye-movements are modulated by reading ability: Evidence from Indian low and high literates. *Journal of Eye Movement Research* 5(1), 1–10.

Mithun, Marianne. 1984. How to avoid subordination. *Berkeley Linguistics Society* 10, 493–509.

Montag, Jessica L. & Maryellen C. MacDonald. 2015. Text exposure predicts spoken production of complex sentences in 8- and 12-year-old children and adults. *Journal of Experimental Psychology: General* 144, 447–468.

Montrul, Silvina. 2008. *Incomplete Acquisition in Bilingualism: Re-Examining the Age Factor*. Amsterdam: John Benjamins.

Morais, José, Jesus Alegria & Alain Content. 1986. Literacy training and speech segmentation. *Cognition* 24, 45–64.

Morais, José, Luz Cary, Jesus Alegria & Paul Bertelson. 1979. Does awareness of speech as a sequence of phones arise spontaneously? *Cognition* 7, 415–438.

Nevins, Andrew, David Pesetsky & Cilene Rodrigues. 2009. Pirahã exceptionality: A reassessment. *Language* 85, 355–404.
Nippold, Marilyn A. 1998. *Later Language Development: The School-Age and Adolescent Years*. Austin, TX: Pro-ed.
Nippold, Marilyn A., Tracy C. Mansfield & Jesse L. Billow. 2007. Peer conflict explanations in children, adolescents, and adults: Examining the development of complex syntax. *American Journal of Speech-Language Pathology* 16, 179–188.
O'Neil, Wayne. 1977. Clause adjunction in Old English. *Linguistics* 17, 199–211.
Pakulak, Eric & Helen Neville. 2010. Proficiency differences in syntactic processing of monolingual native speakers indexed by event-related potentials. *Journal of Cognitive Neuroscience* 22(12), 2728–2744.
Pattamadilok, Chotiga, José Morais, Paulo Ventura & Régine Kolinsky. 2007. The locus of the orthographic consistency effect in auditory word recognition: Further evidence from French. *Language and Cognitive Processes* 22, 700–726.
Paunonen, Heikki. 2006. Vähemmistökielestä varioivaksi valtakieleksi. In Kaisu Juusela & Katariina Nisula (eds.), *Helsinki Kieliyhteisönä*, 13–99. Helsinki: Suomen kielen Ja kotimaisen kirjallisuuden laitos.
Perre, Laetitia, Chotiga Pattamadilok, Marie Montant & Johannes C. Ziegler. 2009. Orthographic effects in spoken language: On-line activation or phonological restructuring? *Brain Research* 1275, 73–80.
Petersson, Karl Magnus, Carla Silva, Alexandre Castro-Caldas, Martin Ingvar & Alexandra Reis. 2007. Literacy: A cultural influence on functional left–right differences in the inferior parietal cortex. *European Journal of Neuroscience* 26, 791–799.
Philp, Jenefer. 2003. Constraints on "noticing the gap": Nonnative speakers' noticing of recasts in NS-NNS interaction. *Studies in Second Language Acquisition* 25(1), 99–126.
Pinker, Steven. 1995. Language acquisition. In Lila R. Gleitman & Mark Liberman (eds.), *An Invitation to Cognitive Science, Vol. 1: Language*. 2nd ed., 135–182. Cambridge, MA: MIT Press.
Pulleyblank, Edwin G. 1995. *Outline of Classical Chinese Grammar*. Vancouver: UBC Press.
Read, Charles A., Yun-Fei Zhang, Hong-Yin Nie & Bao-Qing Ding. 1986. The ability to manipulate speech sounds depends on knowing alphabetic writing. *Cognition* 24, 31–44.
Reis, Alexandra & Alexandre Castro-Caldas. 1997. Illiteracy: A cause for biased cognitive development. *Journal of the International Neuropsychological Society* 3(5), 444–450.
Scott, Cheryl M. 1988. Spoken and written syntax. In Marilyn A. Nippold (ed.), *Later Language Development: Ages 9 through 19*, 49–95. Boston, MA: Little, Brown and Company.
Seidenberg, Mark S. & Michael K. Tanenhaus. 1979. Orthographic effects on rhyme monitoring. *Journal of Experimental Psychology: Human Learning and Memory* 5(6), 546–554.
Seidlhofer, Barbara. 2011. *Understanding English as a Lingua Franca: A Complete Introduction to the Theoretical Nature and Practical Implications of English Used as a Lingua Franca*. Oxford: Oxford University Press.

Stanovich, Keith E. & Anne E. Cunningham. 1992. Studying the consequences of literacy within a literate society: The cognitive correlates of print exposure. *Memory & Cognition* 20, 51–68.

Street, James & Ewa Dąbrowska. 2010. More individual differences in language attainment: How much do adult native speakers of English know about passives and quantifiers? *Lingua* 120, 2080–2094.

Tarone, Elaine, Martha Bigelow & Kit Hansen. 2007. The impact of alphabetic print literacy level on oral second language acquisition. In Nancy Faux (ed.), *Low-Educated Second Language and Literacy Acquisition: Proceedings of the Second Annual Forum, The Literacy Institute at Virginia Commonwealth University, 2006*, 99–122. Richmond, Virginia: The Literacy Institute.

Trudgill, Peter. 2011. *Sociolinguistic Typology*. Oxford: Oxford University Press.

2015. Societies of intimates and linguistic complexity. In Rik De Busser & Randy J. LaPolla (eds.), *Language Structure and Environment: Social, Cultural, and Natural Factors*, 133–147. Amsterdam & Philadelphia: John Benjamins.

Wray, Alison & George W. Grace. 2007. The consequences of talking to strangers: Evolutionary corollaries of socio-cultural influences on linguistic form. *Lingua* 117, 543–578.

Ziegler, Johannes C., Ana Petrova & Ludovic Fernand. 2008. Feedback consistency effects in visual and auditory word recognition: Where do we stand after more than a decade? *Journal of Experimental Psychology: Learning Memory and Cognition* 34, 643–661.

4   ELF and Translation As Language Contact

Anna Mauranen

1   Introduction

At the outset, it might seem that translated language and English as a lingua franca (ELF) have little in common. One is primarily a matter of rendering text into a translator's first language; the other produces spontaneous discourse in a second or additional language. However, if we look at research findings from these two kinds of language use, we find shared strands: in both, traces of at least one other language have been discovered in the primary language of communication. Moreover, observations have been made in both that would seem to suggest parallel processes, such as enhanced explicitness, heavy proportional weight of the most frequent vocabulary, and a tendency towards unusual collocations and multiword sequences. This would seem to warrant a deeper look into the possible connections between these apparently very different kinds of language use: it might tell us something new about multilingual processing, language contact and elements of language change.

Bilingual speakers are no longer seen as two monolinguals in one individual – but languages are nevertheless predominantly viewed as separate and 'complete' in themselves, despite an alternative paradigm questioning this (e.g. Blommaert & Rampton 2011, Canagarajah 2013, Li 2018; see also Cogo this volume). This is an obvious mismatch: most people know more than one language, and so their linguistic repertoires, or idiolects, are heterogeneous in terms of the languages they draw on, but the tacit assumption underlying standard languages is a community of monolingual speakers. Standards are upheld (and renewed) for every language separately, as if each was a self-contained system with no leaks. Leaks are nevertheless inevitable if communities have contacts outside themselves, which is virtually inescapable in today's world, or if they include multilingual speakers, which is also normal in virtually any community. Moreover, standards are in themselves poor representations of internal realities in language communities: they reflect only weakly the heterogeneity in ordinary language practices; nevertheless they are imbued with prestige well beyond the status of just one dialect, style or register, which technically would be a more accurate description of their nature. Moreover, languages spoken in different countries may go by the same name but maintain different regional standards (English, German and Spanish are typical examples). Despite their shortcomings, standards nevertheless exert a strong normative impact on certain bilingual situations, notably language teaching and translation. ELF, however, falls outside standard languages and is regulated only by speakers' bottom-up, spontaneous norms.

To what extent bilinguals' (or multilinguals', I use the terms here interchangeably) repertoires are integrated in their cognition, and to what extent their languages are separate is not entirely clear (despite no lack of competing models and theories); it would seem, though, that there is more variability than is easy to capture with a single model, and that the degree of integration would appear to vary according to a number of individual and contextual factors. What is well established, however, is that multilinguals are different from monolinguals, and that this concerns their first languages as well as their additional languages (cf. Cook 2003, Cook & Bassetti 2011). A useful concept for describing bilingual competence is Cook's (1991) 'multicompetence', which refers to the knowledge of two or more languages in one mind. The concept is easily extendable to include monolinguals, who also know different registers, styles, dialects, etc., and can alternate between them much like multilinguals switch between languages.

This paper suggests that different kinds of cross-linguistic influence, such as those we find in translations and lingua francas, are consequences of language contact in a more general perspective, and that the outcomes of these contact processes manifest themselves at all levels of language. At a collective, macro level of linguistic features, discernible in large corpora, we find that translations, lingua francas and often also learner language exhibit certain similarities in, for example, lexis, collocations and word frequencies. At discourse level we find, for example, enhanced explicitness in both second language use (in this case ELF) and translations. Such phenomena, it is argued, reflect language contact in individual speakers' minds and practices – in other words, their multicompetence. These large-scale phenomena result from cognitive and interactive processes of multilingual individuals in situations where we might expect competition from different parts of their language repertoires.

2   Interference and Bilingual Contexts

It has been known for a long time that learners' first languages influence their use of the languages they are learning or have learned. Weinreich (1953) paid attention to bilinguals using their languages differently from monolinguals and called this 'interference'. Many other terms have also been used since, such as 'transfer' or 'cross-linguistic influence'. The latter term, adopted, for instance, in Odlin (2003) and Jarvis and Pavlenko (2007), is perhaps the most neutral and accurate. The concept of cross-language influence has been a central concern in second and foreign language learning research (SLA) and in translation studies, especially from a normative perspective, which has construed transfer or interference from another language as a major problem. It has nevertheless shown obstinate persistence in output despite the best efforts of generations of educators.

SLA is an active international research field that investigates not only L1 influence or learners' errors, but also numerous other aspects of learner language, as well as processes and progress in acquisition. Despite the field's breadth, the influence of the L1 on the acquisition of an L2 has not ceased to interest researchers. It is studied in terms of processes (e.g. Odlin 2003, Ellis 2007, Nitschke et al. 2010) as well as products, for instance in learner corpora (e.g. Bestgen et al. 2012, Crossley et al. 2015, Wang 2016). Corpus-based L2 studies tend to adopt a normative view of their findings and construe L1-influenced deviations from comparable native-speaker use as indicators of learners' 'problems' and 'difficulties' (e.g. Nesselhauf 2005, Gilquin 2008, Hasselgård & Johansson 2011), which are in need of pedagogic intervention so as to help learners achieve 'native-like fluency and idiomaticity' (e.g. Wang 2016). The SLA field has been severely criticized for imposing this 'deficit model' on learners – that is, for seeing L2 learners as imperfect compared to an ideal native speaker (Firth & Wagner 1997, Jenkins 2000, Seidlhofer 2011) – and for its reluctance to let go of the notion of monolingualism and the implication that the ultimate goal of SLA is a kind of double monolingualism (e.g. Cook 2002, Grosjean 2008, Ortega 2009). Despite critique, the persistent normative notion holds in language education research that L1 influence on an L2 is a problem and steps are to be taken by responsible educators to erase this as completely as possible. A number of scholars nevertheless adopt a more descriptive or theoretical attitude to L1 influence on a learner (e.g. Cook 2003b, Pavlenko 2014, Sharwood Smith & Truscott 2014).

Related worries abound in translation studies. As in learner research, interference is widely regarded as a problem. It is discussed as the systematic bias ('translationese', see e.g. Gellerstam 1996) that is taken to manifest influence on a translation either from the source language or from a source text. Like translation scholars, many linguists not only reinforce the notion that translations are inherently imperfect (similar to the deficit model of learner language), but also suffer from interference to the extent that they cannot be regarded as serious data. Translations should therefore be excluded from language corpora, for instance. The following quotation from Teubert illustrates the attitude:

Translations, however good and near-perfect they may be (but rarely are), cannot but give a distorted picture of the language they represent. Linguists should never rely on translations when they are describing a language. . . . Rather than representing the language they are written in, they give a mirror image of their source language. (Teubert 1996: 247)

Descriptive translation studies, on the other hand, envisage interference as a phenomenon that is typical of translations in general, whether it presents a problem or not. Baker (1993) suggested it could be a translation universal, that is, characteristic of all translations irrespective of any particular source and target language pair. In a similar vein, Toury (1995) posits 'the law of interference' as one of the major regularities in translations. Chesterman (2004) suggests that as interference relates to differences between translations and their sources, it falls within what he calls 'S-universals', or source text-related universals. Eskola (2002, 2004), in turn, regards interference as a translation universal, which manifests itself in differences between translated and comparable non-translated texts in the same language, and which can best be detected by large-scale comparisons. This conceptualization corresponds to target language-related universals, or Chesterman's 'T-universals'. Lanstyák and Heltai (2012) similarly recognize the influence of the source text in translations. Instead of interference, they speak of 'discourse transfer' or 'contact effects' as preferable terms, and depict a translator's output as monolingual, source text-influenced communication. In the non-prescriptive tradition, then, translation studies adopts similar views to more recent and critical views of SLA – cross-linguistic influence is there, but rather than seeking to erase it, it is something we should understand better, and therefore investigate.

Both research traditions, then, use interference (or a similar term) to refer to the influence of one language on the use of another. However, there is a crucial difference between the two perspectives. In SLA and learner language studies, interference refers to the influence of the learner's L1 on their output in the target language, an L2. By contrast, in translation studies the reverse is the case, and the term is used to talk about the influence of the source language, an L2, on the translator's output in their L1. The same phenomenon, then – cross-linguistic influence – is observed in both contexts, but attributed to opposite causes.

I make two suggestions in this paper. First, that we can see both kinds of 'interference' in more general terms as a consequence of language contact, with manifestations at different levels of language. A related point is made by Lanstyák and Heltai (2012), who compare ordinary language contact (e.g. among bilingual speakers, not necessarily learners) and translations, proposing 'contact universals' to cover both bilingual use and translation. It is certainly important to include translations in language contact research, whether we want to look for universals or not. This finds support from the SLA perspective: Cook (2003) observes that, contrary to the usual interpretation, Weinreich's definition refers to 'deviation from the norms of either language' (Weinreich 1953: 1), and thus not just those of an L2. Schmid (2019) argues along similar lines: L1 and L2 affect one another. There is a wider connection to language change: Thomason and Kaufman (1988) proposed that bilingualism is a major context of contact-induced change, since a speaker's L2 brings about change in their L1.

My second suggestion is that any general account of language contact should grant lingua francas a central place, since they are contact languages by definition (e.g. Thomason & Kaufman 1988, Thomason 2001). For lingua franca research, English is currently the most intriguing case on account of its unique position as a global language and its consequent contact with a major proportion of the world's languages, thus in potential contact – with bidirectional influence – with all of them. English is also the language that currently dominates the global volume of translations. Moreover, there is a clear gap in recent research on how English participates in language contact (e.g. in Schreier & Hundt 2013), in respect of effects from either translation or the use of ELF.

3   ELF and Language Contact

Lingua francas are vehicular languages used by speakers who do not share a first language. This traditional definition is perfectly workable for the present purpose. Clearly, much lingua franca use takes place between speakers for whom the language is not their first (or one of them), even though speakers can also find themselves in lingua franca situations using their native languages. Despite the obvious ubiquity of second language use (SLU), and in contrast to learners or translators, relatively little research has been conducted on the use of second languages in contexts outside established L2 varieties, perhaps apart from the study of pidgins or incipient creoles. A notable exception is Cook (e.g. 2003), who employs the term 'L2 user', and since the turn of the millennium, a growing body of research into ELF has emerged, substantially altering the perception of a second language altogether (see, for example, Jenkins et al. 2018).

Second language users, such as most of those using ELF, can be expected to show some similarities to learners, because by definition SLU implies the acquisition of a new language at some stage. It is likely that the similarities are manifest above all in cognitive processes like activation, retrieval or suppression. We can also expect resemblance to contact-induced varieties, which are subject to acquisitional cognitive processes similar to learner language (see Mesthrie & Bhatt 2008: 156ff.). Translators might seem to part company with L2 users here because, as a rule, their primary output language is their L1. Yet, like SLUs, they will have learned at least one additional language at some point, and they engage in bilingual activity as they translate. More importantly, on the receptive side they engage in the same processes as L2 users and learners do in making sense of a non-first language. SLU at the cognitive level can thus be compared to learner language and translation; they all involve bi- or multilingual speakers using one of their languages. We can also view all three as 'hybrid languages', following Trosborg's (1997) characterization of translations. Hybridity has also been invoked in theorizing ELF (Mauranen 2007, Seidlhofer 2011). Hybrid processing results in monolingual output on the surface, while processing a mixture of languages underneath.

Despite similarities in cognitive processes, learners and users cannot be presumed to be identical in their language use, given the inevitably powerful role of the social context. The contexts and purposes of learning an L2 depart radically from those of using one (Mauranen 2012, 2018) and lead to an entirely different orientation to language. Translations, in turn, have their own social purposes and uses, which have little, if anything, in common with learning or SLU.

While there is little empirical research so far comparing ELF and learner language, there is some, notably Laitinen's work (2016, 2018). He has carried out extensive comparisons involving learner English, indigenized varieties of English, ELF and 'core' L1 English. His research is quantitative and structural, which otherwise has been under-represented in ELF research. Laitinen's typological profiling provides clear indications that, in morphosyntactic terms, ELF is a distinct variety type among Englishes. It clearly differs from learner Englishes in both spoken and written modes, but is instead strikingly close to other SLU varieties – that is, World Englishes – and moreover to core L1 English varieties, particularly in writing.

Where lingua francas, specifically ELF, differ from the other contact situations under scrutiny is that they are not confined to contact between two languages; when bilinguals use ELF, they speak English with others from different bilingual backgrounds (say, speakers with German as L1 talk to speakers with Italian as L1). This is more complex than first-order contact between two languages, in Mauranen's terms 'similects', which are parallel idiolects between speakers of the same L1 and English (for example, L1 German speakers using English). ELF is therefore a contact language between similects, a 'second-order language contact' (Mauranen 2012, 2018).

Arguably any language contact, including similects, may involve multilinguals, thus more than two languages. The issue is not usually addressed in SLA or in translation studies, where it can conveniently be shelved. By contrast, it is inescapable in ELF, for which the multilingual nature of the contact is a necessary feature. Multilingualism as a crucial component – or indeed as a superordinate – of ELF has been put forward by Jenkins (2015), who speaks of 'English as a multilingua franca' arguing that multilingualism is the higher-level category of which ELF is a part.

4 Macro Level of Language

Some linguistic features are surprisingly similar in translations and ELF if we look at them in large quantities, visible in big corpora. In this section, I take up three kinds of evidence from mainly corpus-based studies in translation studies and ELF research. Where relevant, I make comparisons with findings from learner language. I will be looking at frequencies, grammatical preferences and what in translation research is known as the loss of 'unique items'.

The relative over-representation of the most frequent lexis in translations was first noted by Laviosa-Braithwaite (1996) in her pioneering research to test Baker's (1993) hypotheses of translation universals by comparing corpora of translations and texts originally written in the same language. Her sample of newspaper texts was very small, but subsequently other researchers have achieved similar results with larger and more diverse databases, such as the Corpus of Translated Finnish (CTF, *Käännössuomen korpus* 2001, Mauranen 1998). Directly comparable and supportive results were obtained by Nevalainen (2005), who discovered a corresponding pattern of proportional over-representation of highly frequent lexis in Finnish translations relative to original Finnish texts. This study was based on altogether 10 million words of the CTF, with ten source languages from seven genres. Another supportive study on the same corpus was carried out by Tirkkonen-Condit (2005), who discovered that lexical sequences or n-grams behave basically like individual words in this respect: highly frequent n-grams are even more clustered at the top end of frequency lists in translations. In brief, these studies have supplied evidence for lexical simplification in translations, conceived as the proportional over-representation of the most frequent lexis.

What happens in ELF? Apparently a very similar phenomenon. Mauranen (2012) compared the Corpus of English as a Lingua Franca in Academic Settings (ELFA 2008) to two corpora with data from English L1 speakers: the Brown corpus (1964) and the MICASE corpus (Simpson et al. 2002). Lexical frequencies ordered by rank in the Brown corpus comply with the general 'power law' pattern laid down by Zipf (1935) for language, and it shows among other things that 135 top-ranking words account for 50 per cent of the entire corpus (i.e. of all the running words that make up the database). In ELFA, by contrast, only forty-four of the most frequent words suffice to make up half of the database – in other words, only a third (33 per cent) of the number of distinct words of Brown. This sounds like a dramatic difference. However, Brown is a written corpus that comprises a wide variety of registers and styles, while ELFA is made up of speech and only academic discourse. It is more directly comparable to MICASE, which is also a corpus of academic speech. Clearly, the difference in mode (written vs. spoken) is striking: MICASE requires only the top fifty-eight words to account for 50 per cent of the corpus, which is well under half (43 per cent) of the number in Brown. MICASE, then, is more similar to ELFA than to Brown. This supports the notion that speech is radically different from writing, as Biber (2009) and Dąbrowska (this volume) have discussed in depth. The mode difference has also been found to hold for academic speech specifically, which resembles spoken language more than it does academic prose (see e.g. Swales & Burke 2003, Mauranen 2004b, Biber 2006, Biber & Gray 2010). Even when this is taken into account, a notable difference remains between ELFA and MICASE. A corresponding tendency was found by Gilner (2016), who compared ELF and English L1 lexis with a different set of corpora: ELFA and VOICE (2013) together were compared to ICE-CORE (see Gilner & Morales 2011). These findings render ELF comparable to translations: it leads to usage where the most frequent lexis is exceptionally prominent. Learner corpora has revealed a similar predisposition favouring the most frequent vocabulary (e.g. Altenberg & Granger 2002, Granger et al. 2002).

Should we conclude from this that language contact is detrimental to lexical richness? Nevalainen (2005: 156), for example, claims that translations 'impoverish the language' lexically by over-representing the most frequent items. The conclusion seems premature, even counter-intuitive, given that contact normally leads to borrowing of different kinds, and lexis is remarkably mobile, adaptable and readily borrowed. A more detailed look yields a more nuanced picture. Lexical distributions in ELF and L1 English speech reveal that, even though relative over-representation is clearly in evidence, the difference levels out already at high-frequency ranks – that is, at about the 200 most common words (Mauranen 2012). If we think of the average person's vocabulary size, we are talking about tens of thousands, not hundreds of words; the estimated average vocabulary comprises about 20,000–35,000 words at minimum. Moreover, the most frequent vocabulary accounts for most usage in any case: approximately 1,900 of the most frequent words account for about 75 per cent of all English usage (COBUILD 1995). These estimates are based on the average native speaker and mean that less than one-tenth of the words we know account for three-quarters of our actual usage. Even if the most frequent lexis accounts for the best part of any running text, the top-level concentration is hardly likely to wreak havoc on the resources of a whole language. Moreover, Ferraresi & Bernardini (2019) recently compared translations and originals in terms of lexical density and non-core vocabulary (i.e. excluding the top 1,000 commonest items), and found no significant difference in lexical complexity between translated EU texts and comparable untranslated texts.

Moreover, words do not occur in isolation. The 'phraseological tendency' has become well known in linguistics since Firth's (1957) notion of collocation began to attract wider attention, and is employed by scholars under varying labels and demarcations, such as lexical bundles (Biber et al. 1999), collocational frameworks (Renouf & Sinclair 1991), units of meaning (Sinclair 1996) or formulaic sequences (Wray 2002). These reflect the tendency of words to co-occur, either by convention or a step further, clustering so firmly that together they come to mean more than the elements separately. Where conventional preferences are not adhered to, amplified variability in patterns can follow, with some resulting expressions imparting a sense of unusualness. This seems to happen in translations: Mauranen (2000) found sequential patterns in translations that diverged from originals in the same language, including collocational tendencies that were sometimes markedly different. For example, Finnish HALUTA 'want to' collocated strongly with OSOITTAA 'show' in translations, as in 'I want to show that...', whereas in original Finnish this never occurred. The typical original collocate of HALUTA was KOROSTAA ('emphasize'), as in 'I want to emphasize that...', while the typical collocate of OSOITTAA was PYRKIÄ 'try', as in 'I have tried to show that...'. Jantunen (2004), in turn, studied degree modifiers and discovered that where originally Finnish texts showed a strong preference for three synonymous modifiers, in translations preference patterns were far less clear and variability more pronounced. In this way, if multiword units are taken to be an integral part of lexical patterning, the idea of overall simplification of lexis is again challenged. It is also important to note that employing fewer individual words to cover large amounts of text in effect means increased variability in combinatorial patterning, because the same frequent forms may engage in novel combinations and thereby enrich the overall lexical range of a text or a language.

Beyond the variability of multiword sequences, translations from different source languages also show divergent degrees of conformity with target conventions, that is, with non-translated texts (cf. Mauranen 2000, 2004a). Intriguingly, translations from other languages than English appear to conform more to target norms than English does. If this tentative finding based on CTF is correct, it supports the notion discussed above that an L2 influences a speaker's L1. Specifically, it alters not only usage, but also L1 intuitions. Why translators' Finnish, in this case, has been modified more by English than by other languages may be attributable to the notable presence of English in Finnish society over several decades, especially compared to other foreign languages: in the media, school, translations and increasingly as a lingua franca in large parts of higher education. Translators working from English may well have internalized this massive influence more than translators from languages less visible in the society. Not only translators are affected in this way; the texts in CTF have also passed through the hands of publishers' editors, who are professional language regulators. We can interpret this as an alteration in collective intuitions about acceptability in Finnish, which has been modified through exposure to English.

Translations thus seem to blur well-established patterns of convention and preference by allowing cross-language influence to spread. Parallel processes can be detected in ELF: not only do conventionally preferred, even fixed patterns become diluted in the sense of becoming more variable, but new preferences also set in (Mauranen 2012, 2018). For instance, the firmly fixed expression *let me say a few words about it* not only acquires alternatives (e.g. *let me say a couple of words about it),* which would suggest it has been interpreted as a productive frame, but it also gives rise to a new preference: *let me say some words about it.* This formulation, functionally equivalent to the conventional form, is attested in speakers from different language backgrounds. It is therefore not transfer or interference from a single other language, but a fairly typical ELF phenomenon, 'approximation' (Mauranen 2012), which can lead to similar manifestations in different speakers' outputs (see also Carey 2013, Mauranen 2018). It is also noteworthy that these new preferences emerge on which speakers from various backgrounds seem to settle. Some possible ways in which and reasons why this may happen are pursued in Sections 5 and 6.

Learners have been found to deviate from conventional sequences and collocations of the target language, and as Pawley and Syder (1983) noted some decades ago, nativelike mastery of idiomaticity is extremely hard for even very advanced learners (see also Nattinger & DeCarrico 1992). Research has since repeatedly confirmed that learners differ in this respect from native speakers (e.g. Wray 2002, Nesselhauf 2005, papers in Granger & Meunier 2008). For the present context, it suffices to note that such tendencies have been attested; whether it makes sense to require such nativelikeness from learners is another matter.

Multiword units are composed not only of strings of words but also of structural properties, thus straddling lexis and structure. Their importance in cross-linguistic borrowing and change has been noted in earlier research, as in 'lexico-syntactic calquing' (Silva-Corvalan 1998): lexical and pragmatic borrowing carry along their structural features, which get adopted together with the lexis. A recent example from Finnish would be the incipient productivity of the calque *pitkässä juoksussa* ('in the long run'), now producing expressions like *pitkässä kuusessa* ('in the long fir tree') in the same function. According to Ellis (e.g. 2017), L2 acquisition is largely a matter of sequence learning. These observations underline the role of multiword units and phraseology in contact, learning and change.

Altered quantitative distributions of grammatical structures have also been found in translations and ELF. Grammatical infelicities are not necessarily at stake: Eskola's (2002, 2004) investigations of several non-finite syntactic structures of Finnish (what she termed 'synthesizing structures') revealed them to be proportionally under-represented in translations. There is nothing ungrammatical about this; it is a distributional phenomenon. Along similar lines, most of the structures that Ranta (2013) compared in ELF and L1 English speech were also basically perfectly grammatical, but with different distributions, like the relative 'overuse' of the *-ing* forms of verbs. Similar tendencies are seen in World Englishes (Meriläinen et al. 2017).

One distributional phenomenon is specific to translation: the relative underrepresentation of 'unique items' or 'untranslatables' of the target language (Tirkkonen-Condit 2004). Tirkkonen-Condit posited that translations use fewer lexical items that are unique to the target language than texts originally written in that language. Typical cases in her study were Finnish verbs of sufficiency, that is, lexical verbs that contain the semantic feature of 'sufficiency', for example MALTTAA ('be patient enough') or USKALTAA ('have enough courage'). Translations displayed proportionally fewer of them than texts originally written in Finnish. Corresponding tendencies have been noted with pragmatic particles in translated Swedish (Gellerstam 1996) and grammatical structures in Finnish (Mauranen & Tiittula 2005). Mauranen and Tiittula (2005) explored bidirectional English-Finnish and German-Finnish translations, looking at grammatically optional vs. obligatory personal pronouns. Finnish, unlike English and German, is a pro-drop language, that is, personal pronouns are optional in certain contexts; translations towards Finnish reflect this by dropping pronouns. Yet much more often pronouns are retained, which results in several times more pronouns in translations. A specific feature of Finnish grammar is the generic person ('null person'), a third-person form with no pronoun and generic meaning: Finnish originals, for example *Ei tarvitse sanoa* ('not-has-to-say'), need translating with a pronoun, as in *You don't have to say it*. Translations into German and English reflect the difference by adding pronouns where either the Finnish pro-drop feature or the generic person structure occurs.

In all, there is evidence not only from lexis, but also from pragmatics and grammar that translations tend to under-represent unique features of the target language. This would seem to support the relevance of the *text* level in translation: the properties of the text at hand affect its translation. Translations nevertheless also make alterations, reduce or add features; this, in turn, supports the interpretation that translators work at the level of *language* in adhering to the norms and conventions of the target language. Altogether, then, the source influences the translation where preferences rather than, say, ungrammatical structures are concerned, which is why we can discern the influence in large numbers rather than in individual cases. As pointed out in Section 2, we meet similarly detectable novel preferences in ELF corpus data.

The linguistic features discussed in this section may with good reason be described as manifestations of hybridity, as they indicate the influence of at least one other language on the one that is currently being used. It is possible to think of behavioural or cognitive processes that might lie behind these large-scale phenomena, and many scholars in translation studies in fact suggest explanations originating in a translator's behaviour or cognition. For example, Toury (1995) talks about how the propensity to translate word by word helps 'the law of interference' seep into translations. Tirkkonen-Condit (2004) attributes under-represented items to a tendency to translate literally, and Eskola (2004) invokes stimuli in the source text that have possible, even if not preferred, translation equivalents in the target language. For learners, reasons attributed to transfer effects, learning processes, individual differences and teaching practices have been common. Beyond those, some scholars have pointed out that certain features may simply be less 'learnable' or inherently hard, among them conventionalized or formulaic language (cf. Pawley & Syder 1983). Wray (2002) even suggests that learning formulaic expressions correctly is impossible on account of the different processes of acquiring an L1 and additional languages.

How macro-level phenomena relate to cognitive processes is discussed in connection with cognition in Section 6, but before that the mediating level of social interaction is taken up in the next section.

5   Micro Level: Social Interaction

Macro phenomena show the aggregate outcomes of myriad interactions between individual speakers. Where language changes – or is maintained – is in these micro-social face-to-face interactions, and it is through these that linguistic changes diffuse and spread (e.g. Milroy & Milroy 1985, Chambers 2009). ELF interactions are therefore ubiquitous sites of potential language change. Translators of course deal with texts, not face-to face interaction, but translations nevertheless show interactional features of the kinds that can be discerned in texts (cf. Hyland 2000).

The most straightforward interactive phenomenon that comes up in both translations and ELF is known as explicitation. The term was suggested by Blum-Kulka (1986), and the phenomenon has thereafter been widely accepted as a translation universal, despite some critical voices (Becher 2010). Blum-Kulka found that translations used more cohesive devices than their source texts, later supported in Øverås (1998), who also found more lexical changes towards explicitness than implicitness. Olohan and Baker (2000) discovered more grammatically optional elements, such as relative pronouns in translations (*he said* **that** *it's all right* vs. *he said it's all right*), while Kujamäki (2000) reported additions to explanations of cultural and contextual features potentially unfamiliar to readers. Mauranen and Tiittula (2005) found more grammatically optional personal pronouns in translated than in untranslated texts: for instance, the first-person singular pronoun forms *minä/mä* appeared 5.9 times every 1,000 words in originally Finnish texts, but 15.0/1000 w in translations from English. Eskola (2004) detected explicitation in syntax – for example, non-finite constructions translated with finite ones. Similarly, in the following example (from the Finnish-English Contrastive Corpus), the Finnish original (FO) shows a nominal construction (*candidacy*), while the English translation (ET) opts for a whole *that* clause:

FO: *Puolueen johto* **oli sopinut** *Kekkosen miehenä tunnetun entisen ulko- ja pääministerin tohtori Ahti* **Karjalaisen ehdokkuudesta** *ja puolueen eduskuntaryhmän enemmistö tuki häntä.*
'had agreed on ... Karjalainen's candidacy'

ET: *The party leadership* **had already agreed** *among themselves* **that** *a known Kekkonen follower, former foreign minister and prime minister Ahti* **Karjalainen,** **should be their candidate.**

This case illustrates the increase of syntactic explicitness, or the degree of 'sentence-likeness' in translation. Enhanced explicitness thus manifests itself in lexical choices, grammatical structures, discourse management and content elaboration – either as a relationship observed between original texts and their translations, or in comparisons between non-translated and translated texts in the same language. Arguably, this is an interactional feature, indicating a translator's audience awareness: spelling things out works towards textual clarity. In this way, it bears close resemblance to Sacks et al.'s (1974) notion of recipient design.

ELF research has found similar practices in face-to-face interaction. Manifestations of explicitness of several kinds have been identified, starting from syntax, as in this case of fronting, or 'left dislocation', where the subject noun is put before the clause, and a pronoun in the clause refers back to the already familiar subject:

> S1: a couple of questions erm **this citizenship** how much does **it** *influence* the people...

In addition to fronting, tails or 'right dislocation' (*in lab studies* **they** *are quite similar* **the genomes**) have also been found for negotiating topics (Mauranen 2007), a preference in verb phrases for the attention-catching, explicit BE + *ing* form (Ranta 2006) and discourse management expressions like metadiscourse (Mauranen 2012). Among the most typical explicitation findings are repetition and rephrasing in dialogue and polylogue (Seidlhofer 2004, Mauranen 2006, Pitzl 2010), and in monologues like lectures (Suviniitty 2012). Explicitation in monologues illustrates the sliding borderline between different kinds of interactivity: translated and other written texts are not categorically distinct from spoken monologues. The mainly qualitative findings on rephrases and repetitions are supported by a quantitative overview (Mauranen 2012), showing that the total number of rephrase indicators is considerably higher in ELF than in comparable English L1 discourse: 78.8 items/1000 w vs. 21.4 items/1000 w, respectively. We can thus talk about explicitation in ELF just as we do in translation.

Dialogic explicitation practices in ELF have also been connected to the more general interactional process of accommodation (Jenkins 2000, Seidlhofer 2011, Mauranen 2012). In interactional linguistics, accommodation refers to the way speakers adjust their speech in accordance with the contingencies of a changing situation (cf. Couper-Kuhlen & Selting 2018), but ELF researchers, drawing on accommodation theory (Giles 1973), also include speakers' convergence or divergence at various levels and kinds of expression, from phonology to discourse. Converging or diverging on speech characteristics between speakers can broadly be seen in terms of willingness to align their situation models, which, according to Pickering and Garrod (2004), is what enables successful communication. Alignment in interaction takes place through automatic processes across levels of linguistic representation like lexical choices, pronunciation or grammar. It is a property of social interaction, but at the same time it is interwoven with cognitive processes.

The connection between social interaction and cognition is perhaps most perceptible in spoken dialogue, in this case ELF. When speakers look for the least common denominator that would support interactional fluency, it is likely that the best guesses would be those that are the most widely shared. High-frequency items are good candidates, as their chances of being known to both parties are the best. In this way, the preference observed at the macro level (Section 4) is produced and reproduced in interaction, which also strengthens already well-entrenched cognitive representations of language. Apart from actual face-to-face interaction, an attempt to ensure that situation models get shared can be conceived analogously in translation, too: for translators, the many forms of explicitation may be a deliberate strategy aimed at accommodating their readers' assumed situation models.

We have thus found signs of enhanced explicitness at discourse level, in individual texts and speech in both SLU and translations. In addition, we have seen that they relate to the macro level of language, as well as to cognitive processes.

6 Cognitive Level

Multilingual individuals processing language are at the heart of language contact. Sajavaara made a pertinent observation some twenty-five years ago in respect of learners and contrastive linguistics:

the interlingual contrast is not housed directly in the two language systems but is mediated through the language learner ..., i.e., it is buried in the minds of bilingual language users. (Sajavaara 1996: 31)

While the present concern is neither with interlingual comparisons nor primarily with learners, the significant point is that 'objective' sets of differences between language systems are far less relevant for speakers than human bilingual perception. Bi- or multilingual processing is where we might expect to find important shared phenomena in SLU, translation and learner language.

Multilinguals operate unavoidably as multilinguals even if they find themselves in a monolingual environment; their whole repertoire is involved in all their communicative activity.

Research in cross-linguistic influence and multilingualism suggests that bilinguals cannot entirely quench other languages than those they are predominantly using at any given time. It is clear that bilinguals are able to operate monolingually (e.g. Paradis 2004) – that is, without overt code-switching – but even if they do not overtly use another language, its elements are still alive in their processing system (e.g. Djikstra & Van Heuven 2002). The L1 affects a speaker's use of a given target language, but so do their other dominant languages (e.g. Winford 2003), and the L1 is also subject to influence from other languages (e.g. Cook 2003b, Section 4 above). It seems, in short, that influences run along multidirectional courses among speakers' linguistic repertoires.

As already noted at the end of Section 4, researchers in translation and learner language have been inclined to offer explanations that invoke behavioural or cognitive processes to tendencies observed in production data. I look at some of the principal tendencies discussed in Sections 4 and 5 at the macro and interactional levels and seek to relate them to cognitive processes in this section: those pertaining to large-scale tendencies like frequencies, and those concerning the interrelations of interaction and cognition, mainly priming.

To begin with frequency, the main observation in all three contact situations was that translators, ELF users and learners were falling upon the most frequent vocabulary items more than comparable, presumably largely monolingual populations using their first languages. This was normatively construed as a problem at the collective level, with strong implications that it is also a 'problem' at the individual level, reflecting simplifying processes in translation and inadequate command of the language in learners. As already observed (Section 4), the differences, although real, only concern a small section of the highest-frequency vocabulary, which accounts for the best part of any language use. From a cognitive viewpoint this means that the bulk of our language experience consists of the most frequent items, both in reception (when others use them) and in production (when we use them ourselves). Therefore, these items ought to be most strongly entrenched in any individual's mind. The same goes for structures: frequent constructions are altogether processed faster and with less effort because people have had more opportunity to practise them (cf. Dąbrowska 2004). It is hard to see how such processes in themselves would be different for L1 and L2, even if different contexts of experience may give rise to divergences in output. For example, a greater quantity and intensity of experience in L1 would mean a greater aggregate amount of activation and would thus keep activation thresholds low in the L1, also thereby probably ensuring and maintaining accessibility to rarer items.

Conversely, some contexts like immigration may provide more activation for an L2, and as non-selected items gradually raise their activation thresholds (e.g. Paradis 2004, Sharwood Smith & Truscott 2014), make the L1 less accessible. Contextual variation therefore means that general predictability for the ease of access of items or structures is relatively low for individual cases.

Very common items, whether lexical or structural, should be strongly represented in a lingua franca because they can be processed faster and more effortlessly by all. As discussed in Section 5, ease of processing benefits interactional fluency, and the ensuing activation of frequent items is apt to enhance their entrenchment even further. The tendency may be additionally augmented by the potentially high processing load brought about by the sheer unpredictability of many ELF encounters, as we may assume that well-entrenched items are most accessible even under heavy processing pressure.

Translators also face a high processing load: receiving input in one language and producing output in another means that they are constantly moving between activation and suppression of items from the languages with which they are working. The Activation Threshold Hypothesis put forward by Paradis (2004) holds that, for a given item to be selected in a multilingual's mind, its activation must exceed those of competing items, which are simultaneously inhibited, and their activation thresholds raised. In contrast to L2 use, there is no one 'more activated language' (Pavlenko 2014: 223) in translation that would be the more accessible overall; translators alternate continually between activation in two languages. If it is also the case that multilinguals' processing systems are non-selective with regard to language, as Paradis suggests, then related items such as translation equivalents should be activated along with items in a source language. This is, of course, exactly what we find in professional translators. Even though most of the research manifesting simultaneous activation in bilinguals has dealt with homographs or cognates across languages, while unrelated words have not shown an equal degree of simultaneous activation (Van Assche et al. 2012), there are also indications that translation equivalents may cause cross-linguistic priming, to which we return later in this section. Overall, then, there seem to be indications of a cognitive basis for an enhanced presence of the most frequent vocabulary in translations and SLU, because the high processing loads imposed by simultaneous pressure to activate and suppress items from different languages would favour the most entrenched vocabulary from each.

Another macro-scale phenomenon described in Section 4 that sheds light on cognition and changing intuitions is the way in which translators use multi-word sequences. As transpired from Mauranen (2000), multiword sequences in translations not only deviated from those in comparable original texts, but the subtler difference emerged that translations from English diverged more from typical Finnish patterns than translations from other languages. It would thus seem that English had had a stronger impact on translators and editors than the other languages, altering their first language intuitions. Although a corpus-based observation, it also ought to reflect the intuitions of the individuals involved, which would appear to fit the observations of bilingual behaviour made by, for example, Weinreich (1953), or papers in Cook (2003) and Cook & Bassetti 2011).

This tallies with accounts from other non-English-speaking countries where 'anglicisms' in translations have struck researchers. For example, Lanstyák & Heltai (2012) report on the increase of certain Hungarian constructions at the expense of others in spontaneous Hungarian use as a consequence of the growing presence of English in Hungarian society. Although all these cases concern English – which is currently particularly conspicuous everywhere – it would seem plausible that all languages act on each other in similar ways in any society that has multilingual speakers.

Several of the phenomena discussed in this paper can be related to the generally automatic, non-conscious process of priming, a tendency of speakers to repeat what they have recently comprehended or produced. Interaction is a central site of priming: alignment with your interlocutor generates priming effects through the brain's strong attuning to its social environment, that is, to other people (e.g. Hari et al. 2016). Conversation thus acts upon the brain. The interface between interaction and cognition is crucial for understanding how linguistic influence passes from one individual to another: we receive enormous amounts of linguistic input daily – why do we later repeat some things from what we have heard or said, but not everything?

As far as ELF is concerned, one of the most intriguing facets of priming from previous research is that it can take place even when the relevant expression is perceived to be ungrammatical. When ELF users accommodate to each other's speech, they may also repeat non-standard forms:

> S1: yeah and they are not **publicised**
> S2: no they are not **publicised** no, but er that's a question of...
> S1: yeah that's ... I most certainly agree that you can't **publicise** in in in the scientific journals... (ELFA corpus 2008)

Here a thesis examiner (S1) and a doctoral candidate (S2) are discussing whether some of the candidate's data has been published or not. S1 produces an approximation of the standard form, as is quite typical in ELF discourse. Whether such priming has persistent effects on the speakers remains an open question if we cannot follow them further, but there are examples of the same approximate forms (e.g. *registrate*) occurring in several independent ELF contexts, as well as on the Internet (Mauranen 2018). While previously familiar items in these encounters undoubtedly get further reinforced, it is also possible that novel items, such as approximations, become salient and learnable. Earlier findings suggest that priming tends to be larger for less frequent than more frequent constructions, possibly on account of the surprise they cause. As Pickering and Garrod (2017: 187) speculate, 'the strong priming of rare forms may reinforce the memory for such forms and hence promote language change'.

For translations, the particularly relevant kind of priming is cross-linguistic priming. Expressions or utterances people have encountered in one language tend to affect their expressions in another (see e.g. Pickering & Garrod 2017). It is therefore a good candidate for explaining in cognitive terms why – or how – we receive and pass on influences, and how texts in one language may prime us to emulate some of its features in another. Kujamäki's (2004) study of student translators showed that source expressions greatly reduced the selection of items most specific to the target language (Finnish, the participants' L1). He constructed a short text including three Finnish-specific lexical items relating to snow and driving conditions (*kinos, hanki, keli*) and had them translated into English and German. The English translations were two compounds *snowbank* (≈ *kinos*), *snowdrift* (≈ *hanki*) and a hypernym *conditions* (≈ *keli*). When students were asked to translate the German and English texts into Finnish, nearly two-thirds used a less target-specific item. This indicates the strength of cross-linguistic priming, and in behavioural terms we could say it supports the influence of the source text on the translator. On the other hand, one-third of the translations rendered the source input with the specific, uniquely Finnish item. This reflects a shift to activating the target language. It would seem, then, that alternate activations take place while moving from source input to target output; the tendency of the source input to activate closely parallel items in the output appears to overpower the tendency to shift more completely to target language activation for most people, even though not all. Cross-language priming would therefore seem to be the cognitive basis for what at the macro level of language manifests itself as the relative underrepresentation of target language-unique lexical or pragmatic items. Since between-language priming has also been found for structural influences, we might hypothesize that structures behave analogously to homographs or cognates across languages (Van Assche et al. 2012): if equivalent structures exist in languages, they should be activated simultaneously. Such processes could therefore underlie the findings in Eskola (2004) and Mauranen and Tiittula (2005). Thus, where translation equivalents exist, or are possible renderings of the source text stimulus, it is not surprising that translators select those over possibilities that are more distant, for example by being single-word renderings or more common but less equivalent structures in the target language.

We have seen in this section that high processing load, changing activation thresholds and priming effects provide a cognitive basis for understanding macro-level effects of the propensity to rely heavily on the most frequent vocabulary, as well as the tendency for approximations and non-standard or non-preferred items to appear and spread. The processes take place in both translations and ELF. The main mediating factors would seem to be interaction in ELF, and the continual need to alternate between textual activation and suppression in translations.

7 Conclusion

We have traced contact-influenced language use in translations and ELF and noted a few similarities. On occasion, learner language has also been included. It is possible to recognize a certain hybridity that ensues from each: language affected by multilingual contact. In itself this is not new, but the present perspective with the three-pronged approach brings together contact influences from quite different settings that are rarely, if ever, investigated together. Some features, like high proportions of the commonest words and 'untypical' collocations, are shared in all three – but their import is also questioned. Translation and ELF both manifest enhanced explicitness in discourse, together with simultaneous simplification and augmented variety in lexis. Translations and learner language show proneness to interference from another language: translations reportedly from the source language or source text; learner language supposedly from their first language. In ELF, such effects from specific other languages have not been teased out, as they would not contribute much to understanding the special characteristics of ELF, which result from complex multilingual influences. The evidence for the priming effect on ungrammatical items in ELF nevertheless testifies to a closely related process. Moreover, a wealth of evidence already accumulated from other sources, together with spot checks (e.g. progressives in Ranta 2013 and in Meriläinen et al. 2017) suffices to corroborate the presence of speakers' L1 in ELF. It is presumably also simplistic to talk about contact between only two languages in translation and SLA. Reality must be fuzzier, as linguistic influences come from many sources and directions to anyone's experience.

This paper has argued that the overarching phenomenon behind the observed effects is language contact. Contact was examined at three levels: cognition, interaction and language as a collective entity. As cognitive processing activates and suppresses items and structures, frequent vocabulary is likely to be strengthened in the process, as it already presumably contains the most robust items in speakers' repertoires; if competing systems are active in a speaker's mind, the most entrenched parts of each are likely to become more salient, other things being equal. Other things may not be equal, though, and priming effects for one thing may clearly alter item salience. Most SLA research (e.g. Ellis 2007, Hawkins & Filipović 2012) seems to assume, at least tacitly, that whole language systems are separate in speakers' minds, even though the assumption is probably not very solid (Cf. Pavlenko 2014, Schmid 2019). Given the considerable uncertainty around this, research methods may also hide processes in multilingual activity. One issue is the nature of frequent vocabulary: we tend to measure it for each language separately, but in an individual's mind the languages, and items from each, may intermingle so that their strongest words originate in different languages. That is, the frequency list of an individual's most entrenched vocabulary may consist of interleaved L1, L2 ... Ln items.

Bilingual text processing, as in translation, is likely to be primed by the source text to foreground items and structures shared in the two languages at the cost of non-shared material. This may result in unusual or infrequent structures in the target text, even new collocations, which may look 'untypical' from their target language viewpoint.

In ELF, priming effects come about mainly through interaction, apt to strengthen items with wide currency, like common lexis and structures. Yet, approximate expressions and innovations also often work well in conversation if they give sufficient clues to their meaning in the context. If interlocutors accept them, they stand a good chance of being reinforced for the speaker, while interlocutors on their part can be primed by them and potentially diffuse them further. Despite this potential, it is uncertain how persistent priming effects are. Pickering and Garrod (2017) argue that priming is more likely to be effective coming from interaction than mere exposure, such as listening to a debate. Chambers (2009) in turn suggested, from a sociolinguistic viewpoint, that not all interaction is equally conducive to the propagation of linguistic innovations, but that peer interaction is more effective than socially asymmetrical interaction. Putting these together would lead us to expect the least priming effect in listening, more in interactions and most in interactions among peers. Nevertheless, in academic contexts where asymmetrical institutional positions seem to override native-speaker status (Mauranen 2013, Hynninen 2016), they may also result in priming – the educational setting may simply prompt it because students tend to orient to what the professor says. This needs further research, as does priming in translation, because clearly priming can effectively take place through texts (e.g. Hoey 2005).

Translations indicate unmistakable priming effects from texts. Clearly, the intense engagement with text in the translation process is quite different from listening to other people talk, and it would seem reasonable to expect the process to exert a special kind of influence. The powerful presence of other languages in, for example, digital and traditional media may also emanate more overall influence than is detectable in small-scale experimental studies or in single-language corpus research (see, however Laitinen & Lundberg in this volume). Individuals' linguistic intuitions are inclined to change on account of extensive exposure to foreign languages. This can feed upwards to the macro level in the shape of greater acceptability of, for instance, English-influenced multiword units in a non-English language community (cf. Mauranen 2000), but need not be limited to single-language influence.

The collective, macro level of language manifests the aggregate effects of the levels below as frequencies, patterns and preferences, and in its turn reflects back those patterns onto individual speakers through many channels. The picture is nevertheless becoming more diffuse with developments particularly from globalization and digitalization in contemporary societies. For any national language this means not only fraying boundaries but also new sources of internal heterogeneity, as sites of text and talk are differentially favoured or accessible to groups divided by, say, age, language and socio-economic or ethnic position. To make sense of the ensuing mixing of languages or their elements, we may have to let go of many assumptions concerning the separateness of languages at each of the levels of contact we have considered here.

The sites of contact we have investigated turn out to share many properties and a general character of hybridity. However, whereas translation and SLA manifest first-order language contact, ELF is different. First-order contacts (similects) come together in ELF interaction and affect each other, constituting second-order contact, which is qualitatively new. In the process, the influences make up what could be depicted as a multidimensional space, a 'contact universe' with multiplex links in innumerable directions. ELF impacts the individual user, individuals in interaction and usage in the aggregate. Moreover, it is regulated from the bottom up only, and any incipient norms (see Low 2016) arise from interaction. Because ELF, unlike national, standardized languages, is unregulated from the top down, it throws new light on how self-organizing patterns take shape, and can potentially show these processes more clearly than regulated languages do.

We can therefore expect that ELF opens a new window to theories of language as a complex dynamic system (see Schneider 1997 and this volume Mauranen 2017, 2019, Vetchinnikova 2017, Larsen-Freeman 2018, Vetchinnikova & Hiltunen this volume). The magnitude and scale of English and its links with nearly all other languages in the world makes its contact potential unique and sets it up as a major driver in changing not only English but the global linguistic landscape. At the same time, it raises questions with regard to other kinds of contact: how simple or bilingual are they? Translations take place between two languages, but translators are usually multilingual; surely their multilingualism affects their work in more ways than one. Overall, multilingual users may have more complex cognitive representations of languages that develop in contact with other multilinguals, even if they are mainly drawing on one language at a given time.

REFERENCES

Aijmer, Karin, Bengt Altenberg & Stig Johansson (eds.) 1996. *Languages in Contrast*. Lund: Lund University Press.

Altenberg, Bengt & Sylviane Granger. 2002. The grammatical and lexical patterning of *make* in native and non-native student writing. *Applied Linguistics* 22(2), 173–189.

Baker, Mona. 1993. Corpus linguistics and translation studies: Implications and applications. In Mona Baker, Gill Francis & Elena Tognini-Bonelli (eds.), *Text and Technology: In Honour of John Sinclair*, 233–250. Amsterdam, Philadelphia: John Benjamins.

Becher, Victor. 2010. Abandoning the notion of 'translation-inherent' explicitation. Against a dogma of translation studies. *Across Languages and Cultures* 11(1), 1–28.

Bestgen, Yves, Sylviane Granger & Jennifer Thewissen. 2012. Error patterns and automatic L1 identification. In Scott Jarvis & Scott A. Crossley (eds.), *Approaching Language Transfer through Text Classification*, 127–153. Bristol: Multilingual Matters.

Biber, Douglas. 2006. *University Language. A Corpus-Based Study of Spoken and Written Registers*. Amsterdam: John Benjamins.

2009. Are there linguistic consequences of literacy? Comparing the potentials of language use in speech and writing. In David R. Olson & Nancy Torrance (eds.), *Cambridge Handbook of Literacy*, 75–91. Cambridge: Cambridge University Press.

Biber, Douglas & Bethany Gray. 2010. Challenging stereotypes about academic writing: Complexity, elaboration, explicitness. *Journal of English for Academic Purposes* 1(19), 2–20.

Biber, Douglas, Stig Johansson, Geoffrey Leech, Susan Conrad & Edward Finegan E. 1999. *The Longman Grammar of Spoken and Written English*. London: Pearson Education.

Blommaert, Jan & Ben Rampton. 2011. Language and superdiversity: a position paper. Available at www.kcl.ac.uk/sspp/departments/education/research/Research-Centres/ldc/publications/workingpapers/abstracts/WP070-Language-and-superdiversity-a-position-paper-.aspx.

Blum-Kulka, Shoshana. 1986. Shifts of cohesion and coherence in translation. In Juliane House & Shoshana Blum-Kulka (eds.), *Interlingual and Intercultural Communication: Discourse and Cognition in Translation and Second Language Acquisition Studies*, 17–35. Tübingen: Narr.

Canagarajah, A. Suresh. 2013. *Translingual Practice: Global Englishes and Cosmopolitan Relations*. New York and Abingdon: Routledge.

Carey, Ray. 2013. On the other side: Formulaic organizing chunks in spoken and written academic ELF. *Journal of English as a Lingua Franca* 2(2), 207–228.

Chambers, John K. 2009. *Sociolinguistic Theory*. Revised ed. Oxford: Wiley-Blackwell.

Chesterman, Andrew. 2004. *Beyond the particular*. In Mauranen & Kujamäki (eds.), 33–49.

Collins COBUILD English Dictionary. 1995. London: Harper Collins.

Cook, Vivian. 1991. The poverty-of-the-stimulus argument and multi-competence. *Second Language Research* 7(2), 103–117.

(ed.). 2002. *Portraits of the L2 User*. Clevedon: Multilingual Matters.

2003. Introduction: The changing L1 in the L2 user's mind. In Vivian Cook (ed.), *Effects of the Second Language on the First*, 1–18. Bristol: Multilingual Matters.

(ed.). 2003b. *Effects of the Second Language on the First*. Bristol: Multilingual Matters.

Cook, Vivian & Benedetta Bassetti. 2011. Relating language and cognition: The second language user. In Vivian Cook & Benedetta Bassetti (eds.), *Language and Bilingual Cognition*, 143–190. New York: Psychology Press.

Couper-Kuhlen, Elizabeth & Margaret Selting. 2018. *Interactional Linguistics: An Introduction to Language in Social Interaction*. Cambridge: Cambridge University Press.

Crossley, Scott A., Tom Salsbury & Danielle S. McNamara. 2015. Assessing lexical proficiency using analytical ratings: A case for collocation accuracy. *Applied Linguistics* 36(5), 570–590.

Dąbrowska, Ewa. 2004. *Language, Mind and Brain. Some Psychological and Neurological Constraints on Theories of Grammar*. Edinburgh: Edinburgh University Press.

Djikstra, Ton & Walter J. B. Van Heuven. 2002. The architecture of the bilingual word recognition system: from identification to decision. *Bilingualism: Language and Cognition* 5(3), 51–66.

Ellis, Nick. 2007. Cognitive perspectives on SLA: The associative-cognitive CREED *AILA Review* 19(1), 100–121.

2017. Chunking in language usage, learning and change: *I don't know*. In Hundt, Marianne, Sandra Mollin & Simone Pfenninger (eds.), *The Changing English Language*. Cambridge: Cambridge University Press.

Eskola, Sari. 2002. *Syntetisoivat rakenteet käännössuomessa*. Joensuu: University of Joensuu.

2004. Untypical frequencies in translated language. In Mauranen, Anna & Pekka Kujamäki (eds.) 2004. *Translation universals – Do they exist?* Amsterdam: John Benjamins. 83–99.

Ferraresi, Adriano & Silvia Bernardini. 2019. Lexical simplification in English and Italian Eurolects: (con/di)vergences. Presentation at the AIA conference, 5–7 September 2019, Padova, Italy.

Filppula, Markku, Juhani Klemola, Anna Mauranen & Svetlana Vetchinnikova (eds.) 2017. *Changing English: Global and Local Perspectives*. Berlin: Mouton de Gruyter.

Firth, Alan & Johannes Wagner. 1997. On discourse, communication, and (some) fundamental concepts in SLA research. *Modern Language Journal* 81, 285–300.

Firth, John R. 1957. General linguistics and descriptive grammar. In John Firth *Papers in Linguistics 1934–1951*, 216–228. Oxford: Oxford University Press.

Garcia, Ofelia & Li Wei. 2014. *Translanguaging: Language, Bilingualism and Education*. London: Palgrave Macmillan.

Gellerstam, Martin. 1996. Translation as a source for cross-linguistic studies. In Aijmer, Altenberg & Johansson (eds.), 53–62.

Giles, Howard. 1973. Accent mobility: A model and some data. *Anthropological Linguistics* 33, 27–42.

Gilner, Leah. 2016. Dominant vocabulary in ELF interactions. *JELF* 5(1), 27–51.
Gilner, Leah & Franc Morales. 2011. The ICE-CORE word list: The lexical foundation of 7 varieties of English. *Asian Englishes* 14(1), 4–21.
Gilquin, Gaëtanelle. 2008. Combining contrastive and interlanguage analysis to apprehend transfer: Detection, explanation, evaluation. In Gaëtanelle Gilquin, Szilivia Papp & Maria Belén Diez-Bedmar (eds.), *Linking Up Contrastive and Learner Corpus Research*, 3–33. Amsterdam: Rodopi.
Gilquin, Gaëtanelle & Sylviane Granger. 2011. From EFL to ESL: Evidence from the International Corpus of Learner English. In Joybrato Mukherjee & Marianne Hundt (eds.), *Exploring Second-Language Varieties of English and Learner Englishes*, 55–78. Amsterdam: John Benjamins.
Granger, Sylviane, Joseph Hung & Stephanie Petch-Tyson (eds.). 2002. *Computer Learner Corpora, Second Language Acquisition and Foreign Language Teaching.* Amsterdam: John Benjamins.
Granger, Sylviane & Fanny Meunier (eds.). 2008. *Phraseology. An Interdisciplinary Perspective.* Amsterdam: John Benjamins.
Grosjean, François. 2008. *Studying Bilinguals.* Oxford: Oxford University Press.
Hari, Riitta, Mikko Sams & Lauri Nummenmaa. 2016. Attending to and neglecting people: bridging neuroscience, psychology and sociology. *Philosophical Transactions of the Royal Society B* 371: 20150365. http://dx.doi.org/10.1098/rstb.2015.0365.
Hasselgård, Hilde & Stig Johansson. 2011. Learner corpora and contrastive interlanguage analysis. In Fanny Meunier, Sylviane De Cock, Gaëtanelle Gilquin & Magali Paquot (eds.), *A Taste for Corpora. A Tribute to Professor Sylviane Granger*, 33–61. Amsterdam: John Benjamins.
Hawkins, John A. & Luna Filipović. 2012. *Criterial Features in L2 English: Specifying the Reference Levels of the Common European Framework.* Cambridge: Cambridge University Press.
Hoey, Michael. 2005. *Lexical Priming. A New Theory of Words and Language.* London: Routledge.
House, Juliane. 2011. Translation and bilingual cognition. In Vivian Cook & Benedetta Bassetti (eds.), *Language and Bilingual Cognition*, 519–527. New York: Psychology Press.
Hundt, Marianne, Sandra Mollin & Simone Pfenninger (eds.) 2017. *The Changing English Language.* Cambridge: Cambridge University Press.
Hyland, Ken. 2000. *Disciplinary Discourses: Social Interactions in Academic Writing.* London: Longman.
Hynninen, Niina. 2016. *Language Regulation in English as a Lingua Franca.* Berlin: DeGruyter Mouton.
Jantunen, Jarmo. 2004. *Synonymia ja käännössuomi.* Joensuu: University of Joensuu.
Jarvis, Scott & Aneta Pavlenko. 2007. *Crosslinguistic Influence in Language and Cognition.* London: Routledge.
Jenkins, Jennifer. 2000. *The Phonology of English as an International Language.* Oxford: Oxford University Press.
  2015. Repositioning English and multilingualism in English as a lingua franca. *Englishes in Practice* 2(3), 49–85.
Jenkins, Jennifer, Will Baker & Martin Dewey (eds.). 2018. *The Routledge Handbook of English as a Lingua Franca.* London, New York: Routledge.

Käännössuomen korpus (Corpus of Translated Finnish). Käännössuomen sähköinen tutkimusaineisto. Käännössuomi ja kääntämisen universaalit –hankkeessa koostanut Joensuun yliopiston kansainvälisen viestinnän laitos 1997–. Availability: Anna Mauranen, University of Helsinki.

Kujamäki, Pekka. 2000. Seitsemän veljen saksannokset ja romaanin saksankielinen vastaanotto – kaksi eri maailmaako? In Outi Paloposki & Henna Makkonen-Craig (eds.), *Käännöskirjallisuus ja sen kritiikki*, 199–227. Helsinki: Yliopistopaino.

2004. What happens to 'unique items' in learners' translations? 'Theories' and 'concepts' as a challenge for novices' views on 'good translation'. In Mauranen & Kujamäki (eds.), 187–204.

Laitinen, Mikko. 2016. Ongoing changes in English modals: On the developments in ELF. In Olga Timofeeva, Anne-Christine Gardner, Alpo Honkapohja & Sarah Chevalier (eds.), *New Approaches to English Linguistics: Building Bridges*, 175–196. Amsterdam: John Benjamins.

2018. Placing ELF among the varieties of English. In Sandra C. Deshors (ed.), *Modeling World Englishes: Assessing the Interplay of Emancipation and Globalization of ESL Varieties*, 109–131. Amsterdam: Benjamins.

Lanstyák, Istvan & Pal Heltai. 2012. Universals in language contact and translation. *Across Languages and Cultures* 13(1), 99–121. doi.org/10.1556/Acr.13.2012.1.6.

Larsen-Freeman, Diane. 2018. Complexity and ELF. In Jennifer Jenkins, Will Baker and Martin Dewey (eds.), *The Routledge Handbook of English as a Lingua Franca*, 51–60. London, New York: Routledge.

Laviosa-Braithwaite, Sara. 1996. *The English Comparable Corpus (ECC): A Resource and a Methodology for the Empirical Study of Translation*, unpublished PhD thesis. Manchester: University of Manchester Institute of Science and Technology.

LePage, Robert B. & Andrée Tabouret-Keller. 1985. *Acts of Identity: Creole-Based Approaches to Language and Ethnicity*. Cambridge: Cambridge University Press.

Li, Wei. 2018. Translanguaging as a practical theory of language. *Applied Linguistics* 39(1), 9–30.

Low, Ee-Ling. 2016. A features-based description of phonological patterns in English as a lingua franca in Asia: Implications for standards and norms. *JELF* 5(2), 309–332.

MacWhinney, Brian. 2005. A unified model of language acquisition. In Judith Kroll & Annette M.B. De Groot (eds.), *Handbook of Bilingualism: Psycholinguistic Approaches*, 49–67. Oxford: Oxford University Press.

Mauranen, Anna. 1998. *Käännössuomi ja kääntämisen universaalit: tutkimus korpusaineistolla*. [Translated Finnish and Translation Universals: A Corpus Study], project research plan, MS, Savonlinna School of Translation Studies.

1999. Will 'Translationese' ruin a contrastive study? *Languages in Contrast* 2(2), 161–185.

2000. Strange strings translated language: A study on corpora. In Maeve Olohan (ed.), *Intercultural Faultlines. Research Models in Translation Studies 1: Textual and Cognitive Aspects*, 119–141. Manchester: St. Jerome Publishing.

2004a. Corpora, universals, and interference. In Mauranen & Kujamäki (eds.), 65–82.

2004b. Talking academic: A corpus approach to academic speech. In Karin Aijmer (ed.), *Dialogue Analysis VIII: Understanding and Misunderstanding in Dialogue*, 201–217. Tübingen: Max Niemeyer.

2006. Signalling and preventing misunderstanding in English as lingua franca communication. *International Journal of the Sociology of Language*, 177, 123–150.

Mauranen, Anna. 2007. Hybrid voices: English as the lingua franca of academics. In Kjersti Fløttum, Trine Dahl & Torodd Kinn (eds.), *Language and Discipline Perspectives on Academic Discourse*, 244–259. Newcastle: Cambridge Scholars Press.

2012. *Exploring ELF*. Cambridge: Cambridge University Press.

2013. Lingua franca discourse in academic contexts: shaped by complexity. In John Flowerdew (ed.), *Discourse in Context*, 225–246. London: Bloomsbury Academic.

2017. A glimpse of ELF. In Filppula et al. (eds.), 223–253.

2018. Second language acquisition, World Englishes, and English as a Lingua Franca (ELF). *World Englishes* 37, 106–119.

2019. Academically speaking. English as the lingua franca. In Ken Hyland & Lillian L. C. Wong (eds.), *Specialised English: New Directions in ESP and EAP Research and Practice*, 9–21. London, New York: Routledge.

Mauranen, Anna & Jarmo Jantunen (eds.). 2005. *Käännössuomeksi. Tutkimuksia suomennosten kielestä*. Tampere: Tampere University Press.

Mauranen, Anna & Pekka Kujamäki (eds.). 2004. *Translation Universals – Do They Exist?*. Amsterdam: John Benjamins.

Mauranen, Anna & Liisa Tiittula. 2005. MINÄ käännössuomessa ja supisuomessa. In Mauranen & Jantunen (eds.), 35–70.

Meriläinen, Lea, Heli Paulasto & Paula Rautionaho. 2017. Extended uses of the progressive form in Inner, Outer and Expanding Circle Englishes. In Filppula et al. (eds.), 191–221.

Mesthrie, Rajend & Rakesh Bhatt. 2008. *World Englishes*. Cambridge: Cambridge University Press.

Milroy, Jim & Lesley Milroy. 1985. Linguistic change, social network and speaker innovation. *Journal of Linguistics* 21, 339–384.

Nattinger, James R. & Jeannette S. DeCarrico. 1992. *Lexical Phrases and Language Teaching*. Oxford: Oxford University Press.

Nesselhauf, Nadja. 2005. *Collocations in a Learner Corpus*. Amsterdam: John Benjamins.

Nevalainen, Sampo. 2005. Köyhtyykö kieli käännettäessä? Mitä taajuuslistat kertovat suomennosten sanastosta. In Mauranen & Jantunen (eds.), 139-162.

Nitschke, Sanjo, Evan Kidd & Ludovica Serratrice. 2010. First language transfer and long-term structural priming in comprehension. *Language and Cognitive Processes* 25(1), 94–114.

Odlin, Terence. 2003. Cross-linguistic influence. In Catherine J. Doughty & Michael H. Long (eds.), *The Handbook of Second Language Acquisition*, 436–486. Oxford: Blackwell.

Olohan, Maeve & Mona Baker. 2000. Reporting *THAT* in translated English. Evidence for subconscious processes of explicitation? *Across Languages and Cultures* 1(2), 141–158.

Ortega, Lourdes. 2009. *Understanding Second Language Acquisition*. London: Hodder Education.

Øverås, Linn. 1998. In search of the third code: An investigation of norms in literary translation. *Meta* 43, 571–588.
Paradis, Michel. 2004. *A Neurolinguistic Theory of Bilingualism*. Amsterdam: John Benjamins.
Pavlenko, Aneta. 2014. *The Bilingual Mind*. Cambridge: Cambridge University Press.
Pawley, Andrew & Frances H. Syder. 1983. Two puzzles for linguistic theory: Nativelike selection and nativelike fluency. In Jack C. Richards & Richard W. Schmidt (eds.), *Language and Communication*, 191–225. London: Longman.
Pickering, Martin J. & Simon Garrod. 2004. Towards a mechanistic psychology of dialogue. *Behavioural and Brain Sciences* 27(2), 169–225.
2017. Priming and language change. In Hundt et al. (eds.), 173–190.
Pitzl, Marie-Luise. 2010. *English as a Lingua Franca in International Business: Resolving Miscommunication and Reaching Shared Understanding*. Saarbrücken: VDM.
Ranta, Elina. 2006. The 'attractive' progressive – why use the -ing form in English as a Lingua Franca? *Nordic Journal of English Studies* 5(2), 95–116.
2013. *Universals in a Universal Language? Exploring Verb-Syntactic Features in English as a Lingua Franca*, PhD thesis. University of Tampere.
Renouf, Antoinette & John McH. Sinclair. 1991. Collocational frameworks in English. In Karin Aijmer & Bengt Altenberg (eds.), *English Corpus Linguistics: Studies in Honour of Jan Svartvik*, 128–143. London: Longman.
Ringbom, Håkan. 1992. On L1 transfer in L2 comprehension and production. *Language Learning* 42, 85–112.
Sacks, Harvey, Emanuel Schegloff & Gail Jefferson. 1974. A simplest systematics for the organization of turn-taking in conversation. *Language* (50), 696–735.
Sajavaara, Kari. 1996. *New challenges for contrastive linguistics*. In Aijmer, Altenberg & Johansson (eds.), 7–36.
Schmid, Monika. 2019. When is a bilingual an attriter? – Bilingualism as a two-way street. Presentation at the 5th International Conference of Applied Linguistics in Lithuania, 26–28 September 2019, Vilnius University, Lithuania.
Schneider, Edgar W. 1997. Chaos theory as a model for dialect variability and change? In Alan R. Thomas (ed.), *Issues and Methods in Dialectology*, 22–36. Bangor: Department of Linguistics, University of Wales.
Schreier Daniel & Marianne Hundt (eds.). 2013. *English as a Contact Language*. Cambridge: Cambridge University Press.
Seidlhofer, Barbara. 2004. Research perspectives on teaching English as a lingua franca. *Annual Review of Applied Linguistics* 24, 209–239.
2011. *Understanding English as a Lingua Franca*. Oxford: Oxford University Press.
Silva-Corvalan, Carmen. 1998. On borrowing as a mechanism of syntactic change. In Armin Schwegler, Bernard Tranel & Myriam Uribe- Etcxebarria (eds.), *Romance Linguistics: Theoretical Perspectives*, 225–246. Amsterdam: John Benjamins.
Sharwood Smith, Michael & John Truscott. 2014. *The Multilingual Mind: A Modular Processing Perspective*. Cambridge: Cambridge University Press.
Sinclair, John McH. 1996. The search for units of meaning. *Textus* 9(1), 75–106. Reprinted in Sinclair, John McH. 2004. *Trust the Text*, 24–48. London: Routledge.
Suviniitty, Jaana. 2012. *Lectures in English as a Lingua Franca: Interactional Features*, unpublished doctoral dissertation. Helsinki: University of Helsinki. HELDA E-thesis. [Online]. Available from http://urn.fi/URN:ISBN:978-952-10-8540-6.

Swales, John M. & Amy Burke. 2003. 'It's really fascinating work': Differences in evaluative adjectives across academic registers. In Charles Meyer & Pepi Leistyna (eds.), *Corpus Analysis: Language Structure and Use*, 1–18. Amsterdam: Rodopi.

Teubert, Wolfgang. 1996. Comparable or parallel corpora? *International Journal of Lexicography* 9(3), 238–264.

Thomason, Sarah G. 2001. *Language Contact*. Edinburgh: Edinburgh University Press.

Thomason, Sarah G. & Thomas Kaufman. 1988. *Language Contact, Creolization, and Genetic Linguistics*. Berkeley, CA: University of California Press.

Tirkkonen-Condit, Sonja. 2004. Unique items – over-or under-represented in translated language?. In Mauranen & Kujamäki (eds.), 207–220.

—— 2005. Häviävätkö uniikkiainekset käännössuomesta?. In Mauranen & Jantunen (eds.), 123–137.

Toury, Gideon. 1995. *Descriptive Translation Studies – and Beyond*. Amsterdam: John Benjamins.

Trosborg, Anna. 1997. Translating hybrid political texts. In Anna Trosborg (ed.), *Analysing Professional Genres*, 145–158. Amsterdam: John Benjamins.

Van Assche, Ewa, Duyck Wouter & Robert. J. Hartsuiker. 2012: Bilingual word recognition in a sentence context. *Frontiers in Psychology* 3, 174. doi: 10.3389/fpsyg.2012.00174.

Vetchinnikova, Svetlana. 2017. On the relationship between the cognitive and the communal: a complex systems perspective. In Filppula et al. (eds.), 277–310.

Wang, Yin. 2016. *The Idiom Principle and L1 Influence*. Amsterdam: John Benjamins.

Weinreich, Uriel. 1953. *Languages in Contact: Findings and Problems*. New York: Linguistic Circle. Reprinted: 1963. The Hague: Mouton.

Winford, Donald. 2003. *An Introduction to Contact Linguistics*. Oxford: Blackwell.

Wray, Alison. 2002. *Formulaic Language and the Lexicon*. Cambridge: Cambridge University Press.

Zipf, George K.. 1935. *The Psychobiology of Language*. Boston, MA: Houghton-Mifflin.

Corpora

ELFA. 2008. The Corpus of English as a Lingua Franca in Academic Settings. Director: Anna Mauranen. www.helsinki.fi/elfa/elfacorpus (25 February 2013).

FECC. Finnish-English Contrastive Corpus. Finland: University of Jyväskylä.

Simpson, R. C., Briggs, S. L., Ovens, J. & Swales, J. M. 2002. The Michigan Corpus of Academic Spoken English. Ann Arbor, MI: The Regents of the University of Michigan. http://quod.lib.umich.edu/m/micase/ (25 February 2013).

VOICE. 2013. The Vienna-Oxford International Corpus of English (version POS XML 2.0). Director: Barbara Seidlhofer. www.univie.ac.at/voice/page/download_voice_xml (25 February 2013).

A Standard Corpus of Present-Day Edited American English, for use with Digital Computers (Brown). 1964, 1971, 1979. Compiled by W. N. Francis and H. Kučera. Providence, Rhode Island: Brown University.

5 Present-Day Standard English
Whose Language Was It Anyway?

Terttu Nevalainen

1 Introduction

The topic of this chapter was inspired by an interview with Barbara Seidlhofer, Professor of English and Applied Linguistics at the University of Vienna and a lingua franca specialist, entitled 'Whose language is it anyway?', where she was quoted as saying that 'the "th" or the third person "s" are usually of no consequence at all in international communication' (Schwarz-Stiglbauer 2013).[1] I will take up the challenge posed by the question 'whose language?' and go back in time to trace the generalization in Standard English of peculiarities like verbal *-s*, mentioned by Seidlhofer. My aim is to provide answers to questions such as whose usage they originally represented and what alternative expressions could have been selected instead but were not. A comparison will also be made with regional and international varieties of English that have in fact adopted some of these alternatives, such as the suffixless third-person singular.

As is well known, but not always acknowledged, Standard English comprises features of various origins that were adopted by speakers of English at different points in time (e.g. Hope 2000). In this respect the situation is similar to that of English in international communication today, except that historical choices were made by a much smaller speaker population and from a much more limited feature pool. To illustrate the complexity of historical processes, I will zoom in on the social history of verbal *-s*, which was originally a northern English form and had to make its way into southern usage to become, later on, part of the canon of Standard English. Variation was involved in all stages of the process, which is another commonality between historical

---

I would like to thank the audience at the ELF and Changing English, 10th Anniversary Conference of English as a Lingua Franca, the external reviewer and the volume editors for feedback and valuable comments on earlier versions of this paper. Any remaining infelicities are of course my responsibility.

[1] As is clear from the text, 'the "th"' here refers to the pronunciation of the English voiced/voiceless dental fricatives, which '[g]enerations of English students recall several hours of practicing the pronunciation of "th" in front of the mirror'.

developments in L1 and various lingua franca uses of English today. Evoking the wider context of my empirical work on the historical sociolinguistics of earlier English, my aim is to show that it is rewarding to connect the past and the present, and not only to use the present to explain the past, as famously suggested by William Labov (1977), one of the pioneers of modern sociolinguistics. I will argue that what appear to be quite different specializations may in fact have a good deal in common at a higher level of sociolinguistic generalization.

This chapter is constructed as follows. By way of general background, Section 2.1 introduces one of the first documented sources promoting (American) English as a potential international lingua franca. Section 2.2 moves further back in time and considers one of the early texts to discuss in any detail the regional basis for a would-be standard variety of English, and Section 2.3 outlines two principal approaches to the historical study of Standard English. In the empirical part of the chapter, Section 3 refers to a number of corpora and databases to tell the story of verbal -*s* in its sociohistorical context; evidence for both the language community at large and individual language users is adduced to demonstrate the range of variation in the process of convergence on a single variant form over time. Section 4 connects the past with the present by discussing the current range of variation in the expression of the third-person present indicative in varieties of English worldwide, some of which have long histories of their own. The attested variants include the suffixless form that was one of the alternatives rejected in mainstream use in the past but that prevails in a large number of varieties of English around the world today, and is indeed of common occurrence in English as a Lingua Franca. Going back to the main findings discussed, Section 5 draws the conclusions from this historical exercise and promotes a broad view of sociolinguistic inquiry into language variation and change, past and present.

2   Background: Projecting Back in Time

According to Jenkins (2017: 594), the term 'English as a Lingua Franca' and its acronym (ELF) were first referred to in public discourse in 1996, which makes ELF a relatively recent field of research. However, if a lingua franca is understood to rise in response to communicative needs in diverse situations of language and dialect contact, the use of English for those purposes is, of course, not new. Adopting the long view, Widdowson (2017: 111) argues that 'since ... different approaches to dealing with this adaptive process [of variable discourse textualization] have a long history, ELF study is not in its essentials new either. It too has its precedents, and tracing them can perhaps reveal more clearly just what these essentials are.'

If the development of Standard English is viewed as a dynamic adaptive process, as Widdowson suggests, its history could be considered part of the history of ELF. This is not to imply that the two would be expected to follow similar lines of development over time. On the level of ideology, for example, there is an irreconcilable conflict of interest between them, manifested in practice in issues such as *code fixation* (Seidlhofer 2017: 96–97), difficult to envisage especially in the context of English as a (multi-)Lingua Franca (Jenkins 2017: 601).[2] In the next two sections I will take a brief look at what kinds of English were first proposed for the functions of 'lingua franca', and for what reasons, at the international level (Section 2.1) and, earlier on, nationally (Section 2.2). Section 2.3 presents the two basic theoretical approaches adopted by language historians who study Standard English. The contact-based diffusionist approach is adopted here.

2.1 Suggestion for American English as a Lingua Franca

Today North American English is the variety of the language that international speakers of English are exposed to around the world. It gained this global position after the Second World War with the rise of the United States as a world power. However, the idea of the suitability of English, and the English spoken by the American population in particular, as an international language was presented much earlier. John Adams, the second president of the United States, wrote to Edmund Jenings from Amsterdam back in 1780:[3]

> You must know, I have undertaken to prophecy that English will be the most respectable Language in the World, and the most universally read and Spoken in the next Century, if not before the Close of this.
>
> American Population will in the next Age produce a greater Number of Persons who will Speak English than Any other Language. And these Persons will have more general Acquaintance and Conversation with all other nations than any other People, which will naturally introduce their Language every where, as the general medium of Correspondence and Conversation among the Learned of all Nations, and among all Travellers and Strangers, as Latin was in the last Century and French has been in this. Let Us then encourage and advise every Body to study English.

The criteria that Adams uses to justify his 'prophecy' include the number of speakers of American English, their contacts with speakers of other languages and hence the usefulness of the language in international communication.

---

[2] By contrast, code fixation is typically part of the theory and practice of English as a Foreign Language (EFL); see e.g. Seidlhofer (2017: 90–91).

[3] The quotes are taken from James Taylor's digital edition of the Adams Papers (2018), pp. 170–171.

Adams is right in his prediction of the impact that American English was to have on the use of English worldwide, and it is noteworthy that he is referring to a variety whose history had already reached an advanced stage of standardization (Anderwald 2016: 1–23). Although the English that he himself writes does not substantially deviate from current Standard English grammar (even if his compounding and especially his capitalization do), he tells Jenings in his letter that he saw the need to propose to the President of Congress that an academy should be founded to regulate the use of the English language.

> I have written to Congress a serious Request, that they would appoint an Accademy for refining, correcting improving and Ascertaining the English Language. After Congress shall have done it, perhaps the British King and Parliament may have the Honour of copying the Example. This I Should admire. England will never have any more Honour, excepting now and then, that of imitating the Americans.

This undertaking never materialized in the form implemented, for example, in France or Spain, but the mere suggestion of it in the lingua franca context shows that code fixation figured prominently in Adams's proposal.

2.2 Suggestion for London English as a Literary Norm

One of the early candidates for a national reference variety of English was sixteenth-century London English (Görlach 1991: 8–9, 13–16, Barber 1997: 10–13, Nevalainen 2003, 2006: 29–44).[4] An often-quoted source is George Puttenham's (1529–1590/91) *The arte of English poesie* from 1589, written as a guidebook for aspiring young poets, or *makers*. Puttenham devotes much space to detailing what the recommended usage is not; the recommendation itself is shown in bold in the quoted passage:

> Our maker therfore at these dayes shall not follow Piers plowman nor Gower nor Lydgate nor yet Chaucer, for their language is now out of vse with vs: neither shall he take the termes of Northern-men, such as they vse in dayly talke, whether they be noble men or gentlemen, or of their best clarkes all is a matter: nor in effect any speach vsed beyond the riuer of Trent, though no man can deny but that theirs is the purer English Saxon at this day, yet it is not so Courtly nor so currant as our Southerne English is, no more is the far Westerne mās [man's] speach: **ye shall therfore take the vsuall speach of the Court, and that of London and the shires lying about London within lx. myles, and not much aboue.** I say not this but that in euery shyre of England there be gentlemen and others that speake but specially write as good Southerne as we of Middlesex or Surrey do, but not the common people of euery shire, to whom the gentlemen, and also their learned clarkes do for the most part condescend, but herein we

---

[4] I use the broad term 'reference variety' instead of 'standard variety' to indicate the uncodified status of a focused set of norms in the speakers' minds before code fixation and prescription (Nevalainen 2003: 132).

are already ruled by th'English Dictionaries and other bookes written by learned men, and therefore it needeth none other direction in that behalfe. (Puttenham 1589, Book III: 120–121)

Puttenham argues that the 'best speech' of his day is found in London and the Home Counties, more specifically at the Royal Court. (This argument was pragmatically justified as the young poet would have been on the lookout for patronage.) Puttenham excludes regional dialects and archaic literary language from his 'Courtly' and 'currant' Southern English, although he admits that in every shire there are gentlemen and others who write 'good Southerne'. He objects to the language of the 'common people', but also suggests a good deal of social fluidity between gentlemen and their learned clerks and the lower social ranks. Fox (2003: 107) summarizes the message conveyed by Puttenham and his contemporaries by saying that '[t]he hierarchy of urbanization, which was mirrored by the hierarchy of educational provision and literacy levels, seems also to have been reflected in the hierarchy of "purity" and "civility" in speech'.

Puttenham does not address the question of where the forms of his current southern English originated. Viewing his own usage and leaving spelling aside, we find that many grammatical features that are now part and parcel of Standard English were already in place in his writing, while certain others were not. Although a construction such as multiple negation was no longer used by writers like Puttenham (*nor in effect **any** speech vsed*), it is a common non-standard feature today. Forms that would not be found today include the use of the second-person subject pronoun *ye* for *you* (*ye shall therfore take*) and of the verbal suffix *-th* for *-s* (*it **needeth** none other direction*). However, it will be shown in the following sections that the language that Puttenham described was not as pure and free from regional and social influences as he made it out to be.[5]

2.3   Approaches to the Historical Study of Standard English

Traditional histories of English often posit a direct line of continuity from a given dialect or variety to present-day Standard English. Referring to writers such as Strang (1970: 161), Hope (2000) calls it the 'single ancestor dialect' or SAD hypothesis. He attributes it to the family-tree metaphor of linguistic transmission, a dominant scholarly tradition in historical linguistics since the nineteenth century. The complementary perspective of dialect contact and

---

[5] The features singled out here have been studied by generations of researchers interested in Early Modern English. My original empirical work is presented within a historical sociolinguistic framework e.g. in Nevalainen & Raumolin-Brunberg (2017; 1st ed. 2003) and in more general terms in Nevalainen (2006); both publications contain extensive references to secondary literature on these topics. See also Section 3.

diffusion is common in many fields of historical research today. Both transmission and diffusion are relevant at different levels of abstraction, and both involve a good deal of idealization. Labov (2007: 347), for one, acknowledges this and writes that '[s]uch a clear dichotomy between transmission and diffusion is dependent on the concept of a speech community with well-defined limits, a common structural base, and a unified set of sociolinguistic norms'. In reality, these conditions are rarely fulfilled, and certainly not in the case of ELF (see e.g. Hynninen & Solin 2017).

I will use the history of verbal -*s* to illustrate the heterogeneity of contacts between speakers of different regional and social backgrounds before the rise of normative grammar in the eighteenth century. In certain respects the contact situation resembled that of ELF at the macro level, about which Mauranen (2017: 9) writes: 'ELF bears certain recognisable affinities with dialect contact; both incorporate contact between speakers of mutually intelligible varieties' or 'lects'. In late medieval England, dialect contacts gave rise to several 'colourless' lects that were based on a pool of linguistic features to which various groups of language users had contributed. Arising from shared communicative needs, these lects were no longer strictly localizable in their written form, and in the course of time, certain feature combinations were focused on and came to be regulated and codified as Standard English (Smith 1996: 68–77, Milroy & Milroy 1999, Nevalainen 2003, Nevalainen 2014, Nevalainen & Raumolin-Brunberg 2017: 158–184).

If, following Mauranen (2017: 10), ELF is understood at the macro level in terms of similects – that is, hybrid, contact-based lects – it lies at the far end of the heterogeneity vs. homogeneity continuum. At the other end come written standard languages with fixed codes, documented in grammar books and dictionaries. This is not simply an issue of the granularity of description – one lect or set of lects being described in greater detail than the other(s). Standard English is a useful concept for a closely regulated, largely fixed variety that has come to be accepted by the language community for certain communicative functions, but it is ill suited to describe the long historical process that was required for such a focused variety to emerge in the first place. As illustrated by English strong verbs, for example, this process did not always lead to grammatically regular systems (Trudgill 2009, Anderwald 2016). The third-person singular present indicative suffix is also a typological misfit in present-day Standard English, which no longer marks number and person contrasts in verbs other than *be*. I will return to this typological aspect in Section 4.

3 The Story of Verbal -*s*

The third-person singular indicative suffix goes back to a stage in the history of English where the language had a relatively complex inflectional morphology, which, moreover, displayed dialectal variation. The present-tense indicative was marked differently in the North, the Midlands and the South; in the third-person singular, -es was in competition with -eþ (later spelled with -th, as in the Puttenham quote in Section 2.2). Their phonetic realization differed in the final consonant, an alveolar fricative in -es and an (inter)dental one in -eþ (see e.g. Holmqvist 1922, Kytö 1993, Ferguson 1996, Nevalainen & Raumolin-Brunberg 2000b, Cole 2019: 131–134 and the references therein).[6]

A Linguistic Atlas of Late Mediaeval English (LALME; McIntosh et al. 1986), which covers the period 1375–1500, indicates that the -es ending was used in the third-person singular in the North and Northern Midlands, down to Lancashire in the west and to Lincolnshire in the east (maps 645, 646). Accepting the received wisdom that the South – the capital region in particular – had a decisive role in leading the process of standardization, the question then becomes when and how the northern suffix percolated into the South in social and regional terms, and how individual language users participated in this process. Answers to these questions can be found in the textual evidence of the period, now increasingly available in digital corpora annotated for metadata (Section 3.1), early grammars and spelling books (Section 3.2) and large databases such as Early English Books Online (Section 3.3). The tail end of the trajectory of the outgoing -th suffix extends to the present day and can be traced, for example, to a variety of print and online media (Section 3.4).

3.1 Corpus Linguistic Evidence for Diffusion

3.1.1 The Helsinki Corpus of English Texts Empirical work on digital corpora has made variation transparent to historical linguistics. The multigenre Helsinki Corpus of English Texts (HC) provides an overall view of the diffusion of verbal -s in the Early Modern English period. The corpus divides the period after 1500 into three seventy-year subperiods (1500–1569, 1570–1639 and 1640–1710), enabling a rough comparison over time. Kytö (1993) analysed the corpus and found that verbal -s had been firmly established, for example, in personal letters before English settlers emigrated to the New World in the seventeenth century. The -s ending was a minority variant (3 per cent of the cases) in the first subperiod correspondence, but by the third subperiod it had become the dominant form, and the differences between the

---

[6] The disappearance of the unstressed vowel in the suffix is linked to the more widespread development of schwa loss in English inflectional endings. For further discussion of the realization of the third-person singular indicative, see Nevalainen and Raumolin-Brunberg (2000b). Following common sociolinguistic practice, I will refer to the suffix as verbal -s (or -th), regardless of whether the vowel is realized or not.

Table 5.1 *The Corpus of Early English Correspondence: its original version (CEEC), Extension (CEECE) and Supplement (CEECSU).*[7]

Completed versions	CEEC	CEECE	CEECSU	TOTALS
words	2,597,795	2,219,422	442,484	**5,259,701**
collections	96	77	19	**192**
letters	5,961	4,923	829	**11,713**
writers	778	308	94	**1,180**
time span	ca. 1410–1681	1653–1800	1402–1663	**1402–1800**

six genres studied (diaries, private and official letters, sermons, histories, trials) had largely evened out.

Unlike the non-localized Early Modern English part of the corpus, the Middle English part allows certain dialect comparisons. Analysing the last subperiod (1420–1500; ca. 210,000 words), we find that the -*s* ending appears in more than 80 per cent of the cases in the North, as opposed to only 1 per cent in East Midland texts and 17 per cent in southern texts (Nevalainen & Raumolin-Brunberg 2000a: 304). This is in keeping with the dialect atlas evidence presented in the introduction to this section.

3.1.2 The Corpus of Early English Correspondence Having established an approximate timeline for the diffusion of -*s* between 1500 and 1700 based on the Helsinki Corpus, we can take a closer look at the process by analysing it in the larger Corpus of Early English Correspondence (CEEC, 1400–1800). As this resource was compiled according to sociolinguistic principles, it will take us further in the quest for the progress and consolidation of verbal -*s* as part of the present indicative paradigm in the South as well. The corpus includes rich metadata on each letter writer and recipient, enabling the researcher to focus on their social and regional origins, family background, education and mobility, for example. The composition of the CEEC is shown in Table 5.1, detailing the number of words, letter collections, letters and writers in each of its component parts. The 2.6 million-word original version of the corpus (1410–1680), with its 778 writers, provides the data for the analysis of verbal -*s* in this section (for bibliographical references to the individual text collections, see Nevalainen & Raumolin-Brunberg 2017: 256–267).

---

[7] For further details, see the Corpus Resource Database (CoRD) entry for the corpus at www.helsinki.fi/varieng/CoRD/corpora/CEEC/. The corpus was compiled by the sociolinguistics and language history project team under my direction, in collaboration with Helena Raumolin-Brunberg. Full citations for the corpora discussed in this chapter are provided in the Primary Sources section.

One of our compilation principles was to select a sizable number of writers from the North, East Anglia, the City of London and the Royal Court at Westminster to enable dialectal comparisons. The latter two were focused on for sociolinguistic reasons because of their different population bases: the City was inhabited by middling and lower social ranks and dominated by commercial interests, whereas the uppermost social ranks, including royalty, resided at Westminster, which was the seat of government and the centre of various political and cultural activities (e.g. Power 1985; see further Nevalainen & Raumolin-Brunberg 2017: 26–52).

Figure 5.1 presents a bird's eye view of the use of verbal -s in these four areas in forty-year periods between 1460 and 1681. All four show an S-shaped curve of diffusion, indicating that verbal -s became the dominant form in all four in the course of the first half of the seventeenth century. But the figure also suggests that there were some deviations in the process. First, since -s was a northern form, we would expect it to have continued there at a high frequency level throughout the period. This was the case in the first forty years, but it was followed by a notable drop in the first decades of the sixteenth century, when -s hardly appears at all in the other areas, East Anglia and the South, represented in the corpus by the City of London and the Royal Court. The fact that -s is not attested in the South is not unexpected as such – this is where -th would have

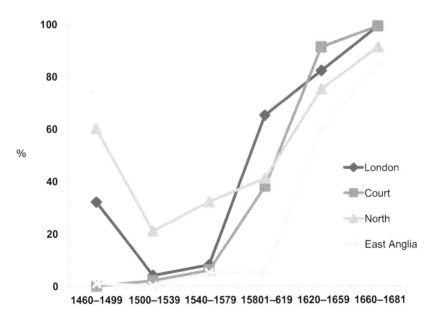

Figure 5.1 Frequency of verbal -s (vs. -th) in the CEEC.

been used – were it not for the first-period peak of -*s* in the City of London. It can be explained by the input of letter writers who were members of a merchant family with notable northern connections. This piece of information goes to show that immigrants enriched the linguistic feature pool of the City by introducing their own dialectal variants (Nevalainen & Raumolin-Brunberg 2017: 177–179).

On the other hand, the significant drop in -*s* use in the North can be understood against the backdrop of its non-use in London and at court: the southern -*th* was spreading to the North at the time. This is seen more clearly when we break the information in Figure 5.1 into two separate diagrams in Figures 5.2 and 5.3. Figure 5.2 presents the dominant -*th* form in the first two forty-year periods, and it clearly shows its increased frequency in the North against the stable background of the Court and East Anglia. This pattern of diffusion would be expected on the basis of what Puttenham (1589) had to say about the dialect hierarchy in the country. However, moving on to Figure 5.3, we can see a different pattern emerging from the 1540s onwards: the rise of -*s* at the expense of -*th* in all four areas studied, and especially in the City of London. The change is only incipient in the more remote and isolated East Anglia, but, as shown in Figure 5.1, it also picks up there in the early decades of the seventeenth century (on East Anglian English, see Nevalainen et al. 2001).

The question now arises of how this sudden U-turn came about. Since it is most notable in the City, we may look into demographic history for some explanations. It turns out that London was a city of immigrants. Against the background of high mortality in Early Modern London, the continued increase

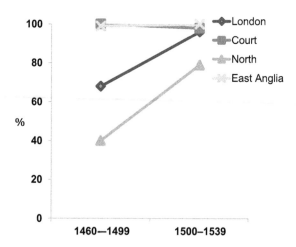

Figure 5.2 Frequency of -*th* (vs. -*s*) between 1460 and 1539.

Figure 5.3 Frequency of *-s* (vs. *-th*) between 1540 and 1619.

in its population was solely due to migration from areas where the birth rate was, unlike in London, higher than the death rate (Rappaport 1989: 76). Rappaport estimates that if London's death rate exceeded its birth rate by 10 per cent in the mid-sixteenth century, 700 immigrants were needed every year to maintain its population at 70,000, and another 700 to account for its net annual increase of 1 per cent. The records show that London's migration field was unusually large, and that one-third of the migrants who became citizens of London between 1551 and 1553, for example, came from the northern counties (Rappaport 1989: 77–80). Research also suggests that the social structure of London was fluid at the time and offered numerous opportunities for social encounters of various kinds (see further Nevalainen & Raumolin-Brunberg 2000a). Although sociohistorical and demographic evidence is indirect, it certainly goes part of the way to explaining the rapid increase in the use of *-s* in the capital region in the latter half of the sixteenth century.

3.1.3 Two Sixteenth-Century Londoners: Individual Variation Despite the fluidity of social structure, there was also distinct occupational and social status segregation in sixteenth-century London, which is why the City and Westminster are treated as two separate localities in the CEEC. It is shown that social status correlated with the selection of verbal *-s*, or, as the case may be, with the avoidance of it (Nevalainen & Raumolin-Brunberg 2017: 133–156, 202–214). Comparing two near-contemporary sixteenth-century Londoners will make these divergent patterns of usage more concrete. Both of them came

Figure 5.4 Thomas Cromwell (painted by Hans Holbein between 1532 and 1533; public domain via Wikimedia Commons).

from relatively humble origins but had vastly different life experiences – and choices of the verbal suffix.

Thomas Cromwell (ca. 1485–1540) was born in Putney, south-west of London, the son of a brewer, but he spent a significant part of his working life at the Royal Court in Westminster, as he rose, first, to become a secretary to Cardinal Wolsey and, later, King Henry VIII's chief minister. He is portrayed with his letters and papers in Figure 5.4. Cromwell was made Earl of Essex in 1540, the very year when, failing to please Henry in solving his marital problems, he was executed for charges of treason, heresy and corruption (Leithead 2009).

In his correspondence, Cromwell was a consistent -(e)th user. Example (1) comes from his official correspondence, a letter to the Duke of Norfolk, and example (2) from a private letter to his wife, Elizabeth. It is, however, noteworthy that the two verbs *have* and *do* are generally slower in taking the -s ending, even after it starts spreading to the South.[8]

1) And as touching your said order surely the kinges highnes **liketh** it veray well. And albeit that he **doubteth** not, but the persons whom ye haue appointed woll do euery thing to the best, yet neuertheles ... ye shall

---

[8] This is a case of *lexical diffusion* where the most frequent verbs adopt the incoming feature last. For Early Modern English, see e.g. Kytö (1993), Nevalainen (1996) and Raumolin-Brunberg (1996), and for Late Modern English e.g. Nevalainen (2018).

understonde that the Kinges highnes at this tyme **dothe** send doun certain of his Counsail to take order in that mater. (CEEC; 22 May 1537, Thomas Cromwell to the Duke of Norfolk; Cromwell PII,56)

2) Elyzabeth I commend me unto you and have sente you by this berer a fatt doo [doe], the one half whereof I pray you may be delyvered unto my gossyp mastres Smyth, and with the rest to use your pleasure. . . . And farther I pray you sende me word in wryting who **hathe** resorted unto you syns my departuer from you to speke with me. (CEEC; 29 November 1525, Thomas Cromwell to his wife; Cromwell PI,314)

The other sixteenth-century Londoner worth introducing in this context is Henry Machyn (1496/1498–1563), a merchant tailor and chronicler who lived and worked in the City of London. Little is known about the details of his early life except that he was admitted to the Merchant Taylors' Company in the City of London in 1530, and that he served as a clerk of his small parish of Holy Trinity-the-Less in Knightrider Street in the City (Mortimer 2008). No portrait of him survives, and it is likely that none was painted of him either.

As is shown by the passages quoted in (3) and (4) from his chronicle, Machyn was an -(e)s user, and he also used the suffix in verbs like *have*.

3) The xij day of aprell waſ sett in ye stoky[s at Westminster] markett a stranger ye wyche he **goyſ** all in red [& **says**] y^t he lord of all lord{s} & kyng of all kyng{s}
(The twelfth day of April was set in the stocks at Westminster Market a foreigner, the which he **goes** all in red and **says** that he is lord of all lords and king of all kings.)
(Machyn 1561-04-12; http://quod.lib.umich.edu/m/machyn)

4) The sam day waſ a goodly maygam at westmỹster
aſ **haſ** ben synef w^t gyant{s} moreſ pykeſ guneſ
& drumeſ & duwyll{s} & iij moreſ dansseſ & bagpypeſ
& wyell{s} & mony dysgyssyd & ye lord & ye lade of ye may
rod gorgyouſ ly w^t mynsterell{s} dyuer playng
(The same day was a goodly May game at Westminster as **has** been seen [since?], with giants, morris pikes, guns, and drums and devils and three morris dances and bagpipes and viols and many disguised. And the lord and the lady of the May rode gorgeously with minstrels divers playing.)
(Machyn 1555-06-03; http://quod.lib.umich.edu/m/machyn)

Machyn's *Chronicle* – or diary, as it is often called – has attracted some scholarly attention over the years. Labov (1972: 285), for example, argues that 'Machyn provides evidence for the lower-middle-class treatment of several important linguistic variables in 16th-century London English'. Among these features is verbal -*s*. However, as we have seen, the form is not common either in the City of London or at Westminster in the mid-sixteenth century. The idea that Machyn was one of a large number of immigrants who arrived in

London during this period receives support from the study Britton (2000) carried out using LALME. He localized Machyn's idiolect to south-west Yorkshire, also identifying him as an -*s* user. Mortimer (2008) traced the family name to north Leicestershire and found it likely that Machyn was born there. Either way, the Machyn evidence supports the argument that immigrants, numerous as they were, continued to use the linguistic features they had acquired early on and were largely responsible for the rapid increase in the use of verbal -*s* in the City of London in the second half of the sixteenth century.

3.2 Evidence from Grammarians and Spelling Reformers: Indexical Layering

We can shed more light on language-user choices by tracing the diffusion of verbal -*s* in indexical terms, that is, by looking for the various meanings that speakers have associated with this particular linguistic feature over time. Introducing a multilayered approach to indexicality, Silverstein (2003: 216–217) discusses, for example, 'Standard' and various 'non-Standard' forms of usage in terms of speaker-focused indexical order. In principle, such indexing processes are no different from speakers identifying different 'varieties' of ELF based on similarities in pronunciation, syntactic features and lexical choices that typically arise from contacts of a particular L1 with English (e.g. Mauranen 2017: 9).

Turning to contemporary sixteenth-century grammarians and spelling reformers for the indexical norms enregistered in the South at the time, a solid baseline is provided by John Hart (ca. 1501–1574), the most notable early English phonetician, who devised a reformed spelling system with the aim of regularizing the English orthography of his day. Hart was born near London, and he modelled the sound vs. letter/graph correspondences of his phonemic system according to the speech of the Court and its surroundings (Salmon 2004b). It therefore comes as no surprise that the dental fricative is the regular third-person present indicative ending in his works (Hart 1551, 1569, 1570), in both formal and informal contexts, with only a handful of instances of the alveolar -*s*, such as *methinks* and *belongs* (Danielsson 1963, II, 174–176).

Importantly, Hart also provides first-hand evidence of another process that coincided with the variation in the third-person suffixes, namely deletion of the unstressed vowel in the southern suffix -*eth*. This vowel syncope was another change diffusing from the North to the South and, besides the third-person singular indicative ending, it affected the -*es* suffixes in plural and genitive nouns, and -*ed* in the past tense and participle forms of verbs (see Nevalainen & Raumolin-Brunberg 2000b for an empirical study). Once the change had run its course, the unstressed vowel only remained in contexts where the noun or verb ended in a sibilant. Today when we talk about vowel insertion into such contexts, we are in fact referring to cases that never underwent vowel deletion.

Reflecting the northern origin of this vowel syncope, in his *Pamphlet for Grammar* (1586: 65), William Bullokar (ca. 1531–1609) mentions the use of -*s* as a poetic contraction of -*eth*. Like Hart, Bullokar was a southerner, born in Sussex (Salmon 2004a), and his observation provides a key to the complex scenario behind the change in the third-person singular indicative suffix in indexical terms: syncope of the unstressed vowel was, as a rule, more advanced in -(*e*)*s* than in -(*e*)*th*. As -(*e*)*s* was spreading rapidly in the South, Bullokar indexed the choice of suffix stylistically and suggested that the syncopated variant -*s* varied with the unsyncopated -*eth* in literary language.

As noted in Section 3.1.3, the diffusion of verbal -*s* was lexically conditioned in that such high-frequency verbs as *have* and *do* took much longer to change than other verbs in the South. Alexander Gill (1565–1635) continues to index *has* diatopically in his *Logonomia Anglica* (1619: 16, 117–118), and he refers to it as the northern variant of *hath*. Gill was born in Lincolnshire, but his career culminated in becoming the headmaster of St Paul's School in London (Campbell 2004). However, reflecting the parallel process of unstressed vowel deletion that accompanied verbal -*s*, he adds that, in other verbs, -*eth* can shorten to -*s* or -*z,* and become -*ez* after a sibilant (1619: 52). As Figure 5.1 indicates, by the early seventeenth century, verbal -*s* had become the norm in personal correspondence both in London and at court. By then -*eth* had receded to a stylistically marked form and continued to be used as an elevated or metrical variant in Gill's reformed spelling.

Finally, Richard Hodges, a London schoolmaster and advocate of vernacular literacy (d. 1657; Hodges 2004), gives further evidence for the stylistic indexing of the two variant forms in *A special help to orthographie* (1643: 26–27). He notes that, while -(*e*)*th* can appear in written language ('with the Learned in their Writings') and in print ('many wel-Printed Books'), it is pronounced -*s* or -*z* in everyday speech.

> Therefore, whensoever *eth*, cometh in the end of any word, wee may pronounce it sometimes as *s*, & sometimes like *z*, as in these words, namely, in *bolteth* it, and *holdeth* it, which are commonly pronounc't, as if they were writen thus, *bolts* it, and *holds* it: save onely in such words, where either c, s, sh, ch, g, or x went before it: as in *graceth, pleaseth, washeth, matcheth, rageth, taxeth*: for, these must still remaine as two syllables. Howbeit, if men did take notice, how they use to speak, in their ordinary speech one to another, they might plainly perceive, that in stead of *graceth*, they say *graces*, and so they pronounce al other words of this kinde, accordingly. (Hodges 1643: 26–27)

Hodges also testifies to stylistic indexing in spoken language, as in *The English primrose* (1644) he transcribes liturgical speech using the syllabic suffix with the dental fricative. Later scholarship finds Hodges' usage overall to be 'real and unaffected' but 'in many ways somewhat advanced' (Dobson 1957, vol. I: 186).

In sum, despite Hart's testimony in the mid-sixteenth century, syncope failed to systematically diffuse to the southern third-person suffix *-eth*, which retained the unstressed vowel and was in due course replaced by the syncopated *-s* (and by the unsyncopated *-es* in sibilant-final verbs) in ordinary speech. The pronunciation of the suffix harmonized with the preceding verb-final sound and was pronounced, as today, voiced /z/ after vowels and voiced consonants, and voiceless /s/ after voiceless consonants (for further discussion of orthoepic, orthographic and phonotactic evidence, see Dobson 1957, Kytö 1993: 129–130, Nevalainen & Raumolin-Brunberg 2000b: 236–238, Walker 2017: 138–140).

3.3 Evidence from Early English Books Online and the Tail End of the Process

The final stages of the diffusion of verbal *-s* in the seventeenth century can be traced by resorting to Early English Books Online (EEBO), a very large digital database that contains facsimiles of about 132,000 titles printed in England, Ireland, Scotland, Wales and British North America between 1473 and 1700.[9] The first release of its full-text version (EEBO-TCP) is freely available and consists of some 25,000 texts. It also comes with an n-gram viewer, which enables one to search the distribution of individual words over time in both original and normalized spelling. The latter option is used in Figure 5.5, which shows the crossing over of *hath* as opposed to *has* and *doth* as opposed to *does* towards the end of the seventeenth century: both take place in print at the turn of the eighteenth century, in *have* slightly earlier than in *do*.

In personal correspondence (CEEC, CEECE) *has* and *does* become the majority forms earlier, in the last two decades of the seventeenth century, and the change is completed in the first half of the eighteenth century (Nevalainen 2018: 103–105). In mainstream speech the change is no doubt even earlier (Walker 2017: 142–143). But this is not the whole story in regional terms, as *hath* and *doth* survived as regional forms in south-western dialects up until the nineteenth century (Wright 1898–1905), and so became, in turn, regional dialect indicators.

---

[9] See https://eebo.chadwyck.com/about/about.htm and www.textcreationpartnership.org/tcp-eebo/ . Altogether some 60,000 texts have been keyed in and are included in the second release of the database at the time of writing. The EEBO n-gram viewer is available from http://earlyprint.wustl.edu/eebotcpngrambrowser.html.

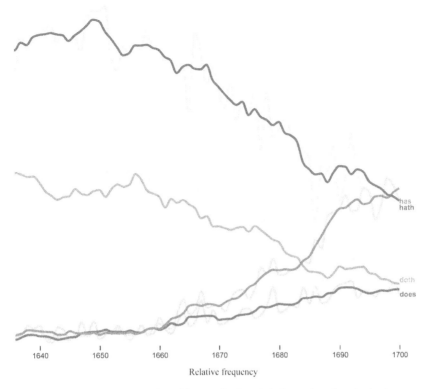

Figure 5.5 Frequencies of *has* vs. *hath* and *doth* vs. *does* in print in the seventeenth century (EEBO).

3.4 Current Media Evidence

As we have seen, the traditional, historical third-person form *-(e)th* was largely replaced by *-(e)s* between the fifteenth and seventeenth centuries in mainstream usage. However, journalese and more recently the digital media have given the recessive *-th* suffix a new lease of life. It is used as a stylistic stereotype with archaic and/or humorous connotations in contexts such as those in (5) and (6).

(5) But what the tabloids **giveth** they may also **taketh** away, and Charles must watch his step. (*Time*, 19 June 2000)

(6) **Cometh** the hour, **cometh** the man with the cheeky grin. (*The Times*, 29 October 2007)

'Cometh the hour' has become something of an internet meme, with endless variations of the kind 'the iceman cometh', 'the taxman cometh', 'the iceberg cometh' and 'cometh English team, cometh uncertainty'.[10] The verb form *cometh* on its own is also of common occurrence. Searching, for example, the electronic catalogue of the National Library of Australia, we get more than 900 hits for books that contain it (Jeffrey Archer's *Cometh the Hour* topping the list), and more than 45,000 results for newspapers and similar content.[11] The tail end of a linguistic change can stretch a long way.

4   Alternative Ways of Saying 'The Same Thing'[12]

Discussing accommodation in social interaction in ELF contexts, Mauranen (2017: 13–14) singles out processes such as morphological regularization and a preference for the most frequent vocabulary as indications of structural simplification. A prototypical instance of morphological regularization is the common use in ELF of the suffixless form in the third-person present-tense indicative (e.g. Jenkins et al. 2011: 289). In morphosyntactic terms, the replacement of the third-person singular *-(e)th* by the originally northern *-(e)s* discussed in Section 3.1 was also the result of a process of simplification in the Early Modern English dialect contact situation. This section introduces the original, more complex northern English system of present-tense verbal inflections – the so-called Northern Subject Rule (Section 4.1) – and then moves on to consider the range of alternative expressions found in varieties of English around the world today (Section 4.2).

4.1   The Northern Subject Rule

We have so far traced the history of verbal *-s* in non-localizable mainstream usage, or *Communis dialectus*, as Alexander Gill (1619) called the language of educated upper social ranks in distinction to country dialects. There was also a third option that was used alongside *-th* and *-s*, namely the suffixless or zero variant. In the Helsinki Corpus data it was a distinct minority form, covering fewer than 2 per cent of the cases (29 instances, to be precise, compared to 1,606 of the total of *-th* and *-s*; Kytö 1993: 118). Example (5) illustrates this option in a letter written by Katherine Paston, a Norfolk gentlewoman, to her teenage son in 1626. In the first sentence she uses *-s* (*remembers*) in the first

---

[10] 'The iceman cometh' is an allusion to Eugene O'Neill's 1939 play of that name and has biblical undertones. It has been widely used in the press and occurs, for example, with reference to the Finnish Formula 1 driver Kimi Räikkönen in a *Guardian* sports page headline in 2011 (www .theguardian.com/sport/2011/nov/29/kimi-raikkonen-lotus-renault-gp). I would like to thank my colleague Mark Shackleton for drawing my attention to these parallels.
[11] See https://trove.nla.gov.au/result?q=Cometh&l-availability=y (Accessed 12 February 2019).
[12] This is an often quoted part of Labov's formulation of the principle of total accountability in variationist sociolinguistics (Labov 1969: 738).

verb but the suffixless form in the second (*take*), with the same subject *thy father*; the zero form reappears in the second sentence (*remember*), with *thy brother* as the subject. On the basis of this example it is difficult to detect a pattern regulating her choice of the zero alternative, which had been attested in East Anglia since the fifteenth century (Bailey et al. 1989, Nevalainen & Raumolin-Brunberg 2017: 179).

5) thy father **remembers** his loue to the and **take** thy wrightinge to him very kindly: thy brother **remember** his louingest loue to the. (CEEC, Katherine Paston, 1626; PastonK, 90)

However, such patterns did exist. In the North, the use of the zero variant could follow the Northern Subject Rule (NSR), which constrains the choice of the verbal inflection depending on the subject of the sentence and its proximity to the verb: full NP subjects favour the inflected form in the singular as well as in the plural, whereas pronoun subjects favour the zero form (*NPs Vs, they V*). With pronoun subjects, the choice is also sensitive to coordinated verbs: if the pronoun subject is not repeated (i.e. the subject pronoun is not adjacent to the verb), the second verb is inflected (*they V and Vs*). These principles are illustrated in examples (6)–(8), drawn from Queen Elizabeth I's translation of Boethius' *De Consolatione Philosophiae* (quoted from Schendl 1996: 150–151). These examples show that the pattern was also found in the South but, as the use of *giue* ('give') instead of *giues* ('gives') in (8) indicates, the rule was not followed consistently.

6) for **wicked men giues** this good turn to dignitie, that **they spot** them with their own infection (Queen Elizabeth I, 1593, *Boethius* 50.23)

7) For if neither they can doo that **they promise** & **wantes** greatest good. (Queen Elizabeth I, 1593, *Boethius* 48.11]

8) My **maydes knowes** their lady, with me **they com**, & whan I parte, **giue** place. (Queen Elizabeth I, 1593, *Boethius* 23.18)

Schendl (1996: 153–156) attributes the presence of these patterns in the capital to migration from the North and the northern Midlands, where the pattern was also productive. In essence, the NSR can be traced back to Late Old Northumbrian (Klemola 2000, Pietsch 2005: 45–62, Cole 2019). However, only the subject constraint is attested, mostly in plural contexts, in the South in the fifteenth and sixteenth centuries (Bailey et al. 1989, Wright 2002). The pattern is found in Shakespeare, with around 10 per cent of the plural NP subjects showing the effect in the *First Folio* (Schendl 2000). As the constraint was not generalized in the South, northern contact influence is only systematically represented in the third-person singular by the replacement of *-th* by *-s* to mark this person and number distinction in the present indicative. But, as Schendl (1996: 153) notes, the rise of verbal -*s* in the singular in the South might have provided some support to the presence of the more complex northern pattern between 1580 and the 1630s.

4.2 Non-Standard Alternatives Worldwide

Tackling the issue of defining ELF, Jenkins et al. (2011: 284) write that, because of the general implications of the worldwide spread of English, '[n]o definition of ELF could be complete without considering its similarities to and differences from the well-established World Englishes paradigm'. This section provides a brief survey of the major Subject–Verb agreement patterns found in Englishes around the world. Other patterns are also reported, and there is a good deal of variation (Pietsch 2005: 13–15, see also Buchstaller et al. 2013), as one might also expect to find in ELF.

The NSR pattern, agreement sensitive to subject type (*Birds sings* vs. *they sing*), continues to be found in some regional varieties of English around the world. According to the Electronic World Atlas of Varieties of English (eWAVE, Kortmann & Lunkenheimer 2013), this pattern continues to be pervasive in Orkney and Shetland English in Scotland, and in Ozark English, which is a rural, working-class variety spoken in the highlands of north-western Arkansas and in south-western Missouri in the United States. It is also found in Bahamian and Appalachian English, and in some south-east American enclave dialects. In general, the varieties in which it occurs are either traditional L1 dialects in Scotland or remote high-contact L1 dialects in the USA (see Figure 5.6).

Another common pattern across varieties of English is generalizing -*s* to all persons (e.g. *I sees the house*). It is pervasive in Newfoundland English in Canada and can be found in Orkney, Shetland, Irish, Welsh and Manx varieties, as well as in south-eastern English dialects. In the USA it occurs in colloquial American English, earlier African American Vernacular English and Bahamian and south-east American enclave dialects. It also occurs in Cape Flats English. The varieties that display this alternative are again either high-contact L1 varieties or traditional L1 varieties (see Figure 5.7).

The third pattern, invariant present-tense forms due to zero marking for the third-person singular (*So she show up and say 'What's up?'*), presents a different profile and, apart from East Anglian English, consists largely of pidgin and creole varieties, as well as indigenized L2 varieties. This highly common pattern, shown in Figure 5.8, is pervasive, for example, in the Hawai'i, Gullah, Bahamian, Belizean, Jamaican, Trinidadian and Barbadian creoles, in Krio and in Guyanese, Cameroon and Ghanaian pidgins. It is also

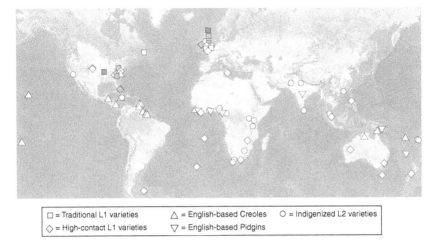

Figure 5.6 Agreement sensitive to subject type (eWAVE Feature 181; the darkest markers show where the feature is pervasive or obligatory).

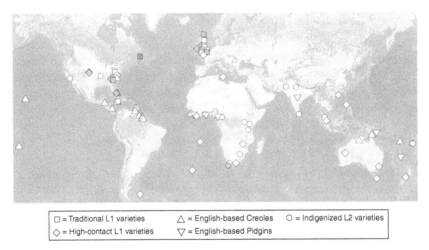

Figure 5.7 Third-person -*s* generalized to all persons (eWAVE Feature 171; the darkest markers show where the feature is pervasive or obligatory).

found in Hong Kong and Malaysian English, in Australian Aboriginal English and in the Torres Strait, Bislama, Pitcairn and Fiji varieties of English. As suggested by the research review conducted by Jenkins et al. (2011: 289), it is also pervasive in ELF.

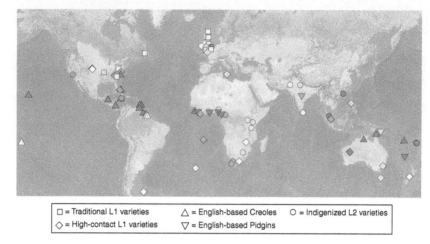

Figure 5.8 Invariant zero marking (eWAVE Feature 170; the darkest markers show where the feature is pervasive or obligatory).

5 Discussion and Conclusion

One of the aims in this chapter was to look for commonalities between linguistic specializations as different as ELF and the historical study of Standard English. My extended case study shows that a natural common ground can be found in certain key concepts and their application, including the prominent roles played in both fields by processes of *language and dialect contact*, *variation* and *structural simplification*, particularly one form of it, *morphological regularization*.[13] I will conclude by assessing all three in the light of my case study.

If we approach Standard English in ELF terms as a dynamic adaptive process, the short answer to the question posed in the title of this chapter is that, historically, it is not the property of any one group of speakers, although it has been appropriated as such by many. At one point, the notion of the 'best speech' was associated with the Royal Court, as Puttenham (1589) suggested. Two hundred years later, John Adams (1780; see Taylor 2018) maintained that, although American English should be further refined and regulated, it had already reached the status of the most respectable and the most universally read and spoken language in the world, and was therefore worthy of being promoted as a lingua franca. Indexing language socially by its speakers, the

---

[13] One must note that, although a degree of simplification is attested in my case study of verbal *-s*, this observation cannot be generalized to all aspects of Standard English (see e.g. Trudgill 2009: 309–315).

numerous accounts of this kind are also careful to specify those whose language Standard English – or 'best speech', in Puttenham's case – is not (Milroy & Milroy 1999).

It follows from the dynamic processual history of Standard English that it has no single ancestor dialect, which makes the 'whose language?' question even trickier to answer diachronically. The different levels of sociolinguistic research from macro to micro offer various historical lines of inquiry to follow (Nevalainen 2015). Based on textual and demographic evidence, research has established that verbal -(*e*)*s* diffused from the North of England to the South and eventually replaced the original southern suffix -(*e*)*th*. In the capital region, the process was associated with migration and social stratification: from the mid-sixteenth century onwards, -(*e*)*s* was typically promoted by members of the mobile merchant community in the City, and it was only adopted with some delay by the influential representatives of the upper social ranks and administrators active at the Royal Court in Westminster. As the form diffused from the spoken language, it took a long time to make its way not only into the written medium, and print in particular, but also into formal spoken contexts such as liturgical speech. Having northern origins, the form was initially indexed both stylistically and socially in the South, especially in high-frequency verbs such as *have*, which retained their southern -*th* form much longer than other verbs.

Analysing the choice of alternative expressions at the micro level of the individual, variation is the norm rather than the exception when language change is under way in the community. Katherine Paston, discussed in Section 4.1, may be exceptional in that she resorts to all three options available to her at the time, but she is certainly not alone in choosing to use more than one variant form. Analysing the proportion of individuals who used both -*th* and -*s* in their personal correspondence between 1560 and 1659, we find that 45 per cent of the writers continued to have a variable grammar in the last twenty-year period (1640–1659), when verbal -*s* had already been established as the majority form in the speech community (see Figure 5.1). When the range of variation was at its widest in the community in the decades around 1600, the proportion of writers with a variable grammar was as high as 60 per cent (Nevalainen & Raumolin-Brunberg 2017: 97).[14] Although only two alternative expressions were studied here, that is enough to show that the choice was not one of either/or, but often enough of more-or-less.

The history of verbal -*s* nicely illustrates the sociolinguistic generalization, also widely attested in ELF communication, that language and dialect contact

---

[14] If a person used the minority form in 10 per cent of the cases or fewer, we interpreted them as having an invariable grammar; that is, an occasional occurrence of the minority variant, either -*s* or -*th*, as the case might be, did not alter the overall impression.

often leads to loss of syntactic complexity. The NSR was never generalized in the South, although the subject constraint triggering the suffixless form after full NP subjects and -*s* after pronouns has been detected in the South as a minority feature, especially in the plural in the sixteenth and early seventeenth centuries. Looking at the varieties of English worldwide today, we find that this system of Subject–Verb agreement is recessive, although it continues to be documented in some traditional European and North American L1 varieties.

The generalization of -*s* to all persons occurs variably in high-contact and traditional L1 varieties. This alternative only marks tense and mood, but not person, and it makes a systematic contrast to the regular past tense marker -*ed*. A simpler but equally regular alternative, found in a wide variety of English-based pidgins and creoles and in indigenized L2 varieties, is to use suffixless forms in all persons. Besides the third-person number contrast, this system neutralizes the mood contrast between the indicative and the subjunctive, and only retains the tense contrast.

This typological option of regularizing the system of zero inflection in the present tense is also common in ELF communication. One of the additional gains for users of this alternative is that it also removes the complication of having to insert a vowel before -*s* to sibilant-final verbs – a historical remnant of the Middle English system that uniformly retained the unstressed vowel in the suffix. We can therefore conclude that, in retaining verbal -*s*, code fixation has made Standard English a less-than-optimal vehicle for lingua franca use. However, as code fixation itself is also a process, it can only slow down ongoing linguistic change, not prevent it. As Trudgill points out, Standard English has undergone very considerable regularization, 'but it has progressed *less far* along the expected regularisation path' (2009: 313, original emphasis). Standard English is more irregular than non-standard dialects, because, Trudgill argues, 'certain forms of regularisation have not *yet* taken place' (2009: 313). It remains to be seen whether verbal -*s* will be among the targets of contact-induced regularization in Standard English, making it more ELF-like in the future.

Primary Sources

CEEC = The Corpus of Early English Correspondence. Department of Modern Languages, University of Helsinki. Compiled by Terttu Nevalainen (project leader), Helena Raumolin-Brunberg, Samuli Kaislaniemi, Mikko Laitinen, Minna Nevala, Arja Nurmi, Minna Palander-Collin, Tanja Säily, Anni Sairio. www.helsinki.fi/varieng/CoRD/corpora/CEEC/.

EEBO = Early English Books Online Text Creation Partnership, phase I: Oxford, Oxfordshire and Ann Arbor, Michigan, 2015. https://github.com/textcreationpartnership/Texts

HC = The Helsinki Corpus of English Texts. Department of Modern Languages, University of Helsinki. Compiled by Matti Rissanen (project leader), Merja Kytö (project secretary); Leena Kahlas-Tarkka, Matti Kilpiö (Old English); Saara Nevanlinna, Irma Taavitsainen (Middle English); Terttu Nevalainen, Helena Raumolin-Brunberg (Early Modern English). www.helsinki.fi/varieng/CoRD/corpora/HelsinkiCorpus/.

Machyn = *A London Provisioner's Chronicle, 1550–1563, by Henry Machyn: Manuscript, Transcription, and Modernization*. An electronic scholarly edition created by Richard W. Bailey, Marilyn Miller and Colette Moore. Ann Arbor: Michigan Publishing. https://quod.lib.umich.edu/m/machyn/.

REFERENCES

Anderwald, Lieselotte. 2016. *Language between Description and Prescription: Verbs and Verb Categories in Nineteenth-Century Grammars of English*. Oxford & New York: Oxford University Press.

Bailey, Guy, Natalie Maynor & Patricia Cukor-Avila. 1989. Variation in subject–verb concord in Early Modern English. *Language Variation and Change* 1(3), 285–300.

Barber, Charles. 1997. *Early Modern English*. 2nd ed. Edinburgh: Edinburgh University Press.

Britton, Derek. 2000. Henry Machyn, Axel Wijk and the case of the wrong Riding: The south-west Yorkshire character of the language of Henry Machyn's diary. *Neuphilologische Mitteilungen* 101(4), 571–596.

Buchstaller, Isabelle, Karen P. Corrigan, Anders Holmberg, Patrick Honeybone & Warren Maguire. 2013. T-to-R and the Northern Subject Rule: Questionnaire-based spatial, social and structural linguistics. *English Language and Linguistics* 17(1), 85–128.

Bullokar, William. 1586. *William Bullokarz Pamphlet for Grammar*. London: Edmund Bollifant.

Campbell, Gordon. 2004. Gil [Gill], Alexander, the elder. In *Oxford Dictionary of National Biography*. Oxford: Oxford University Press. https://doi.org/10.1093/ref:odnb/10729.

Cole, Marcelle. 2019. Subject and adjacency effects in the Old Northumbrian gloss to the *Lindisfarne Gospels*. *English Language and Linguistics* 23(1), 131–154. doi: 10.1017/S1360674317000338.

Danielsson, Bror. 1955, 1963. *John Hart's Works on English Orthography and Pronunciation (1551, 1569, 1570)*, Part 1, *Biographical and Bibliographical Introductions – Texts and Index Verborum*; Part 2, *Phonology*. Stockholm: Almqvist & Wiksell.

Danielsson, Bror & Arvid Gabrielson (eds.). 1972. *Alexander Gill's Logonomia Anglica (1619)*. 2 vols. (Stockholm Studies in English 26, 27). Stockholm: Almqvist & Wiksell.

Dobson, Eric J. 1957. *English Pronunciation 1500–1700*. Vol. 1. Oxford: Clarendon Press.

Ferguson, Charles. 1996. Variation and drift: Loss of agreement in Germanic. In T. Huebner (ed.), *Sociolinguistic Perspectives: Papers on Language in Society, 1959–1994*, 241–260. Oxford: Oxford University Press.

Fox, Adam. 2003. *Oral and Literate Culture in England, 1500–1700*. Oxford: Clarendon Press.

Gil, Alexander. 1619. *Logonomia Anglica*. London: J. Beale.

Görlach, Manfred. 1991. *Introduction to Early Modern English*. Cambridge: Cambridge University Press.

Hart, John. 1551. *The Opening of the Unreasonable Writing of Our Inglish Toung*, ed. by Bror Danielsson (1963). Stockholm: Almqvist & Wiksell.

1569. *An orthographie*. London: W. Serres.

1570. *Methode or Comfortable Beginning for All Vnlearned*. London: Henrie Denham.

Hodges, Richard. 1643. *A Special Help to Orthographie: Or, The True-vvriting of English*. London: Richard Cotes.

1644. *The English primrose*. London: Richard Cotes.

Hodges, Richard E. 2004. Hodges, Richard. In *Oxford Dictionary of National Biography*. Oxford: Oxford University Press. https://doi.org/10.1093/ref:odnb/65660.

Holmqvist, Erik. 1922. *On the History of the English Present Inflections, Particularly -th and -s*. Heidelberg: Carl Winter.

Hope, Jonathan. 2000. Rats, bats, sparrows and dogs: biology, linguistics and the nature of Standard English. In Laura Wright (ed.), *The Development of Standard English, 1300–1800: Theories, Descriptions, Conflicts*, 46–56. Cambridge: Cambridge University Press.

Hynninen, Niina & Anna Solin. 2017. Language norms in ELF. In Jennifer Jenkins, Will Baker & Martin Dewey (eds.), *The Routledge Handbook of English as a Lingua Franca*, 267–278. Abingdon & New York: Routledge.

Jenkins, Jennifer. 2017. The future of English as a lingua franca? In Jennifer Jenkins, Will Baker & Martin Dewey (eds.), *The Routledge Handbook of English as a Lingua Franca*, 594–605. Abingdon & New York: Routledge.

Jenkins, Jennifer, Alessia Cogo & Martin Dewey. 2011. Review of developments in research into English as a lingua franca. *Language Teaching* 44(3), 281–315. doi: 10.1017/S0261444811000115.

Klemola, Juhani. 2000. The origins of the Northern Subject Rule: A case of early contact? In Hildegard L. C. Tristram (ed.), *The Celtic Englishes II*, 329–346. Heidelberg: Carl Winter.

Kortmann, Bernd & Kerstin Lunkenheimer (eds.). 2013. *The Electronic World Atlas of Varieties of English*. Leipzig: Max Planck Institute for Evolutionary Anthropology. http://ewave-atlas.org (Accessed 20 February 2019).

Kytö, Merja. 1993. Third-person present singular verb inflection in early British and American English. *Language Variation and Change* 5, 113–139.

Labov, William. 1969. Contraction, deletion, and inherent variability of the English copula. *Language* 45(4), 715–762.

1972. *Sociolinguistic Patterns*. Philadelphia, PA: University of Pennsylvania Press.

1977. On the use of the present to explain the past. In Adam Makkai, Valerie Becker Makkai & Luigi Heilmann (eds.), *Linguistics at the Crossroads*, 226–261. Lake Bluff, IL: Jupiter Press.

2007. Transmission and diffusion. *Language* 83(2), 344–387.

Leithead, Howard. 2009. Cromwell, Thomas, Earl of Essex. In *Oxford Dictionary of National Biography*. Oxford: Oxford University Press. https://doi.org/10.1093/ref:odnb/6769.

Mauranen, Anna. 2017. Conceptualising ELF. In Jennifer Jenkins, Will Baker & Martin Dewey (eds.), *The Routledge Handbook of English as a Lingua Franca*, 7–24. Abingdon & New York: Routledge.

McIntosh, Angus, M. L. Samuels & Michael Benskin. 1986. *A Linguistic Stlas of Late Mediaeval English*. Vol. I. Aberdeen: Aberdeen University Press.

Milroy, James & Lesley Milroy. 1999. *Authority in Language: Investigating Standard English*. 3rd ed., repr. 2012. London & New York: Routledge.

Mortimer, Ian. 2008. Machyn [Machin], Henry. In *Oxford Dictionary of National Biography*. Oxford: Oxford University Press. https://doi.org/10.1093/ref:odnb/17531.

Nevalainen, Terttu. 1996. Gender difference. In Terttu Nevalainen & Helena Raumolin-Brunberg (eds.), *Sociolinguistics and Language History: Studies Based on the Corpus of Early English Correspondence,* 77–91. Amsterdam & Atlanta: Rodopi.

2003. English. In Ana Deumert & Wim Vandenbussche (eds.), *Germanic Standardizations: Past to Present* (Impact: Studies in Language and Society 18), 127–156. Amsterdam/Philadelphia: John Benjamins.

2006. *An Introduction to Early Modern English*. Edinburgh: Edinburgh University Press.

2014. Norms and usage in seventeenth-century English. In Gijsbert Rutten, Rik Vosters & Wim Vandenbussche (eds.), *Norms and Usage in Language History, 1600–1900: A Sociolinguistic and Comparative Perspective*, 103–128. Amsterdam & Philadelphia: John Benjamins.

2015. What are historical sociolinguistics? *Journal of Historical Sociolinguistics* 1(2), 243–269. doi: 10.1515/jhsl-2015-0014.

2018. Going to completion: The diffusion of verbal -*s*. In Terttu Nevalainen, Minna Palander-Collin & Tanja Säily (eds.), *Patterns of Change in 18th-Century English: A Sociolinguistic Approach* (Advances in Historical Sociolinguistics 8). Amsterdam & Philadelphia, PA: John Benjamins.

Nevalainen, Terttu & Helena Raumolin-Brunberg. 2000a. The changing role of London on the linguistic map of Tudor and Stuart England. In Dieter Kastovsky & Arthur Mettinger (eds.), *The History of English in a Social Context: A Contribution to Historical Sociolinguistics*, 279–337. Berlin & New York: Mouton de Gruyter.

2000b. The third-person singular -(*e*)*s* and -(*e*)*th* revisited: The morphophonemic hypothesis. In Christiane Dalton-Puffer & Nikolaus Ritt (eds.), *Words: Structure, Meaning, Function. A Festschrift for Dieter Kastovsky* (Trends in Linguistics 130), 235–248. Berlin & New York: Mouton de Gruyter.

2017. *Historical Sociolinguistics: Language Change in Tudor and Stuart England*. 2nd ed. London: Routledge.

Nevalainen, Terttu, Helena Raumolin-Brunberg & Peter Trudgill. 2001. Chapters in the social history of East Anglian English: The case of the third-person singular. In Jacek Fisiak & Peter Trudgill (eds.), *East Anglian English*, 187–204. Cambridge: Boydell and Brewer.

Pietsch, Lukas. 2005. *Variable Grammars: Verbal Agreement in Northern Dialects of English*. Tübingen: Max Niemeyer Verlag.

Power, M. J. 1985. John Stow and his London. *Journal of Historical Geography* 11(1), 1–20.

Puttenham, George. 1589. *The arte of English poesie contriued into three bookes: The first of poets and poesie, the second of proportion, the third of ornament*. London: Printed by Richard Field. Ann Arbor, MI: University of Michigan, Digital Library Production Service 2011 April (TCP phase 2).

Rappaport, Steve. 1989. *Worlds within Worlds: Structures of Life in Sixteenth-Century London*. Cambridge: Cambridge University Press.

Raumolin-Brunberg, Helena. 1996. Apparent time. In Terttu Nevalainen & Helena Raumolin-Brunberg (eds.), *Sociolinguistics and Language History: Studies Based on the Corpus of Early English Correspondence*, 93–109. Amsterdam & Atlanta: Rodopi.

Salmon, Vivian. 2004a. Bullokar, William. *Oxford Dictionary of National Biography*. Oxford: Oxford University Press. https://doi.org/10.1093/ref:odnb/3926.

2004b. Hart, John. *Oxford Dictionary of National Biography*. Oxford: Oxford University Press. https://doi.org/10.1093/ref:odnb/12482.

Schendl, Herbert. 1996. The 3rd plural present indicative in Early Modern English: Variation and linguistic contact. In Derek Britton (ed.), *English Historical Linguistics, 1994: Papers from the 8th International Conference on English Historical Linguistics*, 143–160. Amsterdam: John Benjamins.

2000. The third person present plural in Shakespeare's First Folio: A case of interaction of morphology and syntax? In Christiane Dalton-Puffer & Nikolaus Ritt (eds.), *Words: Structure, Meaning, Function. A Festschrift for Dieter Kastovsky* (Trends in Linguistics 130), 263–276. Berlin & New York: Mouton de Gruyter.

Schwarz-Stiglbauer, Margit. 2013. Whose language is it anyway?. *Scilog: Culture and Society* 4(13). https://scilog.fwf.ac.at/en/humanities-and-social-sciences/728/whose-language-is-it-anyway (Accessed 20 February 2019).

Seidlhofer, Barbara. 2017. Standard English and the dynamics of ELF variation. In Jennifer Jenkins, Will Baker & Martin Dewey (eds.), 85–100. *The Routledge Handbook of English as a Lingua Franca*. Abingdon & New York: Routledge.

Silverstein, Michael. 2003. Indexical order and the dialectics of sociolinguistic life. *Language and Communication* 23(3), 193–229.

Smith, Jeremy. 1996. *An Historical Study of English*. London & New York: Routledge.

Strang, Barbara M. H. 1970. *A History of English*. London & New York: Methuen.

Taylor, C. James (ed.). 2018. *Founding Families: Digital Editions of the Papers of the Winthrops and the Adamses*. Vol. 10. Boston: Massachusetts Historical Society. www.masshist.org/publications/adams-papers/index.php/volume/ADMS-06-10 (Accessed 21 January 2019).

Trudgill, Peter. 2009. Vernacular universals and the sociolinguistic typology of English dialects. In Markku Filppula, Juhani Klemola & Heli Paulasto (ed.), *Vernacular Universals and Language Contact*, 304–322. New York & London: Routledge.

Walker, Terry. 2017. 'he saith y^t he thinkes y^t': Linguistic factors influencing third person singular present tense verb inflection in Early Modern English depositions. *Studia Neophilologica* 89(1), 133–146. doi: 10.1080/00393274.2016.1190298.

Widdowson, Henry. 2017. Historical perspectives on ELF. In Jennifer Jenkins, Will Baker & Martin Dewey (eds.), *The Routledge Handbook of English as a Lingua Franca*, 101–112. Abingdon, UK & New York: Routledge.

Wright, Joseph. 1898–1905. *The English Dialect Dictionary*. 6 vols. Oxford: Henry Frowde.

Wright, Laura. 2002. Third-person plural present tense markers in London prisoners' depositions, 1562–1623. *American Speech* 77(3), 242–263.

6 Beyond Language Change
ELF and the Study of Sociolinguistic Change

Janus Mortensen

1   Introduction

Language change has been a key area of interest in sociolinguistics since the foundation of the discipline. Recently, however, it has been suggested that the sociolinguistic notion of change should be broadened to include phenomena that are not necessarily linguistic as such, but which nevertheless concern reconfigurations of language–society relations, for instance in the shifting language ideological value ascribed to particular language varieties in the face of sociocultural change. This broader concept of change, which represents an attempt to pursue a critical interest in social change as well as language change, without giving priority to either of the two sides of the sociolinguistic endeavor, has been referred to as sociolinguistic change (Coupland 2009; Androutsopoulos 2014; Mortensen et al. 2017). In this chapter, I suggest that the development of a wider concept of sociolinguistic change is also of relevance to the study of English as a lingua franca (ELF).

Based on the assumption that the widespread use of English as a lingua franca is likely to lead to increased linguistic variation and variability, language change has been an important area of research in ELF studies since the early days of the field. The Corpus of English as a Lingua Franca in Helsinki (ELFA 2008), the Vienna-Oxford International Corpus of English in Vienna (VOICE 2009), and, more recently, the Asian Corpus of English (ACE 2014) in Hong Kong have been key in the development of the field because they have allowed researchers to test some of the early hypotheses put forward about language variation and change in and through ELF (Seidlhofer 2004: 220), and have helped to produce rich descriptive accounts of how English is "shaped by non-native speakers" (Mauranen 2012, cf. Mauranen 2016).

The interest in language change is reflected in the recent *Handbook of English as a Lingua Franca* (Jenkins et al. 2018), where the concept of "change" – to the extent that it is explicitly touched upon – is commonly discussed in relation to language change (see e.g. chapters by Mauranen 2018; Ranta 2018; Pitzl 2018a; Jenkins 2018). Language change is not the *only* context in which change is addressed in the *Handbook*. Change is also explicitly discussed in several other connections, for example in relation to changing norms for English language teaching, language teaching materials, language attitudes, and language assessment, just as political change, technological change, changing patterns of transnational mobility, and so on are present as an implicit backdrop in many chapters. Nevertheless, on the whole, it seems fair to say that there is no easily discernible orientation towards change as social change in the *Handbook*, just as the interplay between social change and language change is rarely explicitly thematized as a topic of specific theoretical concern.

As we take stock and look forward after ten years of fruitful academic exchanges at annual ELF conferences,[1] I believe it is important to acknowledge that sociolinguistic research that takes an interest in processes of change and the use of English as a lingua franca should not be – and indeed is not – limited to studying "English" as the object of change. It is equally relevant for the field to study the use of English as a lingua franca as the companion – or even possibly the agent – of change *beyond language*, as part of wider processes of social change. This is the perspective that I would like to pursue in this chapter, drawing on research into the internationalization of Danish higher education. While by no means unique, university internationalization offers a good and relatively well-researched case of social change that shows how the increased use of English as a lingua franca is often accompanied by changing language ideological orientations, changing discursive practices, and changes in social norms.

The chapter is organized as follows. I start by offering a discussion of the notion of sociolinguistic change, connecting it to familiar areas of interest within ELF studies. Having established the main ideas behind the concept, I then illustrate the relevance of a sociolinguistic change perspective for ELF studies in more detail, using university internationalization in Denmark as my case. I conclude by arguing that contexts where English is used as a lingua franca generally offer ripe sites for the study of sociolinguistic change in late modernity, which suggests that a research agenda for ELF and sociolinguistic change as sketched in this chapter holds the potential to be of considerable benefit for sociolinguistics and ELF studies alike.

2   Sociolinguistic Change

In a number of publications, Coupland (2009, 2010a, 2014) has called for renewed interest in what he calls *sociolinguistic change*. He makes the point

---

[1] The present chapter is a modified version of a paper delivered as the closing keynote address at *ELF and Changing English*, the 10th Anniversary Conference of English as a Lingua Franca, June 15, 2017, University of Helsinki.

that linguistic change and social change are inextricably linked, and that sociolinguistics needs to treat the two in an integrative manner, much in the spirit of what Dell Hymes once referred to as a "socially constituted linguistics" (Hymes 1974: 196). Within such a framework, which aims to move beyond a view of sociolinguistics as the study of "language variation and change" (LVC; as pioneered by Labov, see e.g. Labov 1994, 2001, 2010; Tagliamonte 2012; Chambers & Schilling-Estes 2013), change is conceptualized as a complex process, involving social change as well as linguistic change. While linguistic change (defined as structural change in language systems) continues to be of potential interest from a sociolinguistic change perspective, it loses the primacy it has traditionally held within the framework of variationist sociolinguistics. This has several implications.

First of all, it opens up new ways of thinking about how language change relates to social change, including the way in which social meaning is ascribed to – or indexed by – particular ways of speaking. We can think of several scenarios (cf. Coupland 2014):

- concomitant change in linguistic form as well as social meaning
  (= language changes, social meaning changes)
- ongoing linguistic change is evidenced, but no reevaluation of the social meaning of particular variants or varieties follows
  (= language changes, social meaning stays intact)
- the language system in a particular context remains "intact," but evaluative dimensions around the system undergo change
  (= language stays intact, social meanings change)

Translating this to an ELF perspective allows us to appreciate that an investigation of "the use of English as a lingua franca" and "change" will not be complete if linguistic change is the only dimension that comes under scrutiny. If we take the much-discussed (s) variable as an example (e.g. Seidlhofer 2004; Cogo & Dewey 2012; Mortensen 2013; see also Nevalainen, this volume), we can imagine a situation in which language users in lingua franca contexts over time gradually begin to display a statistical preference for the Ø-variant (*she run to school*), and come to associate this with the same level of appropriateness, and the same (positive) social values of "prestige" and so on, that have traditionally been reserved for the "received" s-variant (*she runs to school*). This would be an example of concomitant change in language and social meaning. But we may just as easily imagine a situation in which a widespread use of the Ø-variant would *not* lead to a reevaluation of the indexical value of the variant, which might then, despite its extensive use, (still) be associated with "less-than-proper" usage. This exemplifies a situation in which language changes, but social meaning remains intact. Finally, we can imagine a situation in which no particular or conspicuous language change is evidenced (though no language system is, of course, likely to stay completely intact), but where the social evaluation (e.g. the relative status or prestige) attached to particular ways of speaking or particular speakers nevertheless undergoes a shift. This is what Jenkins, at the beginning of the millennium, speculated might happen through a reversal of the values traditionally attributed to "native" vs. "non-native" speakers of English (Jenkins 2000, quoted in Jenkins 2014: 39–40):

> In the days of empire, the natives were the indigenous populations and the term itself implied uncivilized, primitive, barbaric, even cannibalistic ... With the spread of English around the globe, 'native' – in relation to English – has acquired newer, positive connotations. 'Native speakers' of English are assumed to be advanced (technologically), civilized, and educated. But as 'NSs' lose their linguistic advantage, with English being spoken as an International Language [= ELF] no less – and often a good deal more – effectively by 'NNSs' ... perhaps the word 'native' will return to its pejorative usage. Only this time, the opposite group will be on the receiving end.

It would be an overstatement to suggest that we have arrived at this situation today, but there is evidence to suggest that the increased use of English as a lingua franca – and the metalinguistic discourse that unfolds around it – in many contexts seems to be contributing to a partial reevaluation of the status of "native speaker norms" (as reflected by papers in the colloquium on the "linguistic diversity on the international campus" project, organized as part of the 10th Anniversary Conference of English as a Lingua Franca [cf. Jenkins and Mauranen 2018], and similar findings reported in Wang 2013; Mortensen & Fabricius 2014; Karakaş 2015; and other studies). What we see is not a case of clear-cut change from "state-of-affairs A" to "state-of-affairs B." It is more appropriate, I think, to see the situation as one in which multiple norms are vying for position in the language ideological space, making the status of so-called NS vs. NNS varieties more ambiguous.

The concept of sociolinguistic change, says Coupland, "urges us to ask ... questions, where the interest is less in discovering structural change in language systems and more in discovering changing relationships between language and society and their instantiation *at the level of practice*" (Coupland 2014: 70). Turning the focus of attention away from change in language systems to change at the level of practice means that the range of areas in which we may look for change is broadened. As a way of trying to map what these areas are, Coupland suggests that we may think of change along five dimensions where sociolinguistic change might be evidenced: *discursive practices, language ideologies, cultural reflexivity, social norms*, and *mediation/ mediatization*. These dimensions are not necessarily the only areas where we may observe changes in language–society relations, nor the only areas that may be implicated in such change, but they constitute good starting points (as I will illustrate in Sections 3 and 5). It is also important to point out that the dimensions do not exist independently of each other. They constitute overlapping aspects of sociolinguistic change and should be thought of as heuristics that may guide us as we try to describe and theorize sociolinguistic change. Moreover, change is likely to be evidenced in multiple dimensions at the same time (Androutsopoulos 2014: 6). In fact, it is often in the interaction between various dimensions that the richest examples of change are found. In the following, I unpack what is meant by each of these terms and relate them to the field of ELF studies.

3 Sociolinguistic Change and the Study of English as a Lingua Franca

In the three scenarios of change sketched in Section 2, linguistic change and change in social meaning were in effect treated as separate processes that might – but need not – interact. While this sort of approach is convenient for the analyst, it is not the way change is experienced by language users, who tend to encounter the two dimensions (linguistic form and social meaning) as a *unity*, as an integrative part of particular practices. This implies that a sociolinguistic change perspective naturally takes an interest in the formation of social meaning in and through *discursive practices*, as opposed to the abstract meaning of decontextualized forms of speech (e.g. the meaning of postvocalic /r/s in New York). It also means that change in discursive practices – the way language is used in particular settings – will in itself constitute a form of sociolinguistic change, irrespective of whether it involves linguistic change in a more traditional structural sense (e.g. sound change). The use of English as a lingua franca will often involve such change, especially when English is used in contexts where other languages have previously been used. An example of this situation is given in Section 5.2, where the introduction of English as a language of teaching at a Danish university constitutes a change in discursive practice.

A further implication of moving from a language change perspective to an interest in sociolinguistic change is that *language ideology* comes to acquire a natural role as one of the dimensions in which we may look for change. Language ideology can here be taken to refer to "the cultural (or subcultural) system of ideas about social and linguistic relationships, together with their loading of moral and political interest" (Irvine 1989: 255). It is exactly this dimension that Jenkins targets when she talks about a potential reversal of roles in the discourse on "non-native" vs. "native" speakers. In fact, the very emergence of the field of ELF studies, and the (renewed) discourse it has generated about the relevance, utility, and status of different ways of speaking English, also outside specialist circles (cf. Hazel 2016), can be seen as meaningful sociolinguistic change in itself.

A sociolinguistic change perspective also implies that *social norms* – "in the twin senses of what is socially normal and what is socially normative (Piippo 2012)" (Coupland 2014: 76) – come to be seen as a possible dimension of change. Social norms, discursive practices, and language ideology enter into a complex relationship where we may think of norms as the level that mediates between language ideology and practice. Social norms lend a certain sense of continuity to the way that social interaction unfolds in particular contexts. They offer a matrix for what is considered appropriate social behavior and what is not (linguistic and otherwise). Social norms are in many cases implicit – as long as they are not broken, they tend to go unnoticed – but in lingua franca scenarios, it is not uncommon to see social norms becoming the object of explicit metatalk. This is a reflection of the fact that lingua franca scenarios often unfold as part of what I have called transient social communities or transient social configurations (Mortensen 2013; Mortensen 2017; Mortensen & Hazel 2017; cf. Pitzl 2018b). In social configurations of this kind, norms cannot be expected to be shared *a priori* and therefore need to be established in the course of interaction in more profound ways than in other settings.

Another consequence of pursuing an interest in sociolinguistic change is that *cultural reflexivity* comes to feature among the areas that merit analytical and theoretical attention. In explaining how "culture moves through the world," Urban (2001) argues that culture emerges in a perpetual interplay between what he calls "inertial culture" and "accelerative culture." Inertial culture is what allows us to entertain a notion of cultures as relatively durable entities, imagined as they may be (Anderson 1983). Accelerative forces, on the other hand, are what make cultures – and "social space" – evolve. Sociolinguistic change can be seen as a type of cultural change, and therefore it lends itself well to being conceptualized within Urban's framework. The question, of course, is how we can identify accelerative culture and explain where it comes from. In order to account for this, Urban introduces the notion of the *entrepreneur* as someone who "takes something old into a new world, or tries something new out on an old world" (Urban 2001: 2), thereby generating opportunities for what may be called *cultural reflexivity* (though this is not Urban's term). In doing so, the entrepreneur offers a new perspective on existing practices, and opens up the potential for new ways of doing things. ELF studies has arguably been instrumental in generating a level of cultural reflexivity of this sort by challenging existing ideas about English – and English language teaching in particular (Seidlhofer 2004, 2011; Dewey 2012). In the Danish context, "English used as a global lingua franca" was added as a core topic to the national curriculum for English in high schools in 2017. This development was prompted by a growing awareness within the educational system of the fact that English is increasingly being used in lingua franca scenarios, but it was also clearly helped along by the research agenda that was being established within the field of ELF studies. In this sense, the ELF vanguard – as well as English language teachers who have adopted the notion of ELF and introduced it into their teaching – may be perceived as metacultural entrepreneurs, contributing to ongoing sociolinguistic change. But the use of English as a lingua franca does not only participate in generating cultural reflexivity within university halls and school curricula. We also see it playing out in interactions among individuals in many parts of everyday life, where received understandings of the links between language, nation, and nationality may come under scrutiny, as discussed in the analytical sections below (particularly Section 5.1).

Linguistic entrepreneurs also operate in the public domain, for instance in the world of sports, where transnational sports celebrities appear on a daily basis – in English – on television, radio, social media, websites, and so on, thereby contributing to a pluralizing of the linguistic norms that characterize English. This observation points to the fact that a sociolinguistic change perspective necessarily includes an interest in technologically mediated language, that is, language produced and "consumed" under conditions different from face-to-face interaction. This includes an interest in what may be called *mediatization*: "the historical process through which more and more aspects of our lives and socio-cultural understandings are achieved through technologically-mediated systems" (Coupland 2014: 78). This may be seen as a significant condition of contemporary sociolinguistic change, and also one that plays a central role in the sociolinguistics of ELF, though I shall not devote much attention to it in this chapter (but see, for example, Pennycook's work on transnational hip-hop 2007, 2010).

At this point, though the outline has been rather compressed, I hope to have made it clear how a research agenda that takes a broad interest in sociolinguistic change – including the dimensions of *discursive practices, language ideologies, social norms, cultural reflexivity*, and *mediatization* – differs from a research agenda that takes a specific interest in language change, as seen within the variationist paradigm. Researchers who take an interest in language variation and change certainly take social factors into consideration, but they tend to be treated as a more or less static backdrop against which linguistic variation and change, as the primary objects of analysis, play out. From a sociolinguistic change perspective the emphasis is very different. I also hope to have illustrated how the sociolinguistic change approach resonates with many of the research interests found within ELF studies (e.g. language ideology and discursive practice), though these interests are typically not approached from a change perspective – perhaps with the exception of language norms and norms for English teaching.

In the following, I would like to elaborate on my perspective by illustrating the relevance of a sociolinguistic change perspective for ELF studies in more detail. I will do this by using findings from research into university internationalization conducted under the auspices of CALPIU, the Research Centre for Cultural and Linguistic Practices at Roskilde University from 2007 to 2014, and CIP, the Centre for Internationalization and Parallel Language Use at the University of Copenhagen. First, a brief look at university internationalization as a concept and how it may be theorized.

4 University Internationalization and Sociolinguistic Change: The Big Picture

That universities can be characterized as international institutions is nothing new (De Wit 2011; Mortensen & Haberland 2012; De Wit & Hunter 2015). Still, there is reason to claim that the processes that have unfolded across universities in Europe and beyond since the beginning of the 1990s represent a new and distinct form of internationalization, with important implications for the activities that make up the institution of the university, including research, teaching, and administration (Altbach et al. 2009: 2).

One of the distinctive features of contemporary university internationalization is that it is closely linked to processes associated with "globalization." Globalization is, of course, not a new phenomenon either, but the concept nevertheless has considerable value "as shorthand reference to a cluster of changed and still fast changing social arrangements and priorities" (Coupland 2010b: 2). These changes happen under the influence of what Beck calls "the ideology of globalism," by which he means "the view that the world market eliminates or supplants political action ... the ideology of rule by the world market, the ideology of neo-liberalism (Beck 2000)" (quoted in Haberland 2009: 18). Internationalization and globalization are separate processes (Jenkins 2017: 503), but the influence of globalization on current internationalization practices and priorities of universities is obvious to many commentators. As De Wit and Hunter (2015: 43) argue, the second half of the 1990s saw "a gradual shift from political to economic rationales for internationalisation," leading to a situation where "the principal driving force for internationalisation has now become economic" (De Wit and Hunter 2016: 343, cf. Fabricius et al. 2017).

Internationalization has had a profound impact on universities across Europe and beyond. Knight (2008) refers to internationalization as a "key factor" in "shaping and challenging the higher education sector," calling it "a formidable force for change," and she provides a useful list of some of the specific changes internationalization has brought about, including:

- development of new international networks and consortia
- growing numbers of students, professors, and researchers participating in academic mobility schemes
- more emphasis on developing international/intercultural and global competencies

- stronger interest in international themes and collaborative research
- impetus given to recruiting foreign students

(my selection of items from list presented in Knight 2008: 3)

Many of these developments carry the potential to generate sociolinguistic change, and have indeed done so in many cases. The most conspicuous change to follow in the wake of university internationalization in Denmark has been the increased use of English in teaching as well as research dissemination. English has quite simply been the main linguistic conduit for the changes that Knight refers to here – and many others like them, associated with internationalization (cf. Airey et al. 2017).

At a very general level, the use of English as a lingua franca constitutes sociolinguistic change by reconfiguring language–society relations, instantiated in the practices of the university as a societal institution. Not because multilingualism or the use of other languages than the local language are unprecedented phenomena in Danish university history – quite the contrary – but because English comes packaged with a particular ideology; part and parcel, we may say, of a new, market-oriented way of conceptualizing the role of the university in society.

Hartmut Haberland and I have tried to sketch the history of language choice at Danish universities by dividing it into four phases (Mortensen & Haberland 2012). Following Bull (2004), we make the case that different "language regimes" have gone hand in hand with different university types, each based on a distinct legitimizing principle. The medieval and early modern university (fifteenth and sixteenth centuries) was premised on the authority of the church and had Latin, the language of the church, as its dominant language. The enlightenment university (seventeenth and eighteenth centuries) was founded on the principle of reason and made use of Latin, several European languages, as well as Danish (though Danish was not used as a medium of instruction until the second half of the eighteenth century). This linguistic pluralism, we argue, can primarily be seen as a move away from the singular authority of the church. The nineteenth and twentieth centuries saw the birth of the national university as part of a nationalist project. Here Danish was the obvious choice, as a powerful symbol of the unity of the nation, and it ruled almost supreme (especially as a medium of instruction) until English started to enter the institution towards the end of the twentieth century, along with a new market orientation, which we argue constitutes the current "legitimizing principle" of the university.

Since the end of the twentieth century, marketization (Fairclough 1993), internationalization, and anglicization have gone hand in hand at universities in Denmark, sometimes making it hard to distinguish the three processes from one another and to discern relationships of cause and effect between them. This has generated sociolinguistic change along multiple dimensions, all in one way or another relating to the use of English as a lingua franca. In the remainder of the chapter, I would like to discuss some examples of those changes, in order to illustrate what sort of issues a research agenda for "ELF and sociolinguistic change" might take in its scope. My focus is mainly on practices related to teaching, though sociolinguistic change is certainly also evident in other areas of university life, not least research (for examples from the Swedish context, see Salö 2015, 2017).

5   University Internationalization and Sociolinguistic Change: Changing Ideologies, Changing Practices

5.1   Language Ideological Change: The "Domain Loss" Debate and "Parallel Language Use"

Internationalization has affected the language ideological landscape at Danish universities in different ways. One of them concerns the (ideological) position of Danish as "the local language" vs. English as "the global language." The increased use of English in research dissemination and teaching has generated a widespread discourse on so-called domain loss, in which various actors, including politicians, lay commentators, educators, and language professionals have debated whether Danish is in danger of losing its relevance in "domains" associated with research and higher education. Although it may be argued that languages do not really "have" domains, and therefore cannot lose them either (Haberland 2005; cf. Simonsen 2002), and notwithstanding the fact that "science" – or "universities" for that matter – can hardly be constructed as single coherent domains due to the multiplicity of practices and processes these labels encompass (Preisler 2005), this debate is highly interesting since it constitutes a case of sociolinguistic change at the level of language ideology, manifest in metalinguistic discourse. No matter whether Danish will "lose ground" to English (as the domain loss metaphor has it) or not, the arrival of English has upset the sociolinguistic order created during the twentieth century, in which the national language was established as the "natural" language of the university.

The domain loss debate is, of course, about much more than language. Metadiscourse about language change and language loss is normally rife with competing stances and politics of identity, and the domain loss debate is no exception. Preisler (2005) identifies two sides in the debate. On the one hand, we have "the followers." They see the use of English as a purely instrumental affair and embrace the influence of English as a manifestation of internationalization. On the other hand, we have "the concerned," who represent "the educational and cultural elite." They are very critical of the use of English, which they see as a threat to the status of the Danish language and to educational quality (see e.g. Davidsen-Nielsen 2009, 2017).

Among those who criticize the increased use of English and lament the perceived demise of Danish, it is not surprising to find individuals and collectives who subscribe to conservative national worldviews. The right-wing Danish People's Party is a case in point. One of the most striking examples of their engagement in the debate came in 2015 when the party's spokesperson on cultural affairs, Alex Ahrendtsen, achieved wide media coverage during the general election on the basis of a language political proposal that contained two seemingly simple ideas: 1) the introduction of a new tax on the use of English words in advertising and 2) the abolition of state-funded English-medium programs at Danish universities. The first idea was withdrawn the very day it was put forward since it did not comply with the overall party line (Thomsen 2015), but the other was not, at least to my knowledge. If we take a closer look at Ahrendtsen's officially stated reasons for wanting to terminate state-funded English-medium programs, we can make several interesting observations. Extract 1 is a comment by Ahrendtsen taken from an interview-based article from Altinget.dk, an online medium that specializes in Danish politics.

Extract 1 Carpenter Hansen and his daughter's education.

[Original]

Når tømrer Hansen sender sin datter på en videregående uddannelse, har han betalt for, at hun bliver undervist på sit modersmål. Han har ikke betalt for, at der kan komme østeuropæere og andre EU-borgere til Danmark for at blive undervist på engelsk, få SU, få sig en dansk uddannelse – for derefter at smutte igen eller tage jobbet fra tømrerens datter.

[Translation, JM]

When carpenter Hansen sends his daughter off to higher education, he has paid for her to be taught in her mother tongue. He has not paid in order for Eastern Europeans and other EU citizens to be able to come to Denmark to be taught in English, get state educational grants, get a Danish education – only to steal away again afterwards or take the job away from the carpenter's daughter.

(www.altinget.dk/kultur/artikel/df-krav-om-skat-paa-engelsksprogede-reklamer)

This extract clearly illustrates a marketized idea of the university, with education as a product you pay for (in the Danish context through income tax). Ahrendtsen takes internationalization to constitute a threat to the hard-earned privileges of the citizens of the nation state, exemplified by the generic "carpenter Hansen" who, according to Ahrendtsen, is not paying his taxes for the benefit of extra-nationals, but for the benefit of fellow nation-state citizens, his daughter in particular. The perceived encroachment of English on

Danish may, from this perspective, be seen as a symbol of more general concerns related to processes of social change under globalization. To Ahrendtsen this is not simply a matter of linguistic change and the status of one language vis-à-vis another. To him the debate concerns different groups of *speakers* and their relative privileges. In this sense, language ideological contestation can be seen as an indicator not only of (potential) linguistic change but indeed of sociolinguistic change in which social and linguistic change are intimately linked. English (used as a lingua franca) is at the epicenter of this process.

Though it might amount to an overestimation of the phenomenon, Hultgren (2013: 177) makes an interesting point in suggesting that the Nordic debate on domain loss may be seen as a case of what Cameron, following Cohen (1987), calls a "moral panic." As Cameron explains, a society finds itself in a state of moral panic when "some social phenomenon or problem is suddenly foregrounded in public discourse and discussed in an obsessive, moralistic and alarmist manner, as if it betokened some imminent catastrophe" (Cameron 2012: 82). Hultgren notes that "moral panics may be particularly prone to arise in the context of major socio-political destabilization, in this case, globalization," which resonates with the analysis I am pursuing here. Yet, while Hultgren seems interested in conceptualizing domain loss as an empirical phenomenon, treating "lexical borrowing from English into Danish in the Sciences" as a case of language change, it might also be proposed that domain loss is in essence a language ideological construct, which linguists have been heavily involved in establishing (cf. Salö 2016). Under the latter interpretation, the discussion around domain loss could – and should – be analyzed as an example of sociolinguistic change, irrespective of the empirical attestation of bona fide language change.

The debate on domain loss has been accompanied by the coinage of the term "parallel language use," which has gained wide currency not only in Denmark but also in the other Nordic countries (Hult & Källkvist 2016). In a definition available at the website of the Center for Internationalisation and Parallel Language Use, the concept refers to "a situation in which two languages are considered equal in a particular domain, and where the choice of language depends on what is deemed most appropriate and efficient in a specific situation."[2] An earlier definition from the Nordic Council of Ministers states that "the parallel use of language refers to the concurrent use of several languages within one or more areas. None of the languages abolishes or replaces the other; they are used in parallel" (Nordic Council of Ministers

---

[2] http://cip.ku.dk/resurseportal/english/.

2006: 93; see discussion in Holmen 2017 and see Preisler 2009 for an alternative concept of "complementary languages"). As a language ideological construct, the notion of parallel language use may be seen as a compromise that mediates between the two positions in debate about language choice at Danish universities. But the term is not simply about language choice. Its emergence relates to – and is premised on – still ongoing debates about the role of the university under conditions of globalization. Should the university mainly be an institution that serves national interests, or should it be an institution that transcends national borders? Should it be a national public good or a business-like enterprise that uses English in its attempt to attract the best researchers and the most talented students (which is considered important for institutional prestige, as well as revenue). And so on. If we want to understand the contemporary sociolinguistic situation at Danish universities – including the emergence of terms like "domain loss" and "parallel language use," which are both intimately related to the use of English as a lingua franca – we can hardly do this without conceiving of social and linguistic change as two sides of the same coin.

5.2   Discursive Practices and Social Norms: Sociolinguistic Change in Practice

Sociolinguistic change also abounds in the daily practices of the international university, often with important implications for social norms. In some of my previous research, I have detailed how the discursive practices of students reflect – and sometimes challenge – the language ideological assumptions about what constitutes international higher education. In Mortensen (2014) I presented a study of patterns of language choice in three student project groups at a Danish university. The students involved were enrolled on an "international" BA program, and since "English-medium" is commonly treated as a synonym for "international" in the context of Danish higher education, it was unsurprising to find that English (used as a lingua franca) was the dominant language in all groups. What was interesting to find, however, was that the groups had all developed practices in which it was also common for the students to use Danish *or* Danish plus English in conjunction as what Gafaranga and Torras (2001) call a bilingual medium (see also Mortensen 2018). Using the totality of linguistic resources at their disposal, the student groups had developed local discursive practices where language alternation could be imbued with different kinds of indexical meaning (cf. Ochs 1992). This is illustrated in Extract 2 (from Mortensen 2014), in which we see a group getting ready to start a meeting. Five group members are sitting round a table, eating their lunch and waiting for two remaining group members to arrive.

Extract 2 Reproduced from Mortensen 2014: 431.

22	Mette	og Henrik kommer lige om lidt	and Henrik will be here shortly
23	Frida	det er dig der har lasagne med	it's you who brought lasagna
24	Mette	nej det er st- nej det er Paul der har	no it's Paul who's made
25		lavet det	made it
26		men jeg kunne ikke spise det hele	but I couldn't eat it all
27	Frida	⌈nå⌉	oh
28	Mette	⌊nu har han⌋ fået lasagne	now he has had lasagna
29		i tre dage (0.5)	for three days (0.5)
30		så sagde han Mette kan du ikke spise	so he said Mette can't you eat
31		noget af det	some of it
32		jo ⌈sådan skal det da⌉ ikke være vel	well no reason in holding back
33	Frida	⌊??lækkert??⌋	delicious
34		(0.7)	
35	Mette	så nu må vi se	so now we'll have to see
36		jeg ved ikke hvorfor det	I don't know why it
		((referring to some tea she has put on the table earlier))	
37		⌈ser så mærkeligt ud⌉	looks so weird
38	Torben	⌊language policy⌋ Met⌈te⌉	
39	Mette	⌊sorry⌋	
40		(0.5)	
41	Mette	I don't know why it looks so weird	
42		(1.0)	
43	Mette	it looks like (2.1) yeah (.)	
44		I have no words	

As I argue in Mortensen (2014), Torben's utterance in line 38 is treated as a reprimand, which Mette reacts to immediately by apologizing, in English. This displays that Torben and Mette agree that Mette has violated a group norm by speaking Danish, and that the appropriate behavior would have been to use English. Torben may be policing Mette's behavior here in an attempt to ensure that everybody in the group is able to follow the conversation. Yet this cannot be the only explanation, because the group members also use English in cases where only Danish-speaking members of the group are present. With this in mind, I suggest that Torben's reprimand could be seen as an "act of identity" (Le Page & Tabouret-Keller 1985) that positions him as an international student (who speaks English), as opposed to a Danish, non-international student (who speaks Danish) (cf. Mortensen 2014: 432). There may, of course, be other reasons for the use of English in this situation. An orientation to language learning – becoming better at English – might be one such reason. However, there were no explicit goals of language learning built into the curriculum of the program, and the students' English (whether spoken or written) was never specifically evaluated. So, if an orientation to language learning is part of the story here, it would be an orientation established by the students themselves, perhaps implicitly.

I suggest that the meaning of using English vs. Danish discussed above is tied to the local context of the group. It constitutes a social norm, mediating between the level of discursive practice and language ideology. Other students in the same program may be sensitized to similar norms, but it is not a norm that is shared by the surrounding Danish speech community. It does not transpire from my data whether these students know anything about the domain loss debate or the notion of parallel language use – or whether they would care if they did. Still, the extract can be said to encapsulate and at the same time challenge some of the central positions in the language ideological debates that I reviewed earlier. Torben's insistence that English is the appropriate language for this context can be seen as a discursive manifestation of the "follower," who sees English as the "obvious" language of internationalization. Mette's use of Danish does not seem to be language ideologically motivated, born out of a desire to protect or preserve Danish. Nevertheless, the fact that she uses Danish represents a challenge to the idea that education is *either* in English or in Danish, which is otherwise what the notion of parallel language use is often taken to imply. The extract shows that the international university is multilingual, and that English, despite its meta-linguistic billing as "the language of internationalization" is never used as an academic lingua franca in splendid isolation (Haberland & Mortensen 2012; cf. Söderlundh 2012).

The ongoing internationalization of universities also affects the discursive practices of classrooms and lecture halls. In a study published in 2014, Preisler investigates what he calls processes of authentication in the practice of teachers who teach courses in both English and Danish (Preisler 2014: 218). Based on close analyses of classroom interaction, he argues that the sociocultural and linguistic heterogeneity of the international classroom may present a challenge to lecturers, because they cannot rely on shared contextual knowledge when constructing their teacher personas. For one lecturer in particular, this means that a performance that works very well in a Danish-language classroom – in which he stylizes himself as an old-school authoritarian – backfires in a parallel "international" class. As a performative practice, stylization involves the "knowing deployment of socially familiar semiotic material where the speaker strategically complicates and ambiguates her or his relationship with that material" (Mortensen et al. 2017: 10; cf. Coupland 2001, 2007). For as long as the lecturer in question has taught at the university (which amounts to a total of forty years), he has been able to employ this style of humor in his classes, but as a result of social change this particular practice has come under pressure, because mutually familiar semiotic material is in some cases simply harder to come by in the international classroom.

Although teaching in the international classroom does not always result in problems of the sort discussed above (as also shown by Preisler 2014 and several others, e.g. Suviniitty 2012), internationalization invariably brings changes that will affect the discursive practices and social norms of the university. Changing the medium of instruction from the local language to English is a very obvious sort of change, but there is more to it than that. The emergence of new contextual affordances and constraints means that discursive practices are likely to be "read" differently, which in turn will affect the way practices develop. As I have just argued, stylization is a case in point. Under new contextual conditions, acts of stylization that rely on locally familiar stereotypes for their effect simply may not mean the same, and therefore will not *be* the same. As Preisler's example shows, this may also have consequences for social norms, including the social relationship between lecturers and students, which may (but need not) become more "formal" in contexts where humor – through stylization – is not easily achieved.

6   ELF and Sociolinguistic Change: In Conclusion

The majority of what I have discussed in this chapter is not, I believe, radically new to the field of ELF studies. What I would like to suggest, though, is that the perspective I have offered by introducing the notion of sociolinguistic change may go some way towards offering a unified view of the field, constituting a vantage point from which we may begin to unpack and theorize the sociolinguistic complexity involved in the use of English as a lingua franca.

A sociolinguistic change perspective emphasizes that research on ELF and change is not restricted to the study of change in language. By this I do not mean to suggest that language change research is unimportant within the field – quite the contrary. Indeed, if it had not been for an interest in language variation and change, and the corpus-building efforts that resulted from it, ELF research might not have been able to gather the momentum it has. Still, it is striking to note that when change is discussed in relation to ELF, it is predominantly with a view to discussing change in the linguistic system of what we tend to call "English." In other words, English is positioned as the object of change, with the use of English in lingua franca scenarios as the driving force behind that change. What I would like to suggest is that we also need to consider the use of English (as a lingua franca) as the agent or the companion of *social change* in various contexts, and as part of a range of different social processes. A sociolinguistic change perspective attunes us to these complexities, helping us to remember that the nitty-gritty details of language use – which no doubt constitute fascinating objects of study in themselves – are always part of bigger social processes, and that these processes should also fall within the remit of ELF research and sociolinguistic research in general.

The examples I have discussed in this chapter of changing language ideological orientations, changing discursive practices, and changing social norms are all examples of the sociolinguistic change that has followed from the drive towards internationalization at Danish universities. I have not been able to pursue all dimensions and levels of change in this process – for instance, I have not been concerned with how internationalization increasingly involves the generation of new types of technologically mediated talk through the creation of "virtual learning environments," Massive Open Online Courses (MOOCs),[3] and so on. However, despite the limited number of areas I have been able to cover, I believe the examples I have given nevertheless suffice as an illustration of how the study of English used as a lingua franca invariably involves the study of sociolinguistic change, and how the study of the two phenomena might fruitfully inform one another.

In general, contexts where English is used as a lingua franca tend to offer ripe sites for the study of sociolinguistic change in late modernity, quite simply because lingua franca scenarios are premised on increased transnational mobility, involving accelerated flows of people, ideas, goods, semiotic resources, and so on, and because they often, as a result, involve social configurations characterized by a high degree of transience – all hallmarks of the late modern condition, in my view (cf. Lønsmann et al. 2017). The study of scenarios where English is used as a lingua franca has, as such, already helped tremendously in bringing much-needed attention to a number of communicative practices and modes of social interaction typical of late modernity. But, in fact, the processes and practices studied within ELF studies, are, in some ways, nothing more – and nothing less – than particular results of more general processes of sociolinguistic change. Ironically, then, "English" is not necessarily the only or the most interesting object to focus on when we consider the use of English as a lingua franca as a general phenomenon. A comprehensive research agenda for ELF studies and change should move beyond language change as the primary object(s) of interest and approach the study of ELF as part of a bigger picture that involves discursive, social, ideological, and technological change.

In closing the chapter, it seems appropriate to offer a few comments on how the field of ELF studies itself forms part of the processes of change. In talking about *cultural reflexivity* as a dimension of sociolinguistic change Section 3, I pointed out that the ELF vanguard may be perceived as metacultural entrepreneurs, who take "something old into a new world, or [try] something new out on an old world" (Urban 2001: 2), thereby offering a new perspective

---

[3] Some commentators seem to see the use of English in such contexts as a relatively unproblematic extension of the role that English plays in academia already (Montgomery 2013), but there may be room for a more critical examination of the situation.

on existing practices. It is quite obvious to me that ELF studies has always been about trying something new out on an old world, both in relation to the world *out there*, bringing new ideas of language teaching, new ideas about linguistic norms, and so on into the domain of public discourse, *and* in relation to the world *in here* – inside the walls of academia – bringing new perspectives to other academic disciplines, some very closely related, some further afield. Engaging with other fields, whether it is contact linguistics, historical sociolinguistics, cognitive linguistics, big-data digital humanities, neuroscience, or socially constituted linguistics, comes with the added benefit that ELF studies may also be at the receiving end of cultural change, playing host to entrepreneurs who bring something new – or old – into the world of ELF studies. I am confident that the present volume will be successful in achieving this, and I very much look forward to continuing the exchange of ideas and perspectives in the years to come.

Acknowledgments

I would like to thank Nikolas Coupland, Hartmut Haberland, Marta Kirilova, Anna Mauranen, Bent Preisler, Svetlana Vetchinnikova, and an anonymous reviewer for providing thought-provoking and immensely helpful comments for earlier versions of this paper. Any remaining shortcomings remain my responsibility.

Transcription Conventions

⌈ ⌉	Overlap between two or more speakers, upper brackets for the first speaker,
⌊ ⌋	lower brackets for the second speaker
??	Transcriber uncertainty
xxx	Unintelligible word or phrase
(0.3)	Pause, length measured in seconds
(.)	Pause, less than 0.2 seconds
((text))	Transcriber comments
Italics	Danish
Grey font	English paraphrase

REFERENCES

ACE. 2014. *The Asian Corpus of English*. Director: Andy Kirkpatrick; researchers: Wang Lixun, John Patkin, Sophiann Subhan. http://corpus.ied.edu.hk/ace/.

Airey, John, Karen M. Lauridsen, Anne Räsänen, Linus Salö & Vera Schwach. 2017. The expansion of English-medium instruction in the Nordic countries: Can top-down university language policies encourage bottom-up disciplinary literacy goals? *Higher Education* 73(4), 561–576.

Altbach, Philip G., Liz Reisberg & Laura E. Rumbley. 2009. *Trends in Global Higher Education: Tracking an Academic Revolution.* Paris: UNESCO. http://unesdoc.unesco.org/images/0018/001831/183168e.pdf (June 3, 2017).

Anderson, Benedict. 1983. *Imagined Communities: Reflections on the Origin and Spread of Nationalism.* London: Verso.

Androutsopoulos, Jannis. 2014. Mediatization and sociolinguistic change: Key concepts, research traditions, open issues. In Jannis Androutsopoulos (ed.), *Mediatization and Sociolinguistic Change,* 3–48. Berlin: Mouton de Gruyter.

Beck, Ulrich. 2000. *What Is Globalization?* Cambridge: Polity Press.

Bull, Tove. 2004. Dagens og gårsdagens akademiske lingua franca. Eit historisk tilbakeblikk og eit globalt utsyn. In Dag F. Simonsen (ed.), *Språk i kunnskapssamfunnet. Engelsk – elitenes nye latin?,* 35–45. Oslo: Gyldendal Akademisk.

Cameron, Deborah. 2012. *Verbal Hygiene.* 2nd ed. London: Routledge.

Chambers, J. K. & Natalie Schilling-Estes (eds.). 2013. *The Handbook of Language Variation and Change.* 2nd ed. Malden: Wiley-Blackwell.

Cogo, Alessia & Martin Dewey. 2012. *Analysing English as a Lingua Franca: A Corpus-Driven Investigation.* London: Continuum.

Cohen, Stanley. 1987. *Folk Devils and Moral Panics: The Creation of Mods and Rockers.* 2nd ed. Oxford: Basil Blackwell.

Coupland, Nikolas. 2001. Stylization, authenticity and TV news review. *Discourse Studies* 3(4), 413–442.

2007. *Style: Language Variation and Identity.* Cambridge: Cambridge University Press.

2009. Dialects, standards and social change. In Marie Maegaard, Frans Gregersen, Pia Quist & Jens Normann Jørgensen (eds.), *Language Attitudes, Standardization, and Language Change,* 27–49. Oslo: Novus.

2010a. Language, ideology, media and social change. In Karen Junod & Didier Maillât (eds.), *Performing the Self* (SPELL: Swiss Papers in English Language and Literature 24), 127–152. Tübingen: Narr.

2010b. Introduction: Sociolinguistics in the global era. In Nikolas Coupland (ed.), *The Handbook of Language and Globalization,* 1–27. Malden: Blackwell.

2014. Sociolinguistic change, vernacularization and broadcast British media. In Jannis Androutsopoulos (ed.), *Mediatization and Sociolinguistic Change,* 67–96. Berlin: Mouton de Gruyter.

Davidsen-Nielsen, Niels. 2009. Danish under pressure: Use it or lose it. In Peter Harder (ed.), *English in Denmark: Language Policy, Internationalization and University Teaching* (Angles on the English-Speaking World 9), 138–140. Copenhagen: Museum Tusculanum Press.

2017. Ti minutter over tolv. *Kristeligt Dagblad,* sec. Kultur.

De Wit, Hans. 2011. Globalization and internationalisation of higher education. *RUSC. Universities and Knowledge Society Journal* 8(2), 77–164 (Spanish), 241–325 (English).

De Wit, Hans & Fiona Hunter. 2015. Understanding internationalisation of higher education in the European context. In Hans De Wit, Fiona Hunter, Laura Howard & Eva Egron-Polak (eds.), *Internationalisation of Higher Education,* 41–58. Brussels: European Parliament. https://op.europa.eu/s/n60d.

2016. Trends, issues and challenges in internationalisation of higher education: Where have we come from and where are we going? In Simon McGrath and Qing

Gu (eds.), *Routledge Handbook of International Education and Development*, 340–358. New York: Routledge.
Dewey, Martin. 2012. Towards a post-normative approach: learning the pedagogy of ELF. *Journal of English as a Lingua Franca* 1(1), 141–170.
ELFA. 2008. *The Corpus of English as a Lingua Franca in Academic Settings*. Director: Anna Mauranen. www.helsinki.fi/elfa/elfacorpus.
Fabricius, Anne H., Janus Mortensen & Hartmut Haberland. 2017. The lure of internationalization: paradoxical discourses of transnational student mobility, linguistic diversity and cross-cultural exchange. *Higher Education* 73(4), 577–595.
Fairclough, Norman. 1993. Critical discourse analysis and the marketization of public discourse: The universities. *Discourse & Society* 4(2), 133–168.
Gafaranga, Joseph & Maria-Carme Torras. 2001. Language versus medium in the study of bilingual conversation. *International Journal of Bilingualism* 5(2), 195–219.
Haberland, Hartmut. 2005. Domains and domain loss. In Bent Preisler, Anne H. Fabricius, Hartmut Haberland, Susanne Kjærbeck & Karen Risager (eds.), *The Consequences of Mobility: Linguistic and Sociocultural Contact Zones*, 227–237. Roskilde: Roskilde University, Department of Language and Culture.
  2009. English – The language of globalism? RASK. *Internationalt tidskrift for sprog og kommunikation* 30, 17–45.
Haberland, Hartmut & Janus Mortensen. 2012. Language variety, language hierarchy and language choice in the international university. *International Journal of the Sociology of Language* 2012(216), 1–6.
Hazel, Spencer. 2016. Why native English speakers fail to be understood in English – and lose out in global business. *The Conversation*. http://theconversation.com/why-native-english-speakers-fail-to-be-understood-in-english-and-lose-out-in-global-business-54436.
Holmen, Anne. 2017. Parallel language strategy. In Nelleke Van Deusen-Scholl (ed.), *Second and Foreign Language Education* (Encyclopedia of Language and Education, 2nd ed., Vol. 4), 301–311. Cham: Springer.
Hult, Francis M. & Marie Källkvist. 2016. Global flows in local language planning: articulating parallel language use in Swedish university policies. *Current Issues in Language Planning* 17(1), 56–71.
Hultgren, Anna Kristina. 2013. Lexical borrowing from English into Danish in the Sciences: An empirical investigation of 'domain loss.' *International Journal of Applied Linguistics* 23(2), 166–182.
Hymes, Dell H. 1974. *Foundations in Sociolinguistics: An Ethnographic Approach*. Philadelphia, PA: University of Pennsylvania Press.
Irvine, Judith T. 1989. When talk isn't cheap: Language and political economy. *American Ethnologist* 16(2), 248–267.
Jenkins, Jennifer. 2014. *English as a Lingua Franca in the International University: The Politics of Academic English Language Policy*. Milton Park: Routledge.
  2017. Mobility and English language policies and practices in higher education. In Suresh Canagarajah (ed.), *The Routledge Handbook of Migration and Language*, 502–518. New York: Routledge.
  2018. The future of English as a lingua franca?. In Jennifer Jenkins, Will Baker & Martin Dewey (eds.), *The Routledge Handbook of English as a Lingua Franca*, 594–605. Abingdon: Routledge.

Jenkins, Jennifer & Anna Mauranen. 2018. Linguistic diversity on the international campus. *ResearchGate*. www.researchgate.net/project/Linguistic-diversity-on-the-international-campus (May 30, 2018).

Jenkins, Jennifer, Will Baker & Martin Dewey (eds.). 2018. *The Routledge Handbook of English as a Lingua Franca*. Abingdon: Routledge.

Karakaş, Ali. 2015. Orientations towards English among English-medium instruction students. *Englishes in Practice* 2(1), 1–38.

Knight, Jane. 2008. *Higher Education in Turmoil: The Changing World of Internationalisation* (Global Perspectives on Higher Education 13). Rotterdam: Sense Publishers.

Labov, William. 1994. *Principles of Linguistic Change, Vol 1: Internal Factors*. Malden: Blackwell.

2001. *Principles of Linguistic Change, Vol 2: Social Factors*. Malden: Blackwell.

2010. *Principles of Linguistic Change, Vol 3: Cognitive and Cultural Factors*. Malden: Oxford.

Le Page, R. B. & Andrée Tabouret-Keller. 1985. *Acts of Identity: Creole-Based Approaches to Language and Ethnicity*. Cambridge: Cambridge University Press.

Lønsmann, Dorte, Spencer Hazel & Hartmut Haberland. 2017. Introduction to special issue on transience: Emerging norms of language use. *Journal of Linguistic Anthropology* 27(3), 264–270.

Mauranen, Anna. 2012. *Exploring ELF. Academic English Shaped by Non-Native Speakers*. Cambridge: Cambridge University Press.

2016. ELF corpora: Design, difficulties and triumphs. In Marie-Luise Pitzl & Ruth Osimk-Teasdale (eds.), *English as a Lingua Franca: Perspectives and Prospects: Contributions in Honour of Barbara Seidlhofer*, 19–29. Berlin: Mouton de Gruyter.

2018. Conceptualising ELF. In Jennifer Jenkins, Will Baker & Martin Dewey (eds.), *The Routledge Handbook of English as a Lingua Franca*, 7–24. Abingdon: Routledge.

Montgomery, Scott L. 2013. MOOCs and the language barrier: Is open education not so open after all?. *The Conversation*. https://theconversation.com/moocs-and-the-language-barrier-is-open-education-not-so-open-after-all-17423 (June 3, 2017).

Mortensen, Janus. 2013. Notes on the use of English as a lingua franca as an object of study. *Journal of English as a Lingua Franca* 2(1), 25–46.

2014. Language policy from below: Language choice in student project groups in a multilingual university setting. *Journal of Multilingual and Multicultural Development* 35(4), 425–442.

2017. Transient multilingual communities as a field of investigation: Challenges and opportunities. *Journal of Linguistic Anthropology* 27(3), 271–288.

2018. Language regulation in collaborative student writing: a case study. *Language and Education* 32(6), 529–547.

Mortensen, Janus, Nikolas Coupland & Jacob Thøgersen. 2017. Introduction: Conceptualizing style, mediation, and change. In Janus Mortensen, Nikolas Coupland & Jacob Thøgersen (eds.), *Style, Mediation, and Change: Sociolinguistic Perspectives on Talking Media*, 1–24. New York: Oxford University Press.

Mortensen, Janus & Anne H. Fabricius. 2014. Language ideologies in Danish higher education: Exploring student perspectives. In Anna Kristina Hultgren, Frans

Gregersen & Jacob Thøgersen (eds.), *English in Nordic Universities: Ideologies and Practices*, 193–223. Amsterdam: John Benjamins.

Mortensen, Janus & Hartmut Haberland. 2012. English – The new Latin of academia? Danish universities as a case. *International Journal of the Sociology of Language* (216), 175–197.

Mortensen, Janus & Spencer Hazel. 2017. Lending bureaucracy voice: Negotiating English in institutional encounters. In Markku Filppula, Juhani Klemola, Anna Mauranen & Svetlana Vetchinnikova (eds.), *Changing English: Global and Local Perspectives*, 255–275. Berlin: Walter de Gruyter.

Nordic Council of Ministers. 2006. *Deklaration om nordisk språkpolitik* [Declaration on Nordic Language Policy]. DIVA. http://urn.kb.se/resolve?urn=urn:nbn:se:norden:org:diva-607 (June 3, 2017).

Ochs, Elinor. 1992. Indexing gender. In Alessandro Duranti & Charles Goodwin (eds.), *Rethinking Context: Language as an Interactive Phenomenon*, 335–358. Cambridge: Cambridge University Press.

Pennycook, Alastair. 2007. *Global Englishes and Transcultural Flows*. London: Routledge.

2010. Popular cultures, popular languages, and global identities. In Nikolas Coupland (ed.), *The Handbook of Language and Globalization*, 592–607. Malden: Blackwell.

Piippo, Irina. 2012. *Viewing norms dialogically: An action-oriented approach to sociolinguistic metatheory*. Unpublished PhD dissertation. Helsinki: University of Helsinki.

Pitzl, Marie-Luise. 2018a. Creativity, idioms and metaphorical language in ELF. In Jennifer Jenkins, Will Baker & Martin Dewey (eds.), *The Routledge Handbook of English as a Lingua Franca*, 233–243. Abingdon: Routledge.

2018b. Transient international groups (TIGs): exploring the group and development dimension of ELF. *Journal of English as a Lingua Franca* 7(1), 25–58.

Preisler, Bent. 2005. Deconstructing 'the domain of science' as a sociolinguistic entity in EFL societies: The relationship between English and Danish in higher education and research. In Bent Preisler, Anne H. Fabricius, Susanne Kjærbeck & Karen Risager (eds.), *The Consequences of Mobility: Linguistic and Sociocultural Contact Zones*, 238–248: Roskilde: Roskilde University, Department of Language and Culture.

2009. Complementary Languages: The national language and English as working languages in European universities. In Peter Harder (ed.), *English in Denmark: Language Policy, Internationalization and University Teaching* (Angles on the English-Speaking World 9), 10–28. Copenhagen: Museum Tusculanum Press.

2014. Lecturing in one's first language or in English as a lingua franca: The communication of authenticity. *Acta Linguistica Hafniensia* 46(2), 218–242.

Ranta, Elina. 2018. Grammar in ELF. In Jennifer Jenkins, Will Baker & Martin Dewey (eds.), *The Routledge Handbook of English as a Lingua Franca*, 244–254. Abingdon: Routledge.

Salö, Linus. 2015. The linguistic sense of placement: Habitus and the entextualization of translingual practices in Swedish academia. *Journal of Sociolinguistics* 19(4), 511–534.

2016. *Languages and Linguistic Exchanges in Swedish Academia: Practices, Processes, and Globalising Markets*. PhD dissertation. Stockholm: Stockholm University, Centre for Research on Bilingualism.

2017. *The Sociolinguistics of Academic Publishing: Language and the Practices of Homo Academicus*. Cham: Springer/Palgrave.

Seidlhofer, Barbara. 2004. Research perspectives on teaching English as a lingua franca. *Annual Review of Applied Linguistics* 24, 209–239.

2011. *Understanding English as a Lingua Franca*. Oxford: Oxford University Press.

Simonsen, Dag F. 2002. Å velge bort norsk: Om begrepene 'domene' og 'domenetap' anvendt på skandinaviske land. *Norsklæreren* 2, 5–17.

Söderlundh, Hedda. 2012. Global policies and local norms: Sociolinguistic awareness and language choice at an international university. *International Journal of the Sociology of Language* (216), 87–109.

Suviniitty, Jaana. 2012. *Lectures in English as a Lingua Franca: Interactional Features* (Aalto University Publication Series SCIENCE + TECHNOLOGY 19). Aalto: Aalto University, School of Chemical Technology. https://aaltodoc.aalto.fi:443/handle/123456789/7725 (February 23, 2019).

Tagliamonte, Sali. 2012. *Variationist Sociolinguistics: Change, Observation, Interpretation* (Language in Society 40). Malden: Blackwell.

Thomsen, Per Bang. 2015. DF-ordfører: Ja, jeg er blevet banket på plads. News article published on *dr.dk*, the website of the Danish Broadcasting Corporation, June 4, 2015. www.dr.dk/nyheder/politik/valg2015/df-ordfoerer-ja-jeg-er-blevet-banket-paa-plads (June 3, 2017).

Urban, Greg. 2001. *Metaculture: How Culture Moves through the World*. Minneapolis: University of Minnesota Press.

VOICE. 2009. *The Vienna-Oxford International Corpus of English*. Director: Barbara Seidlhofer; researchers: Angelika Breiteneder, Theresa Klimpfinger, Stefan Majewski, Ruth Osimk-Teasdale, Marie-Luise Pitzl, Michael Radeka. www.univie.ac.at/voice.

Wang, Ying. 2013. Non-conformity to ENL norms: A perspective from Chinese English users. *Journal of English as a Lingua Franca* 2(2), 255–282.

Part II

Zooming in on ELF

Introduction
Svetlana Vetchinnikova

While the chapters in Part I of this volume give a wider perspective on the complex relationships between linguistic, social and cognitive processes at play in language contact and change, the chapters in Part II zoom in on specific cases and contexts current right now. All the chapters in Part II are empirical and all work with ELF data. Together they offer a panoramic view of ELF and its potential impact on language change. The focus moves from a broad macro-social angle through the cognitive to the micro-social observations of ELF interaction in different contexts, domains and spaces around the world.

The big sociolinguistic picture is probed by **Mikko Laitinen** and **Jonas Lundberg**, who test the relationship between multilingualism, and ELF use in particular, and the size of social networks. They build on Mauranen's (2012) hypothesis that ELF communication is characterized by weak social ties and as such creates favourable conditions for the diffusion of innovations (Granovetter 1973; Milroy & Milroy 1985). If this holds, ELF speakers can act as agents in the processes of change. To test the hypothesis, Laitinen and Lundberg use a database of over five million tweets geolocated to Sweden from over 110,000 user accounts. They find that user accounts which 'tweet' in languages other than Swedish (the domestic language in this case), and especially those which also use English, a lingua franca in this environment, have more friends and followers, and therefore larger social networks. Accounts which mainly use ELF also have the largest numbers of followers, that is, the truly weak ties. These findings support the hypothesis and suggest that multilingual users, and ELF users in particular, are likely to act as early adopters of innovations and as agents in their diffusion.

Two studies which follow are at the interface between the macro-social and the cognitive. **Svetlana Vetchinnikova** and **Turo Hiltunen** start out from a well-acknowledged fact that ELF interaction exhibits increased variability. They hypothesize that such variability at the communal level can be rooted in individual variation. As other papers in this volume demonstrate, individual language users participating in global ELF communication are highly heterogeneous, coming from a wide variety of social and L1 backgrounds. As a result, their individual languages – or populations of ELF utterances, to use Croft's terminology (this volume) – can be more different from each other than individual languages comprising more traditional local speech communities. It is such heightened individual variation which might be feeding into the variability perceived at the communal level. As a first step in exploring the hypothesis, Vetchinnikova and Hiltunen examine the properties of individual languages in an online ELF environment. They take a linguistic variable – the use of a contracted vs. an uncontracted form, *it's* vs. *it is* – and look at how the two variants are distributed in ten individual corpora of both native and non-native speakers, with one communal corpus used as a point of comparison. They find substantial differences in how the factors of syntactic structure, chunking and priming affect the variation at the individual and communal levels.

Multilingualism is a ubiquitous feature of ELF communication. As Mauranen (this volume) points out, language contact in the minds of individual speakers gives rise to different kinds of cross-linguistic influence. Is there a cognitive effect of multilingualism at a more general level, across different speakers and different language backgrounds? **Peter Siemund** and **Jessica Terese Mueller** seek to track down the much-talked-about multilingual advantages in a population of ELF speakers. More specifically, they examine the effect of a multilingual upbringing on proficiency in later acquired languages, and English in particular, by means of a large-scale questionnaire study. They find that both students and instructors of a German university who were multilingually raised, for example in German and Turkish, tended to rate their proficiency in English slightly higher than those who were raised with only one home language, even though the tendency did not reach statistical significance across all domains of the Common European Framework of Reference for Languages. For example, the difference in the self-assessments was significant with regard to speech, suggesting that multilingually raised ELF users might be enjoying lower levels of anxiety, as Siemund and Mueller point out.

In all the studies which follow, proficiency, or better fluency, becomes an important variable one way or another. **Veronika Thir** picks up the cognitive thread by reporting on an experiment set up to test whether ELF interlocutors are able to draw on co-textual and contextual cues to resolve ambiguity resulting from differences in accents and pronunciations. In the experiment, ELF interlocutors engaged in a communicative task with and without a schematic context, and Thir found that when linguistic and extra-linguistic cues were available, the interlocutors used them to improve understanding. In spoken interaction, fluency can have an impact on the amount of attention that is required for bottom-up processing of the acoustic signal and the corresponding amount that can be freed for top-down processing of the cues available. Thir argues that in conditions of extreme linguistic diversity and ensuing variety of different accents, the ability to draw on communicative resources beyond the acoustic code is crucial.

Introduction 177

The various effects uncovered at the macro-social and cognitive levels prove useful when interpreting the observations of ELF use in interaction reported in the three remaining studies. Multilingualism is very prominent in all of them, intriguingly manifesting itself in different ways and to a different degree and inviting the readers to reflect on the underlying social and cognitive factors.

Rino Bosso's informants were recruited from the same student population as in Thir's study. They live in a university dormitory in Vienna and thus have a possibility of physical contact, but they also interact online via a Facebook group, demonstrating unconventional exploitations of multimodal resources and some covert forms of multilingualism. Bosso finds that the students often use pictures in communicative acts of request for an actual physical object such as a kettle or a ladle. Such household objects are often outside the vocabulary of ELF users, being domain specific and thus low frequency in 'general English'. However, the pictures are used not only to fill a lexical gap, but also as a gloss when such a potential lexical gap is assumed on the part of the target audience. In such cases, a potentially problematic lexical item, such as an Allen wrench, is often flagged, for example with an emoji, and then glossed with a corresponding picture. Here Bosso sees parallels to the flagging of code-switches as potentially problematic items in ELF speech (Hynninen et al. 2017). Interestingly, in his data, the exploitation of multimodal resources is also combined with multilingual resources, since a picture of an unfamiliar lexical item in English can be searched for online using one's L1. Yet, overall, the multilingual resources do not surface very extensively.

Aki Siegel, in contrast, observes how reliance on shared multilingual resources develops over time in spoken conversations between two first-year students, a Thai and a Japanese speaker, in a university dormitory in Japan. She inspects video recordings collected longitudinally over approximately half a year and examines instances of code-switching in word searches using conversation analysis. At the time of the data collection, the students were studying each other's L1s, Thai and Japanese, and they started to code-switch to these languages when experiencing a lexical gap in English. At first the code-switches were flagged and immediately glossed by a translation, but gradually flagging disappeared and a change happened in the positioning of self and other from a non-knower to a knower of her interlocutor's L1. Siegel also notes the use of gaze, head movements and other gestures. In later recordings, the students code-switched not only to their own but also to their interlocutor's L1, showing that they were becoming comfortable in the newly learned language. As Siegel argues, it can be claimed that a change has happened in the speakers' perception of their shared multilingual resources over time. It is interesting to note that most of the code-switches were to Japanese, the language of the country where the interactions took place, with only a few code-switches at the end of the recording period to Thai. To compare, in the ELFA corpus, which is recorded in Finland, most of the code-switches are to Finnish.

Finally in **Alessia Cogo**'s study of advice sessions for refugee/asylum seekers at a London-based charity, which she describes as a super-diverse place, multilingualism manifests itself on a very different scale, suggesting the need to reconceptualize the boundaries between languages. Cogo is interested in the role multilingual resources play in this context. She focuses on two types of interaction – formal and informal – and finds that languages other than English are employed in them differently and to a different extent. Both types of interaction include translanguaging, or free alternation between two or more languages, which enriches interaction and helps achieve comprehension, as well as building rapport, among other things. Yet, formal sessions seem to be dominated by certain ideological considerations which limit the use of such resources. Thus, Cogo argues, while a charity represents a 'safe place' for translanguaging, there is potentially more space for a flexible use of multilingual practices.

These three studies of micro-social ELF interaction provide a good picture of the heterogeneity of ELF contacts and contact circumstances, touching upon written and spoken as well as online and offline communication, privileged and necessity-driven mobility, European and Asian contexts, English- and non-English-speaking countries, as well as a diverse variety of L1 backgrounds and a range of fluency levels. Overall, the chapters in Part II of this volume emphasize the variability of ELF communication and the ensuing need for ways to cope with such variability, giving rise to the emergence of various strategies, as well as multilingual and multimodal practices.

REFERENCES

Granovetter, Mark. 1973. The strength of weak ties. *American Journal of Sociology* 78(6), 1360–1380.

Hynninen, Niina, Kaisa S. Pietikäinen & Svetlana Vetchinnikova. 2017. Multilingualism in English as a Lingua Franca: Flagging as an indicator of perceived acceptability and intelligibility. In Arja Nurmi, Tanja Rütten and Päivi Pahta (eds.), *Challenging the Myth of Monolingual Corpora*, 95–126. Leiden: Brill.

Mauranen, Anna. 2012. *Exploring ELF: Academic English Shaped by Non-Native Speakers*. Cambridge: Cambridge University Press.

Milroy, James & Lesley Milroy. 1985. Linguistic change, social network and speaker innovation. *Journal of Linguistics* 21, 339–384.

7 ELF, Language Change, and Social Networks
Evidence from Real-Time Social Media Data

Mikko Laitinen and Jonas Lundberg[*]

1 Introduction

Can English as a lingua franca (ELF) exert influence on the established varieties of English? This has been one of the core questions in ELF studies in recent years, and Mauranen (2012), for instance, has advocated this view. She has suggested that such a development might be plausible at least in academic settings because academia is often characterized by loose and intermittent social ties. On the macro level, she suggests that weak ties "probably dominate ELF communication" (2018: 11). Her argument, which links weak ties with change, builds on the social network theory. This theory predicts that environments with weak ties create favorable conditions for change, and innovations tend to diffuse in loose-knit social settings more easily than in close-knit networks (Granovetter 1973). In sociolinguistics, the weak social tie model refers to how linguistic variability is embedded in the social structures where it emerges. Loose-knit social networks, in which individuals are primarily linked by weak ties, tend to promote linguistic innovations (Milroy & Milroy 1985). In ELF settings, multilingual individuals might show a greater propensity for weak social ties in general, and ELF users could therefore act as innovators or early adopters and even influence other varieties.

So far, however, little empirical evidence has been presented to test whether ELF users, who are multilingual by definition and often mobile, have larger networks and more weak ties than monolingual individuals. In this article, therefore, we look into network sizes and types among ELF users. Note that we are able to offer an indirect answer to the question posed in the beginning, but we use network data to study whether ELF settings create favorable social conditions for innovations. Our discussion does not deal with a linguistic variable, but we hope that our empirical work on the social embedding of ELF will trigger future studies of ongoing change and ELF.

---

[*] The authors are listed in alphabetical order, both having contributed an equal share to this article. We wish to thank the editors and the anonymous reviewer(s) for their insightful comments on earlier versions of this article. Any shortcomings are our own. We also want to thank Dr. Rafael Messias Martins (Linnaeus University) for his suggestions on visualizing our data for print.

Rather than focusing on academic settings, we utilize freely available big data[1] from one social media platform. We use Twitter, which is a digital application that makes it possible to write and post short micro-blogs, retweet someone else's message, or post links (URL addresses) or multimedia content. Each tweet comes not only with the message itself, but also with diverse metadata: information related to users or geospatial attributes related to the location of the message (see Laitinen 2017a).

As empirical material, we use the Nordic Tweet Stream, or NTS (Laitinen et al. 2017a). The NTS is a cross-disciplinary project of sociolinguists and computer scientists to broaden the empirical basis of ELF. It is a third-generation[2] ELF corpus, which means that it consists of an online data stream that is captured in real time and in massive amounts. The NTS currently covers the area of five Nordic nations (Denmark, Finland, Iceland, Norway, and Sweden). The data collection started in spring 2016, and by January 2019 it had captured 18,043,882 tweets from 382,255 user accounts from 9,191 unique locations in the Nordic region. In terms of richness, the NTS currently consists of nearly one billion metadata points.

To measure network sizes, we use two metadata attributes available for each tweet. These attributes measure the number of one's online friends and followers. Social networks are operationalized as follows: the number of followers indexes truly weak ties (i.e. it requires no action from a user), and the number of friends is an indication of slightly stronger links (i.e. it requires user effort). In a previous study, we suggested that these metadata offer a way of measuring social networks and that they are ideal for research purposes (Laitinen et al. 2017b). First, they are automatically generated and hence they reduce the observer bias. Second, they are freely available to researchers with intermediate computing skills. Third, while we recognize that social networks are always abstractions, friend and follower counts are useful indicators of social networks because of their differing qualities. Milroy (1992: 178) argues that "a tie is 'weak' if it is less strong than the other ties against which it is measured," which also holds true for the follower counts when compared with friends.

Our research question is whether multilingual individuals on Twitter have larger social networks than those who use the domestic languages. We define a

---

[1] We define big data as large quantities of data that come in high velocity and great variety, *viz* both structured and unstructured formats.

[2] We consider first-generation ELF corpora to be corpora such as ELFA (English as a Lingua Franca in Academic Settings) – that is, they represent material from a certain specified genre, such as spoken academic texts. Second-generation ELF corpora are multigenre materials that represent a range of speech situations. These are currently in the making, but one example is the Corpus of English Texts in Sweden (SWE-CE), as detailed in Laitinen (2016).

multilingual individual as someone who uses ELF and other languages more than the main languages of the countries covered.

We propose that our research broadens the scope of ELF studies towards digital humanities (DH) since it intersects computing and ELF. As defined by Kirschenbaum (2010: 56), we regard DH as a methodological outlook rather than "an investment in any one specific set of texts or even methodologies." One core component in this vast field is the improved capture of data, which in our case consists of the big and rich corpus material. These data possess characteristics that are new in ELF. They are proprietary data owned by a private corporation, and using such data requires interdisciplinary collaboration. The material is secondary data that have not been designed for research purposes, but the benefit is that Twitter material is relatively freely available for research. In addition, we are working with messy data, and increasing accuracy requires close collaboration between sociolinguistics and the computer sciences. Lastly, we are fully aware of the limitations related to the sociodemographic scope of Twitter data. Huang et al. (2016) point out that such data do not fully represent the entire population as certain groups – such as young generations in general and, in the case of Twitter, young men in particular – are overrepresented in social media data.

In addition to new forms of data, we utilize a theoretical model that has not yet been widely used in ELF. By combining ELF and social network theory, we make use of variationist sociolinguistics, a field of inquiry that is concerned with investigating linguistic change. According to Weinreich et al. (1968), the essence of the field builds on orderly heterogeneity, and the study of change in social context involves charting for the emergence of innovative linguistic items (actuation), its transition from one stage to another, its embedding in the linguistic and social structures, and its social evaluation. The social network theory is related to examining social embedding of change in the social structures where it emerges by identifying individuals and speaker groups who act as early adopters of innovations or agents of change when a variant diffuses into a population. By adopting a variationist approach, we are able to use a systematic apparatus to investigate variation and change in ELF.

Section 2 discusses the social network theory and presents a set of recent studies that use Twitter as the source for data. Section 3 details the material and methods used. In Section 4 we present the results, while Section 5 discusses the implications of our findings.

2 Theoretical Background

Social network analysis in the variationist paradigm transpires from the idea that individuals form communities and establish interpersonal ties of varying strengths. These personal social networks are not independent of other sociopolitical and cultural frameworks but are closely related to other social variables, such as gender, social layer. Most crucially, interpersonal ties influence the rate at which innovations are adopted and how they diffuse into a community.

The key finding in the social network model is that strong networks with dense and multiplex ties tend to maintain and support local norms and provide resistance to the adoption of competing norms from the outside. Conversely, conditions that are characterized by weak and uniplex ties are important channels for outside influence and hence contribute positively to the spread of innovations. Social organizations that are close-knit tend to inhibit change, while weak ties facilitate it. The model may explain, for instance, why some languages are, in general, more resistant to change than others. Vice versa, the presence of weak ties might explain why ELF could exert influence on the other varieties of English.

This key finding in sociolinguistics builds on Granovetter's (1973: 1365) observation that "only weak ties may be local bridges." He suggests that more people can be reached through weak ties, but not all weak ties serve this function, "only those acting as bridges between network segments" (1983: 229). To explain this somewhat counterintuitive observation of the importance of weak ties, Granovetter (1973) argues that close-knit networks encourage local cohesion and therefore contribute to forming norm-enforcing communities in which adopting an innovation is socially risky. In loose-knit networks, consisting of individuals already on the social fringes, this is not the case, and consequently, early adopters of an innovation tend to be individuals in the margins. In addition, weak ties may be expected to be more numerous among mobile individuals, and they are thus more likely to contribute to the diffusion of an innovation.

In variationist sociolinguistics, network ties have been operationalized in a number of ways. According to Milroy (2004), more interest has been paid to the first-order ties of direct interaction, characterized as friends and kin. Second-order ties are more indirect, consisting of looser acquaintances. In the classic Belfast study, speakers' networks were measured using five indicators to establish how complex and dense a particular tie was. The indicators consisted of (a) having membership in a locally based group, (b) having ties with 2 + households in the neighborhood, (c) sharing a workplace with 2 + individuals from the neighborhood, (d) sharing a workplace with same-sex individuals from the neighborhood, and (e) being involved in voluntary activities with individuals from the same workplace. The responses resulted in a network strength scale, which formed an independent variable, and these values were compared to the eight phonological dependent variables. The results showed that the individuals with strong network ties with the local community also exhibited the highest share of local, vernacular speech.

A large body of variationist sociolinguistic literature exists in which the network-based approach has been applied to contemporary speech communities (for a detailed overview, see Milroy 2004) and to earlier stages of language (see the special issue of the *European Journal of English Studies* (EJES 2000). Although there may be some risk of simplifying the issue, these studies can be roughly divided into two types of characterization of a network. On the one hand, there are studies that set out from an anchor individual, typically in small ethnographically or philologically constructed historical networks (e.g. Fitzmaurice 2000; Bergs 2005; Sairio 2009). On the other hand, some studies have highlighted macro-level foci and have concentrated on large-scale external upheavals that bring about mobility, such as civil wars and urbanization (e.g. Raumolin-Brunberg 1998).

A common denominator in these studies is that they rely on small datasets. This is particularly true in historical networks, but it also applies to Granovetter's (1973: 1368–1371) study. As a way of illustrating this, his methodology used strong ties that were assumed to consist of "friends," while weak ties presumably consisted of "acquaintances," and the empirical data came from a random sample of 100 personal interviews taken from the total sample of 282. While we recognize the importance of carefully constructed personal networks and the fact that online friends and followers can contain a range of social network types (as argued by Boyd & Crawford 2012), the availability of big social media data also forces us to ask if the model could be tested and applied to very large datasets. Such investigations would enable testing if the weak-tie model also holds when the network size is increased substantially to a few hundred or several thousand nodes (Laitinen et al. 2017b). They could also be utilized to provide new answers in fields such as ELF, where technologization in the form of social media is one of the key drivers.

While variationist sociolinguistics has not utilized Twitter data in the ways that we employ here, Twitter has been widely used in recent years. Various monolingual (Scheffler 2014) and multilingual (Barbaresi 2016; Laitinen et al. 2018) Twitter corpora have been compiled. In addition, Eisenstein et al. (2014) used tweets to model the diffusion of lexical innovations in urban and rural areas, while Huang et al. (2016) used them to obtain a more accurate picture of regional dialects in American English. Gonçalves et al. (2018) used Twitter data to explore World Englishes. Various studies have looked into language choice in Twitter geography (Leetaru et al. 2013; Coats 2015, 2016, 2017a), and the role of gender as a background variable has attracted considerable attention (Rao et al. 2010; Burger et al. 2011; Bamman et al. 2014; Coats 2017b).

3   Material and Methods

Our material, the NTS corpus, is a real-time monitor corpus of tweets sent from five Nordic countries. The data collection makes use of the free Twitter Streaming API, and we use HBC[3] as our downloading mechanism. The data capture utilizes the geolocation information, in which we first specify a geographic region covering the five Nordic countries, and then a second filtering process is applied to select only tweets tagged with a Nordic country code (DK, FI, IS, NO, or SE). This second filtering is necessary in order to exclude tweets from neighboring countries (e.g. Germany and Russia) located within the chosen geographic boundary (see Laitinen et al. 2018 for the process).

While tweet data offer an efficient way of capturing data from tens of thousands of individuals, there are limitations. In our case, Twitter users who do not want to share their location are not included. Note that we are not referring to home locations provided by users, which may be misleading or missing (e.g. "Mars," see Graham et al. 2013), but we refer to the geolocation information provided by Twitter. Depending on a user's privacy settings and the geolocation method used, tweets either have an exact location specified as a pair of latitude and longitude coordinates, or an approximate location specified as a rectangular bounding box, which are available in the metadata attached to the message. Alternatively, no location at all is specified. This type of geographic information ("device location") represents the location of the machine or device on which a user has sent a Twitter message. The data are derived either from the user's device itself (using the GPS) or by detecting the location of the user's Internet Protocol (IP) address (GeoIP). The primary source for locating an IP address is the regional internet registries allocating and distributing IP addresses among organizations located in their respective service regions (e.g. RIPE NCC at www.ripe.net handles European IP addresses). Exact coordinates are almost certainly from devices with built-in GPS receivers (e.g. phones and tablets).

Previous studies report that the proportion of geolocated tweets is in general low, between 0.7% and 2.9% depending on geographic contexts (e.g. Barbaresi 2016). In an in-house experiment to test the accuracy of our data (during a ten-day period in August 2017), we compared the number of NTS tweets in which the language tag was Swedish (n = 53,614) with tweets taken from another download project that was attempting to capture all tweets that had been language-tagged as Swedish independent of geolocation (n = 1,880,844). This result indicates that 2.8% of all tweets tagged as Swedish are geolocated

---

[3] https://github.com/twitter/hbc.

to one of the Nordic countries. It should also be noted that GeoIP-based device location can be tricked by using proxy gateways, allowing a user anywhere in the world to "appear" to be located at a particular GeoIP address. The use of proxy gateways to hide the location is probably most common among users with a malicious intent, such as bots.

The presence of bot accounts highlights the fact that big language data are often messy, since they contain material that could skew sampling and result in inaccuracies when used as empirical evidence. Previous sociolinguistic studies rely on a range of methods when it comes to bot accounts. For instance, Huang et al. (2016) recognize their presence but include them in the results (this is also true for Laitinen et al. 2017b). Coats (2017a) utilizes a method in which material from certain types of devices is excluded.

We utilize machine-learning algorithms to increase the accuracy of the data. This algorithm was developed by Lundberg et al. (2018) and it recognizes automatically generated tweets (AGT) written in English and in Swedish. We define an AGT as a tweet in which all or parts of the natural language content are generated automatically by a bot or other type of program. The algorithm makes use of the textual content and nine numerical and nominal properties that can be computed directly from the tweet metadata. We define a bot account as a user account where a majority of all tweets are identified as AGTs. At the time of writing, the AGT-recognition system is operational for data that contain English and Swedish material (for a language-independent tool, see Lundberg et al. 2019). The accuracy rates are over 97%.

In order to increase the accuracy of our data, we restrict ourselves to the NTS Swedish component. The raw dataset contains 5,334,374 tweets from 110,530 user accounts. The timeframe covers the period from November 6, 2016 to February 26, 2018. Figure 7.1 shows the number of identified unique user accounts during the 449 days of data capture.

The gaps in the line show that our downloading mechanism was inoperative for a total of twenty-four days. More importantly, Figure 7.1 shows that on Day 1 (6 Nov.) we captured tweets from 4,043 accounts, and by the end we had identified a total of 110,530 accounts. After the initial increase, the mean increase per day is 193 new user accounts. This suggests that there is a large set of passive tweeters who tweet very seldom.

Figure 7.2 visualizes a cumulative frequency diagram that shows the spread of messages per account. Each point (x; y) shows the tweet and the user counts and should be interpreted so that we have y user accounts with x or fewer tweets. Note that on the y-axis, the scale is logarithmic to base 10. For example, the second step indicates that we have about 47,000 user accounts that have posted a maximum of two tweets during the period. The point at (10^1; 77,765) indicates that we have nearly 78,000 user accounts with a tweet

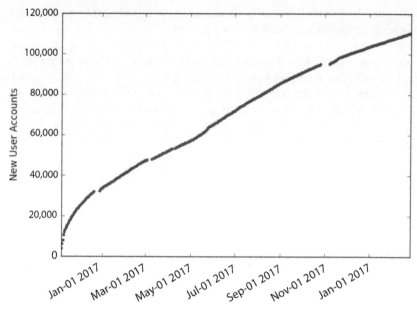

Figure 7.1 The rate of addition of new user accounts in the NTS.

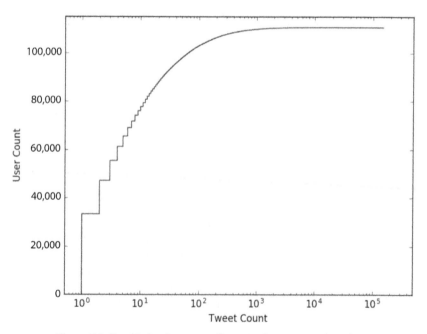

Figure 7.2 Cumulative frequency diagram of user accounts and tweets.

count ≤10. These accounts represent 70.4% of all accounts. Of the accounts, 93.2% have posted fewer than 100 tweets (10^2; 103,020).

The tail end of Figure 7.2 shows the highly active user accounts, and their impact highlights the need for action to increase the data accuracy. For instance, we have ten user accounts each with more than 20,000 tweets during the data capture period. One single user account (userID 461002257, a weather bot) posted more than 150,000 tweets. Notice that 20,000 tweets per 496 days corresponds on average to more than 40 tweets per day.

To prune the dataset, we first exclude verified accounts (i.e. big organizations, celebrities, businesses). This is done by excluding accounts in which the metadata parameter "verified" equals TRUE. Their share is low (2,053 accounts, representing 1.86%, and 57,747 tweets, 1.08%). Second, we exclude bot accounts defined as having 50% (or more) of their tweets identified as AGTs. The number of bot accounts is low (1,187 accounts, share 1.07%), but they generate a rather high number of tweets (342,934, 6.43%). The language distribution of the AGTs is skewed, since 19.6% of all English tweets were identified as AGTs, whereas only 1.7% of the Swedish tweets were AGTs. Finally, since this article is about networking, we exclude all user accounts with fewer than five tweets. As mentioned above, this is a large group of accounts (59,064, share 53.4%) that contribute very little in terms of published tweets (105,421, share 1.9%).

After excluding verified accounts, bots, and accounts with fewer than five tweets, our dataset consists of 48,241 user accounts and 4,828,358 tweets. In Section 4, it is referred to as NTS-Human-Active. This dataset represents active human accounts in Sweden. However, a reasonable question to ask is whether the data represent Swedes and not occasional visitors to the country. Previous studies that use Twitter data have suggested that a great majority of messages in one location, a country for instance, are in fact from residents of that location (e.g. Gonçalves et al. 2018; Lamanna et al. 2018). We can therefore assume that our dataset is reliable, given the general limitations of Twitter data mentioned in the introduction.

With regard to the methods, we utilize three metadata parameters for each tweet. First, our dependent variable is the tweet language. It is automatically generated, and we recognize that automated language identification methods are not entirely accurate. A previous study by Graham et al. (2013) compares the agreement between human coders and Twitter's language recognition system, and their results show that the accuracy of the automated system is high for languages written in the Latin alphabet. Second, as for the independent factor, we utilize the ratio variables of an individual's Twitter friends and followers (see Laitinen et al. 2017b).

4 Results

4.1 The Raw Distribution of Languages

To establish a baseline, we will look first at the share of languages, English/ELF in particular, in the NTS-Human-Active dataset, comparing it with the main language of the country, Swedish, and with other languages. The 48,241 accounts in the dataset were labelled according to the main language of the account. We define the account as (a) predominantly Swedish, (b) predominantly English (ELF), or (c) predominantly Other if the share of tweets per account is more than two-thirds (66.6%). A user account with no dominant language (e.g. an exact 50–50 split) ends up in (d) the Mixed category.

Throughout this section, we will use these four account types as shorthand terms for multilingual and monolingual accounts. It goes without saying that the account types are abstractions and can include a variety of individuals (real or imaginary personae). Since our objective is to mine big data to uncover large quantitative patterns, these terms help us in working with heterogeneous data. So, when we talk about monolingual Swedish accounts, it does not mean the thousands of account holders under this label only know Swedish, but rather that the messages are predominantly in Swedish. Likewise, ELF accounts can include travelers and visitors, but as pointed out in the previous section, Twitter data tend to offer a reliable capture of local language ecologies. In addition, the overall share of English in Swedish Twitter data during more than two years of data capture is much higher than the proportion of people from the prototypical Inner Circle countries living in the country. According to population statistics from the end of 2017, there were 36,470 people who were born in Australia, Canada, Ireland, New Zealand, the United Kingdom, and the USA living in Sweden.[4] That is roughly 0.4% of the total population. The majority of the tweets in English in this dataset are from Swedes and not from visitors from English-speaking countries, for instance.

Table 7.1 shows the language distribution of the account types and the tweets. The main language of Twitter in Sweden is Swedish; 54% of the messages are in Swedish, and 41.1% of the accounts have it as the main language. The share of English of tweets is 19.3%, while 27.9% of the accounts are predominantly in English.

It should be noted that the English accounts generate a slightly smaller proportional share of the tweets than the Swedish accounts. Accounts that are multilingual other than English and Mixed accounts comprise 27% of the accounts and tweets.

---

[4] See www.scb.se/.

Table 7.1 *The count of tweets and accounts in the NTS-Human-Active dataset.*

Account language	Tweets	%	Accounts	%
English	932,410	19.3	13,448	27.9
Swedish	2,607,378	54.0	19,828	41.1
Other	544,921	11.3	5,586	11.6
Mixed	743,649	15.4	9,379	19.4
Total	4,828,358	100.0	48,241	100.0

Table 7.2 *The network sizes for four account types.*

Account, network type	Mean	Median	Range
English, friends	840	321	0; 548,750
English, followers	2,874	337	0; 8,146,448
Swedish, friends	444	230	0; 43,503
Swedish, followers	843	188	0; 356,871
Others, friends	888	256	0; 1,001,126
Other, followers	2,381	253	0; 2,171,359
Mixed, friends	532	242	0; 197,352
Mixed, followers	942	175	0; 377,926

4.2   Network Sizes for ELF Users

Table 7.2 above shows the typical friends and followers profiles for the four user types in the dataset. It includes arithmetic mean values, median, and range for both friends and followers. In general, the median value is a more informative indicator of a typical account, since it better accounts for outliers. The presence of outliers is clearly seen in the range values, where the highest follower count for an English account is several million, while for friends it is more than half a million. It is noteworthy that the outliers for the Swedish accounts are much lower than for the multilingual accounts of English and Other. Note that we have excluded verified accounts of organizations, celebrities, and businesses, which in general tend to have higher friend and follower figures.

If we focus on the mean and median values, the trends are clear. Multilingual users have larger social networks in Twitter than monolingual users, as both the figures for multilingual accounts (English and Other) are considerably higher than for the primarily monolingual Swedish accounts. For the arithmetic mean, the average number of online friends connected with an English account is 840, while for a Swedish account it is 444.

Based on the median values, a typical English account has more than 300 friends and followers, whereas Swedish accounts have around 200. It is noteworthy that the other multilingual accounts, *viz* other than ELF, fall between those who use ELF and those who use Swedish. The mean values for English accounts are nearly 100% larger than predominantly Swedish accounts, and the differences in the median values are some 40% larger for friends, while those for followers are over 70% higher. The fourth category, Mixed accounts that do not surpass the threshold value of two-thirds, shows a fall below the truly multilingual accounts, with median values of 242 friends and 175 followers.

To test whether the median values shown in Table 7.2 are statistically significant, we use the independent one-tailed u-test (Wilcoxon Rank Sum Test). This enables us to examine whether the median values of the dependent variables in the two groups (Eng. and Swe.) as defined by the independent variable (network size) differ from each other at statistically significant levels. The u-test is very similar to the more familiar t-test, the primary difference being that the u-test does not assume known distributions of normality (the Shapiro-Wilk Test). The statistic package used here (R) has an upper limit of 5,000 observations to test the homogeneity of the data for independent samples, and hence we prefer the u-test.

The null hypothesis is that the observed medians are equal. The u-test returns highly significant results for both friends ($W = 105720000$, p-value $< 2.2e-16$) and followers ($W = 110790000$, p-value $< 2.2e-16$). These results enable us to reject the null hypothesis, and we have evidence that the observed medians of the two populations (Eng. and Swe.) differ at statistically highly significant levels.

Table 7.2 also shows that the predominantly English accounts have the largest networks of truly weak ties. In a previous study (Laitinen et al. 2017b), we suggested that the follower count represents truly weak network ties because they require nothing from a Twitter user. The follower category is one-sided and more passive from a personal viewpoint. Friends, on the other hand, represent slightly stronger ties. The results here show that the predominantly English accounts are the only type in Table 7.2, where the median follower count (i.e. truly weak ties) is larger than the friends count.

Figure 7.3 visualizes these findings using a boxplot. It shows that ELF users have larger social networks than other multilingual users and, more importantly, that both of these groups in turn have networks that are larger than those of predominantly Swedish accounts.

The results observed in Table 7.2 and visualized in Figure 7.3 corroborate our initial observations in Laitinen et al. (2017b). In these first results, we utilized data from all of the five Nordic countries and used a dataset that also included bots. These findings showed that the sizes of networks for those who

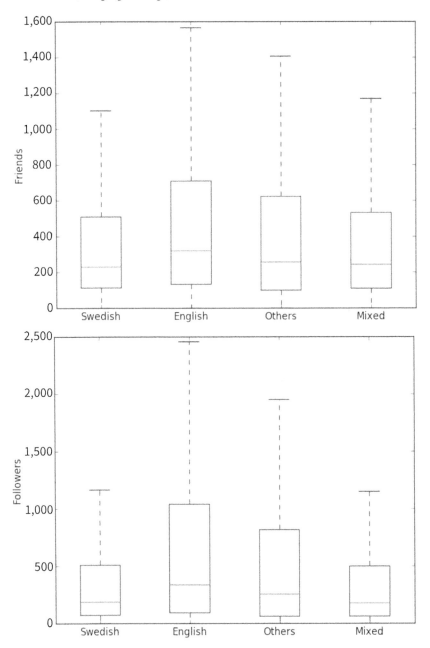

Figure 7.3 Boxplots of the median values for the four account types for friends (top) and followers (bottom).

almost always tweeted in English (99–100% of tweets) were nearly twice the size of the networks of those who rarely or never used English. The added value here is that we are able not only to confirm the first findings, but also to acquire a more accurate picture of networks by focusing on real users and excluding bots.

At this point, a relevant task is to question how valid these numbers are and how real the ties between accounts might be. It is clear that the upper ranges for both friends and followers show non-permanent and passive social ties, as it is cognitively impossible to maintain hundreds of thousands of network ties. However, the median values in this section closely resemble the average sizes of human social networks proposed in social anthropology. On the one hand, Dunbar (1992), drawing on developmental biology, has suggested that the neocortex size in general and the number of neocortical neurons in particular impose an upper limit on an individual's information-processing capacity, which in turn "limits the number of relationships that an individual can monitor simultaneously." According to Dunbar's estimate, the number of social network ties is around 150 nodes. On the other hand, McCarty et al. (2001) investigate the size of personal networks in the USA, and compare two methods that make use of respondents' ability to report the number of individuals they know in specific subpopulations. Their results show "a remarkable similarity between the average network size[s] generated by both methods (approximately 291)."

For our purposes, the network sizes observed in the NTS show noteworthy similarities with these two studies. The median values observed lie within the range of these two estimates, but they show that active multilingualism, defined as online behavior here, clearly plays a role in network sizes.

Figure 7.4 visualizes the accounts using scatterplots that correlate the number of friends with followers per account using a logarithmic scale to base 10. In order to better visualize tens of thousands of accounts, we restrict ourselves to the predominantly Swedish (left) and English (right) accounts. The top part of Figure 7.4 visualizes all the accounts, while the bottom one is zoomed in to the densest concentration. Note that the sharp line at the 5,000 friends mark is brought about by Twitter imposing an upper limit that each individual account can follow, that is, can become friends with.[5] The value used by Twitter is the ratio of followers relative to those who follow an individual. This ratio is not published, and the way to increase the friends count is to gain new followers. Hence, we observe a more direct correlation of friends/followers after the 5,000 mark. Note that more illustrative color

---

[5] https://help.twitter.com/en/using-twitter/twitter-follow-limit.

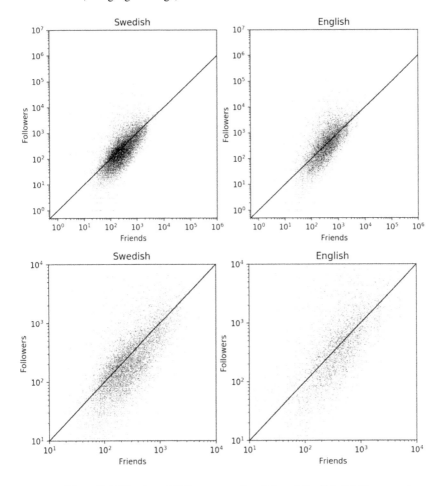

Figure 7.4 Friends and followers per Swedish and English (ELF) accounts (only NTS-Human-Active).

versions of Figure 7.4 depicting trends in big data can be found under the Resources of the book home page.

These visualizations confirm our main finding: accounts with ELF have more friends and followers than the predominantly Swedish accounts. The top part shows friends vs. followers for all of the 13,448 ELF accounts and 19,828 Swedish user accounts. A majority of all user accounts are centered on the median values (about 250 friends and followers), and the numbers of friends and followers for most of the accounts are roughly even, but one should also note that there are numerous outliers. The bottom part of Figure 7.4 is a close-up of the same plot centered on 250 friends and followers. By increasing the resolution, the observations provide additional confirmation of the differences between predominantly multilingual users (English) and predominantly monolingual ones (Swedish), as shown in this section.

4.3 Estimating the Accuracy of Our Big ELF Data

We are utilizing undoubtedly big and rich data, with the original dataset coming from 110,530 user accounts. In the previous sections, these raw data were first reduced to 48,241 human and active accounts, and were reduced even further to 33,276 English and Swedish accounts. This highlights the fact that we need to look beyond mere size in order to determine the added value of the new forms present in the big ELF data. This is widely understood in fields in which the size and scope of data are considered significant (cf. Hiltunen et al. 2017). More importantly, we need to explore ways of estimating the accuracy of our data.

In this section we include parts of the data excluded from the NTS-Human-Active dataset used in the previous section. Figure 7.5 shows three scatterplots (friends vs. followers on a logarithmic scale to base 10) for verified, bot, and

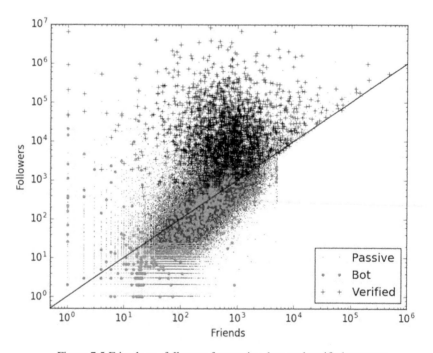

Figure 7.5 Friends vs. followers for passive, bot, and verified accounts.

passive accounts. The label "passive" represents 59,064 accounts with fewer than five tweets. "Bots" represents 1,187 bot accounts, while the label "verified" represents 2,053 verified accounts. Note that a more illustrative color version of Figure 7.5 depicting trends in big data can be found under the Resources of the book home page at [URL].

The first thing to notice is that the passive user accounts behave very much like the active human accounts presented in Section 4.2. The densest concentration resembles that observed in the scatterplots in Figure 7.4, where the median values for friends and followers are around 250. The result suggests that our decision to exclude low-frequency tweeters did not skew the results, since the low tweeting frequency does not imply a substantial change in the number of friends and followers. Low-frequency tweeters tend to exhibit more closely similar reciprocity in their relationships than do more active users (cf. characterized as *acquaintances* by Krishnamurthy et al. 2008). The only noteworthy difference when compared with the more active accounts is that there seem to be a few passive accounts that have an extremely high number (>10,000) of friends and followers. At the same time, we also need to acknowledge that our decision to use five tweets as the threshold limit did not provide any additional information to the observations presented above.

More surprising is the fact that the bot accounts, which are excluded from the results in the previous section, behave very much like the human accounts. The great majority of bot accounts have a few hundred friends and followers. There is a slight tilt towards a higher friend count, most likely because many of these accounts post factual information, such as weather station data, that may have a follower basis. However, this result indicates that the owners of the bot accounts, despite posting a majority of their tweets in an "artificial" way, interact with other accounts in a humanlike manner.

Most importantly, our decision to exclude verified accounts clearly increased the data accuracy. As expected, these accounts behave substantially differently in terms of their friend and follower counts. We should recall that verified accounts often represent well-known artists, companies, or organizations, and that their aim is often to interact with their audience (the so-called *evangelists* in Krishnamurthy et al. 2008). Hence, the verified accounts often have a very high number of followers, much higher than their number of friends.

4.4 A More Detailed Look at the Networks of ELF and Swedish Populations

This section utilizes the data to obtain additional support for our observations concerning social networks of ELF users. The results in previous sections show that multilingual users have larger social networks than monolingual accounts, at least on this social media platform. Section 4.2 shows that the two populations (ELF and Swe.) were statistically significantly different, and the major pattern was also supported by evidence from the accounts labelled as Other – *viz* multilingual with languages other than English – and Mixed. In addition, Section 4.3 shows that we can achieve increased accuracy through our methodological choices. We should recall, however, that these findings were based on a criterion of two-thirds of tweets to define an account. While it is obvious that this is an arbitrary limit, it nevertheless ensures that we deal with clear majorities in language choice and that each account labelled as either Eng., Swe., or Other represents a truly clear-cut account.

This section intends to observe in greater detail how the share of English is distributed with regard to network sizes. We utilize all of the NTS-Human-Active accounts with any share of English; bot, verified, and passive accounts are excluded. Figure 7.6 shows how accounts differ with regard to their share of English.

It visualizes the accounts per their share of English, showing that the large proportion of user accounts geolocated in Sweden (22,081 accounts, share 45.8%) have fewer than 10% of their messages in English. This result is to be expected since Swedish is the major language in the country, as shown in

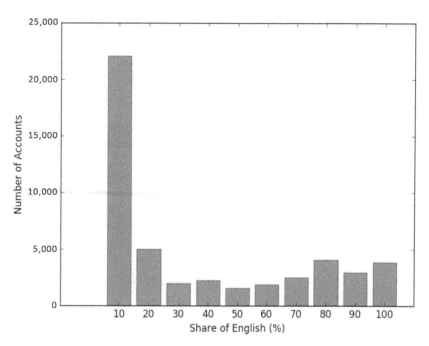

Figure 7.6 Share of English distribution per account type.

Section 4.1, and English is clearly not replacing it, but a noteworthy fact is that over half of the account holders (54.2%) use English to at least some degree (>10%). The lowest number of accounts is in the split (50%) group, while we have more than 3,800 accounts in the dataset that are fully in English. This relatively low share of 100% English accounts may result from the fact that the automated language recognition algorithm used by Twitter occasionally fails to recognize a message, and since the dataset also includes tweets with an unidentified language tag (lang = und), this data-related feature may reduce the proportion of such accounts.

The method used here is based on our previous study in Laitinen et al. (2017b), where we presented a cohort-based algorithm that enabled us to correlate the impact of using English and the network size. This algorithm first divides all users into a number of equal-sized cohorts based on their share of English and then computes the mean and median number of friends and followers for each cohort.

Figure 7.7 shows the ten-cohort division for both friends and followers. Each column represents 5,361 user accounts, and the cohorts are sorted according to their share of English. The number below a cohort indicates the average share of English, while the y-axis indicates the average number of friends and followers in the cohort. It should be noticed that, as a result of the general distribution in the NTS-Human-Active data, the first two cohorts show accounts with no English at all, and the first four cohorts represent user accounts that have no more than 10% of their tweets in English (i.e. the first column in Figure 7.6).

These results show a twofold division of the accounts. On the one hand, for the predominantly Swedish accounts (<10% English), the more that tweets are sent in English, the larger the networks are. This can be seen clearly with regard to both friends (top) and followers (bottom). The individuals with the smallest networks are monolingual tweeters, which is clearly visible in the friend counts. On the other hand, the more multilingual an account becomes, the larger the networks are. Post hoc statistical testing confirms that the pattern observed is statistically significant, since the correlation coefficients for share of English and number of friends and followers give the following result: Followers vs. EngShare: $r = 0.031$, $p < 0.0000001$ and Friends vs. EngShare: $r = 0.025$, $p < 0.00001$. This indicates a weak, but positive, correlation in both cases.

If we briefly compare these bot-free findings (i.e. based on the NTS-Human-Active dataset) to our previous efforts, the results in Figure 7.7 deviate slightly from those presented in Laitinen et al. (2017b). Our first results showed a linear increase in both friends and followers when we increased the share of English, but in these new results we have a drop in friends and followers for primarily monolingual accounts, and then a dramatic increase for the higher shares.

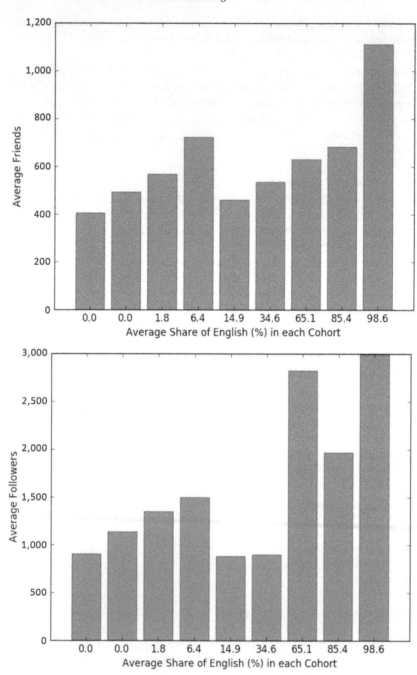

Figure 7.7 Friend cohorts (top) and follower cohorts (bottom) when using a ten-cohort division.

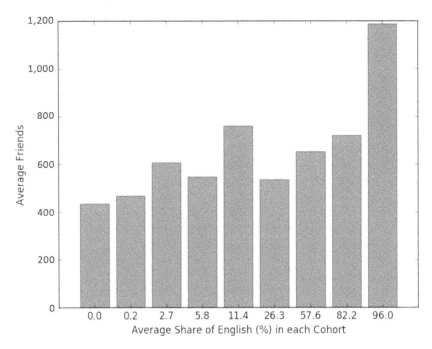

Figure 7.8 Friend cohorts using ten tweets as their threshold value.

We can easily confirm the finding by alternating the independent variables, but the big picture does not change. Those who only tweet in the domestic language (Swedish) in the dataset tend to have smaller networks in general than multilingual account holders. Figure 7.8 visualizes a ten-cohort division, increasing the threshold value for messages sent from five to ten. The visualization confirms the finding.

The general trend remains unaltered, since the occasional tweeting in English for predominantly Swedish accounts shows increased network sizes, but it is only after substantial increases in using English that we start seeing substantial increases in network sizes.

5 Conclusions

The quantitative patterns observed show that multilingual users have a greater number of ties between accounts than monolingual users, and therefore also, most likely, have larger social networks in general. We have observed that, statistically speaking, social embedding of ELF favors weak ties, innovation, and diffusion of change. Larger network sizes and network types suggest that ELF users could be more likely to act as agents of change than the other account types observed here. Hence, it is fair to suggest that the social contexts for multilingual speakers clearly favor linguistic change. The results can be used to suggest a scale based on the sizes of social networks with regard to ELF. This scale can be shown as:

Multilingual with ELF > Multilingual Other > Mixed > Monolingual

This suggests that the size of social networks is larger for each group across the scale from right to left. That is, monolingual users have the smallest networks, and those who occasionally use other languages have larger social networks than monolingual individuals, defined here as predominantly Swedish users. Multilingual social media users have the largest networks, but there is a clear difference between those who regularly use languages other than English and those who use English/ELF. In addition, our findings (Section 4.2) show that ELF users have larger weak-tie networks than any of the other groups investigated here, making them more likely to act as bridges between network segments.

Our results provide empirical evidence relevant to the question presented in the introduction: can ELF exert influence on other varieties of English? As pointed out in the introduction, we are only able to provide an indirect answer to this profound question in English linguistics, since it is beyond the scope of the present study to examine such a broad empirical problem. What our empirical evidence permits us to say is that social embedding of ELF use needs to be taken into account in future studies, and we have illustrated that variationist (and computational) sociolinguistics could offer a useful theoretical and methodological toolbox for this task.

We hope that this finding will result in future network studies of ELF and multilingual environments. Our study is one of the first to provide empirical and quantitative data to support such a finding, but it needs to be pointed out that various previous studies have also suggested that multilingualism in general tends to promote change. This has been suggested by Blake (1992) with regard to the influence of French speakers in post-Norman conquest England and also in present-day settings in urban multiethnolects (Cheshire et al. 2011).

The findings presented here need to be confirmed using other forms of big social media data than Twitter, since it might be the case that Twitter as a platform contains intervening variables that were not accounted for in the operationalization used here. However, it is important to note that the results in Section 4 show that the main finding not only applied to the predominantly English accounts, but was also supported by the observations of the other languages, which included a heterogeneous set of languages in the group labelled as Other. These naturally include a range of languages, from immigrant languages (e.g. Arabic, Turkish) to the other major European languages (French, German, etc.), but the main observation holds.

Lastly, we wish to highlight the methodological side of our study for ELF. As pointed out in the introduction, we have adopted a DH type of approach in which we have combined the expertise of a computer scientist and a sociolinguist with the aim of being able to provide new insights into old questions. This kind of collaboration is needed in various fields, but primarily in the study of ELF. Technologization is one of the key drivers in the global spread of English, and more studies need to adopt DH in the study of ELF, thus complementing small data and more qualitative analyses.

One aspect of DH is dissemination and open data, and we wish to highlight that all of the NTS data used here are available for researchers for replication and manipulation, such as changing the threshold values used in Sections 4.1 and 4.2. At the time of writing, these data can be accessed in-house in the universities with which we are affiliated. In the near future, the objective is to make the data available through an online platform, and we also aim at expanding the geographic scope of our data streaming to other parts of the world where English is used as a lingua franca.

REFERENCES

Bamman, David, Jacob Eisenstein & Tyler Schnoebelen. 2014. Gender identity and lexical variation in social media. *Journal of Sociolinguistics* 18, 135–160.

Barbaresi, Adrian. 2016. Collection and indexation of Tweets with a geographical focus. Tenth International Conference on Language Resources and Evaluation (LREC 2016), May 2016. *Proceedings of the 4th Workshop on Challenges in the Management of Large Corpora (CMLC)*, (2016), 24–27. <hal-01323274>

Bergs, Alexander. 2005. *Social Networks and Historical Sociolinguistics: Studies in Morphosyntactic Variation in the Paston Letters 1421–1503*. Berlin & New York: Mouton de Gruyter.

Blake, Norman. Introduction. 1992. In Norman Blake (ed.), *The Cambridge History of the English Language, Vol. II, 1066–1476*, 1–22. Cambridge: Cambridge University Press.

Boyd, Danah & Kate Crawford. 2012. Critical questions for big data. Provocations for a cultural, technological, and scholarly phenomenon. *Information, Communication & Society* 15(5), 662–679. doi: 10.1080/1369118X.2012.678878.

Burger, John D., John Henderson, George Kim & Guido Zarrella. 2011. Discriminating gender on Twitter. *Proceedings of the Conference on Empirical Methods in Natural Language Processing (EMNLP)*, 1301–1309. Stroudsburg, PA: Association for Computational Linguistics. www.aclweb.org/anthology/D11-1120.

Cheshire, Jenny, Paul Kerswill, Sue Fox & Eivind Torgersen. 2011. Contact, the feature pool and the speech community: The emergence of Multicultural London English. *Journal of Sociolinguistics* 15(2), 151–196.

Coats, Steven. 2015. Non-standard lexical and grammatical resources in Finland Twitter English. A paper presented at Poznan Linguistics Meeting, 19 September 2015, Poznan, Poland. http://cc.oulu.fi/~scoats/poznan1handout.pdf (22.1.2018).

2016. Grammatical frequencies and gender in Nordic Twitter Englishes. In Darja Fišer and Michael Beißwenger (eds.), *Proceedings of the 4th Conference on CMC and Social Media Corpora for the Humanities*, 12–16. Ljubljana: University of Ljubljana Academic Publishing.

2017a. European language ecology and bilingualism with English on Twitter. In Ciara Wigham & Egon Stemle (eds.), *Proceedings of the 5th Conference on CMC and Social Media Corpora for the Humanities*, 35–38. Bozen/Bolzano: Eurac Research.

2017b. Gender and lexical type frequencies in Finland Twitter English. In Turo Hiltunen, Joe McVeigh & Tanja Säily (eds.), *Studies in Variation, Contacts and Change in English 19: Big and Rich Data in English Corpus Linguistics: Methods and Explorations*. Helsinki: VARIENG. www.helsinki.fi/varieng/series/volumes/19/coats/.

Dunbar, Robin. 1992. Neocortex size as a constraint on group size in primates. *Journal of Human Evolution*, 22(6), 469–493.

Eisenstein Jacob, Brendan O'Connor, Noah A. Smith & Eric P. Xing. 2014. Diffusion of lexical change in social media. *PLoS ONE* 9(11), e113114. doi: 10.1371/journal.pone.0113114.

EJES. 2000. *European Journal of English Studies* 4(3).

Fitzmaurice, Susan. 2000. *The spectator*, the politics of social networks, and language standardization in eighteenth century England. In Laura Wright (ed.), *The Development of Standard English 1300–1800: Theories, Descriptions, Conflicts*, 195–218. Cambridge: Cambridge University Press.

Gonçalves, Bruno, Lucía Loureiro-Porto, José Ramasco & David Sánchez. 2018. Mapping the Americanization of English in space and time. *PLoS ONE* 13(5), e0197741. https://doi.org/10.1371/journal.pone.0197741.

Graham, Mark, Scott A. Hale & Devin Gaffney. 2013. Where in the world are you? Geolocation and language identification in Twitter. *The Professional Geographer* 66, 568–578. doi: 10.1080/00330124.2014.907699.

Granovetter, Mark. 1973. The strength of weak ties. *American Journal of Sociology* 78(6), 1360–1380.

1983. The strength of weak ties: A network theory revisited. *Sociological Theory* 1, 201–233.

Hiltunen, Turo, Joe McVeigh & Tanja Säily. 2017. How to turn linguistic data into evidence? In Turo Hiltunen, Joe McVeigh & Tanja Säily (eds.), *Big and Rich Data in English Corpus Linguistics: Methods and Explorations (Studies in Variation, Contacts and Change in English 1)*. Helsinki: VARIENG. www.helsinki.fi/varieng/series/volumes/19/.

Huang, Yuan, Diansheng Guo, Alice Kasakoff & Jack Grieve. 2016. Understanding US regional linguistic variation with Twitter data analysis. *Computers, Environment and Urban Systems* 59, 244–255. doi: 10.1016/j.compenvurbsys.2015.12.003.

Kirschenbaum, Matthew G. 2010. What is digital humanities and what's it doing in English departments? *ADA Bulletin* 150, 55–61. doi: 10:1632/ade.150.55.

Krishnamurthy, Balachander, Phillipa Gill & Martin Arlitt. 2008. A few chirps about Twitter. In Christos Faloutsos, Thomas Karagiannis & Pablo Rodriguez (eds.), *Proceedings of the First Workshop on Online Social Networks (WOSN '08)*, 19–24. New York: ACM. doi: 10.1145/1397735.1397741.

Laitinen, Mikko. 2016. Ongoing changes in English modals: On the developments in ELF. In Olga Timofeeva, Sarah Chevalier, Anne-Christine Gardner & Alpo Honkapohja (eds.), *New Approaches in English Linguistics: Building Bridges*, (Studies in Language Companion Series), 175–196. Amsterdam: John Benjamins. doi: 10.1075/slcs.177.07lai.

Laitinen, Mikko, Jonas Lundberg, Magnus Levin & Rafael Martins. 2018. The Nordic tweet stream: A dynamic real-time monitor corpus of big and rich language data. *Proc. of Digital Humanities in the Nordic Countries 3rd Conference*, Helsinki, Finland, March 7–9, 2018. CEUR-WS.org/Vol-2084/short10.pdf.

Laitinen, Mikko, Jonas Lundberg, Magnus Levin & Alexander Lakaw. 2017a. Utilizing multilingual language data in (nearly) real time: the case of the Nordic Tweet Stream. *Journal of Universal Computer Science* 23 (11), 1038–1056.

2017b. Revisiting weak ties: using present-day social media data in variationist studies. In Tanja Säily, Minna Palander-Collin, Arja Nurmi & Anita Auer (eds.), *Exploring Future Paths for Historical Sociolinguistics*, 303–325. Amsterdam: John Benjamins. doi: 10.1075/ahs.7.12lai.

Lamanna Fabio, Maxime Lenormand, María Henar Salas-Olmedo, Gustavo Romanillos, Bruno Gonçalves & José J. Ramasco. 2018. Immigrant community integration in world cities. *PLoS ONE* 13(3), e0191612. https://doi.org/10.1371/journal.pone.0191612.

Leetaru, Kalev H., Shaowen Wang, Guofeng Cao, Anand Padmanabhan & Eric Shook. 2013. Mapping the global Twitter heartbeat: The geography of Twitter. *First Monday* 18(5). http://firstmonday.org/ojs/index.php/fm/article/view/4366/3654.

Lundberg, Jones, Jonas Nordqvist & Antonio Matosevic. 2018. On-the-fly detection of autogenerated Tweets, arXiv preprint.

Lundberg, Jonas, Jonas Nordqvist & Mikko Laitinen. 2019. Towards a language independent Twitter bot detector. *Proceedings of the Digital Humanities in the Nordic Region (DHN2019)*, University of Copenhagen, March 6–9, 2019.

Mauranen, Anna. 2018. Conceptualising ELF. In Jennifer Jenkins, Will Baker & Martin Dewey (eds.), *The Routledge Handbook of English as a Lingua Franca*. London: Routledge.

2012. *Exploring ELF: Academic English Shaped by Non-Native Speakers*. Cambridge: Cambridge University Press.

McCarty, Christopher, Peter Killworth, H. Russell Bernard, Eugene Johnsen & Gene Shelley. 2001. Comparing two methods for estimating network size. *Human Organization* 60(1), 28–39.

Milroy, James. 1992. *Linguistic Variation and Change. On the Historical Sociolinguistics of English*. Oxford: Blackwell.

Milroy, Lesley. 2004. Social networks. In J. K. Chambers, Peter Trudgill & Natalie Schilling-Estes (eds.), *The Handbook of Language Variation and Change*, 549–570. Oxford: Blackwell.

Milroy, James & Lesley Milroy. 1985. Linguistic change, social network and speaker innovation. *Journal of Linguistics* 21, 339–384. doi: 10.1017/S0022226700010306.

Rao, Delip, David Yarowsky, Abhishek Shreevats & Manaswi Gupta. 2010. Classifying latent user attributes in Twitter. *Proceedings of the 2nd International*

Workshop on Search and Mining User-Generated Contents, 37–44. New York: Association for Computing Machinery. doi: 10.1145/1871985.1871993.

Raumolin-Brunberg, Helena. 1998. Social factors and pronominal change in the seventeenth century: The civil-war effect? In Jacek Fisiak & Marcin Krygier (eds.), *Advances in English Historical Linguistics*, 361–388. Berlin: Mouton de Gruyter.

Sairio, Anni. 2009. *Language and Letters of the Bluestocking Network: Sociolinguistic Issues in Eighteenth-century Epistolary English* (Mémoires de la Société Néophilologique de Helsinki LXXV). Helsinki: Société Néophilologique.

Scheffler, Tatjana. 2014. A German Twitter Snapshot. *Proceedings of LREC, (2014)*, 2284–2289.

Weinreich, Uriel, William Labov & Marvin Herzog. 1968. Empirical foundations for a theory of language change. In Winfred P. Lehmann & Yakov Malkiel (eds.), *Directions for Historical Linguistics*, 95–188. Austin: University of Texas Press.

8 ELF and Language Change at the Individual Level

Svetlana Vetchinnikova and Turo Hiltunen

1 Introduction

It is probably fair to say that empirical descriptions of language in use have been for the most part based on average tendencies, rather than preferences of individual speakers. Individual variation has always been recognized but has seldom been the main focus, except in the fields of stylistic studies and forensic linguistics. In fact, the study of idiolects has been discouraged at least in the field of language change since the seminal publication by Weinreich et al. (1968) who argue that an individual language is not the right place to look for linguistic regularities or change. Labov also clearly stated later that "language ... is an abstract pattern, exterior to the individual" and that "the individual does not exist as a linguistic entity" (Labov 2006: 5).

However, many recent studies indicate a growing interest in the study of variation between individual language users, owing both to the increasing availability of large, diverse and richly annotated data sets and to the finding that these differences do matter in the description of language use. Accordingly, studies have indicated substantial individual differences in grammar (Dąbrowska 2012), collocational preferences (Mollin 2009), n-gram profiles (Barlow 2013; Wright 2017) and lexicogrammatical patterns (Hall et al. 2017). Vetchinnikova (2017) explicitly sets language representation at the individual level against the communal level, at which language is normally described using data aggregated from a population of individuals, and argues that they can be qualitatively different from each other, in the same way as different dialects of a language are both different from each other and from the 'standard'.

Indeed, if, following a recurring line of thinking in this volume, language (or to be more precise, its communal level) is conceptualized as a complex adaptive system (Ellis & Larsen-Freeman 2006; Beckner et al. 2009; see also Schneider and Mauranen this volume), it can be defined as 'a set of variables that interact over time' (de Bot et al. 2007: 7). There is no unanimous agreement on what these interacting variables or elements are. Some researchers, like Schneider (this volume), see language as a system of linguistic units at various levels of abstraction, such as phonemes, morphemes or lexemes, entering into syntagmatic and paradigmatic relations with each other. However, it is also possible to see language as a system of interacting idiolects. We are not the first to suggest this view. For example in their position paper, Beckner et al. (2009: 2) postulate that language seen as a complex adaptive system 'consists of multiple agents (the speakers in the speech community) interacting with one another'. We think these views are not mutually exclusive and depend on the specific timescale and level of representation being modelled. If the latter approach is adopted, the relationship between the communal average and the individual languages must be characterized by the property of emergence characteristic of complex systems, suggesting that these two levels are qualitatively different. If this holds, substantial changes at the individual representation level must bring about change at the communal level.

The issue of individual variation is of particular interest in situations where English is used as a lingua franca (ELF). Typically, in such situations most individual languages are processed as a second language and also experience other effects of multilingual, rapidly changing environments. As a result, they are likely to become more different from each other, and the description of the average might become less informative than ever before. In fact, variability has been recognized as one of the key features of ELF use (Mauranen 2012, 2017; Jenkins 2015; papers in Jenkins et al. 2017). If such variability, at least in part, is brought about by larger differences between individual languages, the description of their properties might bring new insights into the study of ELF, changing English and language change more generally.

This paper contributes to the description of the properties of individual languages and their relationship to the communal average. More specifically, we take a linguistic variable – in this case the use of a contracted vs. uncontracted form, *it's* vs. *it is* – and look at the distribution of its variants and factors influencing the choice in individual and communal corpora collected from an online ELF environment. The factors we examine are: SYNTACTIC STRUCTURE, PRIMING and CHUNKING. Our aim is to investigate whether and how these factors work at the individual and communal levels, and in what way they can have an effect on language change.

2 English Contraction: Morphosyntactic Variation, Reduction and Chunking

Why do we sometimes use contracted forms and sometimes uncontracted? There are a number of social, cognitive and linguistic factors which can influence the choice, as well as a variety of frameworks within which they are explored. In this chapter, we use the term 'contraction' to refer to the process of reducing the expression *it is* to *it's*, as well as to other similar predictable reductions.[1] In our written data, the reduction is orthographically marked with an apostrophe, and the form *it's* corresponds to a phonologically reduced form in spoken language.

The choice between full and contracted forms can be looked at as a case of morphosyntactic variation, together with other linguistic variables such as alternation in the dative (*gave a book to him/gave him a book)*, the genitive (*the girl's eyes/the eyes of the girl*), the comparative (*happier/more happy*), relative pronouns (*that/who*) and particle placement (*switch off the light/switch the light off*) (see e.g. D'Arcy & Tagliamonte 2015 and Gries 2017 for an overview). Since Labov's seminal work (e.g. Labov 1969), morphosyntactic variables like these have been extremely popular in sociolinguistic variationist analyses, given that it is relatively straightforward to determine variable context, or 'different ways of saying the same thing' (e.g. Tagliamonte 2006: 71). The aim of this line of research is 'to understand the mechanisms which link extralinguistic phenomena (the social and cultural) with patterned linguistic heterogeneity (the internal, variable, system of language)' (Sankoff 1988: 157; Tagliamonte 2011: xiv). The main assumption here is that linguistic variation reflects social organization, and by correlating linguistic variables as dependent variables with social factors as independent variables, one can uncover properties of social structure.

Contraction can also be viewed as a case of morphosyntactic or phonological reduction along with, for example, zero complementation in *that*-clauses (e.g. Jaeger 2006) or word-final /t/ and /d/ deletion (Labov 1972; Bybee 2002). In previous studies, reduction has been explained by three interpretations related to frequency effects, which are cognitive in nature, including 1) chunking and ensuing language change, 2) other frequency effects and 3) rational striving for *uniform information density*. These explanations are partly overlapping but also partly distinct. In what follows, we explore previous accounts of the relationship of these factors and contraction.

Phonological reduction as a result of chunking has been extensively discussed by Bybee (e.g. 2002, 2006). For example, Bybee and Scheibman (1999) show that the degree of phonological reduction in *don't* is associated with frequent contexts of use, more specifically when *don't* occurs after the first person singular pronoun *I* and before high-frequency verbs such as *know, think, have, mean* and *feel*. They argue that, through chunking, frequent word combinations become processing units with autonomous storage and undergo changes in their constituent structure. Structural changes also couple with changes in meaning, or more precisely, pragmatic functions, and these processes have also been described in several corpus studies in the neo-Firthian

---

[1] An example of a non-predictable reduction is *won't*, which Huddleston and Pullum (2002: 91) analyse as an inflectional form of *will*.

tradition (Sinclair 1991; Hunston 2007; Cheng et al. 2009). In all cases where *don't* is phonologically reduced the most, the 'hosting' unit has a function which is different from the same combination of words where *don't* is not reduced. For example, all occurrences of *I don't know* in their data are associated with the literal meaning of 'not knowing', but only the reduced instances convey an additional pragmatic function of speaker uncertainty and mitigation of polite disagreement (Bybee & Scheibman 1999: 587). For Bybee and Scheibman, it is the same change of constituent structure which occurs in grammaticalization.

While chunking allegedly starts off as a result of frequency, frequency effects on morphosyntactic variation have also been examined separately from the notion of chunking, as they seem to be able to have an online, synchronic influence on variation too. What sets the two accounts apart is the fact that the frequency effect account does not presuppose the emergence of a unit, which in turn is indispensable in the chunking account. For example, in their study of contraction, Bresnan and Spencer (n.d.) explicitly make a distinction between frequency effects on morphosyntactic variation in compositional and non-compositional language processing. They find that the effect of joint probability of a lexical subject (i.e. excluding pronoun subjects) plus *is/'s* is larger than the effect of other predictors found in previous studies.

Previous corpus studies on morphosyntactic alternation have used a number of other frequency-based predictors, including the joint probability of the preceding word plus the target, and the joint probability of the target plus the following word (e.g. Barth & Kapatsinski 2017). Another measure is conditional probability, that is, the probability of the target given the previous word(s) or the following word(s). A higher probability of the target given its context is expected to lead to reduction (e.g. Jurafsky et al. 2001). Also, surprisal has been used in some studies (Wulff et al. 2018).

Another approach using conditional probabilities is the *uniform information density* (UID) hypothesis (Jaeger 2006), according to which a speaker produces language rationally, maintaining a uniform level of information load or density across the constructions s/he employs. The UID hypothesis predicts that 'elements with high information are lengthened, and elements with low information are shortened', for example contracted, such as in *you are > you're* (Frank and Jaeger 2008: 939). Information density is defined as the conditional probability of the focus element (contracted/uncontracted forms) given the words surrounding it: the more predictable an element is, the less information it contains.

Another factor which works at the cognitive level and is starting to attract more attention is priming (for an early account, see Poplack 1980). In a recent volume edited by Hundt et al. (2017), Pickering and Garrod (2017) and Mair (2017) engage in a detailed discussion on how cognitive research on priming can be integrated with linguistic and, in particular, corpus linguistic research on language change. Pickering and Garrod (2017: 173, see also 2004) define priming as 'a largely non-conscious or automatic tendency to repeat what one has comprehended or produced'. In their account, priming works towards alignment of interlocutors at different levels of linguistic representation, enhancing their mutual understanding. In addition, it contributes to routinization, or the development of fixed expressions with specific meanings which can start out as ad hoc but become conventional over time. Priming is usually studied at very short timescales, for example within a conversation, but can clearly have longer-term effects (e.g. over a week, Kaschak et al. 2011) and, as Pickering and Garrod (2017) argue, can possibly lead to permanent changes. Priming is found in adults, children and non-native speakers, and it works at different levels of linguistic representation, as well as across them. Syntactic priming, or the tendency to repeat the structure of the utterance just comprehended or produced, is very common: for example, passives prime passives (Bernolet et al. 2009), even cross-linguistically (Hartsuiker et al. 2004). Importantly, ungrammatical structures can also prime, leading to increased acceptability after exposure (Kaschak & Glenberg 2004; Luka & Barsalou 2005). Syntactic priming can be enhanced by a *lexical boost* when the constructions priming each other share the specific verb (Branigan et al. 2000) and when the interlocutor is an actual addressee rather than just a passive listener (Branigan et al. 2007). It also appears stronger for infrequent constructions, possibly because surprising forms are learned better (Bernolet & Hartsuiker 2010).

Other corpus studies on priming effects include Szmrecsanyi (2006), who used the term 'persistence', Barth and Kapatsinski (2017) and Mair (2017), who found that the occurrence of *wanna* (< *want to*) can be primed by previous occurrences of *wanna* and *gonna* in the spoken part of the Corpus of Contemporary American English. Gries (2017) suggests using different priming-related factors as autocorrelation effects in multifactorial designs.

In sum, if we leave aside the specific research questions or hypotheses, previous studies have suggested four types of determinants of variation with respect to English contraction: 1) **phonological**, such as preceding segment phonology (Labov 1969; MacKenzie 2012; Barth & Kapatsinski 2017) or, more rarely, rhythmic and segment alternation (Gries 2017); 2) **syntactic**, including different forms of BE – copula, future, progressive and passive (Barth & Kapatsinski 2017), or auxiliary and copula uses (Bresnan and Spencer n.d.) – and the occurrence of the following constituent, often mixing categories from different levels of language organization[2] (e.g. MacKenzie 2012); 3) **lexical or distributional**, which can subsume a variety of factors based on frequencies of words and their combinations, including subject type

---

[2] For example, MacKenzie (2012) used the following categories, mostly following Labov (1969): adjective, *going to* or *gonna,* quotative *like,* locative (e.g. *at work*), noun phrase or clause, progressive verb and not available for coding.

(pronoun vs. full NP) and length of subject; and, finally, 4) **priming**. Still, there is no unanimous agreement on the factors which determine the choice between full and contracted forms, and especially their strength. For Barth and Kapatsinski (2017), this may be due to language redundancy and collinearity among the potential predictors, a point we will discuss in the next section.

3   Individual Variation

Individual variation as one of the possible factors affecting the choice is raised in some papers (Barth & Kapatsinki 2017; Gries 2017; see also the discussion in MacKenzie 2012, section 1.2.3). However, usually the aim is to ensure that individual preferences do not skew the interpretation of central tendencies, rather than actually focus on them. The individual is sometimes included in mixed-effects models as a random effect, because including more than one data point from the same individual violates the assumption of independence. This approach is also taken in Barth and Kapatsinski (2017), whose point of departure is redundancy in language. Indeed, redundancy is what makes language robust, as meaning is inferable from multiple structural layers at the same time, and understanding meaning works through prediction and confirmation of the predicted. Thus, redundancy also means predictability at different levels of abstraction, or structural layers. As Barth and Kapatsinski (2017: 203) put it, 'every feature is predictable from multiple other features', and for this reason they use multimodel inference for inferring grammar from a corpus, instead of the more traditional model selection approach (e.g. Labov 1969). They test a set of models which combine different predictors of contracted/uncontracted BE in different ways and find that there are a number of models which perform almost equally well.

We suggest that part of language redundancy at the communal level and the ensuing difficulty of determining the best predictors for a feature can come from individual variation. Usage-based thinking postulates that language with its characteristic structure arises from the interaction of input and the application of domain-general cognitive properties, such as categorization, analogy, chunking and prediction (e.g. Bybee 2006). Both input and cognition are individual, which, in principle, should lead to an individual version of the language. At the same time, there must be enough overlap between such individual versions to enable social interaction. Presumably, the discrepancy does not result in communicative problems partly due to shallow or approximate processing, as the differences between individual versions simply go unnoticed. Redundancy serves as the other part of the 'safety net': an individual can process language based on his/her own version of the grammar and it will still work. Divjak and Arppe (2013), who study how categorization works and how prototypes can be obtained from near-synonymous exemplars, also mention redundancy: it seems individual learners can pick up very different combinations of synonym properties from exposure and as a result end up with very different prototypes. This, as they put it, 'would make it irrelevant what learners track, as long as they track something' (2013: 245).

If we build our individual versions of the grammar, such grammars might be more consistent (cf. Nevalainen this volume, especially Sections 3.1.3 and 4.1) than an aggregated one. In other words, another way of trying to disentangle language redundancy at the communal level is to divide up a corpus into individual corpora and examine various predictors per each individual instead of in the aggregate. So, while Barth and Kapatsinski (2017: 204) suggest that 'the grammar we induce from a corpus is better thought of as an ensemble of models rather than a single model', we suggest that this might be an ensemble of individual grammars.

4 Data

In contrast to many previous studies studying morphosyntactic variation and reduction in spoken data, our focus is on how this phenomenon is manifested in writing, although in a register that resembles spoken language in many ways: blog comments. We use a corpus which contains ca. seven million words of comments posted on one blog by more than 4,000 individual native and non-native English speakers over a period of seven years (the actual blog posts are not included in the data). We focus on the ten most prolific native and non-native commenters on the blog and extract their individual outputs, ranging between 40,000 and 246,000 words posted, including the author of the blog (Josef), who contributed ca. two million words in comments. The structure of our corpus is summarized in Table 8.1. As can be seen, the data includes four American commenters, one Canadian, two Czech, one Greek, one Swiss and one French, thus forming a typical ELF environment. In addition, we treat comments by occasional contributors to the blog as representing the communal average, or the communal level. We call this subcorpus 'Non24', as it is collected from commenters outside the top twenty-four contributors in terms of volume of output (<400 comments per commenter).

It is important to point out that the Non24 corpus serves as a reference corpus at the communal level. In other words, it is not conceptualized as representative of the whole corpus, or of the genre of research blogs in general; instead, it is simply a sample of language matched to the individual corpora we focus on in terms of time, genre, sociolinguistic context and discursive situation. The only difference from individual corpora is the fact that it is a sample of language from a large number of individuals, where no single individual is over-represented. Most corpus studies rely on such corpora, which are balanced in terms of individual speakers. Thus, by comparing individual corpora to Non24, we aim to show whether individual languages differ from what we generally know about

Table 8.1 *Individual subcorpora and Non24.*

Commenter	N of tokens	N of years active	NS/NNS[3]	Nationality
Josef	1,752,331	8	NNS	Czech
Gary	246,468	8	NS	US
Carol	231,316	8	NS	US
Louis	183,629	3	NS	US
Graham	174,903	8	NS	Canadian
Ruth	160,161	7	NS	US
Agnes	92,861	3	NNS	Greek
Marek	66,950	6	NNS	Czech, lives in Austria
David	41,111	4	NNS	Swiss, lives in Germany
Sabine	39,963	3	NNS	French, lives in Ireland
Non24	3,549,185	8	Both	ca. 4,000 commenters

language based on corpus studies. One of the goals of this research, then, is to examine whether the exploration of individual corpora is worth pursuing in the future and which research questions such exploration seems to suggest.

Using comments written on one blog as data has a number of advantages. In particular, the genre and social context are constant across individuals, so if contacted/uncontracted form is a purely stylistic choice, it should be categorical within one commenter. Also, the genre of blog writing has been described as being situated somewhere between written and spoken modes (e.g. Myers 2009; Mauranen 2013), which makes it a convenient proxy for spontaneous language use similar to much of spoken language, even if it technically represents written language. This is even more true for blog comment threads, which are interactive and less susceptible to norms from above of more formal writing. Such data can even be relevant for reduction accounts, as phonological processing is shown to be at least in some way present in writing and reading (e.g. implicit prosody, Fodor 2002).

5   Methods

Our focus in this study is on the use of contracted vs. uncontracted forms in one specific construction: *it is* vs. *it's*. The decision to concentrate on this form, rather than to include all forms which allow contraction, was motivated by our specific aims of focusing on individual-based variation, as well as assessing the effect of chunking and priming. This aim is easier to achieve by focusing on a single construction, as previous studies have indeed established that the contracted/uncontracted choice depends on the host of the verb (e.g. Labov 1969; MacKenzie 2012). We chose to focus on *it is*/*it's* because it is both frequent, providing enough data to allow for analysis at the level of individual

---

[3] NS: native speaker; NNS: non-native speaker.

speakers, and grammatically versatile, occurring in almost all types of information-packaging constructions, as categorized in Huddleston and Pullum (2002). This exceptional property enables us to undertake a more delicate syntactic analysis and extend the earlier investigations of the syntactic factor in morphosyntactic variation.

Accordingly, our analysis first compares the general tendencies in the use of the variants at both the communal and the individual level, and then moves on to investigate three factors which potentially have an effect on the choice between the variants: SYNTACTIC STRUCTURE, PRIMING and CHUNKING, both at the communal level and within each individual. In what follows, we will describe the procedures undertaken to examine each of the factors one by one.

First, we extracted all instances of *it is* and *it's* from ten individual sub-corpora. In addition, we included 2,000 randomly selected instances from Non24. Then we carefully checked this initial data set and removed all false positives, including cases where the writer had intended to use a genitive form (e.g. *it's* [sic] *major economic partner is China*) or where the contracted form *it's* stood for *it has*. We also removed all instances where the word *it* is a prepositional complement and not the head of subject NP (e.g. *the chaotic nature of it is inseparable*), and cases where contraction would not be possible due to the primary verb *is* occurring at the clause-final position (e.g. *I don't know what it is*) (Biber et al. 1999: 1028). We excluded negative forms *it isn't/ it's not/it is not* because they include a choice between three rather than two alternative forms. Our final data set contained 17,994 instances (Josef 10934, Non24 1690, Gary 1089, Louis 1010, Ruth 835, Carol 766, Graham 559, Agnes 430, Marek 329, Sabine 220, David 132), which we then classified with respect to a number of independent variables:

- PERSON: Possible values include ten individual commenters and Non24.
- PRIMING: The variable is operationalized here as the occurrence of another contracted form in the previous context of ten words. Possible values are *yes* and *no*.
- CHUNKING: The variable indicates whether *it is/it's* is part of a chunk, which is operationalized here as a semi-fixed, five-word[4] n-gram (e.g. ***it is*** *a matter of*, ***it's*** *fair to say*). Importantly, we did not generate a general reference list of n-grams involving *it is/it's* to which individual languages would be compared, but created such a list individually for each speaker. Possible values are *yes* and *no*.
- SYNTACTIC STRUCTURE: Possible values are *cleft, progressive, passive, extraposition* and *copular*.[5]

---

[4] The string *it's* is treated here as consisting of two words.
[5] We have excluded from the plots instances of the construction *going to V* due to a small number of instances (n = 57).

While previous studies have categorized uses of BE into *copular* and *auxiliary*, sometimes using the subcategories *passive*, *progressive* and *future*, we adopted a more fine-grained categorization to better reflect the syntactic differences of the constructions in which *it is/it's* is used. One reason for this is that we wanted to avoid overlap with the variable CHUNKING, which is lexical at its core. Thus, we operationalized syntactic structure in an iterative fashion, using Huddleston and Pullum (2002) as the basis and making distinctions between different information-packaging constructions. While clefts and extraposition constructions also represent copular uses of BE, we categorized them separately, especially because copular uses form the majority of our data. Thus, the category *copular* only contains 'canonical information-packaging constructions', using Huddleston and Pullum's (2002: chapter 16) terminology. These copular uses were further categorized based on the type of the predicative complement into *adjective phrases, noun phrases, prepositional phrases, adverbial phrases* and *clauses*.[6] Extraposition constructions were further divided into *infinitival clauses, declarative content clauses, interrogative clauses, noun phrases* and *gerunds*, based on the type of the extraposed subject. See Table 8.4 in Appendix 8.1 for more details and examples.

In addition, we identified two more categories, which create a syntactic context where the choice between the full and the contracted form is skewed towards the full form. In the first category, a predicative complement precedes *it is/it's*, that is, takes a pre-nuclear position. This often happens in fused relatives, open interrogatives and relativization of predicative complement (see Table 8.5 in Appendix 8.1 for examples). In the second, *it is/it's* participates in a comparative construction, that is, a complement expressing the second term in the comparison which is often elliptical and omits the predicative complement.

Due to scarcity of data in some of the categories, some of the questions examined are exploratory in nature.

6 Results

6.1 Variation between Individuals

The distribution of *it is* and *it's* in our data underlines the importance of looking at the data not only at the communal level but also at the level of individuals, as these two perspectives exhibit considerable differences. At the aggregate level (Non24), the data shows a moderate preference for the full

---

[6] Clauses include *fused relatives, content clauses* and *infinitival clauses*.

ELF and Language Change at the Individual Level

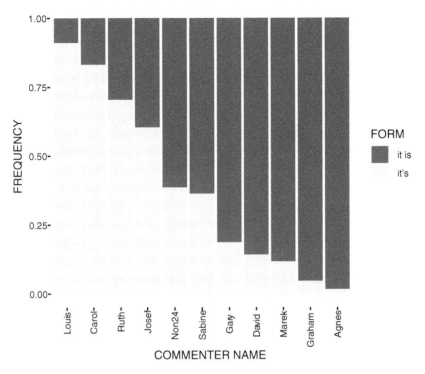

Figure 8.1 Proportions of *it's* and *it is* per PERSON.

form, with 39 per cent (648) of the total instances having the form *it's*, and 61 per cent (1,016) having the form *it is*. However, individual commenters vary greatly between their preferences, as can be seen in Figure 8.1, where the speakers are ordered by the percentage of the full form (shown on the y-axis) from left to right.

Most individual commenters have an overwhelming preference for either the full form (Agnes, Graham, Marek, David and Gary) or the contracted form (Ruth, Carol and Louis). Only Sabine and Josef, the two remaining commenters in the middle, do not show a clear preference towards either variant. It is thus clear that what looks like a variation in the aggregate can be heavily partitioned at the individual level. From this follows that, for some commenters, there is no possibility for any other factors to further influence the choice: for example, Agnes and Graham are categorical in their preference for the full form, which can be a stylistic choice in that it is unaffected by any changes in the conditions. Next, we shall look more closely at the remaining data sets where the influence of other factors can still be considered.

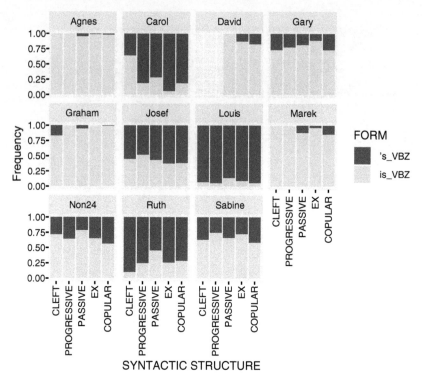

Figure 8.2 Proportions of *it's* and *it is* per SYNTACTIC STRUCTURE, PERSON.

6.2 Syntactic Structure: The Main Categories

Contrary to what could perhaps be expected, SYNTACTIC STRUCTURE does not appear to have a systematic influence on the choice between the two forms. As can be seen in Figure 8.2, there are only very small variations in the proportions across all syntactic structures in all data sets. When subcategories of the largest categories, *copular* and *extraposition,* are considered, the overall picture stays the same. There are some effects visible, but they vary both in the direction of the influence and the syntactic category for different individuals.[7]

---

[7] As mentioned in Section 5, we did not include the *going to* V category in the plots due to low frequency. There are only fifty-seven occurrences of the construction in the whole data set, out of which twenty-three belong to Louis's subcorpus (1.3 instances per 10,000 words). Agnes, David, Graham and Sabine do not use the construction at all and the rest use it only very rarely (fewer than 0.3 instances per 10,000 words). In Non24, the construction occurs seven times, five of which are contracted and two uncontracted. In contrast, all instances in Louis's corpus are contracted. This distribution also suggests individual preferences.

At the communal level (Non24), the contracted form seems to be positively associated with the *copular*[8] category and negatively associated with the *passive* ($\chi^2 = 26.7$, df = 4, $p < 0.05$). However, these associations are not observed in individual corpora. Yet, if we look at the subcategories of *copular* constructions, we see that when BE is followed by a *clause*, all commenters who prefer the contracted form overall show an even stronger preference for contraction, whereas those preferring full forms are unaffected (Agnes, Graham and Marek, but with the exception of Gary).[9] It is possible that we see an effect of chunking here, as structures where *it* functions as subject, BE as copula and clause as complement tend to be idiomatic (Huddleston & Pullum 2002: 962). This is especially true for content clauses, such as (1)–(3):

(1)   *It's just that you haven't really read the paper...* (Josef)

(2)   *It's just that the juxtaposition doesn't work...* (Louis)

(3)   *I think it's because they refuse to believe that...* (Carol)

Here, *it's just that* and *it's because* seem to work as semi-fixed chunks, sometimes allowing a modifier (e.g. *it's always because*), which serve as convenient sentence openers.

Two more trends, this time completely idiosyncratic, can be seen in Carol's usage. First, her overall preference for the contracted form is overruled in clefts, where she uses the full form eighteen times and the contracted one ten times. No other commenter with a preference for contracted forms shows any tendency in this direction: Louis and Ruth are almost categorical in using the contracted form in this category too. In contrast, Carol's overall preference for contraction is even more pronounced in the *extraposition* category (including all subcategories). Given that clefts and extraposition constructions belong to the same higher-order category of BE used as copula, the explanation for the variation is unlikely to be purely grammatical. Another idiosyncratic trend is observable in Josef's data: he prefers to use the full form in progressives, despite his overall preference for contraction.

The reasons for a range of trends reported here are not immediately clear. We have mentioned chunking as one of the possible explanations and will return to it in more detail in Section 6.4. What is clear, though, is that syntax does not have a systematic influence on the variation between the forms in our

---

[8] Note that since we distinguished between different information-packaging constructions, the category *copular* only contains uses of BE as copula in canonical syntactic structures. Clefts and extraposition constructions where BE also serves as copula are analysed as separate categories.

[9] The choice of *it's* in this context is nearly categorical for Carol (10 out of 11 instances), Louis (33/34) and Ruth (12/14), and the probability of the contracted form is considerably higher for Gary (10/19) and Josef (214/252), compared to their general tendencies.

data; instead, what we see is mostly a collection of individual preferences. This finding supports the hypothesis that what we see at the communal level can be quite different from what happens at the individual level.

6.3 Special Syntactic Context

We will now briefly comment on two special categories mentioned in Section 5, where syntactic structure influences the choice quite clearly in favour of the full form: cases where a predicative complement takes a pre-nuclear position (e.g. *to know* **what** *it is really about*) and comparative constructions (e.g. *worse* **than** *it is now*). While the preference for the full form is almost categorical – and for this reason we were originally going to exclude these instances altogether – cases of contraction also occur, suggesting that they should be included in the analysis.

Out of 157 pre-nuclear cases, in only twenty-two the verb is contracted. These include twenty instances where *it's* is part of some conventional phrase: *for what it's worth* (twelve instances), *what it's like* (five), *where it's at* used in an idiomatic sense (two) and *what it's all about* (one). It therefore seems that the dispreferred contraction here can be partly explained by chunking, which increases the likelihood of reduction. At the same time, all but one occurrence belong to commenters who have an overall preference for contraction – Louis, Carol, Josef and Ruth – indicating a tentative possibility of some interaction between the preference for contraction and the use of chunks.

The other category is formed of comparative constructions. In this category, *it's/it is* is part of a structurally reduced subordinate clause expressing the secondary term in the comparison, highlighted in bold in examples (4)–(6) (see Huddleston & Pullum 2002: 1106).[10] As a result of such structural reductions, the predicative complement often does not follow *it's/it is*, just like in pre-nuclear cases. For example:

(4)   *This is as true for the Greeks* ***as it is for us***. (Carol)

(5)   *And as painful* ***as it is*** *to say this...* (Louis)

(6)   *The higher CO2 is,* ***the harder it is to increase it****...* (Josef)

However, not all comparative clauses are elliptical or structurally reduced, and we were interested to see whether the preference for the full form due to the absence of the complement in its habitual position spreads or generalizes to cases where the complement follows *it's/it is* as normal, and in principle

---

[10] For example, the sentence *she is older than I am old is ungrammatical (Huddleston & Pullum 2002: 1108).

nothing precludes the use of contraction (e.g. *My explanation is as elegant as it is simple...* [Non24]).[11] Out of 180 cases of the comparative construction, 108 were pre-nuclear, and the full form was used in all of them. This finding supports the effect of the pre-nuclear position of the predicative complement on the variation between the contracted and the full form. Out of the remaining seventy-two cases where the predicative complement was present and positioned after *it's/it is,* forty-five belong to Josef, which only allows us to look at the variation in his data set. In this syntactic context, Josef used the contracted form six times and the full form thirty-nine times, including twenty-four cases involving a reanalysed construction, *as long/far as,* functioning as a compound preposition (see Huddleston & Pullum 2002: 1134). What is interesting is that this uncharacteristic preference for the full form is also attested here. Whether Josef's preference for the full form in all comparative clauses is another case of an individual preference, or whether it is motivated by generalization from pre-nuclear cases, remains an open question. If the latter is true, the process of generalization can also be studied at the individual level.

In general, it seems that, while overall syntax does not have a systematic influence on the variation, special syntactic conditions can set constraints on the use of the contracted and uncontracted forms.

6.4 Priming

Next, we investigated the effect of PRIMING – more precisely, the possibility that the choice of the contracted form would be primed by a previous use of contraction within the same stretch of discourse (Szmrecsanyi 2006; Barth and Kapatsinski 2017; Mair 2017). As previously described, priming was operationalized as the preceding occurrence of another contracted form within a window of ten words, similar to Barth and Kapatsinski (2017) and Mair (2017). Figure 8.3 shows the proportions of contracted and uncontracted forms separately for cases where there was not a previous occurrence of a contraction ('NO', left bar) and where there was one ('YES', right bar). The left bar only includes instances where there would have been an opportunity for using a contracted form; other instances have been excluded.

As can be seen, the presence of a previous instance of a contracted form clearly increases the likelihood of using a contracted form. The magnitude of this effect varies between speakers: it is smaller among individuals who prefer to contract and larger among those who prefer to use the full form. This is probably because those who contract overall contract very often, even when

---

[11] See Barth and Kapatsinski (2017: 249) for a discussion of a similar issue of the direction of fusion with the preceding word generalizing beyond contexts motivated by co-occurrence: *it's* vs. *cat's*.

220 *Svetlana Vetchinnikova and Turo Hiltunen*

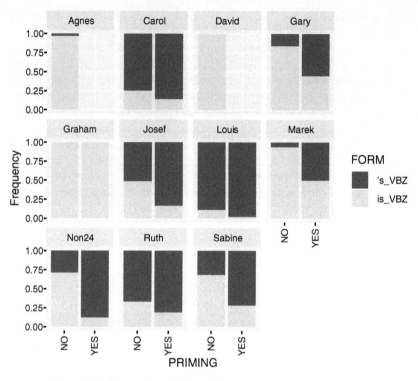

Figure 8.3 Proportions of *it's* and *it is* per PRIMING, grouped by PERSON.

there is no priming context. Still, even for these individuals the tendency to contract is boosted in the presence of the priming context in comparison to their overall proportion of contracted forms.

Interestingly, the greatest difference between priming and no-priming contexts is found at the communal level, that is, Non24 data (nearly sixty percentage points). It is difficult to say why this happens, but one possible explanation is that our operationalization of the priming effect (i.e. previous occurrence of a contracted form or a full form within ten words to the left) not only identifies the priming contexts, but also splits the data into instances produced by those who prefer to contract and those who prefer to use the full form, as Non24 data is very likely to contain both types. In other words, if we find two instances of the contracted form within the span of ten words, this can happen 1) due to priming or 2) because both instances are produced by the same individual who prefers to contract irrespective of priming. If this is indeed the case, studies which use communal data might be exaggerating the effect of priming (in the case of self-priming): one speaker can be using the same form because s/he has a preference for this form overall, rather than due to online priming.

6.5 Chunking

The final variable we look at is whether *it is/it's* is part of a chunk in the use of a specific individual, referred to here as CHUNKING. With more data it should be possible to look at degrees of compositionality, but here we operationalize the variable only in a dichotomous way as compositional vs. non-compositional processing. We also take a very conservative measure of non-compositionality, counting a sequence of words as a chunk if it is a fixed five-gram and occurs in an individual corpus at least three times. The only variation we allow is the variation between *it is/it's*. Five-grams are comparatively rare even in large corpora, and if they recur in a relatively small individual corpus, compositional processing is highly unlikely. However, the conservativeness of the measure needs to be taken into account in interpreting the results.

The fact that we extract five-grams involving *it is/it's* from each corpus individually means that, in our view, chunks can be personal. In other words, we assume that a sequence of words which is processed compositionally by the majority of the population (the communal level) can be processed non-compositionally by a specific individual, and vice versa. Thus, we do not compare individual production against a list of multiword units established at the communal level, and instead create an individual list of chunks using independent criteria, that is, length, fixedness and frequency of repetition. We apply the same criteria of non-compositionality to Non24 data for the purposes of comparison, as chunks are normally identified in corpus linguistics using aggregate data.

Figure 8.4 shows the proportions of the variants separately for instances which are not part of a chunk ('NO') and which are part of a chunk ('YES'). Excluded from the figure are commenters whose data does not contain five-grams that meet the frequency threshold. As can be seen, similar to PRIMING, CHUNKING seems to increase the likelihood of the contracted form across individual speakers. This clearly holds at least for those who prefer to contract in general.[12] Yet the effect reaches statistical significance only for Josef and Carol (Josef: $\chi^2 = 46$, df = 1, p = 1.18e-11; Carol: $\chi^2 = 14.8$, df = 1, p = 0.0001; Ruth: $\chi^2 = 3.6$, df = 1, p = 0.0567; Louis: $\chi^2 = 3.2$, df = 1, p = 0.0738). This

---

[12] Gary's data does not support the tendency; Agnes and Graham use full forms categorically, irrespective of any possible additional factors, as was mentioned in Section 6.1; and David's, Sabine's and Marek's data do not contain chunks according to our criteria, most likely due to the size of their corpora (they have the smallest) and the conservativeness of our operationalization of chunks.

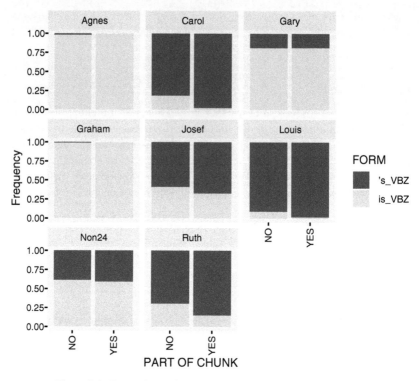

Figure 8.4 Proportions of *it is* and *it's* per CHUNKING, grouped by PERSON.

could be due to the conservativeness of our operationalization: since our criteria for the identification of chunks targeted precision over recall, we can be sure that the 'YES' bar contains chunks only, but the 'NO' bar is likely to contain some proportion of non-compositional instances too. Interestingly, there is no effect in Non24 ($\chi^2 = 0.065$, df = 1, p = 0.7985).

In principle, the results, at least for Carol and Josef, support the hypothesis that chunking can lead to reduction within speaker-specific chunks. According to a usage-based model of grammar, such reduction presumably occurs due to reanalysis of constituent structure and is therefore a sign of grammatical change (Bybee & Scheibman 1999; Bybee 2006). The individuality of personal chunks can be seen in Table 8.2, which lists the four most frequent fivegrams starting with *it's/it is* for each of the commenters.

Thus, chunking, just like priming, seems to have a systematic effect on the variation between the two forms across individuals. This is not very surprising since both chunking and priming have always been proposed as cognitive factors. In this sense, the present study simply confirms that indeed we can see

Table 8.2 *Most frequent five-grams involving it is/it's for each of the individual commenters.*

Carol	Gary	Louis	Josef	Ruth
quite conceivable that, 13	really hard to, 5	going to be, 8	still true that, 104	kind of like, 6
bad enough that, 8	up to the, 5	quite possible that, 5	very clear that, 64	just me, but, 4
simply the case, 6	true that the, 5	a lot easier, 5	clear that the, 29	a matter of, 4
a good thing, 6	also possible that, 5	a lot more, 5	a part of, 29	too bad that, 3

Table 8.3 *Distribution of speaker-specific chunks across syntactic categories.*

	Cleft	Copular	Extraposition	Passive	Progressive
Carol	0	9	71	0	7
Josef	30	721	1,151	21	2

the effect at the individual level. However, as Table 8.2 shows, individuals develop very different repertoires of personal chunks. Thus, the effect of chunking results in individuals contracting in different rather than similar places, irrespective of, for example, syntactic structure.

In fact, it can be tested whether the fact that we did not see a systematic effect of syntactic structure is actually due to the differences between individual chunk repertoires. Unfortunately our data is too scarce to be tested for statistical significance, but a few tentative observations can be made. In Section 6.2 we reported a few miscellaneous effects of syntactic structure on the variation in individual data sets: Carol was shown to prefer contracted forms overall, yet in her data, clefts were associated with a lower-than-expected frequency of contracted forms. Based on Table 8.3, showing the distribution of their personal chunks across syntactic categories, we could hypothesize that Carol's low frequency of contracted form in clefts could be due to the total absence of chunks in this category. Most of her chunks are found in extrapositions, which is the category most strongly associated with *it's* in her data. Following a similar logic, Josef's lower-than-expected rate of contraction in the progressive could tentatively be attributed to the near-absence of chunks.

For example:

(7)   *it is always the majority who must be right...* (Carol, cleft)

(8)   *it is the neoconservatives, not the paleoconservatives, who are to blame...* (Carol, cleft)

(9) *it is the veterinary researcher who first developed a successful IVF technique...* (Carol, cleft)

(10) *it's quite conceivable that the TV producers fabricated this call-girl tale...* (Carol, extraposition)

(11) *it's quite refreshing to see a publication such as...* (Carol, extraposition)

(12) *it's simply the case that news jibes well with strings...* (Carol, extraposition)

(13) *it's promising the people a fixed amount of products...* (Josef, progressive)

(14) *it is rotating and orbiting and moving in many ways...* (Josef, progressive)

Based on Table 8.3 and examples (7)–(14), it is possible to tentatively hypothesize that a heightened preference for contracted forms is associated with categories which are more conducive to chunk formation (copular and extraposition), whereas the categories less conducive to this (such as clefts, passives and progressives) would exhibit lower rates of contraction. As the examples illustrate, the focus of a cleft, as well as the main verb in a progressive structure, is always changing, while the opening part in extraposition can be very repetitive. In our data, extraposition as a syntactic structure especially seems to facilitate chunk formation across all speakers. This agrees with the fact that some of the grammar patterns which belong to a category such as *it is* ADJ *that* (Francis et al. 1998: 480) are described as useful and frequently used, for example, in academic writing (Charles 2004; Groom 2005; Hunston 2010; see also Biber et al. 1999: 1020 on lexical bundles initiating extraposed structures), and are therefore likely to be common in research blogging and blog comments, which is the register our data represents.

What is slightly puzzling in this light is how Carol manages to have chunks in the progressive category, especially as nobody else has any at all. On closer examination, it turns out that many of the instances in her progressive category are actually extraposed structures with a verb phrase instead of a more usual adjective phrase. Most of the instances are variants of the same semi-fixed chunk: *it's/it is becoming increasingly clear/apparent/obvious/more difficult to/that* (n = 10), such as:

(15) *It's becoming increasingly more difficult to see all those distant points...*

(16) *It's becoming increasingly apparent that the cosmological constant is finely-tuned.*

(17) *It's becoming increasingly clear that classical algorithms are maxing out.*

Other verb phrases initiating an extraposed structure are also possible, for example, *it's looking more and more like this isn't the case.*

All cases considered, chunking seems to play an important role in explaining the variation.

7 Conclusions

Normally when we want to describe language regularities, we collect a balanced sample of language from a large number of speakers, making sure that no one is over-represented. The underlying assumption is that language is homogeneous enough across speakers, and we are interested in what they share instead of their idiosyncrasies, as the task of describing idiosyncratic features of all individuals is obviously futile. However, it is also generally agreed that linguistic regularities emerge as a result of the interaction between linguistic, social and cognitive factors. In principle, all these factors should then be observable within each individual too. At the same time, the ubiquity of the cognitive factor does not necessarily presuppose the uniformity of linguistic regularities. All individuals have the same cognitive properties: they chunk, use analogy, make categories and generalize to new instances. However, linguistic regularities which arise from the application of these properties crucially depend on the input to which they are applied. To what extent different individuals infer different regularities from the inputs they receive is a question which has not received much attention. It also becomes especially interesting in ELF settings, where variation in individual language exposure is much higher than in monolingual settings.

In this study, we selected a linguistic variable – *it is* vs. *it's* – and examined the effects of the linguistic (syntactic structure) and cognitive factors (priming and chunking) on the variation in one communal and ten individual native and non-native corpora extracted from the same blog, that is, keeping the social context constant. Importantly, we thus compared individual data sets to a separate corpus with balanced sampling representing the communal level (Non24), instead of to their average. We found that most individuals in our data prefer either the full form or the contracted form. Thus, what the communal corpus probably shows is which preference is in the majority at the population level in this context.

SYNTACTIC STRUCTURE did not have a systematic effect on the variation across all speakers. However, specific syntactic structures seemed to have an effect on specific individuals. Given the chunking patterns of these individual speakers, it is possible that what looks like a syntactic effect might in fact be driven by chunking.

Despite the lack of evidence with respect to the effect of syntactic structure in general, the linguistic factor should not be dismissed, as it can set constraints on the variation which hold across all speakers. In our data, all individuals, irrespective of their overall preference, were influenced by the constraining factor of the predicative in the pre-nuclear position and selected the full form in this syntactic context. There is some initial evidence of generalization from contexts favouring full forms to other instances of the same category working at the individual level, but more research is needed. In principle, since generalization is a cognitive property, it should be possible to trace it at this level. It would be interesting to investigate which categories individuals build and how different such categories can be across individuals.

In contrast, both the cognitive factors of PRIMING and CHUNKING had a more systematic effect across individual speakers. Priming is highly sporadic and it is not clear whether its effects can accumulate and lead to change. Yet, self-priming might be one of the reasons behind the clear individual preferences we observed, along with the fact that they do not seem to become more like each other as usage-based theory would predict, a phenomenon described by Barlow (2013: 471) as 'inbuilt inertia' (see also Szmrecsanyi 2006; Pickering & Garrod 2017). In contrast, chunking facilitates recurrence and can thus easily accumulate. At the same time, chunking also leads to the development of individual chunk repertoires, which can be substantially different across speakers. Thus, while chunking is a common factor influencing variation between the two forms, it may result in different people contracting in different places.

We did not find an effect of chunking on contraction in Non24. One possible reason for this is that Non24 did not contain as many chunks as individual data sets. This is in agreement with an earlier finding that individual languages are more 'fixed' than the communal average, that is, they contain more verbatim chunks: at the communal level the chunks are likely to include variable slots which prevent them from being retrieved with n-gram tools (Vetchinnikova 2017). A possible link between the preference for contraction and the proportion of chunks in one's language (i.e. its degree of 'fixedness' [Vetchinnikova 2017] or 'chunkedness' [Arnon and Christiansen 2017; McCauley and Christiansen 2017]) might be another interesting question for future research.

There has been some discussion in ELF literature on whether non-native ELF speakers process language compositionally or not, since they do not always reproduce standard phraseological units precisely (Seidlhofer 2009; Mauranen 2012; Pitzl 2012; Vetchinnikova 2015). In our data, both native and non-native speakers exhibited personal repertoires of chunks and showed the effect of chunking on contraction, which speaks in favour of non-compositional processing. If so, imprecision or approximation (Mauranen 2005, 2012) introduced by non-native ELF speakers into standard English phraseology can also have a long-term effect and implications for language change. It is also possible to hypothesize that individual repertoires of chunks are overall more different from each other in ELF environments than in, for example, closer-knit, predominantly monolingual communities (cf. Laitinen and Lundberg this volume on social network theory and ELF). However, to test this prediction one would need to compare individual chunk repertoires from samples of ELF and monolingual interactions. We did not pursue this goal here.

Overall, in our study the communal level seemed to be different from the individual. Complexity theory provides a good framework for explaining how the two are related. The communal level is not simply the average of the individual languages: such explanation would question the validity of counting the means, which is not in doubt. Instead, the communal level can be seen as being emergent from the individual, that is, as being qualitatively different from it. This explanation makes both levels important and worthy of investigation in their own right.[13]

REFERENCES

Arnon, Inbal & Morten H. Christiansen. 2017. The role of multiword building blocks in explaining L1–L2 differences. *Topics in Cognitive Science* 9(3), 621–636.

Barlow, Michael. 2013. Individual differences and usage-based grammar. *International Journal of Corpus Linguistics* 18(4), 443–478.

Barth, Danielle & Vsevolod Kapatsinski. 2017. A multimodel inference approach to categorical variant choice: Construction, priming and frequency effects on the choice between full and contracted forms of *am, are* and *is*. *Corpus Linguistics and Linguistic Theory* 13(2), 203–260.

Beckner, Clay, Richard Blythe, Joan Bybee, Morten H. Christiansen, William Croft, Nick C. Ellis, John Holland, Jinyun Ke, Diane Larsen-Freeman & Tom Schoenemann. 2009. Language is a complex adaptive system: Position paper. *Language Learning* 59(s1), 1–26.

Bernolet, Sarah & Robert J. Hartsuiker. 2010. Does verb bias modulate syntactic priming? *Cognition* 114(3), 455–461.

Bernolet, Sarah, Robert J. Hartsuiker & Martin J. Pickering. 2009. Persistence of emphasis in language production: A cross-linguistic approach. *Cognition* 112(2), 300–317.

Biber, Douglas, Stig Johansson, Geoffrey Leech, Susan Conrad & Edward Finegan. 1999. *The Longman Grammar of Spoken and Written English*. London: Longman.

Branigan, Holly P., Martin J. Pickering & Alexandra A. Cleland. 2000. Syntactic co-ordination in dialogue. *Cognition* 75(2), B13–B25.

Branigan, Holly P., Martin J. Pickering, Janet F. McLean & Alexandra A. Cleland. 2007. Syntactic alignment and participant role in dialogue. *Cognition* 104(2), 163–197.

Bresnan, Joan & Jessica Spencer. (n.d.). *Frequency and variation in English subject-verb contraction*. Unpublished manuscript. Stanford, CA: Stanford University Department of Linguistics and Center for the Study of Language and Information.

---

[13] We would like to thank the author of the blog for generously providing his blog data for research purposes.

Bybee, Joan. 2002. Word frequency and context of use in the lexical diffusion of phonetically conditioned sound change. *Language Variation and Change* 14(3), 261–290.

2006. From usage to grammar: The mind's response to repetition. *Language* 82(4), 711–733.

Bybee, Joan & Joanne Scheibman. 1999. The effect of usage on degrees of constituency: The reduction of *don't* in English. *Linguistics* 37(4), 575–596.

Charles, Maggie. 2004. *The Construction of Stance: A Corpus-Based Investigation of Two Contrasting Disciplines*. Unpublished PhD thesis. University of Birmingham.

Cheng, Winnie, Chris Greaves, John McH. Sinclair & Martin Warren. 2009. Uncovering the extent of the phraseological tendency: Towards a systematic analysis of concgrams. *Applied Linguistics* 30(2), 236–252.

D'Arcy, Alexandra & Sali A. Tagliamonte. 2015. Not always variable: Probing the vernacular grammar. *Language Variation and Change* 27(3), 255–285.

Dąbrowska, Ewa. 2012. Different speakers, different grammars: Individual differences in native language attainment. *Linguistic Approaches to Bilingualism* 2(3), 219–253.

de Bot, Kees & Diane Larsen-Freeman. 2013. Researching second language development from a dynamic systems theory perspective. In Marjolijn Verspoor, Kees de Bot & Wander Lowie (eds.), *A Dynamic Approach to Second Language Development: Methods and Techniques*, 5–23. Amsterdam; Philadelphia: John Benjamins.

de Bot, Kees, Wander Lowie & Marjolijn Verspoor. 2007. A dynamic systems theory approach to second language acquisition. *Bilingualism: Language and Cognition* 10(1), 7–21.

Divjak, Dagmar & Antti Arppe. 2013. Extracting prototypes from exemplars: What can corpus data tell us about concept representation? *Cognitive Linguistics* 24(2), 221–274.

Ellis, Nick C. & Diane Larsen-Freeman. 2006. Language emergence: Implications for Applied Linguistics – Introduction to the special issue. *Applied Linguistics* 27(4), 558–589.

Fodor, Janet D. 2002. Psycholinguistics cannot escape prosody. *Proceedings of Speech Prosody*, 83–90. Aix-en-Provence, France.

Francis, Gill, Susan Hunston & Elizabeth Manning. 1998. *Collins COBUILD Grammar Patterns: Nouns and Adjectives*. London: HarperCollins.

Frank, Austin F. & T. Florian Jaeger. 2008. Speaking rationally: Uniform information density as an optimal strategy for language production. *Proceedings of the Annual Meeting of the Cognitive Science Society* 30, 939–944.

Gries, Stefan Th. 2017. Syntactic alternation research: Taking stock and some suggestions for the future. *Belgian Journal of Linguistics* 31(1), 8–29.

Groom, Nicholas. 2005. Pattern and meaning across genres and disciplines: An exploratory study. *Journal of English for Academic Purposes* 4(3), 257–277.

Hall, Christopher J., Jack Joyce & Chris Robson. 2017. Investigating the lexico-grammatical resources of a non-native user of English: The case of *can* and *could* in email requests. *Applied Linguistics Review* 8(1), 35–59.

Hartsuiker, Robert J., Martin J. Pickering & Eline Veltkamp. 2004. Is syntax separate or shared between languages? Cross-linguistic syntactic priming in Spanish-English bilinguals. *Psychological Science* 15(6), 409–414.

Huddleston, Rodney & Geoffrey K. Pullum (eds.). 2002. *The Cambridge Grammar of the English Language*. Cambridge: Cambridge University Press.

Hundt, Marianne, Sandra Mollin & Simone E. Pfenninger. 2017. *The Changing English Language: Psycholinguistic Perspectives*. Cambridge: Cambridge University Press.

Hunston, Susan. 2007. Semantic prosody revisited. *International Journal of Corpus Linguistics* 12(2), 249–268.

2010. Starting with the small words. In Ute Römer & Rainer Schulze (eds.), *Patterns, Meaningful Units and Specialized Discourses*, 7–30. Amsterdam; Philadelphia: John Benjamins.

Jaeger, T. Florian. 2006. *Redundancy and Syntactic Reduction in Spontaneous Speech*. Unpublished doctoral dissertation. Stanford University.

Jenkins, Jennifer. 2015. Repositioning English and multilingualism in English as a Lingua Franca. *Englishes in Practice* 2(3), 49–85.

Jenkins, Jennifer, Will Baker & Martin Dewey (eds.). 2017. *The Routledge Handbook of English as a Lingua Franca* (Routledge Handbooks in Applied Linguistics). Milton Park, Abingdon; New York, NY: Routledge.

Jurafsky, Daniel, Alan Bell, Michelle Gregory & William D. Raymond. 2001. Probabilistic relations between words: Evidence from reduction in lexical production. *Typological Studies in Language* 45, 229–254.

Kaschak, Michael P. & Arthur M. Glenberg. 2004. This construction needs learned. *Journal of Experimental Psychology: General* 133(3), 450.

Kaschak, Michael P., Timothy J. Kutta & Christopher Schatschneider. 2011. Long-term cumulative structural priming persists for (at least) one week. *Memory & Cognition* 39(3), 381–388.

Labov, William. 1969. Contraction, deletion, and inherent variability of the English copula. *Language* 45(4), 715–762.

1972. *Sociolinguistic Patterns*. Philadelphia: University of Pennsylvania Press.

2006. *The Social Stratification of English in New York City*. 2nd ed. Cambridge: Cambridge University Press.

Luka, Barbara J. & Lawrence W. Barsalou. 2005. Structural facilitation: Mere exposure effects for grammatical acceptability as evidence for syntactic priming in comprehension. *Journal of Memory and Language* 52(3), 436–459.

MacKenzie, Laurel E. 2012. *Locating Variation Above the Phonology*. PhD thesis. University of Pennsylvania.

Mair, Christian. 2017. From priming and processing to frequency effects and grammaticalization? Contracted semi-modals in present-day English. In Marianne Hundt, Sandra Mollin & Simone E. Pfenninger (eds.), *The Changing English Language*, 191–212. Cambridge: Cambridge University Press.

Mauranen, Anna. 2005. English as a Lingua Franca – an unknown language? In Giuseppina Cortese & Anna Duszak (eds.), *Identity, Community, Discourse: English in Intercultural Settings*, 269–293. Frankfurt: Peter Lang.

2012. *Exploring ELF: Academic English Shaped by Non-Native Speakers*. Cambridge: Cambridge University Press.

2013. Hybridism, edutainment, and doubt: Science blogging finding its feet. *Nordic Journal of English Studies* 12(1), 7–36.

2017. Conceptualising ELF. In Jenkins, Jennifer, Will Baker & Martin Dewey (eds.), *The Routledge Handbook of English as a Lingua Franca* (Routledge Handbooks in Applied Linguistics), 7–24. Abingdon; New York, NY: Routledge.

McCauley, Stewart M. & Morten H. Christiansen. 2017. Computational investigations of multiword chunks in language learning. *Topics in Cognitive Science* 9(3), 637–652.

Mollin, Sandra. 2009. "I entirely understand" is a Blairism: The methodology of identifying idiolectal collocations. *International Journal of Corpus Linguistics* 14(3), 367–392.

Myers, Greg. 2009. *The Discourse of Blogs and Wikis*. London: Continuum.

Pickering, Martin J. & Simon Garrod. 2004. Toward a mechanistic psychology of dialogue. *Behavioral and Brain Sciences* 27(02), 169–190.

2017. Priming and language change. In Marianne Hundt, Sandra Mollin & Simone E. Pfenninger (eds.), *The Changing English Language*, 173–190. Cambridge: Cambridge University Press.

Pitzl, Marie-Luise. 2012. Creativity meets convention: idiom variation and re-metaphorization in ELF. *Journal of English as a Lingua Franca* 1(1), 27–55.

Poplack, Shana. 1980. The notion of the plural in Puerto Rican English: Competing constraints on (s) deletion. In William Labov (ed.), *Locating Language in Time and Space*, 55–67. New York: Academic Press.

Sankoff, David. 1988. Sociolinguistics and syntactic variation. In Frederick J. Newmeyer (ed.), *Linguistics: The Cambridge Survey,* 140–161. Cambridge: Cambridge University Press.

Seidlhofer, Barbara. 2009. Accommodation and the idiom principle in English as a Lingua Franca. *Intercultural Pragmatics* 6(2), 195–215.

Sinclair, John McH. 1991. *Corpus, Concordance, Collocation*. Oxford: Oxford University Press.

Szmrecsanyi, Benedikt. 2006. *Morphosyntactic Persistence in Spoken English: A Corpus Study at the Intersection of Variationist Sociolinguistics, Psycholinguistics, and Discourse Analysis*. Berlin: Mouton De Gruyter.

Tagliamonte, Sali. 2011. *Variationist Sociolinguistics: Change, Observation, Interpretation*. Chichester: Wiley-Blackwell.

Tagliamonte, Sali A. 2006. *Analysing Sociolinguistic Variation*. Cambridge: Cambridge University Press.

Vetchinnikova, Svetlana. 2015. Usage-based recycling or creative exploitation of the shared code? The case of phraseological patterning. *Journal of English as a Lingua Franca* 4(2), 223–252.

2017. On the relationship between the cognitive and the communal: A complex systems perspective. In Filppula, Markku, Juhani Klemola, Anna Mauranen & Svetlana Vetchinnikova (eds.), *Changing English: Global and Local Perspectives* (Topics in English Linguistics). Berlin: Mouton de Gruyter.

Weinreich, Uriel, William Labov & Marvin Herzog. 1968. Empirical foundations for a theory of language change. In Winfred P. Lehmann & Yakov Malkiel (eds.), *Directions for Historical Linguistics*, 99–188. Austin: University of Texas Press.

Wright, David. 2017. Using word n-grams to identify authors and idiolects. *International Journal of Corpus Linguistics* 22(2), 212–241.

Wulff, Stefanie, Stefan Th. Gries & Nicholas Lester. 2018. Optional *that* in complementation by German and Spanish learners: Where and how German and Spanish learners differ from native speakers. In Andrea Tyler, Lihong Huang & Hana Jan (eds.), *What is Applied Cognitive Linguistics: Answers from Current SLA Research,* 99–120. Berlin, Boston: De Gruyter Mouton.

Appendix 8.1

Table 8.4 *Syntactic categorization used with examples.*

Category	Subcategory	Examples	Inst. total	%
Copular:			10,653:	60:
(canonical)	+ AdjP	...*it's a bit foolish*...[14]	3,738	21
	+ NP (incl. DP)	...*it's nonsense.*	5,599	32
	+ AdvP	...*it is enough for us.*	158	1
	+ PrepP	*It's about physics.*	732	4
	+ Clause	...*it's what's going on right now.*	426	2
		...*it's because he's ignorant/It's as if*[15] *they didn't anticipate*...		
		...*it is purely to encourage a chemical reaction.*		
Progressive		...*it's already happening!*	322	2
Going to V		*It's going to be a major project*...	57	0
Extraposition:			5,391:	31:
	inf. clause	*It's always bad to plan the future*...	2,746	16
	declarative clause	*It's important that they're libertarian!*	2,324	13
	interrogative clause	...*it is unclear just how this will proceed.*	315	2
	NP	*It is funny your remark*...	3	0
	gerund	...*it's nice being able to voice my opinion here.*	3	0
Passive		...*it's affected by new results.*	857	5
Cleft		*It is experimental evidence that is missing.*	377	2
Total			**17,657**	**100**

[14] It was a deliberate strategy to choose short examples for illustration, but in reality the length of the syntactic structures where *it's/is* participates varies widely. For example, in copular uses, predicative complements can be very long and include various modifiers and complements, including clausal ones, as in *It's as simple as measuring how much water you drink every day.*

[15] *As if* here is treated as a conjunction.

Table 8.5 *Pre-nuclear cases and comparative constructions.*

Category	Subcategory	Examples	Inst. total
Pre-nuclear		…who realize just how difficult it is to keep the business afloat…	157
		Whoever claims it is has been brainwashed…	
		Ah here it is…	
		…a cooling tower, no matter what kind of plant it's in, makes steam.	
		…transmogrifying our banking system into the Dracula that it is today!	
		So it is with all chemistry.	
Comparative			180:
	Elliptical	…the press is as controlled in Iran as it is in most of the world.	108
	Complement present	…it will be faster in Firefox much like it is faster in Windows.	72
		The climate, as long as it is a part of science…[16]	
Total			**337**

[16] We have included cases of *as soon as*, *as far as* and *as long as*, which often have reanalysed idiomatic meanings.

9 Are Multilinguals the Better Academic ELF Users?
Evidence from a Questionnaire Study Measuring Self-Assessed Proficiencies

Peter Siemund and Jessica Terese Mueller

1 Introduction

This contribution addresses the question of putative linguistic advantages of multilingual over monolingual speakers, as described inter alia in Agustín-Llach (2017), Bialystok et al. (2012, 2018), Cenoz (2013), Maluch et al. (2015), and Maluch et al. (2016). This is a central and rather hotly debated issue in current studies on bilingualism and multilingualism. The difference between monolingual and multilingual speakers lies therein that multilingual speakers are able to understand and use more than one language, whereas monolingual speakers are those who are only able to understand and use one language. Speakers with multilingual language backgrounds have been found to outperform monolingual speakers in matters of executive control, cognitive reserve, cognitive development, metalinguistic awareness, and language learning. The evidence available, however, is by no means unanimous. We ask here whether comparable performance advantages can also be identified in multilingually raised speakers who use English as a Lingua Franca (ELF) in tertiary education. The research design described in this chapter basically follows that of studies previously and subsequently carried out in the context of Singapore and the United Arab Emirates (Siemund et al. 2014; Leimgruber et al. 2018; Siemund et al. 2020).

Since non-native speakers of English already outnumber native speakers[1] by a wide margin, with a strong tendency towards widening further, it can be

---

We would like to express our gratitude to Anna Mauranen, Svetlana Vetchinnikova, and Jean-Marc Dewaele for their constructive and very helpful comments and criticism on a previous version of this article. All remaining errors and inconsistencies are our own.

[1] Dewaele (2018) argues that the terminological opposition of "native speaker" and "non-native speaker" should be replaced by "L1 user" and "LX user," as the latter terms are devoid of ideological connotations. We here continue using the former terms, since these are more established.

taken for granted that communicative encounters between non-native speakers of English in this language are pervasive. Accordingly, English has come to be used as a lingua franca in various domains of society, including business, tourism, health care, and – last but not least – academia. The individual ELF users, like all speakers in any given society, can be assumed to bring heterogeneous language backgrounds and repertoires to the table, ranging from monolingual upbringings to various forms of bilingualism or multilingualism in the home and other relevant environments in which these individuals are raised.

An increasing number of ELF encounters take place in academia, and since students and instructors require extensive international experience and expertise in modern academia, universities in non-English and non-native English-speaking countries (i.e. countries in the outer and expanding circles, according to Kachru's [1986] definition) increasingly offer programs in English in order to attract international students. As a consequence, administrative staff are also confronted more and more with communication in ELF. There can be no doubt that academic ELF is a register that presents high communicative demands for the uninitiated user, and hence it seems plausible to assume that some speakers can manage these better than others. Competence in academic ELF depends on factors such as proficiency in English, previous exposure to ELF, experience with a wide range of ELF speakers, and the like. If it were possible to show that language background – monolingual vs. multilingual – definitively influences ELF proficiency, this would represent another piece in the puzzle of the debate on multilingual advantages.

We here approach the matter as follows. Section 2 tackles some definitional matters in relation to ELF and lingua franca communication, attempting to identify what they are and what they are not. Section 3 concerns itself with different kinds of multilingual advantages, as described in previous studies. The main point here is to identify which conceptions of advantages can be considered relevant for ELF communication. In Section 4, we introduce the research questions, while in Section 5 we describe the results of a study on language repertoires and academic ELF usage that was carried out at the University of Hamburg in 2016. This study is solely based on self-assessments and does not include more objective tests. It will be shown that multilingually raised ELF speakers consistently provide higher self-assessments than their peers with a monolingual background, although these differences are not always statistically significant. Section 6 discusses these findings and Section 7 summarizes the study and formulates some ideas for future research.

2   Defining ELF

As the present contribution is concerned with multilingual speakers of ELF in academic contexts, it seems appropriate to clarify briefly what the defining characteristics of a lingua franca are. The following considerations are primarily based on Mauranen (2012).

ELF is not a native language, nor is it as a second, third, or foreign language. It is, to put it in the words of Mauranen (2012: 8), "a vehicular language used by speakers who do not share a first language." Thus, it can be any language in a speaker's language repertoire except for their first or native language. Communication between lingua franca speakers and native speakers of the lingua franca represents a special case that goes beyond the present discussion. A lingua franca arises in specific communicative situations in which the speakers lack a common first or native language but nonetheless need to communicate. The definition of a lingua franca is thus largely situation based and does not rest on specific linguistic properties, even though lingua franca speakers employ communicative strategies that allow one to identify them as such. A lingua franca can be completely artificial (e.g. Esperanto) or be recruited from a natural language that has a certain reach or social prestige. The history of mankind knows a considerable number of lingua francas, inter alia, Sanskrit, Arabic, Latin, Greek, French, and English. Lingua francas come in varying degrees of complexity, ranging from simple trade pidgins to erudite languages for academic and other social encounters of high complexity.

Lingua francas are different from learner languages, as Mauranen (2012: 3–4) points out, although the same language – say, English – may be the target of language-learning efforts and be used as a lingua franca. Again, the difference is largely situational and functional. Language learning proceeds within specialized contexts (i.e. the classroom), and it is primarily in this context that learner languages arise and are used. The goal here is to work towards a certain target language norm (e.g. Standard British English). Learners in a classroom tend to share the same language background, or, at least, they used to share one prior to our current age of globalization (see Bonnet & Siemund 2018). The same language or language variety may be employed as a lingua franca in a different context. Lingua franca users may then use this language for ad hoc communication without striving for a normative target.

Lingua franca communication represents a complex language contact scenario, and it is not a simple task to determine precisely which languages are in contact in such situations. Given the above observations, though, we can exclude direct contact between the speakers' first or native languages. What is apparently in contact, then, are the respective contact-based lects of the speakers, but since these are influenced by the substrate of their first or native languages (first-order contact), and perhaps also by further languages in their repertoires, the resulting language contact situation is one of considerable complexity. Mauranen (2012: 29) analyzes this as a situation of contact between what she refers to as "similects" (i.e. the individual, but similar idiolects influenced by the speakers' L1 [or other] substrate), and it is precisely these contact varieties that are actually in interaction in lingua franca communication. In other words, the background languages of the speakers partake in the resulting contact situation as well. We see here a case of second-order language contact, or a contact between hybrids (Mauranen 2012: 29). It is obvious that this contact situation gains in complexity the more languages are involved. Hence, given that multilingually raised individuals possess a broader linguistic repertoire, beginning at an earlier age compared to their monolingually raised peers, it can be presumed that multilingually raised lingua franca speakers may well contribute more complexity to such interactions than their monolingually raised peers.

Although there is no evidence that lingua francas develop their own grammars, as the language contact situations are simply too short and fluid for that to happen, there is convincing evidence that lingua franca speakers – apparently rather unconsciously – employ a set of joint communicative strategies that allow them to communicate successfully in this similect encounter. They mysteriously know what to do to make themselves understood without ever having been taught, much as in other communicative projects (see Clark 1996; Schegloff 2007; Siemund 2018). As Mauranen (2012: 7) points out, there is "a strong orientation to content over form," which is very different from the classroom learning context where the use of correct forms is an important, if not *the* primary educational goal. This content orientation is reflected in observable patterns of language use among lingua franca users, which are characterized by simplification, levelling, explicitness, repetition, accommodation, and enhanced cooperativeness. To quote Mauranen (2012: 56) again, "[c]onstant similect encounters can be assumed to impinge on use by enhancing transparency: simplicity in grammar, complexity in lexis, and explicitness in discourse."

If it is the case that lingua franca speakers tend to place content over form and communicative success over correctness, they can be expected to develop high levels of communicative flexibility and error tolerance. It could therefore be presumed that they generally try to make communication work, rather than pointing out to each other what has gone wrong (but see Kuteeva 2019 for conflicting findings). Moreover, as a consequence of encountering speakers with many different language repertoires and, accordingly, similects, they can also be expected to develop above-average comprehension skills. They can thus be assumed to have – at least on average – communicative advantages in relation to, say, the average monolingual speaker in their encounters with other monolinguals within their language community, as well as second- or foreign-language learners of the language of the monolingual speaker. In the words of Mauranen (2012: 57):

Communicative practices of these kinds benefit interlocutors in both of their roles: that of a speaker and that of a hearer. They allow processing time for both (for example hesitating, repeating, and pausing), assist in mutual comprehension (for example explicitness, approximation), and help achieve positive social goals (for example repetition, co-construction).

Such considerations, however, are quite reminiscent of ongoing and rather controversial debates about the putative advantages of multilingual over monolingual speakers. Here, the hypothesis is that bilingual and multilingual speakers enjoy a host of advantages over monolingual speakers, ranging from mental processing and cognitive development to metalinguistic awareness and issues of language production and comprehension. We will take a closer look at these in the next section.

3   The Multilingual Advantages Debate

If we hypothesize that multilingually raised ELF speakers show advantages in relation to monolingually raised ELF speakers, we first of all need to specify in which senses we use the word *advantage*. This is not at all trivial, as multilingualism and language in general are complex phenomena that can, in principle, produce advantages of very different kinds and in different ways. Needless to say, we also need to consider the possibility that multilingualism may produce negative effects or no effects at all.

On a historical note, the discussion regarding the benefits and deficits of monolingual, bilingual, and multilingual upbringing and education can at least be traced back to the eighteenth and nineteenth century, when policies of nation-building were supported by arguments in favor of a single national language and monolingual development, while discrediting alternative models of linguistic development, as well as linguistic and dialectal diversity. At that time, this made sense politically and economically, since railway traffic suddenly allowed people to interact across longer distances in shorter times, and the invention of the telephone created the first widely distributed virtual networks. Linguistic diversity was conceptualized as a problem and not as something in need of preservation and development. Having said that, the overall trajectory towards monolingualism was in fact set into motion much earlier with the introduction of Protestantism in Europe and the concomitant translation of the Bible into a common language of the people. In addition, compulsory schooling required an academic language upon which to base the syllabus, and print media could be circulated more widely and in higher print runs as a consequence of the invention of mechanical printing. We must not forget, though, that the linguistic model of the educated elite used to be bilingualism, since Latin and French were employed for academic, political, and religious purposes and served as lingua francas. Following the sobering effects of the two World Wars and the ensuing, more critical perspective on nationalism and cultural chauvinism, we can witness a renewed interest in bilingualism and a strong research commitment to showing that bilingual development can be as successful as monolingual development. Some decades later, propelled by globalization and migration processes set into motion by reliable and inexpensive long-distance travel, a new freedom of movement due to the collapse of the Iron Curtain, and continuing wars and human hardship, the scientific question is no longer whether bilingualism and monolingualism are equivalued alternatives, but rather whether and to what extent multilingual models of language development have advantages for individuals and their respective societies, or can be designed in such a way as to produce said advantages.

Steering clear of the trivial observation that knowledge of languages increases one's cultural capital, primarily qua their communicative potential or Q-value in the sense of de Swaan (2001), and thus allows one to gain access to more speakers and different cultures, the ensuing economic, social, and cultural advantages do not represent the focus of attention here. Rather, we are interested in this case in various positive psychological or attitudinal effects related to bilingualism and multilingualism, as well as potentially favorable effects on language acquisition and learning.

3.1 Executive Function (Control) and Cognitive Reserve

The deficit view of bilingualism was seriously questioned in the by-now-classic study by Peal and Lambert (1962), opening up a highly successful strand of research documenting the ability of children to acquire two languages simultaneously and successfully, while bringing to light certain previously unknown positive effects of bilingualism, particularly in terms of executive control (Bialystok 2001, 2018; Martin-Rhee & Bialystok 2008; Bialystok et al. 2012). According to Bialystok et al. (2012: 241), executive control "is the set of cognitive skills based on limited cognitive resources for such functions as inhibition, switching attention, and working memory." It is tested using a variety of tasks – inter alia, the flanker task, the Simon Task, and the Stroop Task – which involve the opposition of congruent and incongruent conditions of certain stimuli (colors, shapes, letters, etc.) and measure the performance (usually reaction times) of subjects in relation to these conditions. Typically, a bilingual subject group is tested against a monolingual control group. The relevant tests have been carried out on both children and adults and tend to report better (i.e. faster) performance in bilinguals over monolinguals. One should bear in mind that these are standard psychological tests that have been used to demonstrate the influences of a host of other factors on executive control, such as level of blood alcohol, tiredness, illnesses, etc.

More recently and based on the above findings, it was hypothesized that bilingualism – due to its positive effects on executive control – also contributes to what is known as cognitive reserve, that is, a cognitive buffer that can help to protect against age-related symptoms of cognitive decline. Generally, it is known that physical, intellectual, and social engagement contribute to cognitive reserve (Bialystok 2012: 246). The hypothesis that bilingualism also contributes to cognitive reserve was tested in Bialystok et al. (2007) on a sample of 184 patients diagnosed with dementia. On average, when controlling for several confounding factors (education, socioeconomic status, etc.), bilingual patients developed symptoms of dementia four years later than monolingual patients. Bialystok et al. (2004) compared younger and older bilingual and monolingual subjects on the Simon Task and found rather strong processing advantages in older bilinguals in comparison to older monolinguals. Craik et al. (2010) represents a similar study on the effects of bilingualism on the onset of Alzheimer's disease, which was able to identify a significant delay in the onset of relevant symptoms in bilingual patients.[2]

Although the differences reported in the above studies typically reach statistical significance, it must be conceded that the practical relevance of the absolute differences sometimes remains a bit difficult to see (being, say, 100 ms faster or slower in the Simon Task). Moreover, several recent replication studies fail to substantiate Bialystok's bilingual advantage hypothesis (Duñabeitia & Carreiras 2015; Paap et al. 2016). Such contradictory findings have led to a renewed interest in the multilingual advantages debate. Lehtonen et al. (2018: 1), using a meta-analytic comparison, soberly conclude that "healthy bilingual adults do not have such a cognitive control advantage. The synthesis of 152 studies and 891 comparisons and several moderator variables does not show systematic advantages across the analyzed cognitive domains, tasks, or bilingual populations." Interestingly, Lehtonen et al. (2018: 413) detect a measurable publication bias, reporting that "small studies with low precision and large, positive effect sizes might be overrepresented in the peer-reviewed literature, or that comparably small studies with large, negative effect sizes are underrepresented."

3.2 Cognitive Development and Educational Attainment

Advantages of bilingualism and bilingual education have also been discussed in education studies, where potentially positive effects are expected to impact cognitive development and educational attainment. In the relevant studies,

---

[2] In spite of these advantages, bilinguals have also been shown to control smaller vocabularies in each of their languages than monolinguals and slower response rates for lexical comprehension and production (see Bialystok 2012: 242 for an overview; Ivanova & Costa 2008; Bialystok et al. 2010). Moreover, monolinguals outperform bilinguals in verbal fluency tasks in which participants generate the highest possible number of words in a limited time span based on phonological or semantic cues.

bilingualism is typically understood in a special sense and is by and large restricted to "cognitive academic language proficiency" (Cummins 2001: 58), which needs to be seen in contrast to "basic interpersonal communicative skills." This opposition essentially boils down to a register difference (academic vs. colloquial language) and should not be confused with the broader term "language competence" (see MacSwan 2000 for criticism regarding the linguistic discrimination of minority and heritage speakers). In other words, "bilingualism" in such studies means, first and foremost, "academic language bilingualism," and only the latter is supposed to positively impact on cognitive development and educational attainment.

In two successive publications, Cummins (1976, 1979) introduced two hypotheses regarding academic language competence in the bilingual speaker, known as the "threshold hypothesis" and the "interdependence hypothesis." They both relate to the level of academic language competence of the languages in the bilingual mind, and specifically whether the observed bilingualism is additive or subtractive. The outcome of additive bilingualism is high levels of competence in both languages (balanced bilingualism). Subtractive bilingualism can lead to dominant bilingualism, where high academic competence is only achieved in one language, while the other language remains at a lower competence level. It can also lead to a situation in which academic competence in both languages is low, sometimes referred to as "semilingualism" – although this term has attracted widespread criticism for its negative connotation and its potential for social stigmatization. After all, these speakers are perfectly fluent language users. What they lack is the academic register.

According to the threshold hypothesis (Cummins 1979: 230), positive cognitive effects can be expected in situations of additive bilingualism, while dominant bilingualism – wherein language competency levels are higher in one language compared to the other – is associated with neither positive nor negative effects. Put differently, a certain level of academic language competence needs to be reached or surpassed before the positive cognitive effects of bilingualism begin to manifest themselves. It is not entirely clear what is meant by "positive cognitive effects," but they are likely to present themselves in the form of higher educational attainment or better school grades (see also Lasagabaster 1998, 2001). Cummins (1979: 233) furthermore suggested a relationship between the languages in the bilingual mind such that academic competence in one language has positive impacts on academic competence in the other. According to this interdependence hypothesis, for example, it is advantageous for heritage language-speaking children to develop their heritage language academically while receiving schooling in the majority language. Here again it remains difficult to operationalize and measure the interdependence between languages. As Berthele and Vanhove (2017: 4–5) point out, several observable datasets measuring heritage and academic language competence are compatible with language interdependence, and what is more, are also consistent with several alternative principles such as language giftedness or more general cognitive skills.

3.3 Metalinguistic Awareness

According to folk wisdom, the learning of further languages is a function of the languages that one already knows, such that previous language knowledge facilitates the learning of new languages. The more languages one already knows, the faster one can proceed in the learning of further languages. The scientific concept behind this intuitively plausible generalization is metalinguistic awareness, which Jessner (2006: 42) defines as the "ability to focus attention on language as an object in itself or to think abstractly about language and, consequently, to play with or manipulate language," or, according to Jessner (2008: 277), "the ability to focus on linguistic form and meaning ... to categorize words into parts of speech; [to] switch focus between form, function, and meaning; and [to] explain why a word has a particular function." Multilingualism is usually taken to increase metalinguistic awareness and multilingual proficiency (see Bialystok 2001; Sanz 2012 for an overview).

A positive relationship between metalinguistic awareness and language proficiency has been documented in several studies. For example, Lasagabaster (2001) finds a significant correlation between metalinguistic awareness and various skills in English (listening, reading, speaking, grammar, and writing). This study was carried out in the Basque Country and is based on 252 bilingual students (Basque, Spanish) who studied English as a foreign language. The strongest effects were measured for grammar and writing, although – contrary to expectation – metalinguistic awareness also had a strong impact on speaking scores (less so on listening and reading). Interestingly, we also find studies that document a negative correlation between bilingualism and metalinguistic awareness, especially in the context of heritage language speakers (Spellerberg 2016).

3.4 Language Acquisition and Learning

More recently, bilingualism and multilingualism have been argued to carry additional positive effects, in that they facilitate the acquisition of additional languages (Cenoz 2013). It appears that "[g]eneral aspects of L3 proficiency [are] more favorable to bilinguals than those studies in which very specific aspects of language proficiency were analyzed" (Cenoz 2003: 80). Such positive effects can present themselves in different ways. The Common European Framework of Reference for Languages (CEFR), apart from distinguishing six proficiency levels, assumes four kinds of language activities. These are:

- reception (listening and reading),
- production (speaking and writing),
- interaction (speaking and writing), and
- mediation (translating and interpreting).

In principle, positive effects of multilingual development could play out in all of these domains. For example, bilingual (or multilingual) speakers learning English as a third or additional language could manifest heightened reception and interaction skills in comparison to a monolingual control group of learners that received the same input. These heightened skills can be expected to become evident in the requisite tasks, that is, a speaker with higher reception skills could draw more information more accurately from a listening or reading exercise. Speakers with multilingual backgrounds may also be the better translators and interpreters, which could be measured on the basis of translation/interpreting speed, but also accuracy.

If there are positive effects of multilingualism on the learning of additional languages, these could also facilitate the acquisition of specific linguistic knowledge. Here, a multitude of phenomena could, in principle, be investigated for positive effects, including:

- lexicon (code-switching, semantic extension, calques),
- grammar (subject-verb agreement, article usage, tense and aspect, word order, etc.),
- phonology (intonation, realization of specific phonemes),
- pragmatic knowledge (politeness, directness, indirectness), and
- alphabetization and scripts (faster learning of new scripts, familiarity with scripts, understanding of script basis).

Positive effects in the above areas of language development (here focusing on English) would be identifiable in higher target-like realizations (or fewer errors) in the linguistic behavior of learners with a multilingual background in relation to those of learners who have grown up in a monolingual environment. Another possibility could be that multilingually raised learners may not differ from monolingually raised learners in regard to the number of errors, but rather regarding the type or quality of errors – for example, higher numbers of errors that do not greatly impede understanding; this would likewise illustrate a positive effect of multilingual upbringings. If, in contrast, multilingual learners merely show different target-like realizations from monolingual learners, but they produce more or less the same number of errors of the same type or quality, they would not in this case demonstrate facilitative effects, but merely different types of cross-linguistic influence.

Most of the above domains have not been explored, but for some we do find data from previous studies.

Generally speaking, studies involving balanced bilinguals learning English as a third language tend to find a positive influence of bilingualism in regard to grammar and vocabulary, as well as overall language proficiency, when compared to monolingual control groups (see Cenoz & Valencia 1994; Sanz 2000). In addition, balanced bilinguals have been shown to process and produce more indirect and polite formulations than their monolingual peers, which may be attributable to heightened metapragmatic awareness (see Safont Jordà 2003). In comparison, studies investigating unbalanced bilingual heritage speakers do not report differences between bilinguals and monolingual controls, nor do they identify any advantages or disadvantages in bilingual speakers (see Sanders & Meijers 1995; Cenoz 2003: 77).

3.5 Summary

In view of the above discussion, we conclude that the controversy about multilingual advantages is still ongoing and that the final word has not been spoken. It seems to be becoming increasingly clear that matters of test design, subject selection, and, rather importantly, the understanding of the word *advantage* are all crucial for determining the outcome of this debate.

The study of executive control in multilingual and monolingual subjects has produced mixed results, with recent replication studies and meta-analyses adding to the skepticism. Interdependence between languages seems to exist, but it remains unclear what the cognitive basis for the observable interdependence is and where exactly it can be expected to present itself. There is little to no evidence for thresholds (Fleckenstein et al. 2018), and they generally remain difficult to define.

Conversely, increased metalinguistic awareness as a consequence of multilingualism appears to be well documented. We consider this as one of the less controversial areas. Moreover, metalinguistic awareness is intuitively plausible – as is increased metacultural awareness as a consequence of travelling and diverse cultural encounters.

When focusing on English language learning, bilingual learners of English, who may be considered future users of ELF, have been shown to have advantages over learners with a monolingual background, especially regarding more general proficiencies and less with respect to target-like usage (Lorenz & Siemund 2019a). Balanced bilinguals here seem to profit more than subjects raised with other forms of bilingualism, such as a form seen in unbalanced bilingual heritage speakers (see Lorenz & Siemund 2019b for an overview).

4 Research Questions

We here transfer the discussion surrounding multilingual advantages, metalinguistic awareness, and language learning into the ELF context, studying the self-assessed proficiencies of academic ELF users in their English. We hypothesize that ELF users with a multilingual background are more skilled in their use of ELF and will therefore report higher English proficiencies than monolingually raised ELF users. This hypothesis is based on the observation frequently made in previous studies that learners of English with a multilingual background enjoy learning advantages over monolingually raised learners. Since the use of ELF presupposes the learning of English as a second or additional language, such learning advantages should carry over to ELF usage.

Specifically, we expect higher proficiencies in the domains of reception or comprehension, both listening and reading. This follows from the assumption of heightened metalinguistic awareness in multilinguals. High levels of metalinguistic awareness can be expected to facilitate the identification and understanding of unfamiliar linguistic structures, independently of whether these are due to incomplete or erroneous acquisition. The present study excludes subjects who acquired English as a native language, but we need to bear in mind that reading comprehension may and certainly does involve texts produced by native speakers of English.

Proficiencies are here measured by self-assessments, and not by way of objective tests. They need to be opposed to objective measures, which are currently not available for the academic context investigated here. Importantly, self-assessments may be biased by language background and cultural background. This needs to borne in mind in the interpretation of the results. For example, as for the context of Singapore, Leimgruber et al. (2018: 301) found that Malays assess their own English language skills as being better than Chinese speakers of English, even though objective measures show the reverse pattern.

5 Academic ELF Users with Multilingual and Monolingual Backgrounds

In a study conducted at the University of Hamburg in 2016 (for further information see Mueller & Siemund 2017; Mueller 2018), students (n = 1,454) and instructors (n = 341) were asked to fill out an online questionnaire via the platform LimeSurvey in either English or German about their multilingual experiences. Specifically, the students and instructors were first asked about the languages in their respective linguistic repertoires, their L1s, as well as the locations of the learning or acquisition of their respective languages. Participants then had the opportunity to rate their own proficiency in various competency areas related to those defined by the CEFR (Council of Europe 2001). Following the questions regarding their individual linguistic repertoire, their attitudes towards the use of ELF, multilingualism, and German as a foreign language were brought into focus.

5.1 Methodology

An online questionnaire of core questions was developed as part of a larger consortium research study focusing on the topic of multilingualism in and around the University of Hamburg, Germany. The project was funded by the Kompetenzzentrum Nachhaltige Universität (Competence Centre for a Sustainable University) of the University of Hamburg and was comprised of four studies with varying foci pertaining to the university setting, each led by teams from various university departments: multilingualism in healthcare at the University Medical Center by the Department of Medical Psychology, multilingualism in research by the Department of German Linguistics, multilingualism in university governance and administration in the Department of Educational Science, and multilingualism vis-à-vis ELF in university instruction in the Department of English Linguistics. The core questions were derived from the linguistic competencies set forth by the CEFR (Council of Europe 2001) and used wording modeled after the descriptions of each of the competency areas of reading comprehension, listening comprehension, spoken production, spoken interaction, and written expression. The CEFR self-assessment grid provides descriptions of can-statements corresponding to each of the CEFR proficiency levels from A1 (beginner) to C2 (mastery) (A1/A2 basic user, B1/B2 independent user, C1/C2 proficient user; see Council of Europe 2001 for comparison).

The methodology and results presented here stem from the study on multilingualism vis-à-vis ELF in the context of university instruction, undertaken by the Department of English Linguistics. The target group specified in this subproject consisted of students and instructors at the University of Hamburg. As it was assumed that instructors would tend to be older than the students, the presumption was that the instructors may have been exposed to fewer languages and perhaps only certain languages compared to the students. More specifically, although it is currently common practice that pupils in German primary and secondary schools are mandated to have English as a first foreign language as part of their core curriculum from the first grade – and some even prior to primary school – this was not always the case in Germany, particularly in East Germany in the former German Democratic Republic (1949–1990), where pupils learned Russian as a first foreign language and were often not exposed to English until much later, if at all. For this reason, the target group was divided between students and instructors, in order to observe whether there may be differences in self-reported multilingualism between participants from younger vs. older generations.

The online questionnaires asked participants first to list languages, dialects, and/or varieties (up to fifteen) in which they possessed any degree of receptive and/or productive proficiency, and then to select which level they would ascribe to their own language competencies and skills in each of the languages listed. The self-assessments of linguistic abilities were based on a six-point Likert scale from one (low or rudimentary proficiency) to six (high proficiency or mastery), which was inspired by the levels A1 through C2 of the CEFR (Council of Europe 2001) and covered each of the following competence areas: listening comprehension, spoken production, reading comprehension, spoken interaction, and written expression.

Overall, 1,454 students and 341 instructors took part in the online survey. Of the students who participated in the survey, 915 chose to indicate their gender: 624 (68.2%) identified as female and 291 (31.8%) identified as male. Of the 1,004 students who indicated their respective age ranges, 725 (72.2%) indicated being between the ages of 21 and 29; 143 (14.2%) between 30 and 40; 73 (7.3%) under 20; 26 (2.6%) between 41 and 50; 28 (1.9%) over 60; and 9 (0.9%) between 51 and 60 (see Figure 9.1).

Regarding the other sample group, 224 of the 341 instructors who participated in the study chose to identify their gender. Of those, 117 (34.45%) identified as male and 107 (31.55%) identified as female. Among those instructors who chose to indicate their age ranges, 92 (38.5%) reported being between 30 and 40; 56 (23.4%) under 30; 46 (19.2%) between 41 and 50; 36

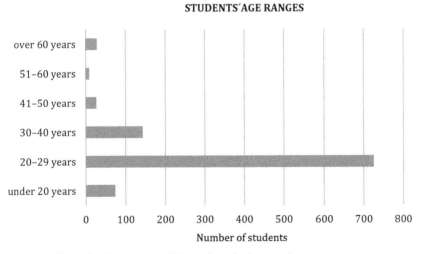

Figure 9.1 Age ranges of the students in the sample.

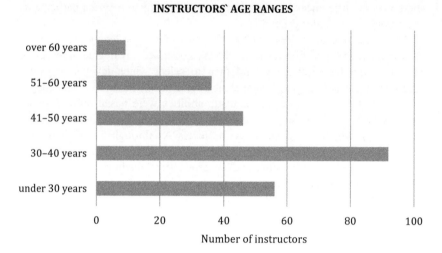

Figure 9.2 Age ranges of the instructors in the sample.

(15.1%) between 51 and 60; and 9 (3.8%) over 60 years of age (see Figure 9.2).

Using the software program SPSS 23 (IBM Corp. 2015), descriptive statistics (i.e. frequencies, means, standard deviations) were initially computed and chi-square tests or Kolmogorov-Smirnov tests were calculated to determine whether the distributions of these results conformed to a normal distribution. In order to determine whether differences in means reached statistical significance, Levene tests for homogeneity of variance were calculated in order to determine whether or not data from independent samples demonstrated similar patterns of variance, and independent t-tests were performed.

5.2   Language Repertoires and Overall Proficiencies

A total of 279 languages, including dialects, varieties, creole languages, pidgin languages, sign languages, one deaf-blind manual alphabet, programming languages, and artificial languages were reported to be used receptively and/or productively by students and instructors. Of these 279 languages, 93 (i.e. 66 languages and 27 varieties or dialects) were identified as "L1s."

5.2.1   Language Repertoires Of those who filled out the online questionnaire, 1,252 students and 290 instructors indicated which and how many languages they make use of receptively and/or productively. Students reported that they were able to understand and or speak between one and fifteen languages, and instructors listed between two and fifteen languages. On

Figure 9.3 Monolingually raised students' (left) and instructors' (right) L1s by frequency.

average, both students and instructors reported possessing receptive and/or productive skills in about five languages. Specifically, students listed on average 5.68 languages (Median = 5; Mode = 4; SD = 2.59), and instructors reported being able to use an average of 5.71 languages (Median = 5; Mode = 4; SD = 2.63) receptively and/or productively.

In total, 929 students (77.6%) and 239 instructors (87.2%) indicated that they had acquired one L1. Figure 9.3 visualizes their L1s by means of word clouds.

Regarding multilingual upbringings, 230 (19.2%) students reported having acquired more than one L1 (i.e. between two and four L1s), and 35 (12.8%) instructors reported having been raised with more than one L1 (i.e. between two and three L1s). These findings are visualized in Figure 9.4.[3]

Due to the fact that we presumed that no participants would be monolingual in the classic sense and that they would only be able to understand and use one language, in the present study, we will compare participants based on their linguistic upbringing, be it monolingual or multilingual. In other words, monolingually raised students and instructors (i.e. those who were brought up using only one language) will be compared to those raised with two or more languages (i.e. two, three, and four), establishing a contrast between monolingually raised ELF speakers and multilingually raised ELF speakers.

Among monolingually raised participants, the following L1s were most frequently identified: German (students: n = 808, 87%; instructors: n = 211, 88.3%), Russian (students: n = 21, 2.3%; instructors: n = 2, 0.8%), English (students: n = 18, 1.9%; instructors: n = 9, 3.8%), Chinese (students: n = 13, 1.4%), Polish (students: n = 6, 0.6%), French (students: n = 5, 0.5%; instructors: n = 2, 0.8%), Turkish, Spanish, and Italian (students: each n = 5, 0.5%).

---

[3] The terms *Plattdeutsch* and *Platt* are colloquial terms for referring to a regional dialect or minority language. However, it is unclear which regional dialects or minority languages are being referred to, as *Plattdeutsch* and *Platt* are general terms that do not differentiate between the two statuses.

Figure 9.4 Multilingually raised students' (left) and instructors' (right) L1s by frequency.

In order to focus only on ELF users, those participants who indicated English as one of their L1s were excluded from further analyses regarding English language proficiency. Once students who indicated speaking English as one of their L1s had been excluded (n = 1,397), 911 (82.7%) reported having been raised monolingually, and 191 (17.3%) identified more than one L1. Once instructors with English as an L1 had been filtered out, 324 remained, and of those, 229 (89.1%) reported having been raised monolingually and 28 (10.9%) multilingually.

5.2.2 Self-Assessment of Language Competencies and Skills Among the 279 languages identified in the linguistic repertoires of the students and instructors, the five languages that were named most frequently overall were the (foreign) languages traditionally offered in German schools: English (students: n = 1,153; instructors = 278), German (students: n = 1,153; instructors: n = 271), French (students: n = 740; instructors: n = 206), Spanish (students: n = 641; instructors: n = 133), and Italian (students: n = 295; instructors: n = 91).

As a trend, multilingually raised participants tended to list more languages in their linguistic repertoires (students, monolingually raised: n = 926; M = 5.54;[4] SD = 2.56; multilingually raised: n = 229; M = 6.43; SD = 2.50; Levene test for homogeneity of variance: F = 0.43; p = 0.84; t(355.65) = −4.81; p < 0.01; instructors, monolingually raised: n = 239; M = 5.54; SD = 2.60; multilingually raised: n = 35; M = 6.66; SD = 2.07; Levene test for homogeneity of variance: F = 1.12; p = 0.29; t(51.05) = −2.88; p < 0.01) and reported being more proficient in each of their languages compared to their monolingually raised peers (see Mueller & Siemund 2017 for further details).

In general, students and instructors rated themselves as possessing "very good" overall proficiency in English, as indicated by their composite scores summing the total of their self-assessed English proficiency levels in the five

---

[4] "M" here refers to the mean.

STUDENTS' ENGLISH PROFICIENCY COMPOSITE SCORES

Figure 9.5 Monolingually raised vs. multilingually raised students' average self-assessed proficiency levels.

domains of the CEFR, which will be elaborated on in further detail in Section 5.3. Their scores ranged from 5 to 30, with a composite score of 5 indicating basic language skills in all five domains, and a score of 30 being associated with mastery in all five domains (instructors: M = 26.68; SD = 3.79; students: M = 24.76; SD = 4.73), and average self-rated language proficiency levels in various languages were consistently higher for multilingually raised students and instructors when compared to their monolingually raised counterparts (Mueller & Siemund 2017). More specifically, when focusing on self-assessed proficiency composite scores in English, multilingually raised participants rate themselves as being more proficient overall when compared to their monolingually raised counterparts (see Figures 9.5 and 9.6).

Multilingually raised students (M = 25.37; SD = 4.2) rated themselves as being significantly more confident in their English language abilities when compared to monolingually raised students (M = 24.67; SD = 4.8; Levene test for homogeneity of variance: F = 2.84; p = 0.09; t(289.12) = −2.00; p < 0.05).[5]

---

[5] A statistically significant Levene test for homogeneity of variance indicates that the variances within the two independent groups (i.e. in this case monolingually raised students and multilingually raised students) are statistically similar. A significant t-test score indicates that there is a significant difference in the mean values of the respective self-assessed proficiency scores between the two independent groups, namely monolingually raised participants and multilingually raised participants.

INSTRUCTORS' ENGLISH PROFICIENCY COMPOSITE SCORES

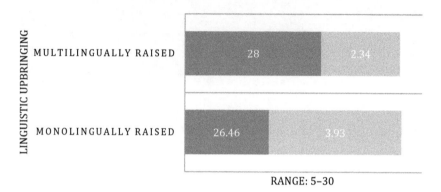

Figure 9.6 Monolingually raised vs. multilingually raised instructors' average self-assessed proficiency levels.

When compared to monolingually raised instructors (M = 26.46; SD = 3.93), multilingually raised instructors rated their overall English proficiency as being significantly higher (M = 28; SD = 2.34; Levene test for homogeneity of variance: F = 5.56; p = 0.02; t(250) = −2.02; p < 0.05).

5.3 CEFR Domains

In order to allow for self-assessments that are based on a standard rating scale, the CEFR self-assessment descriptions were used and applied to the domains of listening comprehension, speaking, reading comprehension, spoken interaction, and writing, which are also defined as language proficiency domains by the CEFR (see Appendix 9.1).

The online questionnaire was programmed in such a way as to allow participants to list each of the languages in which they possessed any degree of proficiency, and subsequently they could choose the proficiency levels for each of their self-identified languages.

5.3.1 Listening Comprehension As seen above, the proficiency domain of listening comprehension refers to participants' perception of their ability to listen to and understand spoken English to varying degrees.

When comparing monolingually raised with multilingually raised students, there appeared to be a slight difference in favor of multilingually raised students. However, upon closer examination, the differences in self-assessed listening comprehension were not statistically significant (Levene test for homogeneity of variance: F = 0.57; p = 0.45; t(293.87) = −1.72; p = 0.09).

Among instructors, as with the students, there was no statistically significant difference between the self-assessed listening comprehension levels of monolingually raised instructors compared to their multilingually raised peers (Levene test for homogeneity of variance: F = 0.10; p = 0.75; t(39.05) = −1.82; p = 0.08). Nevertheless, the multilingually raised instructors confirm the positive trend.

5.3.2 Reading Comprehension The domain of reading comprehension deals with participants' perceived ability to read and understand various types of text to varying degrees in written English.

With reference to self-assessed reading comprehension among monolingually raised vs. multilingually raised students (see Figure 9.7), the latter showed statistically significantly higher self-assessed levels of reading comprehension compared to their monolingually raised peers (Levene test for homogeneity of variance: F = 3.40; p = 0.07; t(305.90) = −2.02; p < 0.05).

The statistically significant difference between monolingually raised vs. multilingually raised students was not seen among instructors in regard to self-assessed reading comprehension (Levene test for homogeneity of variance: F = 7.49; p < 0.01; t(253) = −1.47; p = 0.14), though the overall positive trend remains.

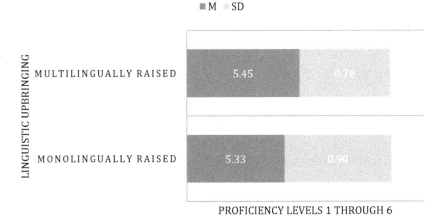

Figure 9.7 Reading comprehension among multilingually raised vs. monolingually raised students.

5.3.3 Spoken Interaction

The domain of spoken interaction describes the degree to which participants feel confident in their ability to engage in conversational interactions in English.

When comparing monolingually and multilingually raised students' self-assessed skills regarding general spoken interaction, there was no statistically significant difference between the two groups (Levene test for homogeneity of variance: $F = 4.87$; $p < 0.05$; $t(1079) = -1.84$; $p = 0.07$).

Just as seen with regard to students' self-assessed spoken interaction skills, there was no statistically significant difference found between monolingually raised vs. multilingually raised instructors (Levene test for homogeneity of variance: $F = 4.94$; $p < 0.05$; $t(252) = -1.82$; $p = 0.07$). The overall positive trend for multilingually raised students and instructors, though, persists.

5.3.4 Spoken Production

Whereas spoken interaction relates to conversational English skills, the domain of spoken production deals with participants' perceived abilities regarding producing coherent speech in terms of monologues, such as giving speeches or presentations – a skill that is often required in the academic context.

When examining self-assessments of their ability to speak coherently at various levels, multilingually raised students reported significantly greater confidence in their abilities when compared to their monolingually raised peers (Figure 9.8; Levene test for homogeneity of variance: $F = 7.69$; $p = 0.01$;

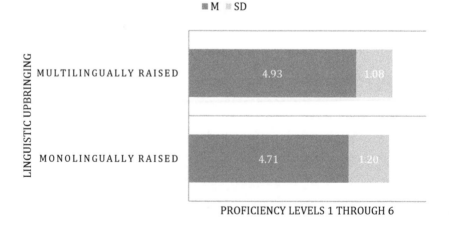

Figure 9.8 Spoken production among multilingually raised vs. monolingually raised students.

Are Multilinguals the Better Academic ELF Users? 255

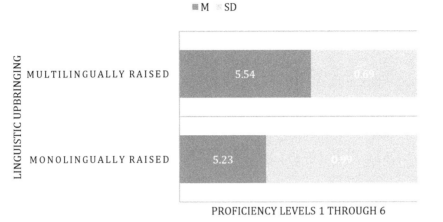

Figure 9.9 Spoken production among multilingually raised vs. monolingually raised instructors.

t(1079) = −2.33; p < 0.05). This difference turned out to be statistically significant.

As with the students, multilingually raised instructors were also significantly more confident in their abilities to produce coherent speech in English compared to their monolingually raised peers (Figure 9.9; Levene test for homogeneity of variance: F = 3.59; p = 0.06; t(41.97) = −2.11; p < 0.05). Calculating the difference also produced statistically significant results.

5.3.5 Written Expression As is the case with spoken production, the domain of written expression is one that is often required of students and instructors in academia to varying degrees. This domain refers to participants' ability to compose understandable written texts in English.

With respect to their self-assessed writing abilities, there was no statistically significant difference between monolingually raised students compared to their multilingually raised peers (Levene test for homogeneity of variance: F = 4.21; p < 0.05; t(1075) = −1.38; p = 0.17), but multilingually raised students again reported higher values.

Unlike the students, among the instructors, those who had been raised multilingually reported significantly higher levels of self-assessed writing ability when compared to their monolingually raised counterparts (Figure 9.10; Levene test for homogeneity of variance: F = 4.26; p < 0.05; t(252) = −2.31; p = 0.05).

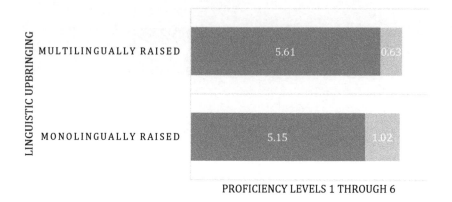

Figure 9.10 Written expression in multilingually raised vs. monolingually raised instructors.

6 Discussion

The research question that we formulated at the outset of this study suggested an influence of language background on self-assessed proficiency in ELF, where language background is broadly defined as monolingual in opposition to multilingual upbringing. This categorization of language backgrounds, of course, represents a simplification, particularly seeing as how we did not detail age of onset, acquisition trajectory, language dominance, or language use of the mother tongues during the acquisition process. Some multilingual competencies or skills in the sample may be additive, others may be subtractive. Some participants may show balanced bilingualism, while others may not. Moreover, in some cases, the background languages are genealogically and/or typologically closely related, whereas in other cases they are more distantly related. In an ideal world, such confounding factors would be controlled for. We also know, however, that subsamples quickly shrink and become meaningless statistically, once a large number of external conditions are factored in. One positive aspect of our sample is that students and instructors define relatively homogenous social groups in terms of educational background.

6.1 Self-Assessed Proficiencies

In the present study, we used self-assessed proficiencies as a proxy for objective proficiencies. This approach, of course, is not without problems, as subjects may overestimate or underestimate certain proficiencies. The advantage of relying on self-assessments is that the sample can be relatively large. With more than 1,500 participants, the sample employed here is comparatively substantial in size and certainly meaningful. Replicating this study with objectively measuring tests would be extremely expensive and time-consuming (see www.mez.uni-hamburg.de for such an approach among secondary school students). Thus, it remains to be seen to what extent the results reported here can be generalized, as we have focused on self-assessed proficiencies in one particular register (i.e. academic ELF).

6.2 Advantages of Multilinguals in the Use of ELF

The idea of a multilingual advantage in ELF proficiency follows from recent and ongoing work on multilingual development, in which a number of areas have been identified where bilingual and multilingual speakers manifest heightened performance in comparison to monolinguals. These include, inter alia, executive function, cognitive development, metalinguistic awareness, and language acquisition and learning. To be sure, the relevant advantages or performance boosts are not necessarily dramatic, and there are also disadvantages, but still, it remains an interesting observation in itself that monolinguals on the one hand and bilinguals/multilinguals on the other show differences in the aforementioned domains. Since ELF communication represents a special case in the use of an additional language, and in and of itself instigates skewing in linguistic performance ("simplicity in grammar, complexity in lexis, and explicitness in discourse" [Mauranen 2012: 56]), we hypothesized that multilingually raised ELF speakers would outperform monolingually raised ELF speakers in general proficiency, or at least in selected areas of proficiency.

In the sample explored here, instructors consistently report higher proficiencies than students, both with a monolingual and a multilingual background. This is certainly not unexpected, as instructors are typically older than students, typically possess more learning experience in and academically related exposure to English, represent the more advanced ELF users in an academic context, and usually have encountered many ELF users with different backgrounds in an international context, and thereby possess arguably higher levels of academic literacy. These highly consistent differences between students and instructors underline the representativeness and reliability of the self-assessments in the present sample, and perhaps of self-assessments in general. Instructors thus possess an advantage over students as a consequence of age and experience with using ELF in an academic setting.

Multilingually raised subjects, both students and instructors, consistently report higher values than monolingually raised subjects. The mean difference for students is 0.7 and for instructors is 1.54, here relying on the composite scores (recall Figures 9.1 and 9.2). This generalization applies to all the CEFR domains investigated here. We find an absolutely consistent overall trend that reaches statistical significance regarding the composite scores, as well as in selected CEFR domains, depending on the group of subjects considered. We interpret this finding as a general advantage of multilingually raised ELF users over their monolingually raised peers. These results nicely tie in with reports from previous studies identifying multilingual advantages in regard to learning additional languages (Cenoz & Valencia 1994; Lasagabaster 1998, 2001; Sanz 2000). However, since we here focused on proficiencies in just one language (i.e. English), these particular results of the study cannot inform the debate surrounding Cummins' (1976, 1979) interdependence and threshold hypotheses, although this tendency was seen across languages in this study (see Mueller & Siemund 2017 for an overview of further language comparisons).

In spoken production, the differences reported between multilingually and monolingually raised students and instructors both reach statistical significance. We did not expect this, hypothesizing instead that a multilingual upbringing would impact most strongly on listening and reading comprehension. This follows from the assumption that knowledge of several languages increases metalinguistic awareness and thus facilitates the identification and analysis of unfamiliar linguistic forms and meanings. Spoken production assesses the ability to speak coherently. The three highest scores – four, five, and six on the scale used here – respectively measure whether subjects are able to "give detailed commentaries about many topics that [they are] interested in," whether they can "present complicated topics thoroughly and in a well structured manner," and whether they think they can "debate topics fluidly, logically and appropriately." We can here only speculate about the reasons why a multilingual upbringing should significantly impact on spoken production, but we may note that the above self-assessment statements essentially capture argumentative skills that in themselves presuppose high levels of language proficiency. High-level argumentative skills, in turn, may be sensitive to metalinguistic awareness, of which speakers with multilingual backgrounds are known to enjoy higher levels. Another interpretation (suggested by Eliane Lorenz, p.c.) could be based on the assumption that speakers with multilingual backgrounds experience lower levels of anxiety when using ELF, hence feel more confident, and therefore report higher production scores than ELF users with a monolingual background. The lower levels of anxiety, in turn, could result from having more extensive experience with languages that multilingually raised ELF users can be assumed to have gathered.

As far as reading comprehension is concerned, only multilingually raised students report statistically significantly higher values. We expected this result as a consequence of higher levels of metalinguistic awareness due to a multilingual upbringing.

Interestingly enough, in written expression only instructors with a multilingual background claim to have higher proficiency scores that are significant in a technical sense. The multilingually raised students in the present sample do not report a similarly strong effect, even though they show the same tendency. We would here like to submit that instructors write substantially more English texts than students and could consequently be expected to be more experienced in this particular CEFR domain.

We also believe that our sample illustrates a fundamental problem in the identification and interpretation of multilingual advantages. Even though there is an overall, statistically significant difference between monolingually and multilingually raised ELF users regarding their self-assessed proficiencies, such significance is not reached in all CEFR domains. The deltas in listening comprehension and spoken interaction, for example, do not reach statistical significance, and with respect to reading comprehension and written expression, only those for either students or instructors do, but not for both. In other words, we find meaningful advantages in selected domains and subsamples. Supposing we merely focused on these statistically meaningful results and ignored the inconclusive values, a strong case for a general multilingual advantage could, in principle, be made. However, there is a danger of positive bias, and a more realistic interpretation of the dataset suggests advantages in some domains, though not in others. These results thus underline the skepticism raised in recent studies (recall the discussion of Lehtonen et al. 2018 in Section 3.1). Multilingualism simply does not work wonders, and monolingually raised subjects are by no means disadvantaged ELF users.

7 Summary and Outlook

This study was meant to provide an overview and critical assessment of the current debate surrounding multilingual advantages. Moreover, its goal was to further inform this debate by discussing new data from a recent online survey on self-assessed ELF proficiencies in tertiary education.

The results demonstrate that the field remains in a state of continuing discussion and controversy, as current research has failed to establish an incontestable multilingual advantage, and several recent replication studies cannot confirm earlier, far-reaching claims regarding such advantages in specific cognitive domains. Nevertheless, in equal measure there appears to be no evidence supporting assertions that would suggest negative consequences of a multilingual upbringing.

The present study revealed statistically significantly higher self-assessed proficiencies of ELF users with a multilingual background in comparison to those raised in a monolingual environment. We interpret this finding in terms of a multilingual advantage. Higher ELF proficiencies emerged especially prominently in the domains of spoken production, reading comprehension, and written production.

Clearly, the current study needs to be replicated using objectively measured proficiencies, as self-assessments can be expected to be skewed in various directions, based on a number of individual and collective factors.

Appendix 9.1

Listening comprehension: How well are you able to able to <u>**understand**</u> each of these languages when you **<u>listen</u>**?

    I am able to... (in these languages)
    1 = understand some words and phrases
    2 = understand simple sentences in everyday situations (e.g., shopping, at work)
    3 = understand the gist of conversations, at work, on the radio/television
    4 = understand when someone gives a presentation or reads the news
    5 = understand longer speeches, films and TV series without much effort
    6 = understand everything or nearly everything effortlessly, even when someone speaks quickly or with an accent

Reading comprehension: How well are you able to **<u>read and understand</u>**?

    I am able to... (in these languages)
    1 = understand some words and phrases
    2 = read short texts (adverts, brochures, menus)
    3 = read texts written in simple language
    4 = read longer texts about current topics (e.g., newspaper articles and reports)
    5 = read long non-fictional texts and literature (e.g., detective stories or romance novels)
    6 = read everything, including specialised scientific articles and literary works

Spoken interaction: How well are you able to **<u>take part in conversations</u>**?

    I am able to... (in these languages)
    1 = say words or phrases
    2 = build simple sentences in everyday situations (e.g., shopping, at work)

3 = take part in conversations about familiar topics
4 = take part in discussions and defend my positions in familiar situations
5 = express myself well in everyday and professional situations and discuss topics with others
6 = effortlessly take part in conversations and express myself appropriately

Spoken production: How well are you able to **speak coherently**?

I am able to... (in these languages)
1 = say some words and phrases
2 = describe my family/career in simple sentences
3 = communicate my experiences and opinions in coherent sentences
4 = give detailed commentaries about many topics that I am interested in
5 = present complicated topics thoroughly and in a well structured manner
6 = debate topics fluidly, logically and appropriately

Written expression: How well are you able to **write**?

I am able to... (in these languages)
1 = write short, simple fixed phrases (e.g., holiday greetings) and personal data/information
2 = write short, simple notes/messages or simple letters (e.g., to thank someone)
3 = write simple personal accounts and longer personal letters
4 = compose detailed texts about many topics that are of interest to me
5 = describe complicated topics thoroughly and in a well structured manner
6 = compose reports, articles, and sophisticated letters in a clear, fluid, stylistically appropriate manner

REFERENCES

Agustín-Llach, M. 2017. The impact of bilingualism on the acquisition of an additional language: Evidence from lexical knowledge, lexical fluency, and (lexical) cross-linguistic influence. *International Journal of Bilingualism.* doi:10.1177/ 1367006917728818.

Berthele, R. & Vanhove, J. 2017. What would disprove independence? Lessons learned from a study on biliteracy in Portuguese heritage language speakers in

Switzerland. *International Journal of Bilingual Education and Bilingualism.* doi:10.1080/13670050.2017.1385590.

Bialystok, E. 2001. *Bilingualism in Development: Language, Literacy, and Cognition.* New York: Cambridge University Press.

et al. 2004. Bilingualism, aging, and cognitive control: Evidence from the Simon Task. *Psychology and Aging* 19(2), 290–303. doi:10.1037/0882-7974.19.2.290.

Bialystok, E., Craik, F. I. M. & Freedman, M. 2007. Bilingualism as a protection against the onset of symptoms of dementia. *Neuropsychologia* 45(2), 459–464.

et al. 2010. Receptive vocabulary differences in monolingual and bilingual children. *Bilingualism (Cambridge, England)* 13(4), 525–531. doi:10.1017/S1366728909990423.

Bialystok, E, Craik, F. I. M. & Luk, G. 2012. Bilingualism: Consequences for mind and brain. *Trends in Cognitive Sciences* 16(4), 240–250. doi:10.1016/j.tics.2012.03.001.

2018. Bilingualism and executive function. What's the connection? In D. Miller et al. (ed.), *Bilingual Cognition and Language: The State of the Science across its Subfields.* Amsterdam: John Benjamins, pp. 283–305.

Bonnet, A. & Siemund, P. (eds.) 2018. *Foreign Language Education in Multilingual Classrooms.* Amsterdam: Benjamins.

Canagarajah, S. 2007. Lingua franca English, multilingual communities and language acquisition. *Modern Language Journal* 91, 923–939.

Cenoz, J. 2003. The additive effect of bilingualism on third language acquisition: A review. *The International Journal of Bilingualism* 7, 71–88.

2013. The influence of bilingualism on third language acquisition: Focus on multilingualism. *Language Teaching* 46(1). doi: 10.1017/S0261444811000218.

Cenoz, J. and Valencia, J. 1994. Additive trilingualism: Evidence from the Basque Country. *Applied Psycholinguistics* 15, 197–209.

Clark, H. 1996. *Using Language.* Cambridge: Cambridge University Press. doi: 10.1017/CBO9780511620539.

Cogo, A. 2012. ELF and super-diversity: A case study of ELF multilingual practices from a business context. *Journal of English as a Lingua Franca* 1(2), 287–313. doi:10.1515/jelf-2012-0020.

Council of Europe. 2001. *Common European Framework of Reference for Languages: Learning, Teaching, Assessment.* Cambridge: Press Syndicate of the University of Cambridge.

Craik, F. I. M., Bialystok, E. & Freedman, M. 2010 Delaying the onset of Alzheimer disease: Bilingualism as a form of cognitive reserve. *Neurology* 75(19), 1726–1729. doi:10.1212/WNL.0b013e3181fc2a1c.

Cummins, J. 1976. The influence of bilingualism on cognitive growth: A synthesis of research findings and explanatory hypotheses. *Working Papers on Bilingualism* 9, 1–44.

1979. Linguistic interdependence and the educational development of bilingual children. *Review of Educational Research* 49(2), 222–251.

2000. *Language, Power and Pedagogy: Bilingual Children in the Crossfire.* Buffalo, NY: Multilingual Matters Ltd.

2001. *Language, Power and Pedagogy: Bilingual Children in the Crossfire.* Clevedon: Multilingual Matters.

de Swaan, A. 2001. *Words of the World: The Global Language System.* London: Blackwell.

Dewaele, J.-M. 2018. Why the dichotomy 'L1 Versus LX User' is better than 'Native Versus Non-native Speaker'. *Applied Linguistics* 39(2), 236–240.

Duñabeitia, J. A. & Carreiras, M. 2015. The bilingual advantage: Acta est fabula? *Cortex* 73, 371–372. doi: 10.1016/j.cortex.2015.06.009.

Fleckenstein, J., Möller, J. & Baumert, J. 2018. Mehrsprachigkeit als Ressource: Kompetenzen dual-immersiv unterrichteter Schülerinnen und Schüler in der Drittsprache Englisch. *Zeitschrift für Erziehungswissenschaft* 1(3). doi: 10.1007/s11618-017-0792-9.

Flynn, S., Foley, C. & Vinnitskaya, I. 2004. The cumulative-enhancement model for language acquisition: Comparing adults' and children's patterns of development in first, second and third language acquisition of relative clauses. *International Journal of Multilingualism* 1(1), 3–16.

Herdina, P. & Jessner, U. 2002. *A Dynamic Model of Multilingualism. Perspectives of Changes Psycholinguistics.* Clevedon: Multilingual Matters.

IBM Corp. 2015. *IBM SPSS Statistics for Windows, Version 23.0.* Armonk, NY: IBM Corp.

Ivanova, I. & Costa, A. 2008. Does bilingualism hamper lexical access in speech production? *Acta Psychologica* 127, 277–288. doi: 10.1016/j.actpsy.2007.06.003.

Jessner, U. 2006. *Linguistic Awareness in Multilinguals: English as a Third Language.* Edinburgh: Edinburgh University Press.

2008. Teaching third languages: Findings, trends and challenges. *Language Teaching* 41, 15–56.

Kachru, B. B. 1986. *The Alchemy of English: The Spread, Functions, and Models of Non-Native Englishes.* Champaign, IL: University of Illinois Press.

Kuteeva, M. 2019. Revisiting the 'E' in EMI: students' perceptions of standard English, lingua franca and translingual practices. *International Journal of Bilingual Education and Bilingualism*, doi: 10.1080/13670050.2019.1637395.

Lasagabaster, D. 1998. The threshold hypothesis applied to three languages in contact at school. *International Journal of Bilingual Education and Bilingualism* 1(2), 119–133.

2001. Bilingualism, immersion programmes and language learning in the Basque Country. *Journal of Multilingual and Multicultural Development* 22(5), 401–425.

Lehtonen, M. et al. 2018. Is bilingualism associated with enhanced executive functioning in adults? A meta-analytic review. *Psychological Bulletin* 144(4), 394–425.

Leimgruber, J. R. E., Siemund, P. & Terassa, L. 2018. Singaporean students´ language repertoires and attitudes revisited. *World Englishes* 37(1), 1–25. doi:10.1111/weng.12292.

Lorenz, E. & Siemund, P. 2019a. Differences in the acquisition and production of English as a foreign language. A study of bilingual and monolingual students in Germany. In E Vetter & U Jessner (eds.), *International Research on Multilingualism: Breaking with the Monolingual Perspective.* Berlin: Springer.

2019b. The acquisition of English as an additional language by multilingual heritage speakers. In M Meyer & U. Hoinkes (eds.), *Der Einfluss der Migration auf*

Sprach - und Kulturräume - The Impact of Migration on Linguistic and Cultural Areas. Bern: Peter Lang.

MacSwan, J. 2000. The Threshold Hypothesis, semilingualism, and other contributions to a deficit view of linguistic minorities. *Hispanic Journal of Behavioral Sciences* 22(1), 3–45.

Maluch, J. T., Kempert, S., Neumann, M. & Stanat, P. 2015. The effect of speaking a minority language at home on foreign language learning. *Learning and Instruction* 36, 76–85.

Maluch, J. T., Neumann, M. & Kempert, S. 2016. Bilingualism as a resource for foreign language learning of language minority students? Empirical evidence from a longitudinal study during primary and secondary school in Germany. *Learning and Individual Differences* 51, 111–118.

Martin-Rhee, M. & Bialystok, E. 2008. The development of two types of inhibitory control in monolingual and bilingual children. *Bilingualism: Language and Cognition* 11(1), 81–93. doi: 10.1017/S1366728907003227.

Mauranen, A. 2012. *Exploring ELF. Academic English Shaped by Non-Native Speakers*. Cambridge: Cambridge University Press.

Mueller, J. T. 2018. English as a lingua franca at the multilingual university: A comparison of monolingually and multilingually raised students and instructors. In A. Bonnet & P. Siemund (eds.), *Foreign Language Education in Multilingual Classrooms*, 359–380. Amsterdam: Benjamins.

Mueller, J. T. & Siemund, P. 2017. Die Sprachen der Lehre: English in the Multilingual University. In I. Gogolin et al. (eds.), Mehrsprachigkeit in der nachhaltigen Universität. Projektbericht, 48–72. Hamburg: Universität Hamburg. URN: urn:nbn:de:0111-pedocs-140469: 46–72.

Paap, K. R., Johnson, H. A. & Sawi, O. 2016. Should the search for bilingual advantages in executive functioning continue? *Cortex* 74, 305–314. doi: 10.1016/j.cortex.2015.09.010.

Peal, E. & Lambert, W. E. 1962. The relation of bilingualism to intelligence. *Psychological Monographs* 76(27), 1–23.

Safont Jordà, M. P. 2003. Metapragmatic awareness and pragmatic production of third language learners of English: A focus on request acts realizations. *International Journal of Bilingualism* 7(1), 43–68. doi:10.1177/13670069030070010401.

Sanders, M. & Meijers, G. 1995. English as L3 in the elementary school. *ITL: Review of Applied Linguistics* 107–108, 59–78.

Sanz, C. 2000. Bilingual education enhances third language acquisition: Evidence from Catalonia. *Applied Psycholinguistics* 21, 23–44.

  2012. Multilingualism and metalinguistic awareness. In C. Chapelle (ed.), *The Encyclopedia of Applied Linguistics*, 3933–3942. Oxford: John Wiley and Sons, Inc.

Schegloff, E. 2007. *Sequence Organization in Interaction: A Primer in Conversation Analysis, Vol. 1*. Cambridge: Cambridge University Press.

Siemund, P. 2018. *Speech Acts and Clause Types. English in a Cross-Linguistic Context*. Oxford: Oxford University Press.

Siemund, P., Schröter, S. & Rahbari, S. 2018. Learning English demonstrative pronouns on bilingual substrate: Evidence from German heritage speakers of

Russian, Turkish, and Vietnamese. In A. Bonnet & P. Siemund (eds.), *Foreign Language Education in Multilingual Classrooms*, 381–405. Amsterdam: Benjamins.

Siemund, P., Al-Issa, A. and Leimgruber, J. 2020. Multilingualism and the role of English in the United Arab Emirates. *World Englishes* 2020;1–14. doi: 10.1111/weng.12507

Siemund, P., Schulz, M. E. & Schweinberger, M. 2014. Studying the linguistic ecology of Singapore: A comparison of college and university students. *World Englishes* 33(3), 340–362.

Spellerberg, S. 2016. Metalinguistic awareness and academic achievement in a linguistically diverse school setting: A study of lower secondary pupils in Denmark. *International Journal of Multilingualism* 13(1), 19–39, doi: 10.1080/14790718.2015.1053891.

10 The Role of Co-Textual and Contextual Cues for Intelligibility in ELF Interactions

Veronika Thir

1 Introduction

Since its beginnings, English as a lingua franca (ELF) research has been concerned with issues of phonological intelligibility among ELF users, that is, among users of English from different linguacultural backgrounds 'for whom English is the communicative medium of choice, and often the only option' (Seidlhofer 2011: 7). Probably the most influential study in this respect is Jenkins (2000), who identified the so-called Lingua Franca Core: a set of pronunciation features that seem particularly important for maintaining phonological intelligibility in ELF communication. Much of the research that followed Jenkins (2000) aimed at providing further evidence to consolidate and refine the Lingua Franca Core (e.g. Deterding & Kirkpatrick 2006, Osimk 2009, Pickering 2009, Deterding 2013). However, little attention has been paid to the contextual conditions under which certain pronunciation features play an important role for phonological intelligibility among ELF interlocutors. This is surprising since contextual effects on phonological intelligibility have been acknowledged for a long time (e.g. Catford 1950, Brown 1989) and studied in various fields of linguistic enquiry (see Section 4). One reason for the lack of ELF studies with regard to this issue – besides ELF research being a comparably young field of linguistic enquiry – may be the impact of Jenkins' (2000) seminal work, which suggested that many non-native ELF users have difficulties drawing on contextual information in the listening process. The study reported on in this chapter investigates contextual effects on non-native ELF users' understanding at the phonological level in more detail. Unlike previous studies, it explicitly focuses on the (un)availability of and non-native ELF users' reliance on contextual information when problems of phonological intelligibility occur in ELF discourse.

2 Intelligibility and Its Relation to Context

The notion of intelligibility has been beset with terminological and conceptual inconsistencies, and different frameworks of intelligibility have been developed in the last decades. One particularly influential framework is the one by Smith (1992), which identifies three different levels of understanding: *intelligibility* ('word/utterance recognition'), *comprehensibility* ('word/utterance meaning (locutionary force)'), and *interpretability* (the 'meaning behind word/utterance (illocutionary force)') (Smith 1992: 76). Intelligibility in the Smith sense thus refers to the process of recognizing meaningful linguistic units such as words and phrases in the stream of speech – what I termed 'phonological intelligibility' in Section 1. This is the sense in which the term 'intelligibility' will henceforth be used in this chapter.

Intelligibility is strongly linked to the phonetic and phonological level, as phonemes constitute the building blocks of speech that help us distinguish, and hence identify, words and morphemes. However, intelligibility is not solely determined by pronunciation; it also depends on the availability of contextual information. That is, speech perception and spoken word recognition are 'interactive' processes during which listeners not only rely on information from the acoustic level (bottom-up processing), but also on information from higher linguistic levels (such as the lexical, the syntactic or the pragmatic) and from extra-linguistic context (top-down processing; cf. Byrd & Mintz 2010). Psycholinguistic evidence has shown that our ability to recognize speech sounds and spoken words also depends on our lexical knowledge (Warren 1970, Luce & Pisoni 1998, Vitevitch & Luce 1999, Altieri et al. 2010) or the syntactic environment of a word (for an overview of previous research findings, see Pisoni & McLennan 2016, Magnuson 2017). Similarly, assumptions about a speaker's intention may lead a listener to 'automatically correct' an unexpected pronunciation and thereby enable them to recognize the intended word (Dascal 1999: 755). This means that the level of intelligibility interacts with the level of word or utterance meaning (i.e. comprehensibility) and the level of pragmatic meaning (i.e. interpretability).

Intelligibility can thus be considered the outcome of a rather complex cognitive process in which different types of contextual information play an important role. One challenge in the investigation of this process is that context itself is a rather tricky notion that necessitates some conceptual enquiry.

3 Co-Textual and Contextual Cues

One fundamental conceptual distinction is the one between 'context' and 'co-text' (e.g. Firth 1957, Catford 1965, Brown & Yule 1983, Halliday 1999, Fetzer 2004, Widdowson 2004, 2011). Whereas context can be defined as 'the extralinguistic circumstances in which language is produced' (Widdowson 2011: 221), co-text denotes 'the intratextual relations [between] linguistic elements' (Widdowson 2011: 222). Widdowson adds that co-textual relations exist at various linguistic levels, such as the phonetic, the phonological, the morphological, the syntactic, the stylistic or the discursive level.

These relations, which are essentially cognitive in nature, need to be distinguished from the actual *physical* co-text of a linguistic element, that is, the linguistic elements that surround it (i.e. what is often understood by the term 'co-text' in linguistic publications; see e.g. Catford 1965, Brown & Yule 1983, Fetzer 2004). For example, knowing that *homework* collocates with *do* constitutes a cognitive co-textual (in this case, collocational) relation in a language user's mind. This relation is physically realized as actual co-text in utterances such as *He did his homework.*

The actual physical co-text of a linguistic element can act as a 'cue' to its identity or meaning due to a co-textual relation in the listener's mind. For example, in the utterance 'He loves his mum and [ded]', the syntactic structure suggests that [ded] is a noun and the word *mum* constitutes a semantic and a collocational cue for *dad* (since *mum* and *dad* are semantically related, and *mum and dad* is a relatively frequent collocation). Therefore, one might assume that the intended word is *dad* (rather than *dead*). Obviously, one needs the necessary cognitive co-text (i.e. the necessary linguistic knowledge) to come to this conclusion. A co-textual cue is therefore defined here as a linguistic signalling device contained in the physical co-text of another linguistic element that, due to a co-textual relation in the listener's mind, facilitates the identification, comprehension or pragmatic interpretation of this element.[1]

Context, in the sense of the extra-linguistic circumstances of language production, is much harder to delimit than co-text. I here distinguish between two basic types: a) the concrete, physical context of an utterance, such as time and place and the objects and people present;[2] and b) the cognitive context of an utterance that each interlocutor brings with them. According to Widdowson (2004), this cognitive context is best understood in terms of schemata, a psychological notion originating in the work of Bartlett (1932), which has been particularly influential in the study of cognition (see e.g. Bobrow & Collins 1975, Minsky 1975, Schank & Abelson 1975, Rumelhart 1980).[3] A schema may be defined as 'a high-level conceptual structure or framework that organizes prior experience and helps us to interpret new situations' (Gureckis & Goldstone 2011: 725).[4] For example, most people's schema of a restaurant includes tables and seats, since this is what they have experienced

---

[1] Co-textual cues are similar to Gumperz's (1982) notion of 'contextualization cues', but the latter are specifically defined as 'contribut[ing] to the signalling of contextual presuppositions' and are therefore restricted to the pragmatic level in their signalling power.

[2] This is essentially what Hymes (1977) terms 'setting' in his SPEAKING heuristic.

[3] Minsky (1975) and Schank & Abelson (1975) use the term 'frame' for what others have called 'schema', but these terms are not always used synonymously (e.g. van Dijk 1977, discussed in Widdowson 1983: 57–58).

[4] For a similar definition, see Bartlett (1932: 201) and Widdowson (1983: 54).

when visiting restaurants in the past. Schemata are to a large extent 'social constructs' (Widdowson 2004: 43) shaped by one's sociocultural experience (see also Tannen 1993). People from different cultural backgrounds will therefore have different restaurant schemata (e.g. some will include chairs, others cushions on the floor).

We draw on schemata to make sense of our experience, including our linguistic experience. Widdowson (1983: 61) therefore speaks of 'schematic anticipation', in that language users 'set up hypotheses, or in my terms schematic projections, to be tested as further information comes in from the discourse process'. In other words, schemata help us infer additional information and anticipate what is to follow. It is in this respect that schematic knowledge can have a facilitative effect on comprehension. For example, if someone talking about their latest trip to a restaurant utters the sentence 'We eventually found a [ʃiːt]', the word will likely be identified as *seat* rather than *sheet*, due to most listeners' schematic knowledge about restaurants. There is empirical evidence that intelligibility problems (or other types of communication problems) might be aggravated (or caused in the first place) if a listener is unable to rely on a relevant schema when processing an utterance (cf. Zielinski 2006, Luchini & Kennedy 2013).

Contextual cues thus fall into two categories: 1) physical cues, that is, elements of the actual physical context of an utterance, and 2) schematic cues, that is, elements of a particular cognitive context (knowledge structure), both of which facilitate the processing of a linguistic element. As with co-textual cues, contextual cues can only aid language comprehension if they are available to the listener. For example, an object can only work as a visual cue if it is in fact visible to the listener. Similarly, a schematic cue can only function as such if the listener possesses the relevant schema to begin with (see also Jenkins 2000, discussed in Section 4).

4 Previous Findings on the Role of Co-Textual and Contextual Information for Intelligibility

Research in various linguistic subdisciplines has found that intelligibility increases when co-textual and/or contextual information is available to listeners. This has been shown for L1 listeners with regard to pathological speech (Garcia & Cannito 1996, Hustad & Beukelman 2001), synthesized speech (see Drager et al. 2006 for an overview of previous research findings) and L2-accented speech (Gass & Varonis 1984, Zielinski 2006).

However, when considering L2 listeners, the situation is a bit more complex. It has been argued in Section 2 that listening constitutes a complex, interactive process in which the input is processed in both a 'bottom-up' and a 'top-down' fashion. This process is assumed to be quick and automatic in L1 listening, but potentially delayed in L2 listeners, especially if they lack linguistic knowledge in the L2 (Vandergrift & Goh 2012: 19). In fact, one widespread view among researchers is that unskilled L2 listeners exhibit 'bottom-up dependency' (Field 2004: 364), in that their 'need to focus upon decoding the input distracts [them] from using context/co-text to build larger patterns of meaning' (Field 2008: 132). Whereas some findings seem to support this view (Hansen & Jensen 1994, Gu et al. 2005), others suggest that unskilled L2 listeners also draw on co-text and context (Tsui & Fullilove 1998, Field 2004), but 'for different purposes' than skilled listeners, namely 'to compensate for parts of the message that they have not understood' (Field 2008: 132).

This has important implications for intelligibility in ELF interactions, where various accents may affect the acoustic signal in such a way that listeners – both skilled and unskilled – *need* to use co-textual and contextual information 'compensatorily' in the process of spoken word recognition. If listeners are able to rely on co-text and context to correct for ambiguities in the input, then pronunciation should not be much of an issue for intelligibility in ELF interactions. This, however, is not what has been found in Jenkins' (2000) seminal study, where pronunciation turned out to be the major cause of communication breakdowns in ELF communication. Jenkins explained this finding by arguing that the type of non-native ELF users she observed 'encounter[s] [difficulties] with top-down skills, particularly in relation to making use of contextual cues, both linguistic and extra-linguistic, and linguistic redundancy', and that this 'force[s] them back to an over-reliance on bottom-up skills which, in turn, leads them to focus too firmly on the acoustic signal' (2000: 20). This assumption is in line with the 'bottom-up dependency' view outlined above, yet Jenkins does not only attribute this kind of processing behaviour to non-native users with limited English skills, but to 'non-bilingual English speakers' (NBESs) in general (Jenkins 2000: 10). These are described as non-native speakers of English from the 'expanding circle' (Jenkins 2000: 19), who are not bilingual in English and who may not strive for fluency or nativelike proficiency in the language (cf. Jenkins 2000: 10), but whose proficiency level 'serves their particular international communicative purpose' (Jenkins 2000: 10). NBESs also include L2 users 'at upper-intermediate level and beyond' (Jenkins 2000: 83), that is, users who arguably qualify as 'skilled' rather than 'unskilled'.

According to Jenkins (2000), NBESs' limited reliance on co-textual and contextual cues in the listening process may be explained by

[their] lack of shared socio-cultural background..., coupled with their mutual lack of access to aspects of the linguistic context, [which] throws them back onto a focus on the acoustic signal. This in turn diverts cognitive resources away from features of the context, which are thence not available to compensate for any limitations in speech perception or production. (Jenkins 2000: 82–83)

Thus, NBESs' over-reliance on the phonetic-phonological code may be due to: a) a lack of linguistic and extra-linguistic knowledge necessary to process an item in a top-down fashion (which Jenkins calls *unavailability* of co-text/context)[5] and b) a cognitive inability to draw on such knowledge (which she calls *inaccessibility* of co-text/context, e.g. due to processing overload).

While Jenkins' observations were seminal for the field of ELF research, it is difficult to set them in relation to subsequent research findings, not least since the category of NBESs is somewhat ambiguous (which Jenkins herself acknowledged) and often not employed by ELF researchers. However, some observations in this respect are possible. Luchini and Kennedy (2013) discuss an instance of miscommunication which supports the assumption that the 'unavailability' of sociocultural knowledge (i.e. cognitive context) makes ELF interlocutors more dependent on the acoustic signal. Interestingly, the instance involved two 'bilingual English speakers'[6] (BESs) (a 'near-native' L1 Spanish listener and an Indian speaker), which shows that Jenkins' assumption might apply to other types of ELF users as well. Similarly, an instance discussed in Deterding (2013) illustrates that all ELF users – even BESs and monolingual native speakers – can have 'gaps' in their linguistic knowledge (i.e. their cognitive co-text), which might occasionally aggravate intelligibility problems. In this case, a BES from Brunei[7] was unfamiliar with a variety-specific idiom, which prevented her from profiting from a co-textual cue in the listening process.

When considering the inaccessibility of co-text and context – that is, situations when a listener is for some reason unable to draw on existing linguistic or extra-linguistic knowledge – more recent studies do not seem to support Jenkins' findings. Experimental research by Osimk (2009) revealed a beneficial effect of syntactic co-text on intelligibility for various European, NBES ELF listeners, suggesting that they accessed their cognitive co-text in the listening process. Studies such as Mauranen (2006), Pitzl (2010) or Kaur (2011) might be regarded as additional evidence that NBESs cannot possibly rely on the acoustic signal alone, since they did not find that pronunciation seriously affected mutual understanding in ELF interactions involving NBESs (though one can only speculate about the reasons for this finding). However, Deterding's (2013) findings regarding ELF interactions involving Asian NBES

---

[5] Cf. my argument in Section 3 on the necessity of cognitive co-text and context for physical co-text and schemata to function as cues in language processing.
[6] All classifications of participants as NBES or BES in the studies mentioned in this section are my own, based on the participant descriptions provided there.
[7] Since 'Brunei English' is 'a newly-emergent variety of English' (Deterding & Sharbawi 2013), the listener can be considered to be from the outer circle, and thus qualifies as a BES (cf. Jenkins 2000: 19).

interlocutors resemble Jenkins' in that here too pronunciation emerged as the major cause of miscommunication.

Clearly, the exact impact of co-textual and contextual cues for intelligibility in ELF communication is still an unresolved matter. There is some evidence which suggests that ELF users might sometimes be particularly dependent on the acoustic input due to an unavailability of cognitive co-text and context on their part. However, findings are inconclusive regarding the assumption that NBES ELF users tend to over-rely on the acoustic signal even if co-textual and contextual cues are available to them. The difficulty in addressing the latter question on the basis of naturally occurring data (the type of data used in most previous ELF studies) is that it restricts the types of co-textual and contextual cues that can be investigated, since only the impact of those cues that happen to be available in the interactions at hand can actually be examined.

The study described in this chapter therefore draws on an experimental approach to investigate different types of co-textual and contextual effects on intelligibility in ELF communication. It presents further empirical evidence with regard to the question of whether (and to what extent) NBES ELF users draw on co-textual and contextual cues when processing each other's accents by analysing instances of unintelligibility in relation to the co-textual and contextual conditions under which they occurred.

5   Data and Methods

The data of this study comprise video recordings of two pairs of NBES ELF users completing a communicative task under two different contextual conditions. Such tasks have been extensively used in investigations of L2 discourse (Ellis & Barkhuizen 2005), for collecting L1 speech data (e.g. Anderson et al. 1991, Grønnum 2009) and also in ELF research (Jenkins 2000, Pickering 2009, Kennedy 2012, 2017). They constitute a useful method to elicit spontaneous, interactive speech data under conditions that can be controlled by the researcher. A further advantage of using such tasks is that participants are using language to achieve a certain goal, and are therefore focused on communication rather than on linguistic accuracy. This was considered desirable in the present study, which, despite its experimental approach, aimed at examining data similar to real-world ELF interactions, in that interactants were 'focused on the interactional and transactional purposes of the talk and on their interlocutors as people rather than on the linguistic code itself' (Seidlhofer 2011: 98).

In the experimental condition, the communicative task was framed within a particular schematic context, which was unavailable in the control condition (see Section 5.2). Each pair completed one task in the experimental condition and one in the control condition, leading to a total of four interactions

Table 10.1 *Speaker information for the two pairs of ELF users.*

		L1	Gender	Age	Proficiency level (self-assessed)[8]
Pair 1	S1	Austrian German	Female	24	Intermediate
	S2	Uzbek/Russian	Female	24	–
Pair 2	S3	Austrian German	Male	54	Advanced
	S4	Romanian	Male	27	Advanced

(see Table 10.2, Section 5.3). The interactional data was triangulated with the participants' notes on the test material and interview data obtained during a 'stimulated recall' (see Section 5.3). This 'introspective method', which has been used extensively in research on L2 acquisition and more recently also in ELF research (Kennedy 2012, 2017), helps 'participants ... recall thoughts they had while performing a task or participating in an event' (Gass & Mackey 2000: 13). It thus allows researchers to 'uncover cognitive processes which might not be evident through simple observation' (Gass & Mackey 2000: 15), and therefore permitted further insights into participants' language processing.

5.1 Participants

Participants were recruited on a voluntary basis via social media. They met for the first time when the recordings took place. Table 10.1 summarizes the speaker information for each of the two pairs.

All participants can be considered NBESs, since they came from expanding-circle countries, did not list English as their L1 and were estimated to be at an upper-intermediate or low-advanced level in English (i.e. close to Jenkins' [2000] participants).

5.2 Tasks and Conditions

5.2.1 The Spot-the-Difference Task and the Two Conditions In the spot-the-difference task, each participant received one of two versions of a picture (or a grid). The two versions differed in exactly twelve aspects, which participants were to identify and record. Since they could not see each other's versions,

---

[8] Participants' proficiency levels were based on self-assessment in a follow-up questionnaire, which asked them to choose between 'beginner', 'intermediate' and 'advanced' for each of their L2s (though from my own impression, S1 seems to have been a bit modest in her estimation). Unfortunately, S2 misunderstood the relevant item in the questionnaire and therefore did not provide an estimate of her proficiency level in English. On the basis of her performance during the tasks and the fact that she was an international MA student in Vienna, it is fair to assume that she was approximately at upper-intermediate/low-advanced level.

they only shared certain aspects of the visual context (i.e. those contained in both versions of the picture/grid), while others (i.e. those only contained in their partner's version) were unavailable to them.

For the spot-the-difference task in the experimental condition (henceforth EC), participants' pictures showed a scene that evoked the schema of a city. The scene included persons and objects one would expect to find in a city, such as a police officer, a pub or a tourist. In order to prime participants further for this schema, the headline 'In the city' was printed at the top of the pictures. This schematic context was supposed to create expectations for (and thereby facilitate the participant's understanding of) certain words their partner would use to describe the depicted scene.

In contrast, no such schematic support was available in the control condition (henceforth CC). Here, participants received a grid, each cell of which contained a different item. The items were not schematically connected, but resembled a random collection of various objects or persons (e.g. a camera, nail polish, a pan). The presentation of each item in a separate cell reinforced the impression that the items lacked a schematic connection. Participants were thus unable to rely on schematic expectations regarding the objects their partner would mention in this condition.

5.2.2   The Map Task and the Two Conditions For the map task, each participant received one of two versions of a map containing a number of landmarks. Version A contained the correct route and some of the landmarks, while version B contained a network of possible routes, and the landmarks missing on version A. Neither version contained all the landmarks. Participants had to mark and label all the missing landmarks on their maps and participant B had to mark the correct route. Again, they could not see each other's maps and thus only shared a certain amount of visual context.

For the map task in the EC, the map was designed to evoke the schema of a zoo. Thus, the headline 'A walk in the zoo' was printed at the top of both maps and the landmarks were items that one would expect to find in a zoo, such as various types of animals.

For the map task in the CC, no such schematic context was available to the participants. That is, the landmarks on the map constituted a seemingly random selection of objects that were not connected via a schema (e.g. a pencil, a church, grapes). Thus, participants were unable to schematically anticipate the items their partner would mention.

5.3   Procedure

Each pair completed both task types, one under the EC and one under the CC (see Table 10.2). They always started with the EC to ensure that a potential

Table 10.2 *Tasks and conditions per pair.*

	Pair 1	Pair 2
Experimental condition (EC)	Spot-the-difference task	Map task
Control condition (CC)	Map task	Spot-the-difference task

facilitative effect on intelligibility of this condition would not have to be attributed to a familiarization effect (which might have to be assumed had participants worked under the EC *after* having worked under the CC). The participants were given a time limit of seven minutes for each task in order to motivate them to work as efficiently as possible.

After finishing the second task, participants completed a follow-up questionnaire to obtain demographic information and information on extra-linguistic factors that might have affected intelligibility, such as language attitudes, familiarity with L2 accents in English in general, and familiarity with their partner's accent. All participants stated that they had had either 'a lot' or 'quite a lot' of contact with English spoken with a non-native accent so far. The Romanian and the Uzbek/Russian speaker had also had 'a lot' and 'quite a lot' of contact with English spoken with an Austrian accent (i.e. their partner's accent), whereas the two Austrian speakers had only had very little exposure to their partner's accent. The speakers' attitudes towards their partner's nation ranged from slightly positive to very positive, and most of them had positive or very positive attitudes towards their partner's accent. Only the female Austrian speaker had a neutral attitude towards her partner's accent.

Immediately after completing the questionnaire, participants took part in the stimulated recall, one after another. Each participant watched the video of the interaction, together with the researcher, while looking at their own and their partner's version of the test material. Thus, they were able to find out whether they had completed the two tasks successfully. The participant was instructed to stop the video whenever they wanted to comment on something or when they remembered that they had not understood something during the interaction. The researcher was also able to stop the video and ask questions. Participants were thus able to provide insights into the sources of miscommunication in the interaction (e.g. a pronunciation issue, a lexical problem) and to point out any instances of 'latent miscommunication' (Linell 1995) that might have otherwise gone unnoticed. They also had the chance to confirm (or not) the researcher's assumptions about when in the interaction miscommunication had taken place. At times, their comments revealed more about their reliance on co-textual and contextual information in the listening process.[9] The recall

---

[9] The researcher was careful not to pose suggestive questions in this respect.

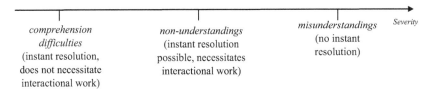

Figure 10.1 Types of miscommunication according to their severity in the experimental data.

was conducted in German with the Austrian participants and in English with the non-Austrian participants.

6 Identification and Classification of Instances of Intelligibility Problems in the Data

Instances of intelligibility (as opposed to comprehensibility or interpretability) problems in the interactional data were identified with the help of participants' comments during the stimulated recall and their notes on the test material. All instances were categorized in relation to a) whether or not a co-textual and/or contextual cue was available[10] to the listener at this point and b) whether or not the listener was drawing on this cue when identifying the problematic word.

Instances of intelligibility problems were also classified according to their 'severity' (cf. Figure 10.1), that is, the extent to which they negatively affected communicative success. It should be noted that the severity scale presented here might not be applicable to other types of interaction, notably naturally occurring ones. Clearly, assessing the severity of an instance of miscommunication is a tricky issue, and always needs to be done in relation to the purpose of the communicative exchange, which varies according to the type of data examined.

As shown in Figure 10.1, *comprehension difficulties* are at the lower end of the severity scale. In such instances, the listener found a particular word hard to understand but was able to recognize it correctly without any further clarification. Thus, the interaction proceeded smoothly as if nothing had happened. At the intermediate level of the severity scale are *non-understandings*. Here, the listener was either entirely unable to identify a word, or was able to make a guess about it but was unsure whether this guess was correct (and indeed, sometimes it was not). They therefore felt the need to seek confirmation or

---

[10] It was assumed that participants' cognitive co-text (linguistic knowledge) was sufficient for the physical co-text of problematic words to function as a cue. The same was assumed with regard to their cognitive context (schematic knowledge), and the schematic context made available in the EC (though this is of course not without problems – see Section 8).

clarification from their partner, which 'disrupted' the flow of the interaction in some way.

Non-understandings need to be distinguished from *misunderstandings* (see e.g. Gass & Varonis 1991, Pitzl 2010, Kaur 2011), which are at the higher end of the severity scale. The crucial difference between these two is that in non-understandings, the listener is instantly aware that they (probably) failed to understand their interlocutor (Weigand 1999: 770). This enables them to request clarification of the problematic item, which greatly increases the chances that the miscommunication will be resolved. In misunderstandings, however, the listener is unaware that they failed to understand their partner (Weigand 1999: 769), and will, therefore, not actively attempt to clarify the issue. Misunderstandings thus seem to have a greater potential for causing more severe or long-lasting communication problems. While they sometimes become apparent later in an interaction, they can also remain undetected for as long as an exchange lasts – which is what happened in my data, resulting in the participants not being able to satisfactorily complete the task at hand.

7   Results

Altogether, sixteen intelligibility problems were identified in 28:07 minutes of interactional data. Two were comprehension difficulties, ten were non-understandings, three were misunderstandings and one was an unclear case. At first glance, this might seem like a lot compared to ELF studies such as Mauranen (2006), Kaur (2011) or Pietikäinen (2018) (though not compared to Deterding 2013).[11] However, it must be remembered that the circumstances of communication in the present study were very different from those in the studies mentioned above, all of which used naturally occurring data. In contrast, the data for this study were elicited under conditions that were basically designed to 'provoke' communication problems of some sort. Moreover, all of the non-understandings in the data could be resolved by the participants, often without much interactional work. The rate of miscommunication reported here is thus less serious than it might initially sound.

---

[11] Mauranen (2006) found only 6 clearly identifiable instances of miscommunication in 5 hours of data, Kaur (2011) only 33 misunderstandings in 15 hours (mean: ~1.1 misunderstanding/30 min) and Pietikäinen (2018) only 46 misunderstandings in about 24 hours (mean: ~1.0 misunderstanding/30 min). However, Deterding (2013) reports 183 tokens of miscommunication in about 10.5 hours (mean: ~35 instances/30 min). Note that all these studies also counted problems at other levels of understanding (i.e. not only intelligibility problems), though Kaur (2011) and Pietikäinen (2018) only counted instances of the type 'misunderstanding'.

Table 10.3 *Comprehension difficulties*

No.	Cond.	Pair	Word	Identified as	Co-text[12]	Contextual cues
7	EC	2	three	three	do you have the birds. (.) er [tri:] birds.	visual context
10	EC	2	basically	basically	now from the penguin <fast> [beɪsɪ] you have to go to the end [...] </fast>	–
9	EC	2	blank	{word signifying sth. like blank/ black}	then n:ow it's like (.) really (.) [blɛŋk] because I only have the PENguin	activity engaged in

7.1 Comprehension Difficulties

There were two cases of comprehension difficulty in the data and one case that may be classified as a comprehension difficulty, or as a fairly non-serious non-understanding (instance 9, in grey font and listed last in Table 10.3). In all cases, either visual cues, co-textual cues or a particular type of cognitive context (a sense of the 'activity being engaged in', i.e. what Tannen & Wallat (1993) call 'interactive frame') seem to have prevented a more severe intelligibility problem.

In instance 7, the visual context helped the listener to assign a word to an ambiguous pronunciation. S4 here asked his partner whether he had a particular landmark (three birds) on his map, pronouncing the /θ/ in *three* as [t]. S3 mentioned during the recall that this pronunciation constituted a cognitive strain for him, but since he too had three birds as a landmark on his map, it was instantly clear to him that the intended phrase was *three birds* (rather than *tree birds*).

Instance 10 illustrates how syntactic co-text can help a listener correctly identify an incomplete word. This instance occurred when S4 was giving S3 directions in the map task. S4 was talking rather fast and therefore reduced the word *basically* to [beɪsɪ], which made it hard for S3 to identify the word.

---

[12] The relevant co-text of a problematic word has been transcribed according to the VOICE transcription conventions (VOICE Project 2007). The word itself has always been phonetically transcribed and marked in bold. Phonetic transcriptions are based on auditory analysis. In case of doubt, the software PRAAT (Boersma & Weenink 2016) was used to identify the nature of a sound.

Nevertheless, S3 was able to guess that the word must be *basically*, probably because its syntactic position indicated that the intended word must be a stance adverbial commenting on *you have to go to the end*.

In instance 9, S3 and S4 were going through their maps to identify spots where one of them was lacking a landmark. When S4 described a particular spot on his map as *blank,* S3 was unable to clearly recognize this word. Yet, he immediately got the gist of the utterance (i.e. that S4 meant something like 'black' or 'blank'), probably due to the syntactic position of the word (allowing him to identify it as an adjective), in conjunction with his sense of the activity in which they were engaging (i.e. identifying empty spots on their maps). Thus, although *blank* was not actually understood at the level of intelligibility (making it a non-understanding at this level), it was instantly understood at the level of comprehensibility/interpretability (making it a mere comprehension difficulty at these levels, if at all). S3 therefore let this intelligibility problem pass (see Firth 1996). This shows that intelligibility of every single word in an utterance is not always necessary to understand its basic underlying meaning, if certain co-textual and contextual cues are present.

7.2 Non-Understandings

7.2.1 Non-Understandings Occurring in the Absence of Sufficient Co-Textual/Contextual Cues

More than half of the non-understandings in the data (six out of ten) occurred in the absence of sufficient co-textual and contextual cues. That is, the co-textual and contextual information available to the listener did not permit them to clearly identify the intended word. As shown in Table 10.4, all but one of these non-understandings occurred in the CC; in these cases (instances 4, 5, 6, 13 and 16), the problematic[13] word was always a landmark (map task) or an item on one of the participants' grids (spot-the-difference task). Since neither the landmarks nor the items in the grids were schematically connected in this condition, no schematic cues were available to the listeners in these instances. They were also unable to draw on visual information, since the respective landmarks and items were not included in their own map or grid. Their last resort, co-text, did not provide enough cues as to the identity of the word either. In instances 4 and 5, the problematic word was embedded in a syntactic structure which allowed the listener to identify

---

[13] It was not always the pronunciation of the word that made it 'problematic'. In instance 1, the speaker actually pronounced *fourth street* according to Standard English pronunciation norms. The confusion between *fourth* and *first* might have arisen due to the sound sequence [θs] in this phrase, which is difficult to perceive due to the phonetic similarity of [θ] and [s]. In instance 6, the non-understanding probably arose because the listener was talking to herself at that moment. In instance 16, the intelligibility problem was caused by ambiguity in the language system (homophony).

Co-textual and Contextual Cues for Intelligibility   281

Table 10.4 *Non-understandings that occurred in the absence of sufficient co-textual and contextual cues.*

No.	Cond.	Pair	Word	Identified as	Co-text	Contextual cues
1	EC	1	fourth	first	okay no it's erm. (.) [fɔːθstriːt]?	–
4	CC	1	herbs	Herbst {German for 'autumn'}	<fast> okay because i have </fast> [hœːb̥z̥] there.	–
5	CC	1	thermometer	–	yeah there's a [θə ˈθœmɒˌmiːθə] @ @	–
6	CC	1	peace	pits {although this word is unknown to S2}	<fast> do you </fast> do you have a [piːs] sign.	–
13	CC	2	zoo	soup	<fast> what is </fast> hh ONE <spel> b: </spel> (.) [sːuː]?	–
16	CC	2	tie	Thai	[taɪ]	–

the part of speech of the intended word, but nothing more, since it was rather neutral in semantic terms ('I have ... there', 'There's a...'). In instances 13 and 16, the speaker did not integrate the word into a phrase or sentence at all, so no syntactic (or semantic) cues were available to the listener. In instance 6, the word *sign* arguably gives some indication as to the first part of the compound *peace sign*, yet *sign* can combine with virtually anything and therefore did not constitute much of a cue for the identification of *peace* either.

Although instance 1 occurred during the EC, no schematic cue was available in this case that would have supported the identification of the problematic word (a number on a road sign in the participants' pictures) over the word that was heard (a different number on a road sign). That is, the schematic context 'city' did not supply any reason to assume that it should be 'fourth street' rather than 'first street'. As the listener's picture contained a road sign with a different text ('3rd avenue'), there was also no visual cue that could have helped her identify the word as *fourth*. The available co-text was also insufficient in order to disambiguate between *first* and *fourth*: both words are numbers which fit the phrase 'it's erm {*number*} street' grammatically and semantically.

7.2.2 Non-Understandings Occurring in the Presence of Sufficient Co-Textual/Contextual Cues

In the remaining four instances of non-understanding, a co-textual or contextual cue that can arguably be considered sufficient to identify the word in question was available to the listener. In two of these instances (Table 10.5), the listener was for some reason not able to draw on the cue.

Instance 2 occurred in the EC when S2 was, for some reason, not able to profit from the available schematic context (city). When S1 was describing the text on a road sign that was part of the city scene in her picture, pronouncing the word *zoo* as [sʉː], S2 was unable to identify the word, although a zoo is something that one might expect to find in a city. However, it is also possible that S2's schema of a city simply does not include a zoo – that is, the schematic cue was unavailable rather than inaccessible to her.

In instance 12, S3 was unable to draw on co-textual cues included in the utterance 'I have a sad person'. S3 here initially understood *sad* as *set*, although the collocation *sad person* is arguably more likely to occur than the combination *set person* and although it makes more sense on a semantic (or schematic) level.

Finally, in the remaining two instances of non-understanding, the listeners did make use of a co-textual and/or contextual cue pointing to the identity of the problematic word (Table 10.6). However, it was the cue itself that

Table 10.5 *Non-understandings where listeners did not profit from a co-textual or contextual cue.*

No.	Cond.	Pair	Word	Identified as	Co-text	Contextual cues
2	EC	1	zoo	–	oh it says (.) <reading> local [sʉː] </reading> here.	schematic context
12	CC	2	sad	set	i have a [sɛd] person.	–

Table 10.6 *Non-understandings where a co-textual and/or contextual cue contributed to loss of intelligibility.*

No.	Cond.	Pair	Word	Identified as	Co-text	Contextual cues
3	EC	1	dog	dark	next comes (.) erm (.) a [dʌg lɪtɫ dɒg]	–
8	EC	2	parrots	birds	<fast> i don'(t) have the [pɛrəts]. </fast>	visual context

contributed to the intelligibility problem by supporting an incorrect identification of the word.

In instance 3, the syntactic and the suprasegmental phonological co-text of the word *dog* seems to have contributed to, if not even caused the non-understanding. This instance occurred in the EC when S2 described the next item on her picture as *a dog little dog*, pronouncing the first instance of *dog* differently from the second one, namely as [dʌg], which is phonetically close to (a non-rhotic pronunciation of) *dark*. While unexpected vowel quality seems to have played a role in this non-understanding, S1 mentioned in the recall that what confused her was her partner uttering the word *dog* twice. It seems that the almost consecutive production of two instances of *dog* and the syntactic position of [dʌg] (between the determiner *a* and the adjective *little*) was what led her to assume that the intended word must be an adjective describing the dog in the picture (*dark*). Moreover, [dʌg] was given tonic stress, which might have reinforced S1's assumption that [dʌg] signified a quality of the dog which S2 wanted to emphasize.

In instance 8, the word-internal and the larger discursive co-text as well as the visual context seem to have contributed to the confusion between *bird(s)* and *parrot(s)*. On the level of phonetics, the intelligibility problem most probably arose because S4 was talking quite fast, making it hard for S3 to distinguish between [pɛrəts] and S4's usual pronunciation of birds ([bɜrdẓ], which S3 had heard a few times by then). Another source of confusion was the preceding turn of the problematic utterance: in this turn, S3 had just informed S4 that one of the landmarks on his map was 'a parrot'. S4 replied (at a rather fast pace) that he did not have any [pɛrəts] on his map. The fact that S4 was using the word *parrot* in its plural form, although S3 had only mentioned a *single* parrot in the previous turn, confused S3, especially because they had talked about *multiple* birds earlier. Thus, word-internal co-text (in the form of an unexpected plural -s morpheme), the preceding discursive co-text and aspects of the visual context (the depiction of a *single* parrot) seem to have contributed to the non-understanding in this instance.[14]

7.3 Misunderstandings

All three misunderstandings in the data occurred in the CC, during a single task involving pair 2 (Table 10.7). They all remained unresolved during the

---

[14] The confusion between *birds* and *parrots* arose two more times later in the interaction. However, it was unclear whether the problem occurred at the level of intelligibility or interpretability in these cases, that is, whether S3 wrongly identified [pɛrəts] as *birds*, or whether he actually recognized the word *parrots* but assumed that what S4 *meant* by it was the three birds talked about earlier. These instances were therefore not included in the total count of intelligibility problems.

Table 10.7 *Misunderstandings*.

No.	Cond.	Pair	Word	Identified as	Co-text	Contextual cues
11	CC	2	pan	pen	[pɛn]. i have a [pɛn].	–
14	CC	2	robe	rope	[roʊp] (.)	–
15	CC	2	cab	cap	er [kɛb].	visual context

interaction, with the participants only becoming aware of them during the recall procedure. One reason why they remained unnoticed was certainly the absence of co-textual and contextual cues that would have pointed participants to their inaccurate understanding (see below). Moreover, S3 and S4 were working through the task extremely quickly (with the exchange lasting only 2:46 minutes), which left them little time to contemplate the accuracy of their understanding. Lastly, there was no 'communicative urgency' to resolve the misunderstandings, since they did not keep the pair from proceeding with the rest of the task.

What is particularly interesting about these misunderstandings is that they all involved the confusion of words forming minimal pairs (*pan/pen, rope/robe, cab/cap*), with two of them being attributable to the loss of a phonemic distinction (/ae/ vs. /ɛ/ in instance 11 and /b/ vs. /p/ in instance 14). Crucially, these confusions all occurred in the absence of co-textual or contextual cues that would have allowed the listener to disambiguate the members of the minimal pair. In all cases, the problematic word referred to an item in the speaker's grid, which could not be anticipated by the listener on the basis of schematic knowledge (since the items in the grids were not schematically connected). The visual context did not provide any helpful cues either, since the relevant item (i.e. a pan, a robe and a cab) was not included in the listener's grid. Finally, the co-text was insufficient to disambiguate the two members of the minimal pair, as the item was either integrated in a very neutral syntactic structure ('I have a...', instance 11) or not integrated in a phrase or sentence at all (instances 14 and 15).

Instance 15 is particularly interesting since it stands in stark contrast to Jenkins' (2000) observations regarding NBESs' alleged over-reliance on the phonetic-phonological code (see Section 4). S4 here described the content of a particular cell on his grid, which was a cab:

1	S4	er [kɛb] (.)
2	S3	[kɛp] (.)
3	S4	<spel> [si: eɪ bi:] </spel>=
4	S3	=<soft> okay </soft>

Although S4 pronounced the final /b/ in *cab* as [b], S3 at first recognized the word as *cap* (line 2). S4 noticed S3's mistake and therefore went on to spell the word, clearly pronouncing 'b' as [biː]. Nevertheless, S3 noted down *cap* on his sheet of paper and confirmed during the recall that he had still believed the intended word to be *cap* at that point. He suggested that he was not properly listening to S4 spelling the word, and that he 'was fixated on *cap*, no matter what [S4] said' (stimulated recall, my translation). In other words, he basically ignored the information in the acoustic signal. But where did his 'fixation' on *cap* come from? One possible explanation is the visual context available to S3 at that point: his grid contained neither a cab nor a cap, but a conceptually related item (a hat), which was in his field of vision during the exchange. This might have incidentally primed S3 for the word *cap*, which illustrates that, just like any language user, a NBES might sometimes pay too little attention to the acoustic signal in favour of information provided by another source.

8   Discussion and Conclusion

English language users nowadays operate in an age of unprecedented linguistic diversity, where reliance on the language code might not always suffice in order to achieve mutual understanding. This is particularly true with regard to the phonetic-phonological level of language, due to the multitude of different accents in which English is spoken all around the world. Research on how ELF users exploit communicative resources beyond the acoustic code to maintain mutual intelligibility is therefore of great relevance. However, such research has remained relatively scarce, not least since it has been argued that a substantial number of non-native ELF users, so-called NBESs, are particularly dependent on the acoustic signal and largely unable to draw on co-textual and contextual information when processing speech. The findings presented here constitute counter-evidence to the latter assumption: in the vast majority of cases where sufficient co-textual and/or contextual cues were available (six out of eight), the NBES interlocutors in this study relied on these cues when attempting to identify a problematic word. Thus, they did not simply 'decode' the speech signal in a bottom-up fashion, but rather seemed to 'interpret' it in relation to co-textual and contextual information. However, as the present study was very small in size – only investigating four exchanges that involved two pairs of speakers – a great deal of empirical research, also of a quantitative kind, is still needed in order to make generalizations about NBES ELF users' ability to draw upon co-textual and contextual cues when processing each other's accents. Nevertheless, it allows for a number of interesting observations.

In this study, suprasegmental, syntactic, semantic and discursive co-text, as well as visual context, all seem to have played a role in a participant's recognition of a word at some point. Those instances involving the beneficial effect of syntactic co-text are in line with Osimk's (2009) findings, whereas the instances involving visual context illustrate the potential significance of non-linguistic resources in face-to-face ELF interactions and the latter's essentially multimodal character – an issue which is explored with regard to written, computer-mediated ELF interactions by Bosso (this volume). The latter instances stand in stark contrast to those observed in Jenkins (2000), where NBESs failed to rely on visual cues in spoken word recognition. A possible explanation is that, being in an instructional setting, Jenkins' participants accorded greater significance to the acoustic code than to extra-linguistic context, whereas the participants in this study were more focused on meaning-making than on form. This would seem to suggest that the purpose of an exchange may affect the processing strategies adopted by NBESs vis-à-vis co-textual and contextual cues (which resonates with Widdowson's (2004: ch. 5) view on language comprehension).

It is more difficult to evaluate the effects of schematic context as operationalized in this study. 'Cognitive contexts' – that is, the schematic representations people bring with them – vary among individuals, and one cannot be absolutely certain whether participants' schemata of 'city' and 'zoo' actually contained the relevant elements that should be evoked by the EC. The fact that seven out of sixteen intelligibility problems occurred in the condition with schematic context seems to suggest that the participants profited little from this type of context. However, in only one of these instances was the problematic word in fact predictable on the basis of the available schematic context (and this type of context thus not exploited). In all other instances, the problematic words were not referring to one of the schematically connected entities on the maps/pictures, or were describing an aspect of an entity that could not be schematically anticipated. In contrast, *all* of the words affected by loss of intelligibility in the CC referred to one of the entities on participants' maps/grids, and one might wonder whether participants would have been more successful in recognizing them had they been schematically connected. Moreover, the more severe intelligibility problems (the three misunderstandings) all occurred in the condition without schematic context, probably because a lack of schematic, visual and co-textual support prevented the listener from noticing their incorrect understanding. Future research should therefore also consider how the absence and presence of co-textual and contextual cues impacts ELF interlocutors' awareness of miscommunication and thereby their interactional work, which in turn affects communicative success as a whole.

Finally, in several instances observed in this study, co-textual and/or contextual information was helpful to the listeners and prevented a more serious communication problem. In others, it misled them by supporting an incorrect interpretation of the acoustic signal, thus contributing to or even causing the intelligibility problem. This illustrates the potential detrimental effect of co-textual and contextual cues on intelligibility, an issue which seems to be much less researched than when co-text and context aid a listener, though it has been documented, for example, in the form of 'mishearings' (Linell 2015). Future investigations of intelligibility in ELF communication should therefore not only consider whether co-textual and/or contextual cues are available and exploited, but also whether they in fact support accurate understanding.

REFERENCES

Anderson, Anne H., Miles Bader, Ellen Gurman Bard, Elizabeth Boyle, Gwyneth Doherty, Simon Garrod, Stephen Isard, Jacqueline Kowtko, Jan McAllister, Jim Miller, Catherine Sotillo, Henry S. Thompson & Regina Weinert. 1991. The HCRC Map Task Corpus. *Language and Speech* 34(4), 351–366.

Altieri, Nicholas, Thomas Gruenenfelder & David B. Pisoni. 2010. Clustering coefficients of lexical neighborhoods: Does neighborhood structure matter in spoken word recognition? *The Mental Lexicon* 5(1), 1–21.

Bartlett, Frederic C. 1932 [reissued 1995]. *Remembering: A Study in Experimental and Social Psychology*. Cambridge: Cambridge University Press.

Bobrow, Daniel G. & Allan Collins (eds.). 1975. *Representation and Understanding: Studies in Cognitive Science*. New York, NY: Academic Press.

Boersma, Paul & David Weenink. 2016. *Praat: Doing phonetics by computer* [Computer program]. Version 6.0.16. www.praat.org/ (retrieved 6 April 2016).

Brown, Adam. 1989. Some thoughts on intelligibility. *The English Teacher* XVIII. www.melta.org.my/ET/1989/main4.html (16 January 2016).

Brown, Gillian & Yule, George. 1983. *Discourse Analysis*. Cambridge: Cambridge University Press.

Byrd, Dani & Toben H. Mintz. 2010. *Discovering Speech, Words, and Mind*. Malden, MA: Wiley-Blackwell.

Catford, John C. 1950. Intelligibility. *English Language Teaching* 5(1), 7–15.

1965. *A Linguistic Theory of Translation: An Essay in Applied Linguistics*. Oxford: Oxford University Press.

Dascal, Marcelo. 1999. Introduction: Some questions about misunderstanding. *Journal of Pragmatics* 31(6), 753–762.

Drager, Kathryn D. R., Elizabeth A. Clark-Serpentine, Kate E. Johnson & Jennifer L. Roeser. 2006. Accuracy of repetition of digitized and synthesized speech for young children in background noise. *American Journal of Speech-Language Pathology* 15(2), 155–164.

Deterding, David. 2013. *Misunderstandings in English as a Lingua Franca*. Berlin: de Gruyter Mouton.

Deterding, David & Salbrina Sharbawi. 2013. *Brunei English: A New Variety in a Multilingual Society*. Dordrecht: Springer.

Deterding, David & Andy Kirkpatrick. 2006. Emerging South-East Asian Englishes and intelligibility. *World Englishes* 25(3–4), 391–409.

Ellis, Rod & Gary P. Barkhuizen. 2005. *Analysing Learner Language*. Oxford: Oxford University Press.

Fetzer, Anita. 2004. *Recontextualizing Context: Grammaticality Meets Appropriateness*. Amsterdam: John Benjamins Publishing Company.

Field, John. 2004. An insight into listeners' problems: Too much bottom-up or too much top-down? *System* 32(3), 363–377.
   2008. *Listening in the Language Classroom*. Cambridge: Cambridge University Press.
Firth, John R. 1957. *Papers in Linguistics: 1934–1951*. London: Oxford University Press.
Firth, Alan. 1996. The discursive accomplishment of normality: On 'lingua franca' English and conversation analysis. *Journal of Pragmatics* 26(2), 237–259.
Garcia, Jane M. & Michael P. Cannito. 1996. Influence of verbal and nonverbal contexts on the sentence intelligibility of a speaker with dysarthria. *Journal of Speech, Language, and Hearing Research* 39(4), 750–760.
Gass, Susan M. & Evangeline M. Varonis. 1984. The effect of familiarity on the comprehensibility of nonnative speech. *Language Learning* 34(1), 65–87.
   1991. Miscommunication in nonnative speaker discourse. In Nikolas Coupland, Howard Giles & John M. Wiemann (eds.), *"Miscommunication" and problematic talk*, 121–145. Newbury Park, CA: Sage Publications.
Gass, Susan M. & Alison Mackey. 2000. *Stimulated Recall Methodology in Second Language Research*. Mahwah, NJ: Erlbaum.
Grønnum, Nina. 2009. A Danish phonetically annotated spontaneous speech corpus (DanPASS). *Speech Communication* 51(7), 594–603.
Gumperz, John J. 1982. *Discourse Strategies*. Cambridge: Cambridge University Press.
Gureckis, Todd M. & Goldstone, Robert L. 2011. Schema. In Patrick C. Hogan (ed.), *The Cambridge Encyclopedia of the Language Sciences,* 725–727. Cambridge: Cambridge University Press.
Gu, Peter Y., Guangwei Hu & Lawrence J. Zhang. 2005. Investigating language learner strategies among lower primary school pupils in Singapore. *Language and Education* 19(4), 281–303.
Hansen, Christa & Christine Jensen. 1994. Evaluating lecture comprehension. In John Flowerdew (ed.), *Academic Listening: Research Perspectives*, 241–268. Cambridge: Cambridge University Press.
Halliday, M. A. K. 1999. The notion of 'context' in language education. In Mohsen Ghadessy (ed.), *Text and Context in Functional Linguistics*, 1–24. Amsterdam: John Benjamins Publishing Company.
Hustad, Katherine C. & David R. Beukelman. 2001. Effects of linguistic cues and stimulus cohesion on intelligibility of severely dysarthric speech. *Journal of Speech, Language, and Hearing Research* 44, 497–510.
Hymes, Dell. 1977. *Foundations in Sociolinguistics: An Ethnographic Approach*. London: Tavistock.
Jenkins, Jennifer. 2000. *The Phonology of English as an International Language*. Oxford: Oxford University Press.
Kaur, Jagdish. 2011. Intercultural communication in English as a lingua franca: Some sources of misunderstanding. *Intercultural Pragmatics* 8(1), 93–116.
Kennedy, Sara. 2012. When non-native speakers misunderstand each other: Identifying important aspects of pronunciation. *Contact* 38(2), 49–62.
   2017. Using stimulated recall to explore the use of communication strategies in English lingua franca interactions. *Journal of English as a Lingua Franca* 6(1), 1–27.

Luce, Paul A. & David B. Pisoni. 1998. Recognizing spoken words: The neighborhood activation model. *Ear and Hearing* 19(1), 1–36.

Luchini, Pedro L. & Sara Kennedy. 2013. Exploring sources of phonological unintelligibility in spontaneous speech. *International Journal of English and Literature* 4(3), 79–88.

Linell, Per. 1995. Troubles with mutualities: Towards a dialogical theory of misunderstanding and miscommunication. In Ivana Marková, Carl F. Graumann & Klaus Foppa (eds.), *Mutualities in Dialogue*, 176–213. Cambridge: Cambridge University Press.

2015. Mishearings are occasioned by contextual assumptions and situational affordances. *Language & Communication* 40, 24–37.

Magnuson, James S. 2017. Mapping spoken words to meaning. In M. Gareth Gaskell & Jelena Mirkovic (eds.), *Speech Perception and Spoken Word Recognition*, 76–96. Abingdon: Routledge.

Mauranen, Anna. 2006. Signaling and preventing misunderstanding in English as lingua franca communication. *International Journal of the Sociology of Language* 2006(177), 123–150.

Minsky, Marvin. 1975. A framework for representing knowledge. In Patric H. Winston (ed.), *The Psychology of Computer Vision*, 211–277. New York: McGraw-Hill.

Osimk, Ruth. 2009. Decoding sounds: An experimental approach to intelligibility in ELF. *Vienna English Working Papers* 18(1), 64–89.

Pickering, Lucy. 2009. Intonation as a pragmatic resource in ELF interaction. *Intercultural Pragmatics* 6(2), 235–255.

Pietikäinen, Kaisa S. 2018. Misunderstandings and ensuring understanding in private ELF talk. *Applied Linguistics* 39(2), 188–212.

Pisoni, David B. & Conor T. McLennan. 2016. Spoken word recognition: Historical roots, current theoretical issues, and some new directions. In Gregory Hickok & Steven L. Small (eds.), *Neurobiology of Language,* 239–253. Tokio: Academic Press.

Pitzl, Marie-Luise. 2010. *English as a Lingua Franca in International Business: Resolving Miscommunication and Reaching Shared Understanding.* Saarbrücken: VDM Müller.

Rumelhart, David E. 1980. Schemata: The building blocks of cognition. In Rand J. Spiro, Bertram C. Bruce & William F. Brewer (eds.), *Theoretical Issues in Reading Comprehension*, 33–58. Hillsdale, NJ: L. Erlbaum Associates.

Schank, Roger C. & Robert P. Abelson. 1975. Scripts, plans and knowledge. In Philip N. Johnson-Laird & Wason, Peter C. (eds.), *Thinking: Readings in Cognitive Science,* 151–157. Tbilisi, USSR.

Seidlhofer, Barbara. 2011. *Understanding English as a Lingua Franca.* Oxford: Oxford University Press.

Smith, Larry E. 1992. Spread of English and issues of intelligibility. In Braj B. Kachru (ed.), *The Other Tongue: English across Cultures*, 75–90. Urbana, IL: University of Illinois Press.

Tannen, Deborah. 1993. What's in a frame? Surface evidence for underlying expectations. In Deborah Tannen (ed.), *Framing in Discourse*, 14–56. New York, NY: Oxford University Press.

Tannen, Deborah & Cynthia Wallat. 1993. Interactive frames and knowledge schemas in interaction: Examples from a medical examination/interview. In Deborah Tannen (ed.), *Framing in Discourse,* 57–76. New York, NY: Oxford University Press.

Tsui, Amy B. M. & John Fullilove. 1998. Bottom-up or top-down processing as a discriminator of L2 listening performance. *Applied Linguistics* 19(4), 432–451.
van Dijk, Teun. 1977. *Text and Context*. London: Longman.
Vandergrift, Larry & Christine C. M. Goh. 2012. *Teaching and Learning Second Language Listening: Metacognition in Action*. New York, NY: Routledge.
Vitevitch, Michael S. & Paul A. Luce. 1999. Probabilistic phonotactics and neighbourhood activation in spoken word recognition. *Journal of Memory and Language* 40(3), 374–408.
VOICE Project. 2007. Mark-up conventions. VOICE Transcription Conventions [2.1]. www.univie.ac.at/voice/documents/VOICE_mark-up_conventions_v2-1.pdf (14 March 2018).
Warren, Richard M. 1970. Perceptual restoration of missing speech sounds. *Science* 167(3917), 392–393.
Weigand, Edda. 1999. Misunderstanding: The standard case. *Journal of Pragmatics* 31, 763–785.
Widdowson, Henry G. 1983. *Learning Purpose and Language Use*. Oxford: Oxford University Press.
  2004. *Text, Context, Pretext: Critical Issues in Discourse Analysis*. Malden, MA: Blackwell.
  2011. Context and co-text. In Patrick Colm Hogan (ed.), *The Cambridge Encyclopedia of the Language Sciences,* 221–222. Cambridge: Cambridge University Press.
Zielinski, Beth. 2006. *Reduced Intelligibility in L2 Speakers of English*. Phd thesis. Bundoora, Victoria: La Trobe University.

11 Exploring the Pragmatics of Computer-Mediated English as a Lingua Franca Communication
Multimodal and Multilingual Practices

Rino Bosso

1 Introduction

English as a Lingua Franca (ELF) has been defined as 'any use of English among speakers of different first languages for whom English is the communicative medium of choice, and often the only option' (Seidlhofer 2011: 7). This definition seems to suggest that communication via ELF can happen via different channels of communication, that is, in oral, written and computer-mediated intercultural communication. Since interactants do not share the same native tongue, they resort to the linguistic resources they share in English and adapt these to their own communicative needs.

Over the last decade, ELF studies have proliferated and reported on the pervasive use of English which 'has been shaped, in its international uses, at least as much by its non-native speakers as its native speakers' (ibid.) and, as argued by Seidlhofer, '[t]his process has obviously been accelerated by the dramatic expansion of communication through the internet' (ibid.).

Since the advent of the Internet, we have been witnessing, in the first place, major changes in the way people establish and maintain relationships with each other, and in the way they go about their daily communicative routines, which are increasingly mediated by digital devices. Furthermore, such devices support sets of multimodal semiotic resources for realizing meaning that have expanded the expressive possibilities available in traditional writing; these may well be exploited to aid mutual understanding, especially when interactants do not share the same linguacultural background, as is the case with Computer-Mediated English as a Lingua Franca (CMELF) interactions. These I consider to be characterized by the flexible adaptation of English, and of other linguistic and non-verbal resources, to the online communicative needs of multicultural social formations.

Internet-based platforms such as chat rooms, blogs and social media are only a few examples of the virtual spaces that offer ELF users the possibility to interact online. Some of these online platforms are global ones that are accessed by huge numbers of users. For example, there were '1.52 billion daily active users on Facebook on average for December 2018' (Facebook

Newsroom 2018). Facebook groups could therefore be ideal virtual settings for investigating CMELF interactions within different kinds of online ELF communities. For example, one of the possibilities that Facebook may offer is that of allowing intercultural communication to take place in virtual settings, without the need for members of the multicultural virtual community to ever meet face to face. In fact, in virtual communities, it is not physical proximity that motivates community formation. Rather, members of a virtual community are brought together by a shared interest in some topic of discussion (Hine 2000). However, it is also possible that multicultural communities of people who live in close proximity, and interact face to face via ELF, decide also to use a Facebook group as an additional virtual space for communicating. I have suggested elsewhere (Bosso 2018) that observing the physical context in which internet users live can also be important for understanding their online interactions, for the physical place and the virtual space are increasingly interrelated in our everyday lives. It is precisely multimodal CMELF use in one such Facebook group that this paper sets out to explore.

2 ELF, Multimodality and Multilingualism

The vast majority of ELF studies to date have examined face-to-face communication and focused on the use of verbal signs in non-scripted, naturally occurring spoken interactions. While the modality of communication this paper aims to explore is written and computer mediated, some of the pragmatic strategies to enhance utterance clarity I will be dealing with have also been investigated in the literature on ELF talk. I will therefore report on some of the main findings in terms of pragmatic strategies which, I believe, signal a continuum between ELF and CMELF in terms of the line of enquiry, regardless of the specific modality of communication that is addressed. I am here referring, in particular, to strategies for 'signaling and preventing misunderstanding in English as a Lingua Franca communication' (Mauranen 2006), and for 'pre-empting problems of understanding in English as a Lingua Franca' (Kaur 2009). As Mauranen (2006) observed, ELF speakers tend to anticipate communicative difficulties by adopting proactive strategies when 'no overt marker of a misunderstanding is in evidence other than seemingly spontaneously arising additional checks, explanations, or clarifications' (Mauranen 2006: 135). Kaur (2009) considered the practice of repeating or paraphrasing overlapping segments in ELF talk as an attempt on the part of the subject utterer 'to pre-empt a problem of understanding rather than to resolve an actual problem as such' (Kaur 2009: 119). However, the pragmatic strategies described above can also be enacted via the exploitation of multimodality and non-verbal signs. Pietikäinen (2018) suggests that ELF couples employ a wide range of pragmatic strategies to pre-empt misunderstandings in spoken interactions, which include the use of extralinguistic features such as pointing, showing and even drawing in order to facilitate mutual understanding. ELF couples tend to adopt these extralinguistic features when one of the partners 'has difficulties with finding the right word, or the right word does not exist in English' (Pietikäinen 2018: 204). Evidence from Thir's experimental study (this volume) also suggests that ELF interlocutors seem to orient to visual cues while recognizing words in the stream of speech, while Konakahara (2016), on the basis of audio- and video-recorded casual ELF conversations, found that disagreement was not only realized verbally in interactions, but was also amplified with hand gestures.

It therefore seems that some ELF researchers have recently started to develop an interest in understanding how non-verbal elements of intercultural communication contribute to the realization of pragmatic meaning, and to the achievement of mutual understanding in ELF interactions. This contribution is likely to be relevant, for we realize discourse and make sense of utterances by relating the verbal signs that are produced to the situational context in which these are embedded (Widdowson 2004), and in which non-verbal devices are also pragmatically relevant. It is perhaps in consideration of the recent interest in paralinguistic and non-verbal devices in ELF talk that Diemer et al. (2016) stress the importance of preserving multimodal features as far as possible in the guidelines for the annotation of their Corpus of Academic Spoken English based on ELF conversations via Skype.

While the studies mentioned above refer to spoken interactions rather than typed, computer-mediated ones, they all raise the issue of the importance of multimodal features in ELF talk, as these appear to be associated with specific pragmatic functions, such as pre-empting misunderstandings or reinforcing disagreement. So far, however, only a few ELF scholars have analysed written, computer-mediated texts. While their studies are indeed focused on the analysis of verbal signs, a few comments seem to signal a potential interest in non-verbal ones. Mauranen (2013) suggests that since 'written text is typically accompanied by visual and auditory material on the web' (Mauranen 2013: 9), it may be particularly well suited for multimodal discourse analysis. Vettorel (2014) briefly touches upon the use of emoticons, and reports that these are used by young ELF bloggers and commenters to 'flag novel words, or words which they use in novel ways' (Vettorel 2014: 179). This comment provides an interesting insight into a possible object of study in multimodal CMELF analysis, namely the use of non-verbal signs for flagging novel, infrequent or difficult words in CMELF interactions. In this sense, flagging verbal signs by means of non-verbal ones could be conceived of as both a multimodal and a multilingual practice. Hynninen et al. (2017) observed glossing as a frequent strategy in flags around code-switching in academic ELF talk, and it would be interesting to see how similar strategies to the ones mentioned thus far are used in virtual environments.

It is perhaps important to clarify here some terminology that I will be using throughout this paper. In the first place, I will be referring to my study participants as ELF users, rather than ELF speakers. The choice of *users* is motivated precisely by the modality of communication that is analysed in this paper, that is, computer mediated rather than spoken. Persons who engage in computer-mediated interactions are normally referred to as users, as their communication is mediated by an electronic tool, be it a computer or a smartphone, via which they access the Internet. My study therefore aims at contributing to previous ELF research by investigating its online manifestations, and the present paper is concerned, in particular, with the analysis of a still under-researched aspect of ELF interactions, namely how ELF users exploit multimodal resources to get pragmatic meaning across.

The reflections made thus far prepare the ground for the research questions that this paper sets out to answer:

1) What are the pragmatic functions of visual devices in CMELF interactions?
2) How are multimodal practices associated with multilingual ones in CMELF interactions?

In the next sections, multimodality in CMELF interactions will be investigated by focusing on naturally occurring Facebook data, produced by a hybrid community of CMELF users, and gathered by adopting the methods of hybrid ethnography.

3   Data and Methodology

The CMELF interactions collected for the aims of this study have been posted to a private Facebook group of students who live in the same student dorm in Vienna. My informants live in close proximity in a building with 306 apartments, a common (or party) room, two communal kitchens, music rooms, shared balconies, a laundry room, a garbage room and long corridors connecting these. One might assume that since students are sharing the same physical place, they will have plenty of opportunities to interact with each other right from the moment they move into the student dorm. However, only a few of them live in shared apartments for couples; the vast majority live alone in small studio flats for single occupancy. The studio flats are equipped with a private bathroom and a small kitchen, so that the residents do not really need to leave their apartments and use the common areas, such as the communal kitchens. Due to the very structure of the physical setting, the possibilities for newcomers to engage in face-to-face contact with other residents therefore seem to be rather limited.

Students may, of course, meet on the balconies, while smoking a cigarette, for example, or in the laundry room, while waiting for their laundry to be washed and dried, and so have the possibility to interact with the few other residents who are present in the same room, at the same time. However, small talk is not the only kind of interaction student dorm inhabitants want to engage in: they may want to organize a party for all the residents in the common room, or they may want to complain about the conduct of other inhabitants, for example, when someone disposes of garbage in the corridors, rather than in the garbage room. Communicating with all the residents in the same place, and at the same time, is not possible, since these students have different schedules at university and they are not always simultaneously present in the physical place. Therefore, they need to find a way of communicating asynchronously, and a Facebook group allows them to do so. These students are therefore members of a hybrid community (HC) 'consisting of people who interact together socially using both online and offline methods of communication' (Gaved & Mulholland 2005: 2). Social relationships in HCs can be established via face-to-face contact in the actual physical place, and then be extended to online spaces (Navarrete et al. 2008: 127). However, what is particularly interesting about the specific HC under investigation is that the reverse consideration seems to apply: it is thanks to the Facebook group that activities such as playing sports or having dinner together can be organized and performed in the physical place. These students happen to live in close proximity but on their own, and it is thanks to the virtual space that they have become a real community.

I first entered the physical setting described above in October 2014, when I moved to Vienna to start my doctoral studies. The first impression I had was of a relatively silent student dorm, with not so many people around. Like most residents, I was also living in a studio flat for single occupancy. It was a nice studio flat, but a very small one, and so I would often leave my room to read on the shared balcony. This is how I happened to meet Pablo, one of the residents, who told me that there was a private Facebook group for students living at the dorm, and that they would share useful information on that platform. He advised me to join, and this is what I did once I got back to my room. From that moment on, I started accessing the Facebook group regularly and, in addition to finding useful information about life at the dorm, such as the working hours of the house technician, I also started to notice some interesting aspects of online communication on this platform. Given the different linguacultural backgrounds of the group members, postings were written in several languages, including German, but those in English greatly outnumbered the postings written in other languages. English was being used as the communicative medium of choice, and it was being shaped by group members to suit their own communicative needs. I asked those members who actively engaged in CMELF interactions for permission to collect their postings. The private Facebook messages I sent to the ninety-four group members who agreed to join the study are the only instances of mediated interaction with my informants. In fact, despite my presence in the physical place, I did not participate in their online interactions in order to avoid any interference in the development of the ethnographic object: naturally occurring, non-elicited CMELF interactions. This way of making ethnography is hybrid: while communication in the virtual space is the ethnographic object, the presence of the ethnographer in the physical place offers the possibility of carrying out interviews in order to 'explore how people design, encounter, and use the Internet in their physical, real world lives' (Jordan 2009: 185). This attention to the physical setting is an aspect that hybrid ethnography shares with more traditional ethnographies. In fact, observing the daily communicative routines of informants in the field setting where they live, and taking field notes, have always been important aspects of ethnographic research, because ethnography 'involves the ethnographer participating, overtly or covertly, in people's daily lives for an extended period of time, watching what happens, listening to what is said, asking questions' (Hammersley & Atkinson 1995: 1). While carrying out my own hybrid ethnography, I myself have been a member of the HC I have investigated, and I have had the chance to interact with my informants face to face, to learn about them and to ask them questions about their use of Facebook as a means for communicating with other HC members. As emerged during an interview with the Facebook group administrator, Samuel, who created the Facebook group for practical reasons, the students needed 'a platform to communicate, to share events, to talk about problems' (from an interview with Samuel). Furthermore, on the online platform, students can post messages that can be viewed by all members of the Facebook group, which seems to be more convenient than knocking on the doors of more than 300 residents in the physical place. As Samuel puts it, 'a Facebook group gives you the possibility to reach a wide audience with really little effort' (ibid.).

During the two-year data collection phase (from late 2014 to late 2016), my informants produced several thousand CMELF utterances. This longitudinal perspective allows a continuous observation of which communicative practices, linguistic and non-linguistic resources are used within the HC to achieve specific communicative goals. One aspect of CMELF communication that came to my attention was the use of non-verbal signs, as it was not only the language that was being adapted to make it suitable for intercultural communication. I had the impression that group members were, over time, developing strategies for enhancing the comprehensibility of their computer-mediated utterances by exploiting multimodal resources. The following sections report on the methodology adopted for analysing CMELF interactions, as well as the findings as to the function of non-verbal signs in these.

4 Multimodality and Computer-Mediated Discourse Analysis

Discourse analysis has traditionally focused on texts constituted by verbal signs and on the function of these in the realization of pragmatic meaning. Texts are not defined in terms of the quantity of linguistic material used in them, but by the function they express, by the underlying communicative intention. As pointed out by Widdowson, texts 'can correspond in extent with any linguistic unit: letter, sound, word, sentence, combination of sentences.... I identify a text not by its linguistic extent but by its social intent.' (Widdowson 2004: 8). It is therefore the exploration of intent, of the purpose for uttering, that is at the very heart of discourse analysis. However, intent may not be solely expressed by means of verbal signs. As suggested by Eco (1976), utterances consist of communicative acts that can result from any production of signals: 'I utter when I draw an image, when I make a purposeful gesture or when I produce an object that, besides its technical function, aims to communicate something' (Eco 1976: 151). Communicative intent can therefore be expressed verbally and non-verbally, and this applies to both spoken and computer-mediated utterances. Quite obviously, the kinds of non-verbal devices employed will vary depending on the channel of communication: while oral, face-to-face interactions allow for the contingent use of gestures and facial expressions, typed, computer-mediated interactions allow for the use of visual devices such as emojis and images.

Current approaches to computer-mediated discourse analysis are increasingly concerned with understanding how both verbal and non-verbal resources are combined for realizing pragmatic meaning, as a consequence of findings in computer-mediated communication (CMC). Research into CMC has revealed that non-verbal signs, such as emoticons, can be used as paralinguistic devices and function as intensifiers, thus complementing and enhancing the meaning expressed verbally (e.g. Derks et al. 2008). Other studies have reported on the use of emoticons as structural markers, thus replacing punctuation marks such as periods and exclamation marks, but never question marks (e.g. Amaghlobeli 2012). Dresner and Herring (2010) have instead pointed to the fact that emoticons can influence the illocutionary force of an utterance: for example, the sequence of verbal signs that seems to express a complaint can be downgraded to a mere assertion by using a winking face at the end of the utterance (Dresner & Herring 2010: 257). In particular, social media platforms, such as Facebook, are conceived of by Herring as Interactive Multimodal Platforms, 'on which two or more semiotic modes – typically, text plus audio, video, and/or graphics – are available to support interactive human-to-human communication' (Herring 2018: 42). The multimodal affordances of social media can be exploited by internet users, who realize specific pragmatic functions by using non-verbal devices. As Herring explains:

graphics on social media sites have evolved from cute or funny images or videos that people share for their entertainment value to **semiotic devices that are used to convey propositional content, in lieu of, or in conjunction with, text**. As such, they can function as propositions within messages or as stand-alone turns in conversational exchanges. These devices include emoticons, emoji, stickers, GIFs, and text-in-image memes. (Herring 2018: 44, bold added)

The potential of such semiotic devices to convey propositional content may be particularly important in intercultural communication, that is, when interactants do not share the same native language and visual resources may aid mutual understanding. These are internet users who have to face a difficult challenge – namely that of working across cultural and linguistic differences – and achieving mutual understanding in this scenario requires an ability to draw on all of the semiotic resources available. In this respect, '[w]orking across differences entails semiotic hybridity – the emergence of new combinations of languages, social dialects, voices, genres and discourses' (Fairclough 2013: 551). While advances in technology, and the advent of the Internet in particular, have provided the circumstances under which intercultural communication has become increasingly more frequent, by offering virtual spaces for intercultural interaction, such as Facebook groups, there are no commonly agreed-upon conventions as to how such interactions should be carried out, that is, via what language(s) or what sets of non-verbal signs. The choice of how to make the most of the semiotic resources that are available to internet users in order to effectively get pragmatic meaning across in online intercultural communication is one that remains with the users themselves. It is precisely the choices made by Facebook users involved in CMELF interactions that will be explored in the next section: in particular, how non-verbal devices are integrated in their computer-mediated utterances to enhance comprehensibility, as well as to establish and manage rapport between interactants.

5   The Function of Images in CMELF

As argued in the previous sections, non-verbal elements of communication are pragmatically relevant: this means that they may express an illocutionary force, just as words normally do, and bring about a certain perlocutionary effect. In particular, one might intuitively guess that non-verbal devices, such as pictures, may prove particularly helpful in allowing mutual understanding in intercultural online communication. In fact, regardless of the topic of discussion, interactants are likely not to share the same exact vocabulary in a language which is not their L1, and using pictures in their online interactions may allow them to tackle this potential threat to mutual understanding. As previously mentioned, some ELF scholars (cf. Mauranen 2006; Kaur 2009) have studied the pragmatic strategies that are employed in ELF talk in order to signal and prevent, or pre-empt, misunderstanding via repeating or paraphrasing verbal signs. One of the circumstances that gives rise to these strategies in ELF talk is, according to Kaur, overlap. While overlap cannot, for obvious reasons, occur in asynchronous CMC as it can during real-time spoken interactions, while looking at my own data I did find some similarities between the strategies described by Mauranen and Kaur of repeating, paraphrasing, clarifying and explaining, to avoid misunderstandings in a proactive way.

However, in my data it seems that non-verbal signs are used in order to avoid potential communicative problems, especially when users utter a computer-mediated communicative act of request and ask on Facebook for specific objects that they need to use in the physical place. In order for their communicative act of request to be successful, they need to make sure that the object they are looking for can be clearly identified by other members of the Facebook group. However, the names of some objects may occur rather infrequently in English, and so be potentially unknown to most HC members. In order to proactively avoid non-understanding or misunderstanding, my informants tend to use a picture in place of the target lexical item, or they accompany the lexical item which refers to the requested object with a picture of the object. Pictures, then, can substitute lexical items, or repeat, clarify and explain what object the user is looking for. In my data it seems that pictures can be used in communicative acts of request, for several reasons, which include filling a lexical gap in the posting produced by the subject utterer, or proactively avoiding misunderstandings. These phenomena will be exemplified in the following excerpts.

6 Communicative Acts of Request and the Exploitation of Multimodality

As members of an HC, my study participants have an important asset: the illocutionary force they express online can lead to perlocutionary effects both in the virtual space and in the physical place. Whether the perlocutionary effect is realized in the online or offline world depends on the kind of communicative act that is uttered online: CMELF communicative acts of the advice-seeking kind, for example, are usually responded to online by means of communicative acts of advice-giving. However, some other kinds of communicative act may bring about some form of exchange that is performed in the physical context to which the HC is bound. This is the case, for example, when communicative acts of request are uttered. Living in close proximity allows HC members, for example, to ask online for objects they intend to borrow from other inhabitants of the dorm, in the physical place. However, asking for objects for daily usage via CMELF in a multicultural HC might not be as easy as it intuitively seems. Most CMELF users are non-native English speakers and it can be expected that there may be some gaps in their knowledge of English vocabulary. For example, the target lexical item in English, corresponding to the object that is being looked for, may be unknown to the subject utterer, or simply may not come to mind during utterance production. This creates a lexical gap in the communicative act of request: while the intention is there, the mention of the required object is not. As a consequence, the illocutionary force of request for an object cannot be expressed, and the perlocutionary effect cannot be achieved. However, another scenario is also possible: the subject utterer may know what the target lexical item in English is, but assume that this is unknown to the target audience. In this case, while the illocutionary force can be expressed, the perlocutionary effect is unlikely to be achieved. In both cases, as we will see in the following excerpts, both multimodal and multilingual practices come into play in strategies that aim at the realization of pragmatic meaning.

The Facebook threads that follow have been anonymized, and pseudonyms are used in place of the subject utterers' real names.

6.1 Filling a Lexical Gap with Images: Focus on the Subject Utterer

6.1.1 Extract 1

Kassandra (F, 19–24, Spanish): Does anyone have something like this? I need it for my knee 😊

The CMELF utterance above, posted in May 2015, can be divided into two communicative acts: the first, the core one, is a communicative act of request, while the second is a description of the motivation for requesting the object. While Kassandra's communicative intention may be easy to infer from the mere observation of the verbal signs in the utterance, this would probably strike us as elliptical: by observing the verbal signs in isolation, it would be impossible to contextualize the utterance, to understand what it is exactly that Kassandra is looking for.

In the verbal components of the communicative act of request above, there is no mention of the requested object, which is, however, pointed to by using the demonstrative 'this', which in turn refers deictically to the picture that follows (Figure 11.1). In the picture, some forms of disinfectant can be seen. Interestingly, the texts that are visible in the picture are in Spanish, which suggests that Kassandra might have searched the Internet for the requested object in her native language and then posted a picture of it, probably because she does not know the target word in English. Even though Kassandra cannot indicate the object she needs verbally, she can nevertheless exploit multimodality. In this sense, the use of this picture results from a multilingual practice: in order to fill a lexical gap in her CMELF utterance, Kassandra draws on other linguistic resources in her multilingual repertoire. It is a case, one might say, of 'hidden' code-switching. The other non-verbal component,

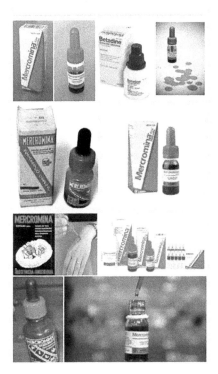

Figure 11.1 Image of disinfectant.

the worried face emoji 😟 at the end of the utterance, reinforces the idea of a serious concern which requires the immediate attention of the audience.

Samuel replies to Kassandra's posting:

Samuel (M, 19–24, German): Oh did you hurt yourself? 😟
Yes, I do have some desinfection… shall I bring it to your room? (what number?)

We can start by analysing the communicative acts in his utterance: he first asks for confirmation of whether Kassandra hurt herself. This is marked both structurally, by means of a question mark, as well as emotionally, by means of the same worried face emoji 😟 Kassandra used in her posting. This moment in which rapport is established is followed by a communicative act of the information-giving kind, 'Yes, I do have some desinfection'. Here Samuel is filling the lexical gap in Kassandra's CMELF utterance, but in so doing he does not translate into English the commercial name of the drug represented in the picture; rather, he uses the hypernym 'desinfection' (disinfection). It is interesting to notice that the term he uses does not conform to standard English morphology, and rather reminds one of the equivalent term *Desinfektion* in his L1, German. One may argue here that he, too, is drawing on his own multilingual repertoire, and the morphology of the target lexical item he puts forward is influenced by his knowledge of his own L1. What we see here is an instance of active co-construction of meaning between interactants who agree on an acceptable term. According to Mauranen,

> there is active co-construction of expressions which the current speaker seems to be lacking [when] participants other than the current speaker initiate the production of an expression that is acceptable. Acceptability is here understood in terms of whether an expression or repair allows the discourse to proceed, and judged by how the discourse moves on – with further clarifications or searches, or with apparent satisfaction with the degree of shared understanding (Mauranen 2006: 135).

It is interesting to infer from Kassandra's reply below that the strategy of mixing verbal and non-verbal signs as she does proves to be successful:

Kassandra: A friend of mine already gave it to me!! 😁 i went skating and i felt. No big deal, but i wanted to desinfect it 😉 thanks samuel! But the way! I am still up for tandem! Let me know 🙂

While Samuel was trying to help Kassandra online, some other member of the HC probably read her Facebook posting and gave her what she was looking for in the physical place. It is also interesting to notice how Facebook emojis seem to be used by Kassandra in order to mark some communicative act boundaries within the computer-mediated utterance: the grinning face, for example, is placed precisely at the end of a communicative act of information-giving ('A friend of mine already gave it to me!! 😁'), the winking face 😉 is placed precisely after a further explanation of the circumstances that brought Kassandra to ask for some disinfectant and, finally, a smiling face 🙂 closes a communicative act in which Kassandra thanks Samuel and invites him on a language exchange they had probably already talked about face to face. As far as non-conformities are concerned, there are two in the second communicative act: 'i felt' (I fell) and 'desinfect it' (disinfect it). While 'felt' might be simply a temporary lapse or a typo, it seems that the non-conformity produced by Samuel, the noun 'desinfection', is picked up by Kassandra and morphologically adapted in order to be used as a verb: 'desinfect'. Interestingly, this non-conformity is reminiscent of *desinfectar* in Spanish, Kassandra's L1. In this sense, while the target term suggested by Samuel does not conform to standard English spelling, it can be understood by Kassandra due to the resemblance to the word *desinfección* in her own L1. Instances of code-mixing and code-switching, as well as the creation of hybrid forms at the intersection between the morphological rules of different languages, are not unusual in ELF interactions, and in intercultural communication more generally. As pointed out by Seidlhofer, ELF users, 'as at least bilinguals, ... have the resources of other languages available to them as well, and ... make use of them as active elements in their linguistic repertoire' (Seidlhofer 2011: 112).

6.1.2   Extract 2

The advantage of carrying out a longitudinal study of CMELF interactions is that the development of certain pragmatic strategies can be tracked over time, and it can be observed whether these occur only as one-offs, or whether they are reapplied by the same user, or even taken up by other HC members and developed into intracommunity pragmatic conventions. As the extract below will show, Kassandra reuses the same strategy discussed in Section 6.1.1 in February 2016, nine months later.

Kassandra (F, 19–24, Spanish): Is anyone selling something like this? Any brand...

Figure 11.2 Image of a kettle.

304 *Rino Bosso*

As pointed out while observing the previous excerpt, again in this case Kassandra seems to be filling her own lexical gap in the CMELF utterance. She probably does not know the word 'kettle' in English, and therefore searches the Internet in her own L1 for images of 'Hervidores de agua'. Once again, she produces a screenshot from her mobile device (Figure 11.2), which she includes in the CMELF utterance and points at by uttering 'something like this'.

Again in this case her strategy proves successful, as a user replies to her message with a communicative act of offering, in which the price and pick-up times of the requested object are specified.

6.1.3   Extract 3

In June 2015 – that is, in the intervening months between the two postings by Kassandra discussed in Sections 6.1.1 and 6.1.2 – another user, Dora, applies a similar strategy to the one already discussed.

Dora (F, 19–24, Romanian): Hey guys, does anyone have one of these i could borrow for a few minutes please? 😊

In the communicative act of request above, the explicit mentioning of the requested object is also lacking, and deictic reference to the picture (Figure 11.3) is realized via the sequence of words 'one of these'. However, unlike Kassandra's postings, there are no screenshots of the internet searches made by Dora, so it is difficult to say whether she searched the Internet for images by using her own L1, Romanian, or whether she typed a collocation such as, for example, 'sweeping and mopping tool' in English.

6.2   Flagging and Multimodal Glossing: Focus on the Audience

In the next extract, produced by Sally in February 2015, we see a different strategy at work.

Figure 11.3 Image of a sweeping and mopping tool.

6.2.1 Extract 4

Sally (F, 19–24, Russian): Hey people! Does anyone have a mixer and a ladle? for those who have no idea of ladle, I attached a picture.. AND last chance does anyone want some cheese, ham and yogurts? In addition you will get some aples ☺

Figure 11.4 Image of a ladle.

In the utterance above, two different communicative acts are present: the first one a request, the second one an offer. While the latter refers back to a previous message posted by Sally the day before, the first one contains a request for two specific objects that are explicitly named: a mixer and a ladle. The user knows what she wants and knows the corresponding target lexical items in English. However, while she does not signal the word 'mixer' as being potentially problematic for her multicultural audience, she seems to assume that some group members will be unfamiliar with the term 'ladle'. She therefore adopts an interesting strategy by glossing this term multimodally: 'for those who have no idea of ladle, I attached a picture' (Figure 11.4).

Samuel replies to Sally's posting, but in so doing he seems to be more interested in her offer than her request.

Samuel (M, 19–24, German): I would take the cheese, ham, yoghurts and apples if possible ☺
Where can I pick it up?
(I'm sorry, but I have no mixer or ladle...)

6.2.2 Extract 5

In the posting that follows, produced by Samuel in March 2015, while a communicative act of request for an object is uttered, as was the case with all the postings already discussed, the combination of verbal and non-verbal elements differs in one important respect from those uttered by Kassandra (Sections 6.1.1 and 6.1.2) and Dora (Section 6.1.3): the object that is asked for is both mentioned verbally in English and represented visually. In this respect, Samuel aligns with the strategy adopted by Sally (Section 6.2.1):

Samuel (M, 19–24, German): Does anybody has a juice squeezer (see photo) which I could borrow tonight or tmr morning? ☺
Thanks!

Figure 11.5 Image of a juice squeezer.

In this case, the term 'juice squeezer' seems to be seen by Samuel as being potentially problematic for the audience, so he flags it verbally and realizes deictic reference to the picture (Figure 11.5) by uttering '(see photo)'. In this respect, he 'glosses multimodally' the problematic lexical item provided in English. As mentioned in Section 2, the practice of verbal glossing is one that has already been investigated in spoken ELF studies. Hynninen et al. (2017) observed glossing in the co-text of code-switches, that is, when foreign words are used within an ELF utterance. However, in the excerpt above there is no code-switching; in fact, it is a lexical item that is already in English which is glossed multimodally.

6.2.3 Extract 6

Similar considerations can be made as to the posting below, also uttered by Samuel, but in June 2015, three months after the posting in Section 6.2.2.

Samuel (M, 19–24, German): Does anybody have an Allen wrench ☺ the thing in the photo 😉) in size M6?

Samuel perhaps considers the term 'Allen wrench' to be problematic, potentially unknown to his audience, and therefore he signals this multimodally, that is, both verbally and non-verbally. Once again, an English item is flagged, as this was probably assumed by the subject utterer to be unintelligible for the target audience. It therefore seems to be important to mention here the function of emojis: the verbal flagging of the problematic lexical item 'Allen wrench' is accompanied by the use of the 'slightly smiling face' emoji: 'Does anybody have an Allen wrench ☺'. The use of this emoji seems to signal Samuel's assumption that the term might be problematic for the audience, as is also manifest in the following sequence, 'the thing in the photo 😉', by means of which Samuel realizes deictic reference to the picture (Figure 11.6), both verbally and by means of the 'winking face' emoji.

Daniel replies to Samuel's request by asking for clarification as to what Samuel needs an Allen wrench for, and Samuel explains, but also informs Daniel that he has already received what he was looking for.

Figure 11.6 Image of an Allen wrench.

Daniel (M, 19–24, Turkish): lol man ☺ why do you need it
Samuel (M, 19–24, German): for repairing my new bike ☺ - but I already got one!

As can be inferred from Samuel's posting in reply to Daniel's, while the interaction goes on in the virtual space, the requested object is obtained in the physical place, as was also observed in relation to the interaction between Samuel and Kassandra (Section 6.1.1). Therefore, the strategy of using images to proactively avoid misunderstandings seems to be a successful one, one that allows HC members to enhance utterance clarity in their CMELF interactions and achieve the desired perlocutionary effect in the physical place.

7   Discussion

In this paper I have discussed the interrelationship between multimodal and multilingual practices in CMELF interactions. In particular, on the basis of an analysis of several computer-mediated interactions between ELF users of different linguacultural backgrounds, I have shown that they seem to be aware of both their own gaps in their knowledge of English vocabulary, and the assumed gaps in the vocabulary knowledge of their multicultural audience. Practical communicative needs, such as having to ask for an object, lead them to develop pragmatic strategies for avoiding misunderstandings: they therefore resort to images in order to realize deictic reference to the requested object, and so manage to effectively express the illocutionary force of request. As evidence from the examples in Section 6 has shown, these strategies see verbal and non-verbal signs as intertwined in the CMELF utterance. While some users may explicitly state that part of the audience may be unfamiliar with a certain lexical item, as was the case in Sally's posting, other users may decide not to put this into words, but rather to provide the audience with sufficient visual cues as deemed necessary to allow understanding. This is what Samuel does, as he realizes deictic reference to a corresponding picture, which in turn functions as a multimodal glossing device. The longitudinal perspective of this study also allows us to appreciate who first used a given strategy: Sally used it first and Samuel was involved in the interaction. Subsequently, Samuel uses and adapts this strategy in his own postings.

Another scenario that involves the use of pictures in communicative acts of request is that of the subject utterer not knowing the target lexical item in English, which corresponds to the object being requested. In two different instances, Kassandra creates an elliptical CMELF utterance in which the requested object is not mentioned verbally. The mentioning function is realized non-verbally by means of the objects represented in the screenshots she posted to the Facebook group. As closer scrutiny of these screenshots has shown, the multimodal practice of searching the Internet for images may be understood to be multilingual: Kassandra carries out her searches in Spanish, her L1, to then embed the images she finds in her CMELF utterances. Therefore, she is drawing on all linguistic and semiotic resources available to her in order to produce CMELF utterances. While there might be indications that some other users, such as Dora, may be applying the same multimodal and multilingual method during utterance production, there is no clear evidence of this, as was the case with Kassandra's screenshots.

8   Concluding Remarks

The present paper has put forward an interdisciplinary approach for investigating CMELF interactions, one that is informed by ethnographic methods for data collection, and by computer-mediated discourse analysis for the actual multimodal analysis of CMELF utterances. While it was not the purpose of this paper to provide the reader with an overview of CMELF, for which a much larger number of HCs around the world would have to be analysed contrastively, my ethnographic approach has led me to focus on a specific HC, and on a specific communicative act, namely the communicative act of request. In particular, as my research questions have indicated, my research interest is in investigating the pragmatic function of visual devices, as well as in observing whether there is a connection between multilingual and multimodal practices in CMELF interactions. On the basis of the observations made thus far, the following concluding remarks can be made:

1. The excerpts discussed in Section 6 show that virtual spaces on Interactive Multimodal Platforms may increasingly develop into particularly rich sites for the exploitation of different semiotic resources, both verbal and non-verbal. In the multicultural Facebook group under investigation in this study, ELF is the default means of verbal communication, and pragmatic meaning is also realized by drawing on a number of other languages and other semiotic resources. CMELF users can be said to exploit the semiotic hybridity allowed by the medium to get pragmatic meaning across.
2. The importance of visual aids for interpreting the meaning of CMELF utterances is at times crucial, as these are not solely used for rapport

management or for the sake of conveying the tone of the message. Both emojis and pictures are used in CMELF utterances as part of proactive strategies to avoid misunderstandings:

a. Emojis have been found to function as structural markers within CMELF utterances, and to delimit the boundaries between different communicative acts within these, thus enhancing utterance clarity. Furthermore, emojis may also be used to flag a potentially problematic term in communicative acts of request.
b. Pictures can be used to realize multimodal glossing of an infrequent lexical item, or as a visual paraphrase of this. Furthermore, pictures can also be used for filling a lexical gap in the CMELF utterance, when the subject utterer does not know, or cannot recall, a corresponding target lexical item in English. In particular, it has been shown that some users retrieve pictures of the target lexical items by searching the Internet in their own L1. This is therefore both a multimodal and a multilingual practice, in that it is multimodality which allows ELF interactants to make use of their multilingual repertoires in novel and creative ways.

The observation and contrastive analysis between different data sets of CMELF interactions may potentially provide interesting insights into the processes that lead to the realization of pragmatic strategies that support mutual understanding in online intercultural interactions via ELF. A longitudinal perspective seems to be apt for observing the impact of such strategies on processes of language variation and change.

REFERENCES

Amaghlobeli, Natia. 2012. Linguistic features of typographic emoticons in SMS discourse. *Theory and Practice in Language Studies* 2(2), 348–354.

Bosso, Rino. 2018. First steps in exploring computer-mediated English as a Lingua Franca. In Xavier Martin-Rubió (ed.), *Contextualizing English as a Lingua Franca: From Data to Insights*, 10–35. Newcastle upon Tyne: Cambridge Scholars.

Derks, Daantje, Arjan Bos & Jasper von Grumbkow. 2008. Emoticons and online message interpretation. *Social Science Computer Review* 26(3), 379–388.

Diemer, Stefan, Marie-Louise Brunner & Selina Schmidt. 2016. Compiling computer-mediated spoken language corpora. *International Journal of Corpus Linguistics* 21 (3), 348–371.

Dresner, Eli & Susan Herring. 2010. Functions of the nonverbal in CMC: Emoticons and illocutionary force. *Communication Theory* 20, 249–268.

Eco, Umberto. 1976. *A Theory of Semiotics*. Bloomington and London: Indiana University Press.

Facebook Newsroom. 2018. Facebook statistics. Available at: http://newsroom.fb.com/company-info/ (last accessed 30 January 2019).

Fairclough, Norman. 2013. *Critical Discourse Analysis: The Critical Study of Language*. 2nd ed. New York: Routledge.
Gaved, Mark & Paul Mulholland. 2005. Grassroots initiated networked communities: A study of hybrid physical/virtual communities. *System Sciences, 2005. HICSS '05. Proceedings of the 38th Annual Hawaii International Conference on System Sciences*.
Hammersley, Martyn & Paul Atkinson. 1995. *Ethnography: Principles in Practice*. 2nd ed. London: Routledge.
Herring, Susan C. 2018. The coevolution of computer-mediated communication and computer-mediated discourse analysis. In Patricia Bou-Franch & Pilar Garcés-Conejos Blitvich (eds.), *Analyzing Digital Discourse: New Insights and Future Directions*, 25–67. Cham: Palgrave Macmillan.
Hine, Christine. 2000. *Virtual Ethnography*. London: Sage.
Hynninen Nina, Kaisa Pietikäinen & Svetlana Vetchinnikova. 2017. Multilingualism in English as a lingua franca: Flagging as an indicator of perceived acceptability and intelligibility. In Arja Nurmi, Tanja Rütten & Päivi Pahta (eds.), *Challenging the Myth of Monolingual Corpora* (Language and Computers 80), 95–126. Leiden: Brill.
Jordan, Brigitte. 2009. Blurring boundaries: The "real" and the "virtual" in hybrid spaces. *Human Organization: Summer 2009* 68(2), 181–193.
Kaur, Jagdish. 2009. Pre-empting problems of understanding in English as a Lingua Franca. In Anna Mauranen & Elina Ranta (eds.), *English as a Lingua Franca: Studies and Findings*, 107–123. Newcastle upon Tyne: Cambridge Scholars.
Konakahara, Mayu. 2016. The use of unmitigated disagreement in ELF casual conversation: Ensuring mutual understanding by providing correct information. In Kumiko Murata (ed.), *Exploring ELF in Japanese Academic and Business Contexts: Conceptualization, Research and Pedagogic Implications*, 70–89. London, New York: Routledge.
Mauranen, Anna. 2006. Signaling and preventing misunderstanding in English as lingua franca communication. *International Journal of the Sociology of Language* 177, 123–150.
— 2013. Hybridism, edutainment, and doubt: Science blogging finding its feet. *Nordic Journal of English Studies* 13(1), 7–36.
Navarrete, Celene, Esperanza Huerta & Thomas Horan. 2008. Social place identity in hybrid communities. In Alessandro Aurigi & Fiorella De Cindio (eds.), *Augmented Urban Spaces: Articulating the Physical and Electronic City*, 125–137. Aldershot: Ashgate Publishing.
Pietikäinen, Kaisa. 2018. Misunderstandings and ensuring understanding in private ELF talk. *Applied Linguistics* 39(2), 188–212.
Seidlhofer, Barbara. 2011. *Understanding English as a Lingua Franca*. Oxford: Oxford University Press.
Vettorel, Paola. 2014. *English as a Lingua Franca in Wider Networking: Blogging Practices*. Berlin: De Gruyter Mouton.
Widdowson, Henry. 2004. *Text, Context, Pretext: Critical Issues in Discourse Analysis*. Oxford: Blackwell Publishing.

12 Development of Shared Multilingual Resources in ELF Dyadic Interaction
A Longitudinal Case Study

Aki Siegel

1 Introduction

The current study investigates changes in the use of code-switching during word search sequences and self-and-other positioning regarding the knowledge of linguistic items in English as a lingua franca (ELF) interaction between two speakers over time. ELF is used in this paper to refer to English used as a contact language between speakers from different linguistic and cultural backgrounds (Archibald et al. 2011). In addition, language, as used in this study, refers to interactional resources for co-constructing meaning in social life (Brouwer & Wagner 2004), and does not refer to the entire linguistic system or categories with clear-cut entities.

ELF interactions are often cases where English is the only option for communication between speakers of different L1s (Seidlhofer 2011). However, accumulating studies have shown that ELF interaction can be multilingual (e.g. Cogo 2012, Mauranen 2012, 2014, Cogo 2017, Hynninen et al. 2017, Pietikäinen 2017). Pitzl (2016) argues that ELF speakers often have multilingual resources available to them and these resources can overlap. Jenkins (2015) also notes that additional languages to ELF interactions "may not be shared from the start (nor do interlocutors necessarily know from the start what they do in fact 'share')," and they are "resources that are discovered as they emerge during the interaction" (Jenkins 2015: 64).

A few longitudinal ELF studies have discussed the increasing use of additional languages over time (Kalocsai 2009, Smit 2010). For instance, in Smit's (2010) study of ELF classrooms, initially the teacher immediately translated certain terms in German, but later in time the students showed that translations for these particular German terms were not necessary anymore. In Kalocsai's (2009) study, exchange students talked about using multiple languages in their conversations as they learned each other's L1s. These studies suggest that ELF-focused interactions can become multilingual over time through the development of interactional resources. However, studies have yet to explore how these changes occur in and through interactions between two speakers over time. The aim of this study is therefore to explore how an ELF-focused interaction between two speakers can develop into a multilingual interaction over time and how these changes can be observed.

2 Background

2.1 Code-Switching in ELF Interactions

Many ELF studies looking at multilingual use have analyzed the speakers' use of code-switching during interactions (e.g. Cogo 2012, Mauranen 2012, 2014, Pitzl 2016, Cogo 2017, Hynninen et al. 2017, Pietikäinen 2017), while others have analyzed the cross-linguistic awareness of the hearer (Hülmbauer 2009, Mauranen & Mauko 2019). Code-switching refers to "the mixing, by bilinguals (or multilinguals), of two or more languages in discourse, often with no change of interlocutor or topic" (Poplack 2001: 2062). ELF studies have identified various functions of code-switching. For instance, Cogo (2009) identifies code-switching as an accommodation strategy used by the speakers in order to facilitate communication. Other functions of code-switching in ELF interactions include: displaying cultural membership (Pölzl 2003, Klimpfinger 2007, 2009, Cogo 2009, 2012, Cogo & Dewey 2012), specifying an addressee (Klimpfinger 2007, 2009, Cogo 2012), displaying linguistic trouble or appealing for assistance (Klimpfinger 2007, 2009, Mauranen 2014, Hynninen et al. 2017), introducing an idea or expression that is normally referred to in the language switched into (Klimpfinger 2007, 2009, Mauranen 2014, Pitzl 2016, Hynninen et al. 2017), reinforcing social relationships (Kalocsai 2011, Mauranen 2014), and managing the conversation (House 2016).

When using code-switching in ELF interactions, speakers often "flag" the code-switching through the use of repetition, hesitation, and translation (Hynninen et al. 2017). Translations are commonly used in order to enhance explicitness to help hearers keep track of the conversation (Cogo 2012, Mauranen 2012, Hynninen et al. 2017). For instance, Cogo (2010) describes an ELF conversation where a speaker introduces a French idiom in English first ("blue flower"), and then in French ("*fleur bleue*"), to pre-empt understanding issues. Cogo (2012) also identified speakers providing English translations to include specific people who were perceived not to understand the non-English utterances during a multilingual, multiparty business interaction. A similar phenomenon is reported by Greer (2008) in his study of bilingual discussion groups, where participants translated words for certain members prior to any initiation of repair, and even after the person had displayed comprehension. These findings suggest that there is a tendency for speakers to ascribe certain language preferences to others.

However, some studies have documented cases where code-switching is done without translation (e.g. Mauranen 2014, Pietikäinen 2014, Hynninen et al. 2017), even when code-switching into a third language that is neither of the speakers' L1 (e.g. Cogo 2009). Pietikäinen (2014) discusses how in conversations between ELF couples, code-switching has often become automatic (i.e. no flagging), and in some cases the speakers do not even notice that they are code-switching. In these studies, the speaker perceives the hearer as understanding the non-English utterance that they are code-switching into, and at the same time the hearer understands or presents themselves as understanding the code-switched utterance.

2.2   Word Searches

Code-switching in ELF interactions is frequently found during word searches (Klimpfinger 2007, Cogo 2009). Word search, as used in this paper, refers to a case where "a speaker in interaction displays trouble with the production of an item in an ongoing turn at talk" (Brouwer 2003: 535). As a result, the speaker often moves on to a side sequence in order to locate a certain word or phrase (Jefferson 1972). The start of a word search sequence is usually initiated during the speaker's turn through hesitancy and an embodied display of difficulty in finding or producing an appropriate word or phrase to complete the turn. Hesitancy or indication of "trouble" is often shown through pauses, word cut-offs, sound stretches, or "uh"s and "uhm"s (Schegloff et al. 1977, Goodwin 1983, Schegloff 1984).

In addition, previous studies have shown the critical role of the speaker's gaze during word searches (Goodwin 1983). Goodwin and Goodwin (1986) analyzed gaze during word searches using conversation analysis (CA) and demonstrated how the use of gaze can reflect the speaker's participation in the word search. For example, while the speaker is conducting a solitary word search, their gaze tends to go elsewhere than the interlocutor's eyes and the speaker displays a "thinking face." During the ongoing word search, the hearer can shift their gaze towards the speaker to indicate co-participation in the word search. If the speaker fails to locate the word they are looking for, they often solicit assistance from the interlocutor by seeking mutual gaze. Mutual gaze is also used when the speaker presents a candidate solution and attempts to solicit a response from the interlocutor.

Code-switching during word searches is often identified in the position of the sought-for word (Funayama 2002, Greer 2008, Mori and Hasegawa 2009, Greer 2013). In addition, during word searches in ELF interactions, speakers are often found code-switching to their L1s (Hynninen et al. 2017). This corroborates with Greer's (2013) study of bilingual interactions, where he found speakers code-switching to their stronger language first to complete their word search, then switching back to or providing a translation in the hearer's perceived preferred language. He argues that the use of code-switching during word searches explicates the speaker's own language preference, as well as the recipient's perceived language preferences.

Summarizing the studies above, the findings suggest that the ways in which code-switching is used during word searches reflect (a) the speaker's own linguistic preferences and (b) their perception of the hearer's linguistic preferences. Moreover, additional languages to English may or may not be a shared resource among the interlocutors. However, little empirical research has been conducted regarding interactional changes that occur over time in relation to (a) the speaker's own linguistic preferences, (b) the ascription of certain language preferences and competencies to others, and (c) additional languages besides English as a shared resource.

2.3 Epistemics in Interaction

In order to understand the ways in which speakers position themselves and their interlocutors on the grid of linguistic knowledge, analyzing the epistemics of the speakers will be of importance. The way knowledge is managed in interaction is referred to as epistemics, and it is the different ways in which commitment is shown towards what one is saying and in which the speaker's attitudes towards knowledge are reflected (Kärkkäinen 2003). Kamio (1994, 1997) describes the knowing and unknowing positions as being on a continuum, and interactants as having domains of information ("territories of information") that are relatively close to or distant from them compared to their interlocutor. He further argues that this concept encompasses the understanding of not only who knows, but also who has the right to know and express the information (Kamio 1997). Drawing on these ideas, Heritage (2012b) addresses relative epistemic access on a scale ranging from more knowledgeable (K+) to less knowledgeable (K−). In addition, he differentiates between epistemic status and epistemic stance and notes:

> If epistemic status vis-à-vis an epistemic domain is conceived as a somewhat enduring feature of social relationships, epistemic stance by contrast concerns the moment-by-moment expression of these relationships, as managed through the design of turns at talk. (Heritage 2012b: 6)

In other words, epistemic stance refers to the positioning in terms of knowledge displayed in the moment of an utterance, while epistemic status refers to the positioning in terms of knowledge at the social relational level. Heritage (2012a) demonstrates that the K+ and K− positions are displayed through the sequential organization of talk, and the giving and receiving of information are "kept track minutely and publicly" (Heritage 2012a: 48). In Raymond and Heritage (2006), this notion is exemplified during a conversation between a grandmother and another interlocutor, where the grandmother claims more knowledge of the grandchildren over the interlocutor, thus presenting her ownership of the grandchildren and her identity as their grandmother. Therefore, knowledge and situated identities are closely connected and become apparent through the orientation of the participants.

Applying this perspective to the previously mentioned studies by Cogo (2010, 2012) and Greer (2008), it can be said that some participants in multilingual interactions are positioned as non-knowers of a certain language by others. However, the non-knower position can also be displayed by the speaker themselves. Hosoda (2006) analyzed word search sequences between L1 and L2 Japanese speakers, and found the L2 speakers positioning themselves as novice Japanese speakers by explicitly requesting support and thus positioning their L1 interlocutor as the Japanese language expert at that moment. In contrast, Kurhila (2006) found L2 speakers attempting to locate the word by themselves first and then turning to the L1 speaker for help during word search sequences. She claims that by conducting a solitary word search first, the speaker displays that they are potentially in the K+ position and have the linguistic competence to resolve the problem alone. Therefore, analyzing interactions in detail from a participant-oriented perspective – for example using CA – can reveal the participant's perception of their own knowledge and their perception of others' knowledge.

2.4   Conversation Analysis

CA is a method developed by Sacks et al. (1974) for studying a wide range of interactional aspects in the social world. Previous studies have demonstrated CA's ability to display how code-switching functions as contextualization cues (Auer 1984, 1998). CA is not able to elucidate the actual cognitive state of individuals, or to understand why one used a particular language at a certain point. Rather, the assumption of CA is that participants in talk display their own cognitive state through their utterances, and at the same time display their understanding of the interlocutor's utterances (Drew 1995). Therefore, by using CA, the analysis can illuminate the turn-by-turn organization of the interaction as it unfolds, in particular how participants respond to code-switching during word search sequences.

CA was not originally intended to be used for tracking change, and CA's classical assumption is that the speakers' skills remain the same (Brouwer & Wagner 2004). However, recent CA studies, especially from the field of second language acquisition, have demonstrated its potential in tracking change in the participants' language use in interaction over time (e.g. Young and Miller 2004, Hellermann 2006, 2007, Huth 2006, Hellermann & Cole 2008, Hellermann 2009, 2011, Ishida 2009, 2011, Pekarek Doehler & Pochon-Berger 2011, Hauser 2013, Dings 2014, Watanabe 2017).

Building on previous work, the current study adopts an exploratory perspective, focusing on the use of code-switching during ELF interactions between two speakers. Using CA and analyzing the data from an unmotivated perspective (Seedhouse 2004), longitudinal changes in the participants' self-and-other positioning of linguistic preferences during word search sequences was observed.

3   The Study

3.1   The Data

These data were collected in a dormitory at an international university in Japan. In the on-campus university dormitory there were approximately 3,000 residents, mostly first-year students, at the time of data collection. At that time, roughly half of the residents were Japanese and the other half were non-Japanese students from approximately ninety countries around the world.

The two participants in this study are Yoko from Japan (L1 Japanese, L2 English) and Jacy from Thailand (L1 Thai, L2 English) (both pseudonyms). Both participants had entered the university and the dormitory in late March of 2010. In addition, Jacy started studying Japanese from April 2010, and Yoko started studying Thai from October 2010. Yoko had had six years of formal English language education in Japan prior to entering the university. Therefore, English was the main language of communication between the two participants.

The participants made recordings using a video camera in their dormitory rooms or in the shared kitchen. The instructions given by the researcher were limited to the positioning of the camera so that all participants would be visible, and the approximate length of the recording of thirty minutes. The researcher asked the participants to talk freely to each other, and thus no specific instruction was given regarding the content of the interaction. In addition, the researcher was not present during the recordings. The recording dates and lengths are displayed in Table 12.1. In total, approximately 143 minutes of recordings were collected.

Table 12.1 *Recording date and length.*

Date	Length of recording (approximate time in minutes)
July 14, 2010	35
November 30, 2010	37
December 13, 2010	38
February 1, 2011	33

Table 12.2 *The number of word search sequences (WS) and the number of WS that include code-switching (CS).*

	Total number of WS	Total number of CS	CS to Japanese only	CS to Thai only	CS to Thai and Japanese
Jul	9	3	3	0	0
Nov	12	8	3	5	0
Dec	15	9	4	3	2
Feb	13	2	2	0	0

The video recordings were transcribed using CA conventions adapted from Jefferson (2004), and gaze and head movements are described above the speech using conventions adapted from Burch (2014). In addition, screen grabs are shown below the utterance to illustrate the gaze. However, in Excerpt 1, Jacy's gaze is not visible and therefore not marked in the transcript. Non-English words that were used in the interactions are displayed in italics. Translations are provided underneath the non-English words in Excerpt 4; translations for Japanese are marked with a star (*) and translations for Thai are marked with a hash tag (#). Transcription conventions are described in Appendix 12.1.

Table 12.2 displays the number of word search sequences identified from the recordings, whether code-switching was used or not, and if so, to which language. In total, forty-nine word search sequences were identified and analyzed. Of these, code-switching was used in twenty-two sequences: Japanese in twelve sequences, Thai in eight sequences, and both Japanese and Thai in two sequences. Japanese was used during the word search sequences in all recordings, while Thai was used only in November and December. Code-switching was used in various ways during the word searches, for instance, to indicate an ongoing word search, to invite assistance, and as a candidate word. Code-switching to Japanese was frequently found throughout the recordings, and there were several instances when Yoko would teach Japanese to Jacy, and Jacy would teach Thai to Yoko.

4   Analysis and Discussion

The analysis focuses on word search sequences where Yoko displays trouble producing the next utterance and uses code-switching. A line-by-line explanation of the interaction will be presented first, followed by analysis in terms of the epistemic positioning of the participants.

Excerpt 1 is from the first recording Yoko and Jacy made in July, four months after entering the university. Excerpt 1 starts when Yoko is explaining about her volunteer project; Yoko code-switches and uses a Japanese word, *ondoku*. *Ondoku* refers to a read-aloud activity, a frequently used classroom activity in Japan, where students are asked to read aloud a textbook entry. In this sequence, we can observe Jacy's self-and-other positioning as a non-knower of the word *ondoku*.

Excerpt 1 July: Ondoku.

```
         y:      +gz up————+thinking face
1   Yoko:        my project is (0.5)
         j:      +starts music
         y:      ———
2                (0.8)
         y:      +turns head +gz down————
3   Yoko:        .hh huhuhu (.) >my< project is
         y:      ——————————
4                (0.3) <ondoku>.
5   Jacy:        [>ondoku?<
         y:      +gz at J————+gz up-
6   Yoko:        [ehn ondoku is (1.0)
```

"ehn ondoku is"   (1.0)
Jacy   Yoko

```
         y:      +gz turn————+gz down————
7                °like° (0.5) reading books?
```

"like"   "reading books?"

```
         y:      ——————————+gz at J
8                (0.3) very: (.) loud
```

"loud"

```
         y:      ———
9                (2.0)
         y:      ——————————
10  Jacy:        °ah°::: (0.3) °story° ( )=
         y:      +nod————
11  Yoko:        =mmh: mmh:
12  Jacy:        ah ↑huh↓::
```

In line 1, Yoko begins her explanation of the project she is involved in. She is looking up while talking, and then she pauses while displaying a thinking face, indicating an ongoing, solitary word search. Jacy then starts playing music on her computer (line 2). After responding with laughter, Yoko restarts her story while looking down (lines 3, 4). After a slight pause, she then slowly utters a Japanese word, *"ondoku"* (read aloud), with a falling intonation. Yoko then starts to provide an explanation, *"ondoku* is" (line 6), while looking at Jacy. This overlaps with Jacy's utterance, *"ondoku"* with a rising intonation, and she other-initiates other-repair of the word *"ondoku"* (line 5). Yoko, however, pauses and gazes upwards, displaying another ongoing word search. Yoko completes the search with a candidate solution, "reading books very loud" (lines 7–8). Jacy provides her understanding of *ondoku* (line 10: not fully audible), which is then confirmed by Yoko (line 11).

Yoko's action in line 4, where she code-switches into Japanese first and then provides the explanation in English right after, is similar to claims from previous studies that speakers use their L1 to gain processing time in order to access the sought-for word (e.g. Mauranen 2014). We can also observe that, despite starting the clarification turn in line 6, Yoko does not move on to the actual explanation until after Jacy completes saying *"ondoku"* (line 5) and there is a one-second pause while Yoko displays thinking (line 6). Mazeland and Zaman-Zadeh (2004) studied other-initiated word-clarification repairs in Finnish-as-a-lingua-franca interactions. They found that word-clarification is not done as the first option to solve a recipient problem; rather, it is done after other types of repair, such as hearing repair, have been unsuccessful. Svennevig (2008) also found that other-initiated repairs are almost always dealt with as a problem with hearing first, and only afterwards are they treated as problems with understanding or acceptance. Given these studies, in line 6 it can be assumed that Yoko is treating Jacy's other-initiation of repair as an understanding or recognition problem of the Japanese word, rather than a problem with hearing. The repair suggests that Yoko is positioning Jacy as a K– of the word *ondoku*. In addition, in line 10 Jacy displays a change of state ("ah") and her version of the definition, showing that Jacy was in fact unfamiliar with the word *ondoku* prior to Yoko's explanation.

As shown in Table 12.2, there were nine word searches in the recording made in July. Of the nine, there were three cases where the participants used Japanese. One of these cases is displayed in Excerpt 1. The other two cases involved Jacy searching for the Japanese words *tojiru* (close) and *miru* (see), and soliciting Yoko's assistance. These are simple Japanese words that Jacy seems to have had difficulties producing.

Based on the small sample size, it is difficult to claim that the phenomenon shown in Excerpt 1 is a general feature between Yoko and Jacy in July. However, analyzing the sequence using the perspective of epistemic stance, the findings indicate the self-and-other positioning of Yoko in the relative K+ position and Jacy in the K− position of Japanese items in the recording made in July.

Slight changes were observed in their second recording, made in November, four months after the first recording. Excerpt 2 is taken from the November recording. In this segment, Yoko is telling Jacy about needing permission from the university office to put up a poster on the campus bulletin board. When explaining the object that she needs to submit to the university office, Yoko code-switches to Japanese and uses *iraisho,* which can be translated as "request form." The word *iraisho* is not a commonly used word in everyday conversations, but it is used more frequently in a business context. The two speakers move on to a side sequence to negotiate the meaning of *iraisho.* Although Yoko code-switches into Japanese in both Excerpts 1 and 2, and explains the meaning of the word in English, her actions right after the code-switch are slightly different between the two excerpts, suggesting an increase in Japanese words as a shared resource.

Excerpt 2 November: Iraisho.

```
           j:     gz at Y─────────────────
           y:     +gz follow hand move─+gz at J
1   Yoko:         we had to: reserve the board,
           j:     +nod─────────
           y:     ────+turn head +gz up───
2                 (0.3) but- (0.7) he sa:id
```

(image: Yoko and Jacy, labeled "he said")

```
           j:     ─────────────────────
           y:     ─────────────────+gz forward
3                 (.) you need (0.5) ↑iraisho.
           j:     ───
           y:     ───
4                 (0.8)
           j:     ─────────────────
           y:     +gz at J ─────────
```

```
5   Yoko:   °>iraisho<°? (0.3) °irai::sh-°
```

[image: Yoko gesturing, caption "iraisho?"]

```
            j:      ———
            y:      ———
6                   (0.5)
            j:      ——————————————————————————
            y:      ——————————————————+gz at hand
7   Yoko:   add (0.4) °something° (.) de-
```

[image: caption "de"]

```
            j:      ——————
            y:      ——————
8   Jacy:   °permission°=
            j:      —————————+nod & turn head
            y:      +nod turn head +gz at J——————
9   Yoko:   =>yeah yeah< permission form
```

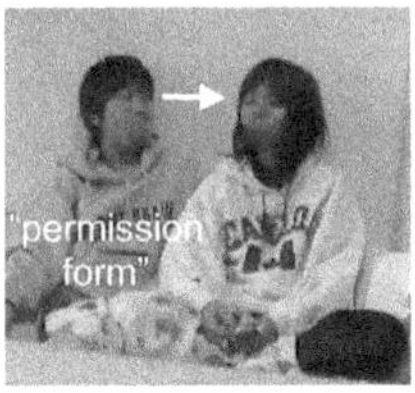

[image: caption "permission form"]

```
            j:      ——————
            y:      ——————
10  Jacy:   $iraisho$ hhu hh
            j:      ——
            y:      ——
11  Yoko:   $iraisho$
            j:      —
            y:      —
12  Jacy:   hhhh
```

In line 2, Yoko disengages her gaze from Jacy and looks upwards, while displaying that she is recalling what the university office worker said to her. She completes her turn by code-switching into Japanese, *"iraisho"* (request form) (line 3). When there is no response from Jacy (line 4), Yoko turns her head towards Jacy and repeats "*iraisho*" in a quick and soft voice, but with a rising intonation to solicit a response (line 5). When there is no immediate response again, Yoko starts to repeat "*iraisho*" again more slowly, but she cuts off (line 5). When there is still no verbal response from Jacy (line 6), Yoko starts to provide an explanation (line 7). However, she pauses and uses a general extender, "something" (line 7) (Hynninen et al. 2017), indicating that she is having trouble producing the appropriate word. Yoko disengages her gaze and starts to gesture by making her thumb and index finger parallel (line 7). Here, Yoko is possibly presenting an iconic gesture of the stamp on the poster that indicates the university office has approved it. Seeing this, Jacy joins the word search and provides a candidate word, "permission" (line 8). Yoko accepts the candidate word with "yeah" and restates "permission form" (line 9). The two speakers then repeat "*iraisho*" with laughter (lines 10, 11).

Lines 1–3 in Excerpt 2 are similar to lines 1–4 Excerpt 1 in the way that Yoko is telling a story, pauses, displays thinking, and ends her turn by code-switching to Japanese with a falling intonation. However, the actions after the code-switching are contrastive. In Excerpt 1, line 6, Yoko immediately begins to explain the meaning of the Japanese word for Jacy, while in Excerpt 2, line 4, Yoko waits for Jacy's response and repeats the potentially troublesome source, taking the silence as an indication of a problem with hearing, at first. Yoko's action of repeating "*iraisho*" could also be her testing whether Jacy knows the word. Either way, up to line 4, Yoko is positioning Jacy as a potential knower of the Japanese word *iraisho*. In addition, Jacy is able to provide an approximate word, "permission," to complete Yoko's word search to explain *iraisho*. This assistance by Jacy may be due to Yoko's gesture and their shared knowledge of the university setting and rules regarding posters, and not Jacy's Japanese knowledge per se. However, the way in which Yoko displays her orientation towards Jacy as a potential knower of the word *iraisho*, and Jacy's involvement in the word search, is contrastive to what has been observed in Excerpt 1. That is, Jacy is self-and-other positioned in the relative K+ position.

In November, there were twelve word search sequences, and of these Japanese was used in three cases. Besides the case displayed in Excerpt 2, one case involved Yoko displaying on ongoing word search with *nani* (what is it), and the other case involved Jacy using *nani* (what is it/what) to prompt Yoko to complete her solitary word search. Therefore, again, the corpus is not large enough to make strong claims that the phenomenon identified in Excerpt 2 is the general trend between the two participants. However, Jacy using Japanese to prompt Yoko to complete her turn also suggests Jacy's increasing use of Japanese.

In the final recording made in February, a further change in self-and-other positioning in terms of a Japanese word was observed, as displayed in Excerpt 3. Excerpt 3 begins when Yoko is sharing her experience volunteering in Thailand. In Excerpt 3, line 11, Yoko explicitly invites Jacy to join her word search and asks for the translation of a Japanese word, *kyushokuhi*, which means "school lunch fee."

Excerpt 3 February: Kyushokuhi.

j: gz at Y————
y: gz down————
1 **Yoko: AH:: in Tubkadard**
j: ——
y: +gz forward
2 **(1.6)**
j: ————————
y: ————————
3 **Yoko: students (0.6) are**
j: ——
y: ——
4 **(4.0)**
j: ——————————————
y: ——————————————
5 **Yoko: have difficulties (0.5) with**
j: ———
y: +gz down
6 **(1.5)**
j: ————
y: +gz at J
7 **Yoko: mmh::**
j: ————
y: ——+gz down
8 **(1.4) (1.0)**
j: ————————
y: ——+gz at J
9 **Yoko: food. ah:**

j: ———
y: ———
10 **Jacy: AH:[::**
j: ——————————————
y: ——————————————
11 **Yoko: [>how to say< *kyushokuhi*.**

j: +gz up
y: ——
12 **(1.4)**

```
          j:      +gz at Y─────
          y:              ─────
13   Jacy:      meal (.) (fee)?
          j:              ─────
          y:              ─────
14   Yoko:      ↑uh:: meals fee
          j:      ─
          y:      +gz forward
15   Jacy:      °uh:°
```

From line 2 through line 8, Yoko pauses multiple times and signals thinking or difficulty with producing her utterance. In lines 6–8, Yoko shifts her gaze down at the table and then looks at Jacy while saying, "mmh," displaying thinking and possibly inviting Jacy to join the word search. When there is no response from Jacy, Yoko tries to complete her turn while gazing down, gesturing a circular shape on the table and uttering "food" with a falling intonation (lines 8–9). Although she completes her sentence, Yoko displays that this is not the word she was searching for by immediately uttering an elongated "ah," accompanied by gazing towards Jacy and indicating that she is still having trouble locating the appropriate word (line 9). Jacy displays that she understands Yoko by using a loud "ah" (line 10). However, Yoko explicitly asks for help to locate the specific word by saying "how to say *kyushokuhi* (school lunch fee)" (line 11). In response, Jacy displays thinking with a 1.4-second silence, while disengaging her gaze from Yoko (line 12). Jacy then provides a candidate word, "meal fee" (however, not fully audible), with a rising intonation, suggesting some uncertainty and prompting confirmation (line 13). Yoko accepts this with no hesitation through a high-pitched "uh" and "meals fee."

Comparing Excerpt 3 to the previous two excerpts, there are again similarities at the beginning of the excerpts, where Yoko displays thinking or searching for a word and then completes it with a candidate word with a falling intonation. However, in Excerpt 3, Yoko does not use Japanese for the candidate word, as in Excerpts 1 and 2. Instead, she uses an approximate word in English ("food") and then explicitly seeks Jacy's help for a translation (lines 9, 11). Yoko's action in line 11 indicates that she positions Jacy as a Japanese user who would know the Japanese word *kyushokuhi*, as well as its English translation. At the same time, Jacy is able to meet these expectations of Yoko's and provide the translation.

In the recording made in February, there were two cases where code-switching was used. The other case of code-switching into Japanese besides Excerpt 2 was when Jacy was rejecting Yoko's other-repair candidate word by saying, "*jyanaiyo*" (that's not it). Although a small sample size, these examples demonstrate that both Yoko and Jacy recognize some Japanese words as a shared resource that both speakers can use for their communication increasingly more often compared to the initial recording made in July.

In addition to English and Japanese, Thai was also used by the participants. As displayed in Table 12.2, Thai was used during the interactions between Yoko and Jacy in ten word search sequences. These cases were identified only in the recordings made in November and December. In addition, in almost all of the word search sequences, Thai was used for a word search marker: *arai na*, which can be translated as "what is it." Both Jacy and Yoko used this phrase. There was one case, however, when Thai was used for a candidate word to complete a word search, as exemplified in Excerpt 4.

Excerpt 4 displays a case in which the speakers used both Japanese and Thai during the word search sequence. The segment starts when Yoko begins a new topic about Christmas being only two weeks away. Yoko code-switches into Thai, using *wan yut*, which means "Saturday Sunday," as a candidate word for her word search. However, the use of this word by Yoko becomes a problematic source and the two speakers negotiate the meaning. In the excerpt, Yoko displays preference towards using Thai in completing her word search, as well as providing a repair when Jacy initiates other-repair.

Excerpt 4 December: Wan Yut.

```
        j:      gz at Y————————————————
        y:      gz up———————————————————
1       Yoko:   a::nd (0.9) I expected that (.)
        j:      ————————————————————————
        y:      ——————————————+gz right +gz up
2               toda:y is ah:: (0.7)     wan ↑yut
```

```
        j:      —
        y:      —
3               (1.6)
        j:      +stick out head (continue gz)
        y:      +gz at J
4       Jacy:   huh?
        j:      —
        y:      —
5               (0.9)
        j:      —
        y:      —
6       Yoko:   wan ↑yut
```

```
       j:      ———
       y:      ———
7              (0.5)
       j:      —————————
       y:      —————————
8      Jacy:   >°wha°< wha:?
       j:      ———————
       y:      ———————
9      Yoko:   wan yut
       j:      ———
       y:      ———
10             (1.1)
       j:      ———————
       y:      ———————
11     Yoko:   wan ↑yut
       j:      ———
       y:      ———
12             (0.5)
       j:      —————————
       y:      —————————
13     Jacy:   °douiuimi°
               *what does that mean*
       j:      ———
       y:      ———
14             (0.6)
       j:      —————————————————
       y:      ———+gz up +gz at J
15     Yoko:   wan (0.6) saoati
               #Saturday Sunday#
```

```
       j:      —————————————————
       y:      —————————————————
16     Jacy:   ah wan ↓yut (0.4) whha
               #holiday#
       j:      —————————————————
       y:      —————————————————
17     Jacy:   hh [huhu $wan ↑yut$
18     Yoko:      [↓yut
       j:      +gz down
       y:      ———
19             (0.5)
       j:      ———+gz at Y—————————
       y:      ————————————————————
20     Jacy:   .hh $imiwa(h)kara(h)naiyo::$[hhh
               *I don't understand the meaning*
```

Development of Shared Multilingual Resources in ELF   327

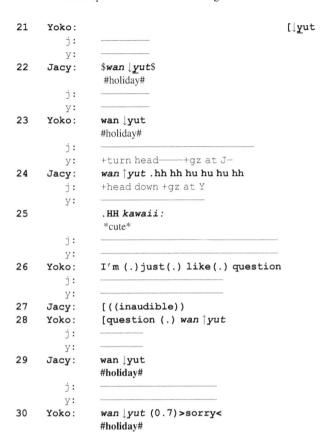

In line 2, Yoko displays that she is searching for a word through sound stretches, pauses, and by moving her gaze away from Jacy. She then provides a candidate word, "*wan yut.*" However, Jacy other-initiates repair through an open class repair initiator, "huh?" (line 4) (Drew 1997). Yoko repeats "*wan yut*" with the same intonation as in line 2, displaying that she understands that Jacy is possibly having trouble hearing the word. However, Jacy still displays non-understanding with "wha," which could be a repetition of "*wan*" or an open class repair initiator "what" with the final sounds cut off (line 8). Yoko continues to provide repair by repeating "*wan yut*" in lines 9 and 11, slightly changing the intonation in line 9. Jacy then explicitly requests the meaning in line 13. She does this by using Japanese "*douiuimi,*" which means "what does that mean?"

Yoko then starts another repair, "*wan,*" and then quickly moves her gaze away from Jacy and back to provide a candidate word, "*saoati,*" which can be translated as "Saturday Sunday" in Thai (line 15). Jacy then finally displays that she has understood with "ah" and by providing her version of the pronunciation "*wan yut*" (line 16). Jacy starts laughing, echoes Yoko's version of "*wan yut*" and says "*imiwakaranaiyo*" (I don't understand the meaning) in Japanese (line 17). During Jacy's response, Yoko repeats "*yut*" with a falling intonation similar to the pronunciation provided by Jacy (lines 18, 21). Jacy says "*wan yut*" again, which Yoko repeats with a similar pronunciation (line 23). Jacy then repeats Yoko's version of "*wan yut*" and starts laughing again (line 24). At the end of her laughing turn, Jacy says "*kawaii*" (cute) in Japanese. Yoko tries to explain that the pronunciation was different since it was a question (lines 26, 28). But Jacy again provides her sample pronunciation of "*wan yut*" (line 29), which Yoko repeats and says "sorry" (line 30).

As seen in Table 12.2, the use of three languages in one word search sequence is not a frequent case in the collection. However, a few interesting observations can be made of this particular sequence. First, Yoko is using Thai, Jacy's L1, to complete her word search (line 2) and to self-repair (line 15). Yoko is thus displaying that she is becoming more comfortable using Thai, and that she has the proficiency to self-repair in Thai. Moreover, lines 18–23, where Jacy repairs Yoko's pronunciation, can be seen as the two speakers "doing pronunciation" (Brouwer 2004) and Jacy displaying her Thai expertise. However, Yoko also attempts to defend her pronunciation by saying that the rising intonation was due to it being a question (lines 26, 28). Therefore, Yoko is displaying her increased confidence and preference towards using Thai during word search sequences, which was not identified in July.

Along with the above, Jacy is using Japanese, Yoko's L1, to initiate repair (line 13) and to respond to Yoko's pronunciation (lines 20, 25). By responding in Japanese, Jacy displays that she is becoming more comfortable speaking in Japanese. In addition, code-switching into Japanese during her laughter in lines 16–25 seems to bring a rapport-building function (Kalocsai 2011). That is, even though Jacy's laughter could potentially be received as laughter at Yoko's mistake, there seems to be no negativity between the two participants.

Finally, Yoko and Jacy's multilingual use in interaction is similar to Cogo's (2012) study on "super-diversity," and possibly reflects the multilingual interactional context in which the two participants are situated (i.e. an international university dormitory). Yoko and Jacy's actions also resonate with the exchange students in Kalocsai's (2009) study, where they code-switched to various languages when they talked, calling it "Erasmus English." In fact, students at this international university also mentioned learning each other's L1s and using several languages when they talked, calling it "AP language," taking the acronym of the name of the university. Therefore, Yoko and Jacy using each other's L1s could be seen as them displaying membership of the international dormitory and mutually accommodating each other (Cogo 2009).

To summarize the analyses from an epistemic perspective, in July, Yoko and Jacy both positioned Jacy as a non-knower of Japanese during the word search sequence. In November, Yoko explored the possibility of Jacy knowing a Japanese word and initially positioned Jacy in the K+ position. However, Jacy required support, such as Yoko's gesture, in order to reach a mutual understanding. In December, Jacy used Japanese words to initiate repair and respond to Yoko's reply, presenting herself as a knower of certain Japanese words. Then in February, Yoko positioned Jacy as a possible knower of a Japanese word, and Jacy was able to adhere to this through the word search sequence. In terms of Thai, in July, there was no use of Thai during word searches. However, during November and December, both Yoko and Jacy used Thai during the word searches. In December, Yoko presented candidate words and self-repaired in Thai during the word search sequence, and exhibited herself as a knower of certain Thai words. Thus, the speakers presented their perception of a gradual increase in their own linguistic resource, as well as their shared linguistic resources of words in Japanese and Thai during the word search sequences. Although these perceptions were sometimes inaccurate, as seen in Excerpts 2 and 4, the excerpts reflect how the speakers explore the boundaries of their overlapping linguistic resources.

In addition, code-switching during the word search was flagged by Yoko during the interaction in July when she immediately attempted to provide a translation, while in November and onwards, unsolicited translations were not identified. The change in flagging behavior between Yoko and Jacy aligns with Smit (2010) and Pietikäinen's (2014) findings on non-flagged code-switching use between speakers who have established a mutual recognition of the interactional resources they share over time. Pitzl (2016) discusses how speakers in ELF interactions, in theory, have "individual multilingual repertoires (IMRs)," which are "all the linguistic resources a person has at their disposal" (Pitzl 2016: 298), and a "multilingual resource pool (MRP)," where the individual multilingual repertoires overlap and both speakers can potentially share the same linguistic resource. Although it is impossible to actually identify the boundaries of the IMR or MRP, Pitzl's (2016) broad concept gives us a starting point to understand why speakers would flag code-switching with some speakers and not with others. That is, speakers may learn other languages and also recognize that they share some interactional resources over time.

This study is not claiming that the participants have full access to the language system or that they share identical linguistic resources. In addition, the code-switched words are different in all of the examples, and the sample size is limited. However, the self-and-other positioning of the participants on a grid of knowledge during the interaction can be seen as gradually changing over time. In other words, the participants' perception of Japanese and Thai as a readily referable linguistic resource for communication between them gradually changed over time.

5   Conclusion

The current study investigated changes in multilingual use by ELF speakers during word search sequences over time. The analyses displayed changes in the speakers' self-and-other positioning of knowing a code-switched word: from a non-knower, to a possible knower, and then to a knower. In addition, the data demonstrated emergent use of a third language during a word search that was not initially used, indicating changes in linguistic resources and preferences.

Previous studies have discussed languages other than English as shared resources that may not be available from the speakers' first encounters, but may instead be discovered or learned through multiple encounters over time (Smit 2010, Pietikäinen 2014, Jenkins 2015). The current study is one of the few studies to capture the changes in the speakers' perception of shared resources in ELF interaction over time. The findings indicate that speakers can increase their use of additional languages in ELF interactions as they learn each other's L1s, and this increase in shared linguistic resources is recognized by the interlocutor. The study builds on accumulating research demonstrating multilingual use in ELF interactions, and suggests the need for more studies that track the same speakers longitudinally, which will be valuable to understand the changes in interactional features over time.

Appendix 12.1 Transcription conventions.

(Adapted from Jefferson [2004] and Burch [2014].)

(.)	Short, untimed pause
(0.3), (2.6)	Duration of silence in seconds
CAPS	Relatively high volume
↑word, ↓word	Pitch rise or fall in the next phrase
$word$	Smiley voice
A: word[word B: [word	Overlapping talk
ha ha, huh, heh	Laughter, depending on the sounds produced
(h), (hh)	Laughter within a word
.hhh	A dot-prefixed row indicates inbreath
wo:::rd	Colons show extension of the sound before it
Word	Underlining indicates some form of stress
A: word= B: =word	Latching speech
°word°	Utterance that is quieter than the surrounding talk
>word word<	Inward arrows show faster speech
?	Question mark indicates rising intonation
(word), ( )	Word or parts of a word transcriber is unsure of or was inaudible
((sobbing))	Other details of the conversational scene

Special conventions

Gz	Gaze
+	Place where action begins, description of action
——	Holding gaze or continued action
word	Translation of a Japanese word
#word#	Translation of a Thai word

REFERENCES

Archibald, Alasdair, Alessia Cogo & Jennifer Jenkins. 2011. *Latest Trends in ELF Research*. Newcastle upon Tyne: Cambridge Scholars Publishing.

Auer, Peter. 1984. *Bilingual Conversation*. Amsterdam & Philadelphia: John Benjamins.

1998. *Code-Switching in Conversation: Language, Interaction and Identity*. London & New York: Routledge.

Brouwer, Catherine E. 2003. Word searches in NNS–NS interaction: Opportunities for language learning? *The Modern Language Journal* 87(4), 534–545. doi: 10.1111/1540-4781.00206.

2004. Doing pronunciation: A specific type of repair sequence. In Rod Gardner & Johannes Wagner (eds.), *Second Language Conversations*, 93–113. London: Continuum.

Brouwer, Catherine E. & Johannes Wagner. 2004. Developmental issues in second language conversation. *Journal of Applied Linguistics* 1(1), 30–47.

Burch, Alfred R. 2014. Pursuing information: A conversation analytic perspective on communication strategies. *Language Learning* 64(3), 651–684.

Cogo, Alessia. 2009. Accommodating difference in ELF conversations: A study of pragmatic strategies. In Anna Mauranen & Elina E. Ranta (eds.), *English as a Lingua Franca: Studies and Findings*, 254–273. Newcastle upon Tyne: Cambridge Scholars Publishing.

2010. Strategic use and perceptions of English as a Lingua Franca. *Poznań Studies in Contemporary Linguistics* 46(3), 295–312. doi: 10.2478/v10010-010-0013-7.

2012. ELF and super-diversity: A case study of ELF multilingual practices from a business context. *Journal of English as a Lingua Franca* 1(2), 287–313. doi:10.1515/jelf-2012-0020.

2017. ELF and multilingualism. In Jennifer Jenkins, Will Baker & Martin Dewey (eds.), *The Routledge Handbook of English as a Lingua Franca*, 357–368. London, New York: Routledge.

Cogo, Alessia & Martin Dewey. 2012. *Analysing English as a Lingua Franca: A Corpus-Driven Investigation*. London: Continuum.

Dings, Abby. 2014. Interactional competence and the development of alignment activity. *The Modern Language Journal* 98(3), 742–756. doi: 10.1111/modl.12120.

Drew, Paul. 1995. Conversation analysis. In Jonathan A. Smith, Rom Hareé & Luk van Langenhove (eds.), *Rethinking Methods in Psychology*, 64–79. London: Sage Publications.

1997. "Open" class repair initiators in response to sequential sources of troubles in conversation. *Journal of Pragmatics* 28(1), 69–101.

Funayama, Izumi. 2002. Word-searches in cross-linguistic settings: Teaching-learning collaboration between native and non-native speakers. *Crossroads of Language, Interaction, and Culture* 4, 33–57.

Goodwin, Marjorie Harness. 1983. Searching for a word as an interactive activity. In John N. Deely & Margot D. Lenhart (eds.), *Semiotics*, 129–137. New York: Plenum.

Goodwin, Marjorie Harness & Charles Goodwin. 1986. Gesture and coparticipation in the activity of searching for a word. *Semiotica* 62(1/2), 51–75.

Greer, Tim. 2008. Accomplishing difference in bilingual interaction: Translation as backwards-oriented medium repair. *Multilingua-Journal of Cross-Cultural and Interlanguage Communication* 27(1–2), 99–127.

2013. Word search sequences in bilingual interaction: Codeswitching and embodied orientation toward shifting participant constellations. *Journal of Pragmatics* 57, 100–117.

Hauser, Eric. 2013. Stability and change in one adult's second language English negation. *Language Learning* 63(3), 463–498. doi: 10.1111/lang.12012.
Hellermann, John. 2006. Classroom interactive practices for developing L2 literacy: A microethnographic study of two beginning adult learners of English. *Applied Linguistics* 27(3), 377–404.
 2007. The development of practices for action in classroom dyadic interaction: Focus on task openings. *The Modern Language Journal* 91(1), 83–96.
 2009. Looking for evidence of language learning in practices for repair: A case study of self-initiated self-repair by an adult learner of English. *Scandinavian Journal of Educational Research* 53(2), 113–132.
 2011. Members' methods, members' competencies: Looking for evidence of language learning in longitudinal investigations of other-initiated repair. In Joan Kelly Hall, John Hellermann & Simona Pekarek Doehler (eds.), *L2 Interactional Competence and Development*, 147–172. Bristol: Multilingual Matters.
Hellermann, John & Elizabeth Cole. 2008. Practices for social interaction in the language-learning classroom: Disengagements from dyadic task Interaction. *Applied Linguistics* 30(2), 186–215.
Heritage, John. 2012a. The epistemic engine: Sequence organization and territories of knowledge. *Research on Language and Social Interaction* 45(1), 30–52.
 2012b. Epistemics in action: Action formation and territories of knowledge. *Research on Language and Social Interaction* 45(1), 1–29.
Hosoda, Yuri. 2006. Repair and relevance of differential language expertise in second language conversations. *Applied Linguistics* 27(1), 25–50. doi: 10.1093/applin/ami022.
House, Juliane. 2016. Own-language use in academic discourse in English as a lingua franca. In Kumiko Murata (ed.), *Exploring ELF in Japanese Academic and Business Contexts*, 59–70. London: Routledge.
Hülmbauer, Cornelia. 2009. "We don't take the right way. We just take the way that we think you will understand" – The shifting relationship between correctness and effectiveness in ELF. In Anna Mauranen & Elina E. Ranta (eds.), *English as a Lingua Franca: Studies and Findings*, 323–347. Newcastle upon Tyne: Cambridge Scholars Publishing.
Huth, Thorsten. 2006. Negotiating structure and culture: L2 learners' realization of L2 compliment-response sequences in talk-in-interaction. *Journal of Pragmatics* 38 (12), 2025–2050.
Hynninen, Niina, Kaisa S. Pietikäinen & Svetlana Vetchinnikova. 2017. Multilingualism in English as a Lingua Franca: Flagging as an indicator of perceived acceptability and intelligibility. In Arja Nurmi, Tanja Rütten & Päivi Pahta (eds.), *Challenging the Myth of Monolingual Corpora*, 95–126. Leiden: Brill.
Ishida, Midori. 2009. Development of interactional competence: Changes in the use of *ne* in L2 Japanese during study abroad. In Hanh Thi Nguyen & Gabriele Kasper (eds.), *Talk-in-Interaction: Multilingual Perspectives*, 351–385. Honolulu: National Foreign Language Resource Center, University of Hawaii at Manoa.
 2011. Engaging in another person's telling as a recipient in L2 Japanese: Development of interactional competence during one-year study abroad. In Gabriele Pallotti & Johannes Wagner (eds.), *L2 Learning as Social Practice:*

Conversation-Analytic Perspectives, 45–86. Honolulu: National Foreign Language Resource Center, University of Hawaii at Manoa.

Jefferson, Gail. 1972. Side sequences. In David Sudnow (ed.), *Studies in Social Interaction*, 294–338. New York: The Free Press.

2004. Glossary of transcript symbols with an introduction. In Gene H. Lerner (ed.), *Conversation Analysis: Studies from the First Generation*, 13–23. Philadelphia: John Benjamins.

Jenkins, Jennifer. 2015. Repositioning English and multilingualism in English as a lingua franca. *Englishes in Practice* 2(3), 49–85.

Kalocsai, Karolina. 2009. Erasmus exchange students: A behind-the-scenes view into an ELF community of practice. *Apples – Journal of Applied Language Studies* 3(1), 25–49.

2011. The show of interpersonal involvement and the building of rapport in an ELF community of practice. In Alasdair Archibald, Alessia Cogo & Jennifer Jenkins (eds.), *Latest Trends in English as a Lingua Franca Research*, 113–138. Newcastle upon Tyne: Cambridge Scholars Publishing.

Kamio, Akio. 1994. The theory of territory of information: The case of Japanese. *Journal of Pragmatics* 21(1), 67–100.

1997. *Territory of Information*. Vol. 48. Amsterdam: John Benjamins.

Kärkkäinen, Elise. 2003. *Epistemic Stance in English Conversation, Pragmatics and Beyond New Series*. Amsterdam & Philadelphia: John Benjamins.

Klimpfinger, Theresa. 2007. "Mind you sometimes you have to mix" – The role of code-switching in English as a lingua franca. *Vienna English Working Papers* 16(2), 36–61.

2009. "She's mixing the two languages together" – Forms and functions of code-switching in English as a Lingua Franca. In Anna Mauranen & Elina Ranta (eds.), *English as a Lingua Franca: Studies and Findings*, 348–371. Newcastle upon Tyne: Cambridge Scholars Publishing.

Kurhila, Salla. 2006. *Second Language Interaction*. Amsterdam; Philadelphia: John Benjamins.

Mauranen, Anna. 2012. *Exploring ELF: Academic English Shaped by Non-Native Speakers*. Cambridge: Cambridge University Press.

2014. Lingua franca discourse in academic contexts: Shaped by complexity. In John Flowerdew (ed.), *Discourse in Context: Contemporary Applied Linguistics*, 225–245. London: Bloomsbury Academic.

Mauranen, Anna & Ida Mauko. 2019. ELF among multilingual practices in a trialingual university. In Jennifer Jenkins & Anna Mauranen (eds.), *Linguistic Diversity on the EMI Campus: Insider Accounts of the Use of English and Other Languages in Universities within Asia, Australasia, and Europe*. Abingdon & New York: Routledge.

Mazeland, Harrie & Minna Zaman-Zadeh. 2004. The logic of clarification: Some observations about word-clarification repairs in Finnish-as-a-lingua-franca interactions. In Rod Gardner & Johannes Wagner (eds.), *Second Language Conversations*, 132–156. London: Continuum.

Mori, Junko & Atsushi Hasegawa. 2009. Doing being a foreign language learner in a classroom: Embodiment of cognitive states as social events. *IRAL – International Review of Applied Linguistics in Language Teaching* 47(1), 65–94. doi: 10.1515/iral.2009.004.

Pekarek Doehler, Simona & Evelyne Pochon-Berger. 2011. Developing "methods" for interaction: A cross-sectional study of disagreement sequences in French L2. In Joan Kelly Hall, John Hellermann & Simona Pekarek Doehler (eds.), *L2 Interactional Competence and Development*, 206–243. Bristol: Multilingual Matters.

Pietikäinen, Kaisa S. 2014. ELF couples and automatic code-switching. *Journal of English as a lingua franca* 3(1), 1–26.

2017. *English as a Lingus Franca in Intercultural Relationships: Interaction, Identity, and Multilingual Practices of ELF Couples*. Unpublished doctoral dissertation. Department of Modern Languages, University of Helsinki.

Pitzl, Marie-Luise. 2016. World Englishes and creative idioms in English as a lingua franca. *World Englishes* 35(2), 293–309. doi: 10.1111/weng.12196.

Pölzl, Ulrike. 2003. Signalling cultural identity: The use of L1/Ln in ELF. *View [z]–Vienna English Working Papers* 12(2), 3–23.

Poplack, Shana. 2001. Code-switching (linguistic). In Neil J. Smelser and Paul B. Baltes (eds.), *International Encyclopedia of the Social and Behavioral Sciences*, 2062–2065. Amsterdam: Elsevier Science.

Raymond, Geoffrey & John Heritage. 2006. The epistemics of social relations: Owning grandchildren. *Language in Society* 35(5), 677–705. doi: 10.1017/S0047404506060325.

Sacks, Harvey, Emanuel Schegloff & Gail Jefferson. 1974. A simplest systematics for the organization of turn-taking for conversation. *Language* 50(4), 696–735.

Schegloff, Emanuel. 1984. On some gestures' relation to talk. In J. Maxwell Atkinson & John Heritage (eds.), *Structures of Social Action: Studies in Conversation Analysis*, 266–296. Cambridge: Cambridge University Press.

Schegloff, Emanuel, Gail Jefferson & Harvey Sacks. 1977. The preference for self-correction in the organization of repair in conversation. *Language* 53(2), 361–382.

Seedhouse, Paul. 2004. *The Interactional Architecture of the Language Classroom: A Conversation Analysis Perspective*. Malden: Blackwell.

Seidlhofer, Barbara. 2011. *Understanding English as a Lingua Franca*. Oxford: Oxford University Press.

Smit, Ute. 2010. *English as a Lingua Franca in Higher education: A Longitudinal Study of Classroom Discourse*. Vol. 2. Berlin: Walter de Gruyter.

Svennevig, Jan. 2008. Trying the easiest solution first in other-initiation of repair. *Journal of Pragmatics* 40(2), 333–348.

Watanabe, Aya. 2017. Developing L2 interactional competence: Increasing participation through self-selection in post-expansion sequences. *Classroom Discourse* 8(3), 271–293.

Young, Richard F. & Elizabeth R. Miller. 2004. Learning as changing participation: Discourse roles in ESL writing conferences. *The Modern Language Journal* 88, 519–535.

13 The Role of Translanguaging in ELF Advice Sessions for Asylum Seekers

Alessia Cogo

1 Introduction

This chapter explores the role of multilingual resources in English as a lingua franca (ELF) advice practices at a UK charity supporting refugees and asylum seekers. Previous research has highlighted how multilingualism is an essential aspect of ELF (Jenkins 2015), and the role of multilingual resources has received increased attention in the latest conceptualizations and linguistic analysis. However, the contribution and nature of multilingualism in relation to ELF need to be further investigated, especially in relation to the functions of multilingual resources. This paper addresses the role of multilingual resources in ELF conversations, focusing on their functions in high-stakes environments such as advice services for refugees and asylum seekers.

The context of exploration is a London-based UK charity supporting refugees and asylum seekers and providing advice services for them. Advice sessions are interesting contexts of intercultural negotiations and high-stakes situations for the migrants seeking advice. In this chapter, I first explore the theoretical framework on which the research was based, and then explain the linguistic ethnographic approach taken to collect and analyse the data. The qualitative analysis of the data shows the complexity of advice practices in relation to the use of multilingual resources in ELF, and demonstrates how translanguaging can be used for at least three functions: pedagogical, explanatory and interpersonal.

2 Theoretical Framework: ELF and Translanguaging Practices

In recent years, a growing body of work has emphasized the need for a theoretical shift in applied and sociolinguistics in the way we conceptualize language, from a view that prioritizes 'reified systems' to a conceptualization of language as 'social practice' (Heller 2007; Blommaert 2010). Rather than working with homogeneity, stability and boundedness as the starting assumptions, 'mobility, mixing, political dynamics and historical embedding are now central concerns in the study of languages' (Blommaert & Rampton 2011: 3).

The notion of translanguaging has been introduced to emphasize the permeability of languages and linguistic repertoires (García 2009; García & Li 2014). In this sense, translanguaging is essentially about a paradigm shift in the study of language, which involves fundamental changes to the way language is conceptualized. This position developed against an additive view of bilingualism as two linear wholes that can be separated and counted, which no longer holds (Grosjean 1982). In this view, meaning-making is not confined to the use of 'languages' as a discrete and fixed set of resources, but to translanguaging as a holistic practice where signs are available for meaning-making in repertoires that extend beyond socially constructed 'languages'. In translanguaging, therefore, meaning is not necessarily in the very act of switching from one language to the other (as in the code-switching, more structural view of language alternation), although this is also possible, but in the full use of resources, which is normalized without functional or diglossic separation (García 2009). However, more recent research has focused on translanguaging as an umbrella term, which includes code-switching practice and functional separation, rather than keeping these as completely separate language alternation phenomena.

Translanguaging is also viewed from a social perspective, within a social justice and pedagogical fairness approach. Conteh maintains that translanguaging needs to be theorized for pedagogy as a 'predominantly social', rather than linguistic, practice, and thus related to identity, culture and context (Conteh 2018, 2019). Then the emphasis shifts from merely exploring linguistic diversity per se to translanguaging, which allows for appreciation of the learner's/speaker's cultural background, especially when translanguaging includes 'minority' languages and disadvantaged communities (like the refugees in this study). Conteh and Brock (2011) have also identified the 'safe places' where bilingual education can take place successfully in communities of minority language speakers, and how educators and family can support the development of a safe place. To this, other researchers have also added the potential for change and creativity. García and Li (2014) posit the idea of 'translanguaging spaces' where individuals critically and creatively engage their own experiences and those of others, often with transformative effect.

Translanguaging, then, is a possible practice of any multilingual, independently of proficiency in socially constructed languages. In other words, both equal bilinguals – that is, bilinguals that have similar competence in all languages in their repertoire – and emergent bilinguals – those at the early stages of learning a language – can engage in translanguaging to communicate (Blommaert & Rampton 2011; Lewis et al. 2012), independently of how proficient a speaker is in any 'language'.

Research in ELF has also contributed to highlighting its multilingual nature and addressed translanguaging practices as an aspect of ELF (Cogo 2018). Researchers have engaged in conceptualizing ELF from a multilingual perspective (cf. Seidlhofer 2011; Mauranen 2012, 2013; Jenkins 2015) and in identifying multilingual practices that are both used in a more *overt* way, by the obvious use of resources pertaining to different languages (words from Spanish or Arabic used in a code-switching mode in ELF conversation), and *covert* resources, which involve multilingual resources in a more cognitive way, where the influences of the L1 or other resources are not visible in conversation but are present in the cognitive repertoire of participants (Cogo 2016a). Even in this apparently 'only English' mode, the multilingual influence is still present.

In this perspective, ELF research has begun to explore the flexible and dynamic use of multilingual resources in highly mobile or super-diverse contexts (Cogo 2012), especially focusing on the speakers and their repertoires. The notion of *repertoire* (cf. Blommaert & Backus 2011) has become more important for ELF research as it moves away from analysing 'complete' language knowledge to the whole range of sociolinguistic and cultural resources (such as any bit of language) that speakers may know and bring into the exchange. Repertoire entails moving away from conceptualizing the dynamic and changeable translanguaging practices as deficient realizations of monolingual communication. Through translanguaging, all the linguistic resources that speakers have learnt or encountered in their lives may become relevant and may possibly be used in their communication. These can range from resources learnt formally in educational environments to entirely informal pieces of language and mere exposure to different languages. This collection of resources is strictly linked with the biographical experiences of individual users, and the repertoires are therefore also dynamic and fluid, as they constantly change with the addition of new resources, the temporary loss or underuse of others and the exposure or loss of exposure to still other resources.

Translanguaging practices may also take place with different kinds of users. For instance, work on translanguaging in ELF business discourse (Cogo 2012) has shown how business professionals can engage in translanguaging to cover various functions, such as to expand and clarify meaning, or to conceptually refer to a specific idea, such as when a specific concept is not easily translatable or simply without functional identification – that is, because translanguaging is the common practice in that context. While functional separation resembles code-switching in the structural sense, these practices all connect to the idea of a flexible and fluid use of resources, which may or may not serve specific functions in the exchange. So code-switching for specific functions can become part of the wider translanguaging practices of a community of speakers.

However, research has focused particularly on the potential for translanguaging, especially in relation to resistance to monolingual ideologies and practices, but less on how the use of multilingual resources is actually limited by constraints related to the context, the ideological pressures of the institutional requirements and the societal discourses (see Blackledge & Creese 2010; Dorn et al. 2014). For instance, in research concerning BELF contexts, translanguaging practices have been shown 'to be kept for the internal and informal kind of communication, the emergent, un-regulated and non-ratified practices' (Cogo 2016b: 46), rather than the written and more formal documents. This is something that came out quite prominently in the data collected among asylum seekers for this project, where the extent of translanguaging practices is clearly influenced by the local, national and institutional discourses and ideologies that circulate in relation to immigration in the local context.

This paper ascribes to García and Li (2014)'s translanguaging perspective, which implies a flexible and dynamic view of multilingual resources and the permeability of languages. This perspective is not in opposition to code-switching, but is in addition to this view and includes it as one possible multilingual practice, alongside more flexible and dynamic uses of resources. Studies have shown that translanguaging may cover specific functions, such as pedagogical, explanatory and interpersonal. In the pedagogical context, translanguaging can be used to encourage participation in class activities, to engage learners and to facilitate the management of tasks (Creese & Blackledge 2010; Cenoz & Gorter 2011). Translanguaging is also used for interpersonal functions, such as creating rapport and establishing solidarity among speakers (Cogo 2012; Vettorel 2014), but also for an explanatory function, where it can be used to expand on meaning or engage in negotiation of non-understanding (Cogo 2009).

3 The Focus: Formal and Informal Advice for Migrants

This study was conducted in a charity supporting refugees and asylum seekers in London, UK. The charity helps migrants in difficult situations, independent of their status (i.e. whether they are old or new migrants, residents, destitute migrants, asylum seekers, refugees, etc.), by offering support for their basic needs, such as food, clothing and shelter, and also by offering advice to support them through the hurdles of life and migration in the UK.

The advice support is the focus of this chapter. Advice and advocacy services constitute a considerable part of the work done by migrant charities. The aim of the services is to help vulnerable people from refugee and migrant backgrounds to address their experiences of destitution and exclusion. The kind of help they seek from the advice sessions is related to their immigration status, but not only to do with this. They deal with issues of poverty, problems with accommodation and lack of knowledge and skills. Underlying all this is the perceived need for the advisor to help them with their English skills when dealing with external agencies or providers of help.

There are a number of reasons for my focus on advice sessions within the ecology of the charity. First, these sessions provide the opportunity to examine ELF in action in a high-stakes environment, in contrast to the majority of ELF studies so far, with some exceptions (Guido 2012). Second, these events are also characterized by time pressure, because the advisors are busy and have to attend to many migrants per day. Therefore, the sessions are supposed to be efficient moments of crucial problem solving. So, in this context, it is interesting to explore to what extent speakers exploit multilingual/translanguaging practice and go beyond language separation, and for what purposes, if any.

The following questions directed this study:

1. What are the differences between multilingual/translanguaging practices used in formal and informal advice sessions?
2. What are the functions of the multilingual/translanguaging practices used in formal and informal advice sessions?

The research questions presuppose a distinction between formal and informal advice sessions – the first are carried out by officially designated advisors or case officers that take on a list of migrants according to the issue and their expertise (some advisors would deal with accommodation issues, some with benefits, others with funding, etc.); the second are informal advice sessions, which are carried out ad hoc by volunteer migrants that have lived in the country for a while and are familiar with the issues that a fellow migrant is facing. Different levels of engagement with multilingual resources were noticed in these two kinds of advice service, with more use of multilingual resources in informal sessions, especially with 'minority languages', and only limited use of multilingual resources in formal sessions. Therefore, the interest lies in seeing which functions are covered by these resources and whether there is a difference between the functions covered in formal and informal sessions.

4   Methodology

A number of data sources were collected, including audio recordings of advice sessions, interviews with staff, volunteers and users at the charity, a focus group and observations. The quantity of data collected and the participants involved are listed in Table 13.1.

The main data set for this paper is the recordings of advice sessions (both formal, in the form of audio recordings, and informal, in the form of observations/vignettes), which help to answer the first research question. The audio recordings, interviews, focus group and observations contribute to answering the second research question.

Table 13.1 *Data collected.*

Quantity	Kind of data collected	Participants
19	Advice and advocacy sessions (6 hours and 22 seconds in total)	Advocate/advisor and migrant
7	Interviews (20–40 minutes in length each)	Researchers and advisors/migrants
1	Focus group (1 hour and 16 minutes)	Researchers and volunteers/staff
1 month	Observations: 1 month of notes/progress sheets collection from three charity centres	All staff, volunteers, stakeholders and migrants

The advice sessions are meetings held at the charity between a migrant and an advisor. Sometimes the advisor is a volunteer and at other times a charity member of staff. The advisor can also be shadowed by a volunteer who is doing advisory training or similar. After the session the advisor normally fills in a progress report form, which includes information about the migrant receiving advice, the issue addressed, any actions taken and any further comments of relevance to the case discussed. However, apart from these typical advice sessions, the staff and volunteers also find themselves offering informal advice to migrants, especially when catching up with them about their situation or when quickly checking something for them (by making a phone call or searching the Internet). Informal advice is also given out by peers, when migrants befriend each other and help each other to solve daily issues of different kinds. This kind of informal advice is very frequent and is not normally recorded in progress forms or other kinds of documentation, but it is noted in the observations and, as shown later in some vignettes, it is equally important for the migrants, and for this project it is important to provide an ecological understanding of the charity's linguistic practices.

Two kinds of interview were carried out: one with the advisors and one with the migrants. The aims of the interviews were related to the advice sessions that they had just taken part in and more generally about advice services in the charity. The participants answered questions general questions about their work in the charity, and specifically in relation to the linguistic resources or strategies used and the motivation for their use. Similarly, the focus group session was carried out with the staff and volunteers at the charity, and it was a general discussion about advice services and their view of the services – what worked and what did not work.

The methodology adopted in this study is that of linguistic ethnography (Copland & Creese 2015), a qualitative approach which privileges the study of sociolinguistic phenomena from the point of view of the participants and sees them embedded in the wider social context and structures. Linguistic ethnography provides a suitable methodology for this study for various reasons. First, it provides a snapshot of the charity practices at any one moment, by combining both linguistic- and ethnographic-oriented data (such as the data collected in this study), thus offering in-depth understanding of the complex sociolinguistic relations at work in such an organization at that time. Second, ethnography is also a historical method and therefore allows researchers to make connections with past and future practices, power relations and expectations – and it therefore sees current practices as dynamic and flexible (for instance, by the time of writing, some of the practices in place at the beginning of the researcher's time working with the charity had already slightly changed). Third, this methodological approach also allows, and in fact encourages, collaboration with the participants/volunteers as novice researchers. This study is based on linguistic ethnography within community-based practices, which involves collecting data and discussing the context and the findings with the people[1] who are familiar with the charity and have been involved with it on a long-term basis. Finally, the researcher and author of the paper is also a participant/volunteer in the charity, and this ethnographic perspective has allowed access to people and places, as well as a deeper understanding of the context.

A total of twenty-one staff and volunteers took part in the project and around 200 migrants were present during the data collection at the three charity centres. All these participants were part of the observation notes, but a limited number took part in the audio recordings of the advice sessions, interviews and the focus group.[2] The staff, volunteers and migrants together speak a wide range of languages, with staff/volunteers speaking Arabic, English, Farsi, French, German, Italian, Norwegian, Polish and Spanish, and migrants speaking mainly Albanian, Arabic, English, Farsi, French, German, Italian, Pashto, Russian, Somali, Spanish, Tigrigna and Urdu.

5   Data Analysis

From the observation data it is noted that in the open space of the charity premises, multilingual practices go on at all times and the charity itself seems to be 'a multilingual ELF safe space', where charity users, staff and volunteers capitalize on, adapt and experience various kinds of multilingual resources.

---

[1] This study was conducted with the help of three volunteers who collaborated with the main researcher/author of this paper in setting up the study and collecting data in the charity. These are Ali, Aileen and Lounja. They have been invaluable cooperators without whom the data collection would not have been possible.

[2] All participants (staff, volunteers and migrants) had been informed about the research project on exploring the advice services, and were reminded about the aim of the project before the data collection or recording started. Both the researcher's institution and the charity taking part in the study approved all ethical procedures.

The general atmosphere is one of appreciation and engagement with multilingualism in the safe space of the informal charity environment, although, as explored later, this is not free from contextual and ideological constraints.

The initial observations showed the extent of the difference between the formal and informal advice offered at the charity in relation to multilingual resources. The formal advice sessions would seem to make less use of overt multilingual resources and more use of negotiation and covert multilingual resources. On the other hand, the informal advice and peer conversations showed use of multilingual resources between volunteers who could speak the languages of the migrants or were learning them (for instance, Arabic, which is one of the most common), or between more expert migrants from the same linguistic background who tried to help new migrants with advice. In the following section I will first show vignette examples from the observations of informal advice (which were not audio recorded, but were noted as part of the observation collection of data), and then give examples from the transcripts of recorded formal advice sessions, interviews and the focus group.

5.1   Informal Advice Sessions

The following observations (in Vignette 1) were collected by one of the volunteer researchers and they highlight how informal advice is a common practice among peer migrants, not only between volunteers and migrants.

> Vignette 1: A normal day at the centre, with lunch being served at 12 noon, after which advice sessions going on in different parts of the hall, ESOL classes start at 1:30 and various groups of clients gather around tables in the hall. The Kurdish people on one, the Syrians, the Nigerian women and their kids, a couple of Albanian from Kosovo and the Iranians. I went around and asked some of them what they were talking about: mainly life in London, how to make applications for different services, immigration issues, some parenting advice and education matters. They mainly spoke their local languages and English. I talked with S and B (volunteers) about these groupings and they were very positive about the impact of the group discussion, and the emotional and mental support work done by the group members.

Vignette 1 reproduces common reflections on the natural group formation in the charity, whereby migrants naturally gravitate towards people with a similar sociocultural background who speak their language. Staff and volunteers at the charity see these groups, and the languages spoken in them, as positive ways of peers providing emotional and practical support, especially more experienced migrants advising more recent ones. Though staff and volunteers do encourage migrants to learn English, go to ESOL classes and practise as much as possible, they also recognize the value of the migrants' group support and encourage informal advice in their language.

In the following vignette, the informal peer-to-peer advice session is the focus of analysis. V is a migrant volunteer who moved to the UK about ten years ago, speaks Urdu and English, has leave to remain in the country and has done various applications for refugee status and related administrative matters. M is a migrant who arrived in the UK a few months earlier. Urdu is his main language. He speaks little English at the moment of the recording.

> Vignette 2: V is helping M fill in the travel permit application. He does that by sitting at a table next to M and opening up the paper application in front of them. From the beginning of the exchange V and M translanguage with Urdu and English. When the actual work on the application begins V continues with translanguaging practices in a more translation mode: he reads the statements/questions in English and then translates them in Urdu. This is the kind of information the application contains: 'Contact address in the UK for correspondence', 'Contact name in the UK if different from that of the applicant', 'Home Office reference number – this will usually be given on your status letter'. The whole exchange resembles a teaching moment –V reads in English, translates the questions, and he also translates the key words various times; M repeats the words in English and Urdu. While translanguaging with V, M is also learning English. V explains the questions in general and some of the words, while placing more emphasis on and repeating the key words in the application.

Vignette 2, reporting on the observation of an informal advice session, seems to recall the origins of translanguaging research in the eighties, when the term 'translanguaging' was coined to describe classroom practices and the pedagogical advantages of dual literacy (Lewis et al. 2012). Although these kinds of episodes are very common (twelve episodes were observed), they are not happening in a formal classroom but in a peer-to-peer mode, or a volunteer-to-migrant mode, and the use of translanguaging with the 'minority' language, Urdu, falls between the pedagogical function of learning English through Urdu and the meaning-making function, specifically of explaining meaning through translation and paraphrasing in another language. V and M use translanguaging in all these functions – that is, the pedagogical, the paraphrasing and the word concept explanation – sometimes clearly separating them and sometimes in conjunction.

In the last vignette, an informal advice session is carried out with A, a French-English bilingual advisor, and a migrant from North Africa. The vignette also reports on the informal interview carried out afterwards which reflects on the session.

> Vignette 3: After the advice sessions conducted in French the advisor (A) explains to me that the migrant only speaks French and that she needs to call the solicitor to enquire about the migrant's case. A explains that she often takes on the cases of people who only speak French as she is fluent in the language, but that in this occasion she had difficulties understanding the migrant because his French is from Mali. She said that after the initial difficulty she now finds herself to, in

her own terms, 'trans-sound'. For her to 'trans-sound' is similar to 'translate' or 'trans-literate' but with sounds. She explains that she needs to tune in her listening to be able to understand him.

Vignette 3 is one of the many examples of informal advice conducted in a language other than English. If the advisors can speak one of the languages of the migrants, advice is sometimes given in Arabic, French, Italian or other languages. Translanguaging practices do happen in this situation and the functions covered are mainly those of explaining a term or a sentence or a concept, with translanguaging and translation being the main forms taken. This vignette also shows how the advisor tries to be flexible with the kind of linguistic resources available in the session between the two participants; she emphasizes the need to accommodate (or trans-sound) her listening skills for them to be able to understand each other.

5.2 Formal Advice Sessions

In this part I analyse two formal advice sessions. Extract 1 involves S, the advisor, and C7, a migrant from Algeria with accommodation problems. One of the problems is that there are rodents in the room where she lives.

Extract 1

1	S	so you want to call this number?
2	C7	yes
3	S	and what is this? this is your address?
4	C7	no no this eh number is the officer commissar office
5		
6	S	ok
7	S	the council (.)this is for what council?
8	C7	ehm
9	S	Rotteram?
10	C7	yes yes
11	S	ok ok ehm did you receive a letter from them?
12	C7	no no just I wait (.) tell me people I want to
13		cause this letter take more time the court to get this letter
14		
15	S	but the court letter is about what?
16	C7	what? the: the landlord need take me out
17	S	eviction?
18	C7	eviction yes but
19	S	but did you receive the letter?
20	C7	no no no
21	S	you didn't receive the letter?
22	C7	no no no I want-I wait
		[lines deletion]
23	C7	because I have problem with this landlord mhm because my
24		my bedroom I have mouse

25	S	ah no:
26	C7	[taking phone from bag] <Sp>mira<Sp>
		<Sp>look<Sp>
27	S	<Sp>hablas espanol?<Sp>
		<Sp>do you speak Spanish?<Sp>
28	C7	<Sp>si hablo espanol<Sp> French
		<Sp>yes I speak Spanish<Sp>
29	S	ehhhh
30	C7	<Sp>lo que quieres<Sp>
		<Sp>whatever you want<Sp>

The conversation starts with some difficulties on the part of the advisor with finding out what the migrant's needs are. From lines 1 to 22 the advisor is trying to find out how she can help S and seems to think that S is being evicted (lines 16–18). Eventually S clarifies that the letter of eviction never came (line 22, emphatic repetition of 'no no no') and explains to the advisor that the problem is that the accommodation is infested by rodents (line 24, 'my bedroom I have mouse').

While C7 is explaining her problems to S, she takes the phone from her bag because she wants to show S the pictures of the room and the rodents. While doing that, she says 'look' in Spanish ('mira' in line 26). It is at this point that the advisor realizes that S may speak Spanish and checks that with her in line 27 ('do you speak Spanish?'). S replies affirmatively ('si' in line 28), and she also starts adding other languages, such as 'French'; her intonation seems to suggest that she could continue with a list of languages, but the advisor interrupts with an exclamation of surprise ('ehhh' in line 29). After that S explicitly adds that any language would be fine by her, with her 'whatever you want' ('lo que quieres' in line 30).

This extract is particularly important in various ways. First, it represents the moment that both advisor and user realize they have another resource in common that they can draw on in their session – this becomes relevant in the rest of the session (see Extract 2), where Spanish and English are used in a translanguaging way, and with the addition of Spanish the advisory session becomes more effective, as C7 uses Spanish and English translanguaging to explain how the rodents have affected her life and her family. Second, it is in this moment that S shows her positive orientation towards her language knowledge: she seems to suggest that she knows many languages and is proud of that, as indicated by her saying 'lo que quieres' in line 30. This utterance can be translated as 'whatever you want' or, more liberally, 'any language you like, I can speak'. This changes the dynamics of the conversation, as from now on the advisor and C7 start translanguaging. What before this moment resembled a difficult conversation in English (from lines 1 to 22), where the advisor was trying to understand what the problem is and what is needed, from this moment onwards (line 23, including Extract 2) the conversation moves flexibly between and through linguistic resources in a translanguaging mode. Third, this is the moment where S starts using her phone to display the pictures of the room where she lives, to explain the problem and provide evidence of it. The use of the visual input also becomes relevant to the rest of the session and part of the negotiation of meaning in the translanguaging mode.

Another important aspect of this extract is that the advice session starts to liven up, with more dramatic effects such as louder and smiling voices (lines 8, 9, 20 in Extract 2), when advisee and advisor discover they can also use Spanish to communicate (together with other languages: French, etc.), and the more informative/factual discussion of the case leaves some space for the narrative to happen. The possibility of translanguaging in ELF opens up spaces for more in-depth discussion of the case, by showing the pictures and expressing emotional response, but also for some more descriptive narrative of the situation of the migrant, their family, their daughter and other aspects. This serves a more personal function of relationship-building and creating personal connections among the translanguaging participants.

In Extract 2, C7 clarifies that she lives in a small room with her husband and daughter, and she shows pictures on her phone to demonstrate the poor state of the room to the advisor. This situation is giving her stress and stomach problems and creating problems for her daughter too.

Extract 2

1	C7	I have more photos [showing photos]
2	S	but … it's terrible … horrible
3	C7	<Sp>si si ahora es invierno<Sp> I have damp I
4		need every day every day pfff
		<Sp>yes yes now it's winter<Sp>
5	S	ok so
6	C7	the problem the this I have my stomach the
7		stress when I see my mouse <Sp>este dia no como
8		nada [.] no toco nada nada mi hija NO @no
9		quiere tocar nada@ salimos fuera<Sp>
		<Sp>that day I don't eat anything [.] I don't
		touch anything my daughter NO @she doesn't want
		to touch anything@ we go out<Sp>
10	S	<Sp>cuantos anos tiene tu hija<Sp>
		<Sp>how old is your daughter<Sp>
11	C7	<Sp>tiene die-nueve<Sp>
		<Sp>she is te-nine<Sp>
12	S	<Sp>nueve<Sp>
		<Sp>nine<Sp>
13	C7	<Sp>nueve anos<Sp>
		<Sp>nine years<Sp>
14	S	you your daughter
15	C7	my husband

16	S	and your husband
17	C7	yes
18	S	three people in this room?
19	C7	my daughter? <Sp>duerme conmigo mi marido y
20		todo ... tiene miedo @ todo el dia asi ... yo
21		estoy<Sp>
		<Sp>she sleeps with me my husband and everything ... she is afraid @ all day like that ... I am<Sp>

The conversation develops from the pictures that C7 is showing. S comments on the state of the room ('terrible' and 'horrible'), and the rest of the narrative is a translanguaging event where C7 moves from the pictures to the explanation of her sickness with gestures (putting her hands on her stomach) and explaining the situation to S. This is accompanied by a certain level of performance, or dramatism, when C7 explains how unwell she gets at seeing the rodents in the room, and how her daughter also cannot eat and they have to leave the room. The whole story is told with emphasis and the repetition of Spanish 'nada', which provide particular prominence to the narrative. This part adds to the clarification that what C7 is asking for is not help with 'eviction', which was the original non-understanding, but help with complaining about the landlord not taking care of the accommodation. The translanguaging part then has a clarification function; it helps the advisor get a general understanding of the issue before proceeding with the action of making a phone call to the authorities. It also provides more in-depth understanding of the consequences on the health of the migrant, which is relevant for putting pressure on the authorities to take action to address the accommodation problem (in fact, the advisor then uses C7's sickness in her phone call).

Another point is that, from line 14 onwards, the advisor chooses to switch to English. This is possibly because the advisor needs to sort out the problem with the accommodation officer and the conversation with the officer is normally carried out in English. This advice session is then imagined to generate a later exchange (between the advisor and the accommodation officer), which is expected to be in English only and, though in the future, still influences the choice of languages used in the advice session.

In Extract 3 this is also shown.

Extract 3

1	C7	tu eres espanola?
		are you Spanish?
2	S	no (.) mi marido es espanol
		no (.) my husband is Spanish
3	C7	ah por eso hablais espanol
		ah that's why you speak Spanish

4	S	si
		yes
5	C7	entiendo
		I understand
6	S	ok I call the centre to see what they can do
7		(.) ehm:
8	C7	yo when I came here no hablo ingles ya eh
9		[ahora hablo
		me when I came here *I didn't speak English*
		[now I speak
10		[xs you speak English well
11	S	@ si si @
	C7	@*yes yes*@
12	S	I like [how you speak
13	C7	si I understand nooo:
		yes I understand *nooo:*
14	S	you are very good you speak English Spanish and
15		[French
16	C7	[French yes
17	S	you speak Arabic?
18	C7	yes
19	S	amazing @@@ (.)

At this point of the conversation the participants have been translanguaging for a while and the advisor knows why C7 speaks Spanish (she lived in Spain for a while), but C7 does not know why S speaks Spanish. This is probably what motivates the question on line 1 about whether S is Spanish. When S replies that she is not but her husband is Spanish, C7 clearly shows that her reason for asking was to find out why S speaks Spanish (line 3 'ah that's why you speak Spanish'), and now she understands ('entiendo' in line 5) why that is.

The advisor seems to want to go back to the issue in hand, the accommodation and the call to the centre to sort it out (lines 6–7), but C7 takes advantage of a hesitation moment (line 7, '(.) ehm') to return to the discussion of languages learnt. She adds that when she arrived here she did not speak any English (line 8, 'yo when I came here no hablo ingles'), but that now she does (line 9, 'ahora hablo'). This description of her language-learning experience sounds like a proud summary of a learning trajectory. She draws attention to the difference between when she arrived with little English knowledge and now when she can speak English. This episode becomes even more interesting since the advisor is there to help her because her English is supposedly not good enough to sort out the issue by herself. S picks up on the proud formulation of language knowledge and encourages C7 by complimenting her on her English (line 10), to which S replies affirmatively ('yes yes' in line 11), but also makes a modest addition that she just understands English (line

13). The multilingual appreciation of C7 becomes the topic in the next few lines when S continues to compliment her for her language knowledge, listing the languages she knows. C7 adds the language 'French' in an overlap with the advisor (lines 15/16), which shows how keen she is to demonstrate her knowledge and 'show off' her multilingualism.

This extract also emphasizes how translanguaging can also serve as a way to create personal connections and emphasize the common experience, that is, that both are related to Spanish in some way through their life trajectories. This is also possible because the charity is seen as a safe translanguaging space. So, while English is the language of the institutional immigration system, of external help and legal requirements, the internal space of the charity can be used as a safe translingual setting, where using the participants' repertoires, rather than English only, is not only permitted but seen in a positive light (Li 2011).

Extract 4 is from a different conversation. This is a formal advice session with a migrant (H) from Ivory Coast. H is waiting for the advisor (J) to arrive and is chatting with T (a volunteer who is shadowing J). When J comes into the room, T explains what they were discussing: where H is from.

Extract 4:

1	T	we were just chatting about eh where she is
2		from
3	J	ah
4	T	from Ivory Coast
5	J	yes remember I saw you last week where Maba
6		took the bus
7	H	mhm
8	J	yeah yeah yeah because they were talking their
9		language from Ivory Coast which
10	H	-Jula
11	J	=Jula
12	T	is it like a mixture with French
13		[and something else?
14	J	[that's what I thought
15	H	no::
16	J	no that's what I thought but it woul-no: I
17		couldn't recognize anything
18	T	can you say something in Jula?

This is a moment just before the advice session starts, and though it is not part of the advice session proper, it is of interest here as just after discussing H's situation with her family, T asks her where her family is – Ivory Coast, where she is from. At this moment J comes into the room and the question of H's first language becomes relevant. As a matter of fact, J had already noticed H speaking her language (lines 8–9) when she saw her at a bus stop (lines 5–6).

It is here that H, who up until that moment has kept rather quiet, interrupts J to tell her the name of her language, 'Jula'[3] (line 10). T thinks it may be a kind of creole, which includes French (the official language of the country), but H denies it and the volunteer asks her to say something in her language, which she goes on to do.

This exchange is an example of the various moments in the charity's communication practices where languages become a topic of conversation. Even when those languages are not shared by the participants and remain a covert resource as translanguaging cannot happen, as in this example, multilingual resources can still be of interest to the exchange. The volunteers who were going to help H in the advice session do not speak Jula and cannot use any other language apart from English for the advice session. However, talking about Jula is a way of getting to know the migrant and her background, and it is a symbolic acceptance of diversity in this context. The exchange is a way of invoking and remembering the language which the participants had heard (or used) at the bus stop in a covert way. When translanguaging is not possible, other ways of creating connections and building relationships are sought out by talking about languages and multilingualism.

6   Discussion and Conclusions

Overall, the charity is a super-diverse space, with staff, volunteer and users from all over the world in a linguistic ecology which provides a safe place for the use of multilingual resources. Communication is done mainly in ELF and all the various activities at the charity show flexible use of translanguaging practices, but this paper has focused on one of them: the advice sessions.

The analysis presented in this chapter exemplifies the role of multilingual resources in ELF advice sessions and relates to the original two research questions (RQ) as follows. In relation to the extent that multilingual resources are used in the ELF advice sessions (RQ1), the data showed that they are used in both formal and informal advice sessions, but the informal sessions tend to contain more translanguaging with 'minority languages', because they are carried out by experienced migrants from the same linguistic background, with peers who are less experienced with life and practices in the UK. While the formal sessions do occasionally show translanguaging practices, they remain with the well-known (mainly European) languages and, with some exceptions, most are in a monolingual mode. In situations where the formal advice may not show translanguaging practices, the participants may still include references to

---

[3] Although French is the official language of Ivory Coast, Jula is one of the local languages.

linguistic diversity in the meta-comments around the languages used by the participants in the charity.

In relation to the functions of translanguaging practices in the advice sessions (RQ2), the data showed that practices can cover at least three functions: first, the pedagogical function, especially in the informal advice session, where translanguaging is used by the migrants to learn or teach English in an informal way, while helping their less experienced peers. This is when the expert migrant helps the new migrants to navigate the difficulties of life in the new context, but also to understand key English discourses in their own community, or English that they will encounter in their life in London. Second, there is the enhancing meaning function, that is, the spontaneous and dynamic use of translanguaging as making meaning and enhancing understanding, when the conversation carried out in English only is not enough, and by translanguaging the participants get a deeper understanding of the issue at hand. Third, there is the more interpersonal function of building rapport, sharing migration backgrounds and creating special connections among the participants by sharing personal narratives through translanguaging.

Although this is beyond the scope of this paper, it is also possible to infer (mainly from interview data that could not be analysed here) that the different functions relate to the aspects that affect the use of multilingual resources, such as language ideologies and temporal and spatial understandings of the specific language ecology. Despite the multilingual safe space, there are certain services within the charity where multilingual resources are less obvious, and where access to them or the legitimization of using them is limited for various reasons. First, linguistic limitation, especially when the advisor and the user do not share the same linguistic knowledge and repertoire. Second, topic limitation, when the topic of discussion cannot be solved between the migrant and advisor, but would need the input of an outside agency or institution that specializes in solving the issue (e.g. the local council, another charity offering specific services, an aid agency), and for this reason the topic is then discussed in the language that needs to be used with the external agencies: English. Third, written mode limitation, when the formality of the advice session means that the discussion and decisions need to be reported and written in a progress form for the migrant's case to be documented in case another advisor needs to continue with the work. Cases often do not get resolved in one session, and although the same advisor tries to continue working on the same case, this is not always possible. This means that a written report needs to be done in English so that the case can be taken over by anybody in the charity. Fourth, local limitation: because the charity is based in the UK, the understanding is that the official language is English. Although the charity space is very multilingual friendly, across the external space outside the charity and the national space (the immigration authorities, local authorities and the regulations concerning migrants in UK) the dominant language ideology is 'English only'.

In terms of this study, this means that what happens during the advice sessions over the course of an hour, as well as across weeks or months, and in the organization but also in the spaces outside it (the local institutions, the government or others), may influence what happens in the communications with the migrants. It would be interesting, therefore, in future work to explore how the relationships across the temporal and spatial scales affect the language choices and the access to resources in multilingual ELF encounters. In this paper, it was possible to glimpse at how time and space scales, as projected into the future, limit the resources that can be used during the advice session. The advice practices were tailored towards the needs, requirements and expectations of different groups outside the exchange itself, that is, the local authorities, the external charities or aid organizations, national immigration services, etc.

In a more general sense, there is an overall acceptance of sociocultural diversity, and the charity offers a safe place where friendly, convivial and cooperative relationships are encouraged in the ethos of helping migrants. Naturally this should not obscure the tensions and power struggles that go on within the services offered by the charity and also with the institutions outside it, the local and national regulations and immigration requirements. Even in a super-diverse ELF context like this one, where ELF translanguaging practices are welcome, there are limitations to accessing or performing these practices that are ideological or spatiotemporal, among others, which emphasizes the complexity of ELF practices and the role of multilingual resources in ELF.

REFERENCES

Blackledge, Adrian & Angela Creese. 2010. *Multilingualism. A Critical Perspective*. London: Continuum.
Blommaert, Jan. 2010. *The Sociolinguistics of Globalization*. Cambridge: Cambridge University Press.
   2012. Complexity, accent and conviviality: Concluding comments. *Tilburg Papers in Culture Studies* 26, Tilburg: Tilburg University.
Blommaert, Jan & Ad Backus. 2011. Repertoires revisited: 'Knowing language' in superdiversity. *Working Papers in Urban Language and Literacies* 67.
Blommaert, Jan & Ben Rampton. 2011. Language and superdiversity: a position paper. Available at www.kcl.ac.uk/sspp/departments/education/research/Research-Centres/ldc/publications/workingpapers/abstracts/WP070-Language-and-superdiversity-a-position-paper-.aspx.
Cenoz, Jasone & Durk Gorter. 2011. A holistic approach to multilingual education: Introduction. *Modern Language Journal*, 95(3), 339–343.

Cogo, Alessia. 2009. Accommodating difference in ELF conversations: A study of pragmatic strategies. In Anna Mauranen & Elina Ranta (eds.), *English as a Lingua Franca: Studies and Findings*, 254–273. Newcastle-upon-Tyne: Cambridge Scholars.

2012. ELF and super-diversity: A case study of ELF multilingual practices from a business context. *Journal of English as a Lingua Franca* 1(2), 287–313.

2016a. Conceptualizing ELF as a translanguaging phenomenon: covert and overt resources in a transnational workplace. *WASEDA Working Papers in ELF (English as a Lingua Franca)* 5, 61–77.

2016b. Visibility and absence: Ideologies of 'diversity' in BELF. In Marie-Luise Pitzl & Ruth Osimk-Teasdale (eds.), *English as a Lingua Franca: Perspectives and Prospects. Contributions in Honour of Barbara Seidlhofer*, 39–48. Berlin: De Gruyter Mouton.

2018. *ELF and Multilingualism. The Routledge Handbook of English as a Lingua Franca*. London: Routledge, 357–368.

Conteh, Jean. 2018 Translanguaging as pedagogy: A critical review. In Angela Creese & Adrian Blackledge (eds.), *The Routledge Handbook of Language and Superdiversity*, 473–487. London: Routledge.

2019. Translanguaging. Key concepts in ELT. *ELT Journal* 72(4), 445–447.

Conteh, Jean & Avril Brock. 2011. 'Safe spaces'? Sites of bilingualism for young learners in home, school and community. *International Journal of Bilingual Education and Bilingualism* 14(3), 347–360.

Copland, Fiona & Angela Creese. 2015. *Linguistic Ethnography: Collecting, Analysing and Presenting Data*. London: Sage.

Creese, Angela & Adrian Blackledge. 2010. Translanguaging in the bilingual classroom: A pedagogy for learning and teaching? *Modern Language Journal* 94 (1), 103–115.

Dorn, Nora, Martina Rienzner, Brigitta Busch & Anita Santner-Wolfartsberger. 2014. 'Here I Find Myself to Be Judged': ELF/Plurilingual Perspectives on Language Analysis for the Determination of Origin. *Journal of English as a Lingua Franca* 3 (2), 409–424.

García, Ofelia. 2009. Education, multilingualism and translanguaging in the 21st century. In Ajit Mohanty, Minati Panda, Robert Phillipson & Tove Skutnabb-Kangas (eds.) *Multilingual Education for Social Justice: Globalising the local*, 128–145. New Delhi: Orient Blackswan (formerly Orient Longman).

García, Ofelia & Wei Li. 2014. *Translanguaging: Language, Bilingualism and Education*. London: Palgrave Macmillan.

Grosjean, François. 1982. *Life with Two Languages: An Introduction to Bilingualism*. Cambridge, MA: Harvard University Press.

Guido, Maria Grazia. 2012. ELF authentication and accommodation strategies in crosscultural immigration encounters. *Journal of English as a Lingua Franca* 1(2), 219–240.

Heller, Monica (ed.). 2007. *Bilingualism: A Social Approach*. London: Palgrave.

Jenkins, Jennifer. 2015. Repositioning English and multilingualism in English as a Lingua Franca. *Englishes in Practice* 2(3), 49–85.

Lewis, Gwyn, Bryn Jones & Colin Baker. 2012. Translanguaging: Origins and development from school to street and beyond. *Educational Research and Evaluation* 18(7), 641–654.

Li, Wei. 2011. Moment Analysis and translanguaging space: Discursive construction of identities by multilingual Chinese youth in Britain. *Journal of Pragmatics* 43(5), 1222–1235.

Mauranen, Anna. 2012. *Exploring ELF in Academia*. Cambridge: Cambridge University Press.

2013. Lingua franca discourse in academic contexts: Shaped by complexity. In John Flowerdew (ed.), *Discourse in Context: Contemporary Applied Linguistics*. Vol. 3, 225–245. London: Continuum.

Seidlhofer, Barbara. 2011. *Understanding English as a Lingua Franca*. Oxford: Oxford University Press.

Vettorel, Paola. 2014. *English as a Lingua in Wider Networking: Blogging Practices*. Berlin: De Gruyter Mouton.

Index

(s) variable 154, *viz also* verbal -*s*
"best speech" 6, 127, 144–145

accommodation 107–108, 111, 140, 237, 312, 329
act of identity 165
A-curve 18, 38
Adams, John 125–126, 144
advantage, bi-/multilingual *viz* multilingual advantage
advice services 336, 341
American English 125–126, 142
anglicism 55, 111
approximation 104, 112–113, 226
asylum seekers 336, 339
attainment, educational 240–241
attractor 19, 39
auto-organization 16, 28–30, 38

Biber, Douglas 84–85, 87, 89, 101–102, 213, 224
bifurcation 17–18, 27, 38
big data 180, 183, 188, 193–195, 200
bilingual *viz also* multilingual
 bilingual ELF speaker (BES) 272
 medium 164
 non-bilingual ELF speaker (NBES) 271–273, 284–286
blog 211–212, 225, 291
 comments 211–212, 224
borrowing 54, 102, 104
 grammatical 50
 lexical 50, 104, 163
bot 185, 187, 190–192, 194–197
bottom-up
 dependency 271
 processing 268, 270, 285, *viz also* top-down processing
brain imaging 79
butterfly effect 18, 26
Bybee, Joan 17, 28, 207–208, 210

call as construction 37–38
calque 50, 104, 243

Cape Flats English 142
catastrophe theory 27
chaos
 and order 18, 24–26, 29, 38–39
 theory 17, 27, 39, *viz also* Complex Dynamic Systems (CDS)
charity 336, 339–343, 350–353
chatroom 291
China English 24
chunk 213, 217, 221–224, 226–227
 formation 224
 personal 223
chunking 28, *viz* Chapter 8, *viz also* chunk
City of London 131–132, 135–136
classroom 84, 166, 235–237, 311
 international 166
cleft 68, 213–214, 217, 223–224
code-mixing 302
code-switching 243, 293, 302, 306, 337–338, *viz* Chapter 12, *viz also* translanguaging
 vs. translanguaging 337–339
cognitive
 development 234, 238, 240–241, 257
 properties, domain-general 210
 reserve 234, 239–240
Common European Framework of Reference for Languages (CEFR) 242, 246–247, 251–252, 258–259
communicative
 difficulties 292
 isolation 47–48, 69
 medium of choice 267, 291, 295
 needs 124, 128, 291, 295, 307
 practices 168, 237, 296
 routines 291, 296
 task 273
communicative act 297, 299–309
 of advice-giving 299
 of information-giving 302
 of offer 304
 of request 299–300, 304–305, 309

356

Index

community
  hybrid 294–295
  monolingual 226, 237
  multicultural virtual 292
  speech 30, 44–45, 47–49, 88
  transient 157
comparative construction 214, 218–219
  correlative 28
competence, language 315, 337
  academic 235, 241–242
  bi-/multilingual 96, 256
competency area, language 241, 246–247
complementizer 87–88
Complex Adaptive Systems (CAS) 16–18, 205, *viz also* Complex Dynamic Systems (CDS)
Complex Dynamic Systems (CDS) 16–40
complexity
  (as a property of a complex system) 17, 19–20, 39–40
  lexical 102, 237
  linguistic 39–40, 44, 80, 82–83, 88, 236–237
  of ELF practices 353
  of language contact 236–237
  societal 86, 236
  sociolinguistic 167
  syntactic 83, 88–89, 146
Complexity Science 16.*viz* Complex Dynamic Systems (CDS)
Complexity Theory 16, 227, *viz also* Complex Dynamic Systems (CDS)
compositionality 25, 28 *viz also* non-compositionality; language processing, compositional and non-compositional
comprehensibility 268, 277, 280, 298, *viz also* intelligibility
comprehension 82, 237–238, 269–270, 286
  difficulty 277–280, *viz also* miscommunication
  listening 245–247, 252–253, 258–259, 261
  reading 76, 245–247, 252–253
computer-mediated communication 291, 293–294, 297
  Computer-Mediated English as a Lingua Franca (CMELF) 291, 293, 296, 308–309
  discourse analysis *viz* discourse analysis, computer-mediated
constituency 228
constituent structure 207–208, 222
contact language 44–45, 51, 99
context 269, 271
  cognitive 269–270, 272, 286
  extralinguistic 268, 286
  inaccessibility of 272
  physical 269–270

  unavailability of 273
  visual 275, 285
  vs. co-text 268–269
contraction 206, *viz* Chapter 8
control, executive 234, 239–240, 244
conversation analysis 313, 315–316
Cook, Vivian 96–99, 109, 111
copula 29, 36–37
copular BE 213–214, 216–217, *viz also* copula
corpus 96–97, 100–102, 129, 167
  ARCHER Corpus 84
  Asian Corpus of English (ACE) 152
  British National Corpus (BNC) 29
  Brown Corpus 101
  Corpus of Early English Correspondence (CEEC) 130–131, 133
  Corpus of English as a Lingua Franca in Academic Settings (ELFA) 101–102, 152, 180
  Early English Books Online (EEBO) 129, 138–139
  Helsinki Corpus of English Texts 129
  individual *viz* individual corpus
  International Corpus of English (ICE) 31, 33, 102
  Kolhapur Corpus 31
  learner 97, 102
  Michigan Corpus of Academic Spoken English. (MICASE) 101
  Nordic Tweet Stream (NTS) 180, 184, 187, 201
  reference *viz* reference corpus
  South Asian Varieties of English (SAVE) corpus 37
  Vienna-Oxford International Corpus of English (VOICE) 102, 173
co-text 269, 271
  cognitive 269, 273
  inaccessibility of 272
  physical 269
  unavailability of 273
  vs. context *viz* context, vs. co-text
creole 52, 60, 64, 69, 142
Cromwell, Thomas 134–135
cue
  contextual 270, 273, 280–287
  co-textual 269, 273, 280–287

Dąbrowska, Ewa 76, 80, 82, 109, 205
Danish People's Party 162
dialect contact 124, 127–146
diffusion 30, 38–39, 127–128, 182
  lexicosemantic 30, 35
digital humanities 169, 181

discourse analysis 297
  computer-mediated 297, 308
  multimodal 293
discourse marker 19
domain loss 161, 163, 166
do-support 22–23
drift 29
Dynamic Model 20, 23, 28

Earlier African American Vernacular English (EAAVE) 25–26, 142
Early Modern English (EModE) 20–21, 25, 129, 140
East Anglia 131–132, 141
East Anglian English 132, 142
education *viz also* attainment, educational
  higher 103, 153, 159, 161, 164
  tertiary 234, 259
Electronic World Atlas of Varieties of English (eWAVE) 15, 142–143
Ellis, Nick C. 17–18, 97, 104, 113, 206
embedding 88–89
emergence 206, 208, 227
emergentism 18, 28, 38–39, *viz also* emergence
English
  American English *viz* American English
  Cape Flats English *viz* Cape Flats English
  China English *viz* China English
  Earlier African American Vernacular English *viz* Earlier African American Vernacular English (EAAVE)
  Early Modern English *viz* Early Modern English (EModE)
  East Anglian English *viz* East Anglian English
  Hong Kong English *viz* Hong Kong English
  Indian English *viz* Indian English
  Middle English *viz* Middle English (ME)
  New Englishes *viz* New Englishes
  New Zealand English *viz* New Zealand English
  Nigerian Pidgin English *viz* Nigerian Pidgin English
  Old English (OE) *viz* Old English (OE)
  Philippine English *viz* Philippine English
  Postcolonial Englishes *viz* Postcolonial Englishes
  Singaporean English *viz* Singaporean English
  Singlish *viz* Singlish
  South Asian Englishes *viz* South Asian Englishes
  Standard English *viz* Standard English
English Language Complex (ELC) 20
English-only 350, 352–353

entrenchment 30, 109–110
entrepreneur 157–158, 168–169
entropy 39
epistemics 314, *viz also* stance, epistemic
Eskola, Sari 98, 104, 106, 112
esoteric language 51–53, 55, 57, 63–64, *viz also* exoteric language; neogenic language
ethnography
  ethnographic object 296
  hybrid 296
  linguistic 341–342
evolution 26, 28–29, 40, 48, 69
exoteric language 5, 51–57, 62–65, 69, *viz also* esoteric language; neogenic language
explicitation 106–108
exposure, print 76, 80
extralinguistic feature 293
extraposition 214, 216–217, 223–224

Facebook 291, 296–297, 300
  group 292, 294–296, 298–299, 308
first language (L1) 48, 82, 96, 109–111, *viz also* language, native
fixedness 221, 226
flagging 293, 304–306, 312–313, 329
fluidity 127, 133, 338
focus group 340–343
focus on form 89
fractal 19, 39
frequency effects 207–208

Garrod, Simon 108, 112, 114, 208–209, 226
gaze 313, 317
generalization 123, 142, 145–146, 219, 226
Germanic 20, 24–26, 49, 67, 69
Germanic Main Stress Rule 24
globalism 159
globalization 115, 159, 163–164, 236, 239
grammar
  development 80, 82
  mental 75
grammaticalization 208
Granger, Sylviane 97, 102, 104
Granovetter, Mark 179, 182–183
Gumperz, John J. 54, 269

Hart, John 136–138
Heltai, Pal 98, 111
heritage language 80, 241–242
high-stakes context 336, 340
Hodges, Richard 137–138
Hong Kong English 143
humor 139, 166–167
Hunston, Susan 208, 224

Index

hybridity 100, 105, 113, 115
 semiotic *viz* semiotic hybridity
Hymes, Dell 60, 154

idiosyncrasy 37, 217, 225
illiterate 77, 79–81
indexicality 136–138, 154, 164
Indian English 21, 28, 31, 33–36, 38
individual corpus 211–212, 217, 221
individual differences 205
individual languages 205–206, 211, 213, 226–227
influence
 cross-linguistic 96–98, 109, 243, *viz also* interference; transfer
 source text 98
information packaging constructions 213
inheritance 45
intelligibility 267–268, 270–271, 273, 277, 286–287, *viz also* comprehensibility; interpretability
interaction, spoken 246–247, 252–254, 259, 292–293, 299
interactional work 278, 286
interactor 46
interference 48, 96–98, 104–105, 113, *viz also* influence, cross-linguistic; transfer
internationalization 153, 159–162, 166–168
interpersonal function 336, 339, 352, *viz also* translanguaging functions
interpretability 268, 277, 280, *viz also* intelligibility
interview 183, 274, 340–344
intrusive *as* 37–38
intuition 103, 110–111, 114
it is ADJ *that* 224

Japanese 316–330
Jenkins, Jennifer 100, 124–125, 142–143, 155–156, 267, 271–273

K+, K– 314–315, 320, 322, 329
knowledge, shared 166
koiné 67
Kolhapur Corpus 38
Kujamäki, Pekka 106, 112
Kytö, Merja 129–130, 138, 140

Labov, William 124, 128, 135, 181, 205, 207
Laitinen, Mikko 16, 100, 180, 183–187, 190, 197
language
 esoteric *viz* esoteric language
 exoteric *viz* exoteric language
 heritage *viz* heritage language

native 99, 236, 291, 298, *viz also* first language (L1)
neogenic *viz* neogenic language
oral 86, 88–89
standard 67–68, 95–96, 128
language acquisition
 L1 48
 L2 96–97, 104, 115, 242, 257
language change 35, 45–47, 69, 145, 181, 205–207, 226
 actuation, transition and evaluation 181
 social embedding of 181
language choice 160, 164, 183, 353
language competence 241
language contact 47–49, 70, 96, 98–100, 102, 108, 113, 124, 145, 236–237, *viz also* dialect contact
 first- and second-order 100, 115, 236–237
language ideology 155–158, 161–166, 338–339, 352–353
language policy 15
language processing
 compositional and non-compositional 208, 221, 226, *viz also* compositionality; non-compositionality
 left-lateralized 79–80
 multilingual 108–110
 online 78
 phonological 76, 78–79, 81, 212
language representation, levels of
 communal and individual 205–206, 209
language shift 64–65, 68–70
languaging 16
Lanstyák, Istvan 98, 111
Larsen-Freeman, Diane 16–20, 28, 115, 205
learner language 96–101, 108–109, 113, 236
lexicon 46, 55, 81, 86, 243
lineage 45, 48–49
Lingua Franca Core (LFC) 267
lingueme 45–50, 53–54, 68
 schematic 50, 52, 69
 substance 49–52, 69
Linguistic Atlas of Late Mediaeval English, A (LALME) 129, 136
linguistic feature 48–49, 96, 100, 105, 136, *viz also* extralinguistic feature
 -based description 15
 pool 47, 128, 132
linguistics
 applied 17
 cognitive 46, 169
 contact 169
 contrastive 108
 corpus 221
 English 200

Index

linguistics (cont.)
  forensic 205
  historical 127, 129
  interactional 107
  socially constituted 154, 169
  sociohistorical 46
  sociolinguistics *viz* sociolinguistics
  usage-based 17, 46–47, 210, 226
listening
  comprehension *viz* comprehension, listening
  L1 270–271
  L2 270–271
literacy 77–89, 127, *viz also* illiterate
  acquisition 76, 88
  vernacular 137
longitudinal 22, 296, 307, 309
  study 303, 311

Machyn, Henry 135–136
Mair, Christian 208–209, 219
marketization 160
Mauranen, Anna 16, 101–106, 128, 179, 236–238, 292, 302
mediatization 155, 158
metalinguistic
  abilities 81–82
  awareness 234, 238, 242, 244–245, 257–258
  discourse 155, 161
  knowledge 77
Middle English (ME) 20–21, 25, 49, 129, 146
migrant 60, 81, 132–133, 136, 336, 339–353
migration 48, 69–70, 133, 141, 145, 239
Milroy, James 23, 106, 145, 179–180
Milroy, Lesley 23, 106, 145, 179, 182–183
miscommunication 272–273, 276–278, 286, *viz also* comprehension difficulty, mishearing, misunderstanding, non-understanding
mishearing 287
misunderstanding 278, 283–284, 286, *viz also* miscommunication
monolingual
  individual 200
  -ly raised ELF speakers 237, 245, 248–259
  practice 339
  speaker 234
monolingualism 97, 238
multilingual
  advantage 234–235, 238–244, 257–260
  individual 179, 181
  -ly raised ELF speakers 234, 237, 248–259
  practice 300, 307, 338

  resources 336–353
  speaker 234
multilingualism 4–5, 53, 100, 234–247, 293, 336
  receptive 53
  symmetric/asymmetric 53, 63
multimodality 286, 292–293, 300, 309
  multimodal features 293
  multimodal practice 300, 307–309
  multimodal resources 294, 296
multi-word unit 95, 103–104, 110, 221

nationalism 84, 160, 238
nativization, structural 20
neo-Firthian tradition 208
neogenic language 51–52, 56–64, *viz also* esoteric language; exoteric language
networks
  close-knit and loose-knit 179, 182
  of relations 23–24
  social *viz* Chapter 7
  social network theory 179, 181–183
  trade 58, 60
New Englishes 20–21, 34, 36
New Zealand English 28
n-grams 101, 205, 213
NICE properties 21
Nigerian Pidgin English 21
non-compositionality 221, *viz also* compositionality; language processing, compositional and non-compositional
non-linearity 17, 19, 41
non-understanding 277–283, 327, 339, 348, *viz also* miscommunication
norm, norms 15, 83, 96, 105, 128, 137, 145, 182, 236
  social 153, 155, 157, 164, 166–168
Northern Subject Rule (NSR) 140–142, 146

Old English (OE) 20, 87
orthography 85, 136
  effects on phonological representations 78–79
overrepresentation 101–102

Paradis, Michel 109–110
parallel language use 164, 166
passive tense 80, 209, 213, 217, 224
Pavlenko, Aneta 96–97, 110, 114
perpetual dynamics 18, 20
persistence 209
Philippine English 28
phoneme awareness 76–77, 80, 89

Index

phonology 24, 83, 243
  phonological awareness 81
  phonological competitor 77
  phonological intelligibility 267–268
  phonological processing *viz* language processing, phonological
  phonological representation 77, 81
  phonological short term memory 81–82
  phonological typology 50
phonotactics 26–27
Pickering, Martin 108, 112, 114, 208–209, 226
pidgin 51–53, 59–62, 64, 66
Pitzl, Marie-Luise 15, 107, 152, 157, 226, 272, 311–312, 329
polysemy 31, 33–34
Postcolonial Englishes 20, 23
practice (language) 95, 157
  communication 351
  communicative *viz* communicative practices
  discursive 153, 155–158, 164–168
  monolingual *viz* monolingual practice
  multilingual *viz* multilingual practice
  multimodal *viz* multimodality, multimodal practice
  translanguaging *viz* translanguaging practice
pragmatic
  function 21, 207–208, 293, 308
  meaning 268, 293–294, 297–298, 300, 308
  strategies 292, 298, 303, 307
preference, linguistic 103–105, 107–108, 140, 154, 205, 214–226, 314, 316, 330
priming 78, 112–114, 208–210, 213, 219–221
  cross-linguistic 110, 112
  self-priming 220, 226
  syntactic 209
production 80, 82–83, 109, 238, 243, 269
  spoken 246–247, 254–255, 258, 260
proficiency 81, 241–260, 271, 337
  level 243, 246–247, 252
  self-assessed 245, 250–252, 256–257, 259–260
progressive aspect 68, 113, 209, 213, 217, 223–224
pronunciation 267–268, 271
prosody, implicit 212
Puttenham, George 126–127, 132, 144–145

Queen Elizabeth I 141

Raumolin-Brunberg, Helena 128–133, 136, 141, 145
reanalysis 21, 219, 222
reception 243, 245
recursion 20, 87

reduction 206–208, 212, 218
  phonological 207–208
reductionism 15–16, 18
redundancy, language 210–211, 271
reference corpus 211
reflexivity, cultural 155–157, 168
register 88, 95–96, 211, 235, 241, 257
  spoken 84
  variation *viz* variation, register
  written 84–86
regularities, linguistic 205, 225
regularization 25, 146
  morphological 140, 144
repair 302, 312, 319, 327–329
  other-initiated 319
  other-repair 319, 324–325
  self-repair 328–329
repertoire 338
  individual chunk 223, 226–227
  linguistic 95, 237, 337
  multilingual 309, 329
replacive lengthening 26
replication 45–47
replicator 45–46
resources, linguistic 164, 291, 329–330, 338, 347
  multilingual *viz* multilingual resources
  multimodal *viz* multimodal resources
  semiotic *viz* semiotic resources
  shared 314, 320, 329–330
restructured variety 68
restructuring 36, 38–39
richness, lexical 75–76, 102
routinization 209
Royal Court 127, 131, 144

SAD hypothesis 127, 145
salience 113
sampling 225
schema 269–270, 275, 280–282, 286
  schematic anticipation 270
  schematic context 273, 275, 281–282, 286
  schematic cue 270, 280–281
Schendl, Herbert 141–142
S-curve 22–23
second language (L2)
  acquisition (SLA) *viz* language acquisition: L2
  use (SLU) 99–100, 108, 110
Seidlhofer, Barbara 100, 123, 157, 226, 291, 303
self-and-other positioning 311, 316, 318, 320, 322, 329–330
self-assessment 235, 245–260
self-organization 17, 39

semiotic
  hybridity 298, 308
  modes 297
  multimodal resources 291
  resources 168, 298, 308
side sequence 313, 320
similect 115, 128, 236–237
simplification 68, 101, 103, 113, 140, 144, 237
Sinclair, John 102, 208
Singaporean English 19, 28, *viz also* Singlish
Singlish 19, 21, *viz also* Singaporean English
Smith, Larry E. 268
social
  organization 55–57, 62–63, 69
  structure 49–50, 55, 62, 133, 179, 181, 207
social change 51, 63, 152–154, 163, 166
social media 158, 181, 183, 291, 297
social networks *viz* networks, social
society
  egalitarian 56–57, 62–63
  illiterate 86
  large-scale 56–58, 64–65, 70
  of intimates 83, 88
  small-scale 54, 56–57, 63, 67
  stratified 56–57, 61–63, 70
sociolinguistics
  historical 124, 169
  variationist 23, 154, 181–183, 200, 207
source language 52, 68, 97–98, 103, 110, 113
South Asian Englishes 37
speaker
  native (NS) 47, 97, 104, 155
  non-native (NNS) 152, 209, 235, 271, 291
speech perception 268
speech processing 80
spelling 78, 127, 136–137
  error 77–78
spoken language 75, 79, 102, 137, 145, 207, 211–212
spoken word recognition 268, 271
stance, epistemic 314, 320
Standard English 20, *viz* Chapter 5
standardization 25–26, 68, 83–84, 126, 129, *viz also* standard language
stimulated recall 274, 276–277, 285
stylization 166–167
subordination 82, 87–88
super-diversity 328
syncope 136–138
synonym 31, 103, 164, 211
  near-synonym 31, 210
syntagmatic relations 19, 206
syntax, hypotactic 87
Systems Science *16.viz* Complex Dynamic Systems (CDS)

Tagliamonte, Sali 154, 207
target language 98, 104–106, 109, 112, 114
Thai 316–317, 325, 328–330
Tirkkonen-Condit, Sonja 101, 105–106
top-down processing 268, 270, 272, *viz also* bottom-up processing
Toury, Gideon 98, 105
transfer 96–98, 104, 106, *viz also* influence, cross-linguistic; interference
transient
  community *viz* community, transient
  social configurations 157
transitive
  complex 31–36
  ditransitive 36
translanguaging *viz* Chapter 13
  as translation 344
  functions 336, 338–339, 344, 348, 352
  practice 339, 345, 351–353
  space 337, 350
translation 312–313, 344–345, *viz* Chapter 4
  studies 97–98, 100–101, 105
transmission
  horizontal/vertical 49
  language 20–21, 69, 127–128
  of polysemy 33
trouble, linguistic 312–313, 319–322
  source 322, 325
Trudgill, Peter 20, 44, 68, 87, 128, 146
T-unit 82
tweets *viz* Chapter 7
Twitter *viz* Chapter 7
typology 50
  sociolinguistic 44, 49, 51, 69–70

underrepresentation 104–106, 112
uniform information density (UID) 207–208
university, international 164, 166, 316, 328
upbringing, linguistic
  monolingual 235, 249, 256
  multilingual 235, 238, 243, 249, 256

variability 83, 103
  in ELF use 206
  linguistic 152, 179
variable, linguistic 135, 206–207, 225
variation 45–46, 55, 124, 152, 217–219, 221, 225–226, 309, *viz also* sociolinguistics, variationist
  determinants 209
  dialectal 129
  individual 133, 145, 205–206, 210, 214–215

Index 363

language variation and change 18, 40, 46, 124, 152, 154, 158, 167
morphosyntactic 208, 211, 213
register 84–86, 89
verb
  double modal 21
  modal 21–22, 24
  semi-modal 21
  strong 25, 128
  weak 25
verbal -s viz Chapter 5, viz also (s) variable
verbalization 46
Vetchinnikova, Svetlana 17–19, 115, 205, 226, 293, 311–313
visual word form area 79
vocabulary 53–54, 75–76, 88–89, 244, 296, 298, 300
  most frequent 95, 102, 109–110, 113–114
  size 76, 86, 102

Weinreich, Uriel 96, 98, 111, 181, 205
Widdowson, Henry G. 124–125, 270–273, 286, 293, 297
word order 24, 243
word search viz Chapter 12
  sequence 311, 313, 315–317, 319–325, 328–330
working memory 79, 239
  load 83, 89
World Englishes 15, 100, 142 viz also English
writing 75–76, 80, 83–84, 86, 88–89, 242
  ability 255
  speech and 88, 101
writing system, alphabetic 76, 80–81, 89
written language 75, 80–82, 88–89, 137, 212

zero form 140–142, 146

Lightning Source UK Ltd.
Milton Keynes UK
UKHW020235191220
375322UK00008B/142